COUNSELING PARENTS OF
THE EMOTIONALLY
DISTURBED CHILD

COUNSELING PARENTS OF THE EMOTIONALLY DISTURBED CHILD

Compiled and Edited by

ROBERT L. NOLAND

Professor of Psychology
University of Dayton
Dayton, Ohio

CHARLES C THOMAS • PUBLISHER
Springfield • Illinois • U.S.A.

Published and Distributed Throughout the World by

CHARLES C THOMAS • PUBLISHER

Bannerstone House

301-327 East Lawrence Avenue, Springfield, Illinois, U.S.A.

Natchez Plantation House

735 North Atlantic Boulevard, Fort Lauderdale, Florida, U.S.A.

©*1972, by* CHARLES C THOMAS • PUBLISHER

ISBN 0-398-02371-9

Library of Congress Catalog Card Number: 71-172462

Printed in the United States of America
ROO-2

Contributors

H. A. ABRAMSON, M.D.

BETTIE ARTHUR, Ph.D.

BETTY BASAMANIA, M.S.S.

EILEEN BERRYMAN-SIMPSON, M.A.

JAMES BLACK, M.D.

MURRAY BOWEN, M.D.

T. BERRY BRAZELTON, M.D.

HILDE BRUCH

GEORGE CHALPIN, M.D.

FLORENCE L. CRISS

GUY DA SILVA, M.D.

ROBERT H. DYSINGER, M.D.

JOYCE EDWARD

PAULA ELKISCH, Ph.D.

RICHARD EMERSON, Ph.D.

O. SPURGEON ENGLISH, M.D.

MARY E. ERIKSON, M.S.W.

ERNA FURMAN

RAY C. GOODWIN

KENNETH H. GORDON, JR., M.D.

AL B. HARLEY, JR., M.D.

ROBERT HIRSCH, M.D.

RICHMOND HOLDER, M.D.

MARGARET S. H. JOHNSTON, M.A.

H. BEVAN JONES, D.P.M.

EUGENE W. KANSKY, M.D.

WILLIAM S. LANGFORD, M.D.

MORTON LEVITT, Ph.D.

DEREK H. MILLER, M.D.

MAISEN MOE

ELMA OLSON, M.A., M.S.S.

M. M. PESHKIN, M.D.

E. LAKIN PHILLIPS, Ph.D.

JULES RISKIN, M.D.

BEN O. RUBENSTEIN, M.S.W.

VICTOR SZYRYNSKI, M.D., Ph.D.

BEATRICE TALBOT

JAMES L. TITCHENER, M.D.

BJORN URDAHL

EZRA F. VOGEL, Ph.D.

ANN L. VROOM, Ph.D.

NIC WAAL

JACK C. WESTMAN, M.D.

J. R. WILKES, M.D.

THEODORE H. WOHL, Ph.D.

BENJAMIN B. WOLMAN, M.D.

Introduction

W ITH the publication of this book we complete our planned three volume work dealing with the counseling of parents of exceptional children. In our first book, *Counseling Parents of the Mentally Retarded: A Sourcebook* (Charles C Thomas, Publisher, 1970), we dealt with the special problems facing parents of the seven million mentally retarded children in our society. In the selection of articles we attempted to provide the reader with the attitudes, information and skills thought to be most useful in helping parents face the challenges of mental retardation. In the second book in this series, *Counseling Parents of the Ill and the Handicapped* (Charles C Thomas, Publisher, 1971), we compiled and edited a collection of articles dealing with counseling parents of children having quite diverse illnesses and handicaps (e.g. visual, speech and hearing defects; epilepsy and cerebral palsy; cardiac and respiratory illnesses; leukemic and terminal conditions). In these volumes, emphasis was on counseling and therapy of the *parents* rather than on the diagnosis, classification and treatment of the child. This frame of reference was continued in the conceptualization and design, and in the selection and compilation of articles for this third and final volume.

We are now witnessing an almost revolutionary change in attitudes about the role of parents and, indeed, the entire family unit, in contributing to the child's emotional distress. We are now very aware of the need to deal much more intensively, much more comprehensively, with the parents and the wider family of the disturbed child if the therapy is to succeed. This volume is an attempt to collect and present in one book some of the best writing available on the role of the parent in child and adolescent psychotherapy, and on the rationale and techniques of parent counseling and therapy represented in current professional practice.

In our society we certainly are considered "child-centered" and we are said to be very responsive to the plea "heal the hurt child." While the seminal insights of Freud and Adler and, more recently, Dreikurs, Bettelheim, Redl and Wineman have been in print and widely publicized for many decades, it was not until recently that the major helping professions recognized just how much parents influence the psychological perception and adjustment of their children, and how important it is for parents of children with major handicaps to receive comprehensive instructional and therapeutic counseling. While much more can and should be done, we are today witnessing the ripening of the seeds of wisdom and determination planted by these and other giants in the child care specialties. There are now psychiatrists, psychologists, social workers, nurses, mental health technicians and others who specialize in child and adolescent psychotherapy. There are also special institutions, hospitals and clinics for children. The younger person with emotional problems is no longer considered a "tag-a-long" extension of adult treatment ideas and services. Youths with problems *are* being helped.

However, as we have written elsewhere, reason demands that we recognize the harsh reality of the world of emotional illness.

> There are many emotional illnesses for which the word short-term "cure" is inapplicable and for which the goal of relative "adaptation" must be substituted. Thus for the child, the parents, the parent-counselor, reason and realism must rule over emotion and phantasy, sensitive objectivity must replace the anarchy of subjective feeling, and developmental planning and implementation must replace either apathetic fixation or blind impulsivity.

Parents of emotionally disturbed children are in many ways like other parents; they have their own unique assets and liabilities, their own self-concepts, their own hopes and fantasies regarding their children. They did not expect that their child would be emotionally disturbed, but on the other hand they are not rendered different as a result of their child's problem. Each parent will bring to the situation his own differential perceptions of the child, his own assets and limitations for playing his role in the situation. Some will accept the challenge with fervor and skill of remarkable proportions; others will be overwhelmed, guilt-ridden, impotent. To most parents, though, it is a painfully difficult, threatening, and highly ego involving experience to face the reality of major illness or handicap in a child.

Recent studies on the diagnosis, treatment and education of handicapped children continue to emphasize the importance of the parents' adjustment to and role in the child's overall maturation and psychological adjustment. Both research and clinical and social case studies have furthered our knowledge of the gross and subtle interaction patterns existing between the emotionally disturbed child and his family, thus focusing more and more on the need for improved methods of parent education and counseling. It has long been known that children can, and often do, reflect the emotional and social adjustment patterns of their parents. This being so with the normal child, imagine the degree to which this relationship could be magnified in the case of the emotionally disturbed child. From the frame of reference of the parent, the child's condition is very likely to affect the parent's personality and adaptation. The parents' past successes and failures in important challenges; their present mental health; their age, physical health and socioeconomic status are examples of major factors which will affect their capacity to adapt to the child's disability. One crucial additional factor is selective perception; one parent may perceive a relatively minor emotional problem in his child as a near-overwhelming catastrophe, while another is able to accept a much more emotionally disturbed child without fatal strain on his psychological security and adaptational abilities.

A distinction should always be made — despite their interactional nature — between the socioeconomic and rehabilitative efforts of the parents in caring for their child and those both tangible and intangible psychological and emotional cues which reveal genuine love and acceptance or masked rejection of the child as a real and fully accepted member of the family unit. All parents probably make many mistakes in the child-rearing process. If the overall relationship, however, is one of genuine and openly-communicated love and respect for the child, then many mistakes can apparently be made without disrupting the positive growth tendencies of the child. It is apparent, however, that similar mistakes made in dealing with the mentally disturbed child will be more deleterious to the psychological health and self-concept of the child. Certainly the parents face more difficult child-rearing conditions in such a case in any event. If the parents become overly concerned about the impact of their behavior they may transmit, rather than their deep feeling of love and concern, the characteristics of fear, guilt, anxiety, indecision, inhibition, etc., thus increasing the probability that the child is going to retain his psychological handicap.

Not only must the parents face the challenge of some degree of role reorientation in order to maximize their effectiveness with the child, but so too might other children in the family be forced into some adaptational requirements. This, of couse, depends upon such factors as the nature and severity of the emotional disturbance, its social stimulus value, etc. The parents will face other adaptational requirements with, for example, their near relatives, neighbors, the school and the local community.

Parents of children with serious emotional illnesses usually come in contact with representatives of several of the following fields: medicine and medical specialties; clinical and counseling psychology; rehabilitation specialties; social casework; education, and special education. Some representatives of these disciplines are — in addition to their expertise in child diagnosis and treatment — well trained and experienced in the parent-counsling area. Still others do not possess the skill nor the confidence in the parent-counseling relationship which they possess in their specific area of specialization. Then again there are professional workers in many of the aforementioned fields who have never really thought that much about anyone in the family other than the child with the emotional illness. Thus, while some counseling of the highest quality and value is being carried on with parents of emotionally disturbed children, there is much room for continued upgrading of this activity. Often the attitudes and explanation of the family physician, the pastor or rabbi, may have — at least initially — as great an effect on the parents as the psychiatrist or psychologist trained in this specific area. This is not to suggest that it is only the psychiatrist and psychologist who are proficient in parent-counseling and therapy. Indeed, experience suggests that the situation is sometimes the reverse. That is, the over-reliance on the initial view that the child should be treated, almost as if in a vacuum, with no contact between the therapist and the child's parents, has more than once prevented certain of these therapists from ever establishing a therapeutic relationship with the parents or other members of the family.

A perusal of the literature reporting on parental reactions to interviews of this sort indicates that in far too many cases the parents leave the counseling session with mixed feelings of frustration, confusion, bewilderment, denial and guilt. Accompanying the feelings may be incomplete information, misunderstood information and selectively perceived information. That some parents may be using defensive reactions such as denial, insulation, projection, displacement and selective perception is somewhat understandable. It seems, however, that some of the unfortunate parental reactions are the result of counseling interviews which failed. That is, some of the primary goals of the counseling session were not reached because of an incorrect or changed diagnosis; evasion or distortion of the child's condition and prognosis; seemingly brutal callousness and frankness in the initial informing session, and perhaps no provision for the very important follow-up interviews with the parents. Well-prepared and well-conducted parent interviews are an important part of the treatment and rehabilitative procedures of people functioning in any sort of counseling relationship with parents of emotionally disturbed children, be they family physicians, pediatricians or other medical specialists, or psychologists, social workers, rehabilitation experts, or educators.

In hopes of furthering this professional interest in parent-counseling and therapy, the writer has collected this series of articles from the world's literature dealing specifically with the counseling of parents of emotionally and mentally ill children and adolescents. We approached the task of selecting appropriate articles from a fourfold frame of reference:

1. We need not impute to the parents either gross culpability, or assign to them guilt feelings, to realize and to proclaim that parental and family patterns of attitudes and behavior are often at the root of childhood emotional and mental

disturbances.

2. The phenomenological reaction of the parents to the child's illness or disability may well be as crucial, and in some cases more so, as the actual disorder in terms of impact on the child.

3. The child's illness or disability may serve as a source of severe disruption, especially psychologically, to parental and family adjustment.

4. A therapeutic-type relationship with a competent professional in the field is needed if the parents are to make an objective, integrative and wholesome adaptation to the child's disability. Such an adaptation would imply that all relationships would be considered (i.e. parent-child; parent-parent; parent-family) as in need of psychological maintenance, not just the issue of the child's care.

As there is already available voluminous information regarding problems relating to diagnosis, classification and treatment of the emotional and mental illnesses represented in this book, such topics will be given only peripheral treatment. The major criterion used in selecting articles for this collection was the relevance of the article to the topic of *counseling parents* of emotionally disturbed children. Some exceptions to this will be found in the rather general and introductory articles of the first part of the book. In the final analysis, however, the articles were chosen with the hope and the belief that the interested reader would find the insights and techniques shared by the authors to be of value to them in contacts with parents who look to them for so much.

The readings in the collection are divided into four sections. Part I deals with articles covering the *rationale of,* and *significant issues in, parent therapy.* Included here are articles on topics such as family interaction in adolescent therapy; examples of distortion in parental counseling; and the family in psychosomatic process. Part II contains six articles on *the mother in therapy.* Included are several articles dealing with the simultaneous treatment of the mother and the child, as well as others dealing with special problems (e.g. very young children; psychosomatic cases). In Part III we have included articles from the very sparse literature dealing with *the father in therapy.* In addition to an opening article on the psychological role of the father, several other articles chronicle the role and treatment of fathers of schizophrenics. Included here, as in the previous section, are articles on group therapy. The last section is on *group therapy with parents*. These articles show the approaches and techniques used by different therapists in groups composed of both parents of emotionally disturbed children. Included are articles showing the approaches used with parents of children in day care and in residential units; of neurotic and psychotic children; of drug addicts and of psychosomatics. The book concludes with a listing of *additional selected readings,* including most of the other titles which we were able to locate on this important topic.

It is our hope that this collection of articles will serve as a useful and convenient source of information and insights for professional and para-professional personnel involved in the counseling and therapy of parents of emotionally disturbed individuals. It is believed that this book will be helpful in college courses in certain areas of psychiatry, clinical and counseling psychology, casework and psychiatric social work, vocational rehabilitation, and in special education courses dealing with the exceptional child and his parents.

R. L. NOLAND

Acknowledgments

THE editor wishes to express his appreciation to the authors who so graciously consented to the inclusion of their articles in this sourcebook. To the extent that there is merit in collections such as this, it is obviously due to the scholarly, creative, and empathic efforts of the authors whose works are presented in this volume.

Thanks are also due to the editors and publishers of the following journals for permission to reprint articles from their periodicals:

American Journal of Orthopsychiatry
American Journal of Psychiatry
American Journal of Psychotherapy
Annals of Allergy
Canada's Mental Health
Canadian Psychiatric Association Journal
Children
Hospital and Community Psychiatry
International Journal of Group Psychotherapy
Journal of the American Academy of Child Psychiatry
Journal of Pediatrics
Mental Hygiene
Psychiatric Quarterly
Psychiatry
Psychoanalytic Study of the Child
Psychosomatic Medicine
Psychotherapy and Psychosomatics
Quarterly Journal of Child Behavior
Social Casework
Social Work

R.L.N.

Contents

PART I

Rationale and Significant Issues in Parent Therapy

Chapter

PART II

The Mother in Therapy

PART III

The Father in Therapy

COUNSELING PARENTS OF THE EMOTIONALLY DISTURBED CHILD

PART I

RATIONALE AND SIGNIFICANT ISSUES
IN PARENT THERAPY

Chapter 1

The Marital Relationship of Parents of Emotionally Disturbed Children: Polarization and Isolation*

EZRA F. VOGEL

FEW studies of factors affecting the personality of children have considered childhood development in the context of the dynamics of the family as a group. The child's internal processes, or his relationship with his mother and, more recently, with his father have instead been the focus of investigation. The present study examines the dynamics of one crucial relationship within the family, the marriage relationship, in order to provide a broader background for considering the personality development of emotionally disturbed children. It looks at this problem with the sociological perspective that considers the dynamics of the group structure, not simply the internal dynamics of the persons involved.

The data for this chapter† were taken from an intensive study of eighteen families, who were seen for a period of from one to four years by an interdisciplinary team of psychiatrists,

*NOTE: Reprinted by permission of the author and *Psychiatry, 23*:1-12, 1960.

†The data for the present analysis are taken from a larger study on families and mental health which is directed by John Spiegel and Florence Kluckhohn; the author wishes to thank the directors for their guidance and assistance in writing this report. The research is a project of the Laboratory of Social Relations of Harvard University. It is financed by the National Institute of Mental Health and by the Pauline and Lewis G. Cowan Foundation. For other reports of the project, see John P. Spiegel, "The Resolution of Role Conflict Within the Family," *Psychiatry* (1957) *20*:1-16; and Florence Kluckhohn, "Variations in the Basic Values of Family Systems," *Social Casework* (1958) *39*:63-72. More detailed evidence for the conclusions in the present paper is presented in the author's Ph.D. thesis, *The Marital Relationship of Parents and the Emotionally Disturbed Child;* Harvard Univ., 1958.

psychologists, psychiatric social workers, sociologists, and an anthropologist. Nine of these families had emotionally disturbed children and were seen in the psychiatric clinic for regular treatment of mother, father, and child. Nine families with relatively healthy children were matched with the disturbed families for size of family, socioeconomic status, ethnic background, and duration of marriage, and were seen in their homes for a comparable period of time. Of each group of nine, three were Irish-American, three were Italo-American, and three were old-American. All the families except one were of working-class background.

In all the families with an emotionally disturbed child, the marriage relationship of the parents was found to be more disturbed than in the families with relatively healthy children. While the disturbed partners often had very similar internal conflicts, in manifest behavior one spouse acted out one side of the conflict, the other, the other side of the conflict. Although at a deeper level they shared the same fundamental conflicts, in relationship to each other they behaved as if they were polar opposites (1). Together they formed a complete system in which each formed a complete system in which each consciously expressed a side of the conflict that the partner did not (2); this polarization was accompanied by a marked isolation.

The pathological process of polarization and isolation can be illustrated by a comparison of a "disturbed" and a "nondisturbed" family. Both families are lower middle-class Catholic Irish-Americans, have five children, and are living in the Boston area. In the D family, the polarization and isolation are particularly striking, but in the O family, despite problems and some polarization, they are minimal.

---

(1) This formulation owes much to the general statement of Parsons and others that each member in the nuclear family has internalized all the different roles in the family but that behaviorally he orients himself primarily to only one of these roles. Talcott Parsons, Robert F. Bales and others, *Family Socialization and Interaction Process;* Glencoe, Ill., Free Press, 1954.

(2) In terms of a general theory of deviance, on one set of standards one person was a compulsive conformist, the other compulsively alienated. On the basis of conflicting standards, their roles were reversed. Talcott Parsons, "Deviant Behavior and the Mechanisms of Social Control," Ch. 7 pp. 249-325; in *The Social System;* Glencoe, Ill., Free Press, 1951.

THE "DISTURBED" D FAMILY

Mrs. D took the initiative in bringing her family to the clinic, immediately talking freely to her therapist on a wide variety of topics although the focus was ostensibly on her oldest son's stuttering and other nervous symptoms. She assumed that she and her therapist had the same basic outlook on life, but that her husband's outlook was very different. Mrs. D's therapist accepted this analysis and commented in the early staff meetings that Mrs. D was "well motivated" and would be a good case for treatment, but that Mr. D was a source of difficulty for his wife and was probably not "well motivated" for treatment. Mr. D also acted on the assumption that the therapists would be more sympathetic with his wife, and was extremely reluctant to come to the clinic for treatment. When he first came, he did not talk freely; he volunteered nothing and offered the briefest possible answers to the therapist's questions. His entire behavior reflected his hesitancy in coming to a clinic which would presumably not be sympathetic to his point of view and would side with his wife in any internal family problem.

From the beginning, Mrs. D came to the clinic well dressed, a relatively new, neatly tailored clothes, which the therapist thought in good taste and very becoming. Mr. D, in contrast, frequently came in his work clothes, and was not very neat, and not always particularly clean.

Similar differences were present in the areas of disagreement between Mr. and Mrs. D. Mr. D was in favor of living fairly close to their relatives and visiting them frequently, but Mrs. D was opposed. Mr. D wanted his wife to be home taking care of the children, but she wanted to be more independent and to get away from the home and family — to work, shop, visit, or just have fun. For example, when she once took a trip to another city, ostensibly to visit a relative, she had a wonderful time vacationing and was not at all pleasant in greeting her husband on her return. Mr. D thought she should have been home taking care of the family instead of going away for a good time.

During therapy, Mrs. D became pregnant, and wanted to give the baby an unusual name, one that implied higher social class. Mr. D argued that it was silly for "just plain people" to give such a fancy name to their child.

Mrs. D had a higher IQ than her husband and considered herself better educated and more interested in academic pursuits. Mr. D admitted that he had no such interest in education and reading, although he was somewhat reluctant to express this to a therapist who was relatively well educated.

These differences in the expressed attitudes of Mr. and Mrs. D correspond in large part to the differences between the typical rural Irish value-orientations and the American middle-class value-orientations. One of the staff's early formulations of the D case was that Mr. and Mrs. D were really extremely different, that it was surprising that they had married, and that the marriage probably had taken place only because Mrs. D had become pregnant before marriage. It was felt that the family tensions resulted from these basic differences. But since Mrs. D's sister, also Catholic, had been divorced, the staff wondered why the D's never seriously considered divorce.

As more material accumulated, this early formulation gradually became clearly inadequate. While on the surface Mr. and Mrs. D seemed different, each expressed the differing attitudes quite defensively and was ambivalent at a slightly deeper level; in fact, both were more alike than one would have imagined from the content of their therapeutic interviews. For example, although Mrs. D was well dressed, at times she seemed defensive in her overemphasis on her appearance. Shortly after she purchased an attractive new coat, she kept it on while sitting in the waiting room before her therapeutic hour, even though it was warm and she was sweating. Although Mr. D seemed to value appearance less, he did so defensively, wearing his old clothes for treatment even though he knew others did not; he had newer clothes and it was not always necessary for him to come directly from work.

During the course of therapy, as some of the defenses began to wear thin, the other side of the ambivalences gradually appeared. For example, in one home visit by the therapist, Mrs. D felt embarrassed by and deliberately paid no attention to what her father-in-law, the incarnation of lower-class Irish culture, was saying, and expected the therapist to do likewise. When the therapist laughed at one of the father-in-law's jokes, Mrs. D seemed surprised, asked to have the joke repeated, and then laughed herself. Although she had greatly stressed her desire to be completely independent from relatives, during the course of therapy the D's moved to a two-family house, and her mother moved into the other half of the house with Mrs. D's approval. While Mrs. D expressed a desire for independence, she later confessed in therapy that she had difficulty "standing on my own two feet."

The same type of ambivalence was also seen in Mr. D. Although he steadfastly renounced middle-class value-orientations, he gradually began making more friendly overtures to his therapist in terms of their sharing the same ideas. He began to play golf with one of his superiors at work, which both he and his wife took as a move in the direction of middle-class American life. Although he had apparently been satisfied with his position at work, he began discussing the possibilities of starting some sort of independent business enterprise. The therapists doubted that this was a real possibility, but Mr. D actually went ahead with this plan. While in relation to his wife he had upheld the idea of being close to his family, it gradually became clear that he also had many ambivalences toward his family and many doubts about the desirability of being too close to them. Perhaps the greatest step during the course of treatment, however, was the decision to move from an apartment house in a poor neighborhood to a two-family house in a middle-class neighborhood of private housing with large lawns.

Until the time of their move to the new neighborhood, there had been considerable tension between Mr. and Mrs. D; immediately after the move the tension suddenly seemed to disappear. Mrs. D said she was amazed and pleased with the interest her husband was taking in the new house and neighborhood, and Mr. D felt that his wife was being more cooperative and that there were fewer problems between them. In a sense, Mr. D had attempted to make the leap toward middle-class life, and Mrs. D at first welcomed him into this new pattern. But within a few weeks it began to be clear that they were not fully able to take these middle-class roles, and tension recurred between Mr. and Mrs. D which was polarized in the same way.

Except for this brief interlude, they behaved in relation to each other as if they had opposite sets of value-orientations, and by so doing were able to avoid recognizing their own internal conflicts. On the conscious level each thought of himself and his partner as possessing a relatively consistent set of value-orientations, which afforded them a level of ego integration that permitted them to function. Each could not recognize consciously in himself the other side of the conflict, but could see it very clearly in and project it on to his spouse.

Although these conflicts were expressed in periodic fights between Mr. and Mrs. D, the prevailing mood was one of silence and discontented resignation. They had actually made an explicit verbal agreement not to discuss certain topics, assuming that any such discussion would certainly end in an explosion. Once during the years of therapy, when Mr. D was drunk, he did bring up a forbidden topic — Mrs. D's premarital affair with a man who symbolized non-Irish middle-class culture — and it did lead to a violent argument. Regarding many other topics, Mr. and Mrs. D had no explicit verbal agreement, but avoided discussion, which they thought would only lead to arguments without improving the situation. This included virtually all the topics about which they had strong feelings, such as Mr. D's work, his family, or Mrs. D's not spending time at home with the children. Mrs. D continually repeated that she could not talk to her husband since he simple could not understand her; Mr. D's conviction about the lack of value in talking was sufficiently generalized so that he felt very reluctant to talk either to his wife or to his therapist about things that really mattered to him.

Mr. D's job kept him away from home for long hours, although the work was not particularly hard or economically rewarding. When he was home, he spent relatively little time talking with his wife, and they almost never performed household tasks in cooperation with each other. Even when Mrs. D was well into her pregnancy and had difficulty carrying the heavy laundry basket to the laundry room, Mr. D steadfastly refused to help.

Although his lack of contact was doubtless a reflection of the annoyances which each felt toward the other, the minimization of the opportunities for friction made it possible for them to avoid serious arguments. They almost never tried to work through problems, because it only led to Mrs. D's steadfastly upholding her side of the argument, and Mr. D's defending his side. Yet the irritability they felt did occasionally erupt despite their attempts to avoid it.

This pattern of conscious polarization, mutual annoyance, and reduction of potentially dangerous interaction to an absolute minimum had considerable stability. The therapist tried to help Mr. and Mrs. D work through their problems, but despite temporary therapeutic success, the pattern between them remained, with only mild changes, during several years of therapy.

THE "NONDISTURBED" O FAMILY

Mr. and Mrs. O, whose children evidenced no serious emotional problems, apparently had developed a less pathological relationship, despite great external and internal pressures. Mr. and Mrs. O were also making accommodations to the conflicts between Irish and American value-orientations, and they also had internal conflicts. Furthermore, Mrs. O's neurotic conflicts were severe enough to interfere seriously with her relationships with relatives and neighbors, and Mr. O's brother and Mrs. O's father had recently had psychotic episodes. But the relationship between Mr. and Mrs. O did not involve the same rigid and hostile polatization, nor did it require the same degree of distance as did that between Mr. and Mrs. D.

Mr. and Mrs. O occasionally quarreled, about Mr. O's family, about their friends, about church participation, and so forth. Mrs. O was inclined to become very upset and excited easily, and one of her husband's main complaints was that she exaggerated too much. Mrs. O complained, on the other hand, that her husband always took things to lightly and tried to overlook too many things. For example, early in the course of home visits, Mrs. O began complaining terribly about Mr. O's parents, and Mr. O defended them. Another time, Mrs. O became upset because she was afraid that Mr. O's brother was becoming psychotic, and Mr. O felt that his wife was too excited and shouldn't take things so seriously. After such arguments, Mr. O usually went out drinking with his friends somewhat more. Mrs. O gave him implicit permission to do this (for example, by calling up his place of employment the following day to say he had fever and chills and hence could not come to work), and then gradually began to apply pressure to him to spend more time at home. He in turn gradually obliged, and they attempted to talk over their difficulties and come to some agreement. Although the arguments did recur, Mr. and Mrs. O did not retain a hostile polarization over a long period of time.

Another example of their accommodation to each other can be seen in their attempts to reconcile the American attitudes about independence with the traditional Irish preference for lineal organization. Early in their contacts with the interviewers, Mr. and Mrs. O were increasingly interested in becoming independent from both sets of parents. During the course of the four years of research, they did become increasingly independent. At first this process focused on their declaring their independence from Mr. O's parents and was accompanied by a considerable number of arguments, with Mrs. O attacking and Mr. O defending his parents. Gradually, however, Mr. O stopped defending his parents and began to agree with his wife, first jokingly and then somewhat more seriously, although his complaints were less severe than those of his wife. Experimentation followed concerning the appropriate relationship with Mr. O's parents, which involved alternation between long periods of no contact and periods of very frequent visiting. Toward the end of the four-year period, the situation seemed to become slightly more stabilized, with relatively infrequent visiting. Although Mr. and Mrs. O did argue about this problem, they did not remain as polar opposites.

During the period when Mr. and Mrs. O first considered increased independence from his parents, particularly when Mrs. O became annoyed while visiting her in-laws, she would urge that they move farther from their parents. Mr. O kept saying they could not afford it, but when a friend of his offered him an unusually good buy, Mr. O was seriously interested and suggested that they visit the house. But then Mrs. O was not willing to see the house and began offering many reasons why the place might not be good and why she was not interested. For a considerable length of time after that she did not talk about moving. Here again, Mr. and Mrs. O's temporary polarization had neither the rigidity nor the hostility that existed in the D case.

Although Mr. and Mrs. O argued, even in front of guests, they also joked with each other and discussed important things relatively frequently. They usually socialized separately rather than as a couple, but this was characteristic of their social group, and compared to their friends they spent considerable time together. Although Mr. and Mrs. O were in the same economic group as the D's, Mr. O, unlike Mr. D, was not willing to move to a nicer home if it would require more money, and hence longer hours.

The joking between Mr. and Mrs. O was a relatively effective way of expressing their complaints to each other, and often led to the desired change. Mr. and Mrs. D were not able to regard these problems with any sense of humor. When Mr. and Mrs. O had serious problems, the tensions were often directed outside the nuclear family. When Mrs. O became upset or angry, her affect was generally directed toward her mother-in-law, rather than toward her husband. Although Mr. O temporarily was annoyed with his wife when she criticized his mother, the husband-wife tensions greatly decreased when he joined his wife against his mother. Mr. D continued to defend his parents to his wife, so that the tensions were absorbed in the husband-wife relationship instead of being dissipated outside the nuclear family.

Because the internal conflicts in the O family were not so severe and their defenses were less brittle, each spouse was able to recognize both the Irish and the American aspects of his own character. In the D family, these conflicts were so severe that neither spouse could integrate both aspects into his own character, and one spouse had become the symbol of what was ego-alien.

THE HOSTILE EQUILIBRIUM

In some of the disturbed cases the marital difficulties were obvious in the beginning, and the spouses complained bitterly about each other. In other cases, difficulties were massively denied, especially at the beginning of contact, and the spouses carefully avoided any mention of marital problems. But whether readily verbalized or massively denied, the disturbances were reflected in certain common attitudes and behavior between the spouses.

Perhaps the most general indication of disturbance was the severe disappointment of the partners with each other and with their marriage. Both husband and wife had persistent fantasies of having married someone else, of not having married at all, or of getting divorced. They often talked longingly of other people who were happily married or of single people who had good times. Sometimes their fantasies of having been married to someone else or of being single were so strong that they almost acted as if the fantasies were true (3). In contrast, the couples in the control families talked eagerly about their own courtship, about how they met each other, their dating experiences, their decision to get married, and the preparations for their marriage.

In all the disturbed marriages there were periodic explosions of hostility, manifested by physical assaults, arguments, refusal to help, or complete avoidance. But between these occasional explosions, there were long periods of armed truce during which both partners would exert considerable energy in trying to control their hostility. These periods were characterized by tension, indirect expressions of annoyance, and lack of contact. Often, the spouses were expert at doing just those things — frequently without conscious design — to which the partners reacted with particular sensitivity and great irritation.

However, the partner aroused was sometimes slow to express the anger felt toward the spouse. Often, the way a spouse irritated the partner appeared so insignificant or innocent that it did not

(3) There was a much more persistent and active type of fantasy than that described by psychoanalytic writers as the normal disappointment when the spouse does not live up to the idealization of the parent image. See, for example, John G. Flugel, *The Psycho-Analytic Study of the Family;* London, Hogarth, 1950; and Edmund Bergler, *Unhappy Marriage and Divorce;* New York, Internat. Univ. Press, 1946. With the exception of one case, however, these relationships did not take the extreme form noted in schizophrenic families. See Lyman C. Wynne, Irving M. Ryckoff, Juliana Day, and Stanley I. Hirsch, "Pseudo-Mutuality in the Family Relations to Schizophrenics," *Psychiatry* (1958) *21*-205-220.

Although it would be fruitful to analyze the developmental background of the spouses, the present analysis deals only with the effects of this disappointment on the patterning of relationships between them.

seem legitimate to express anger in return. Sometimes, although a spouse sensed that the partner was behaving offensively, the clever culprit had disguised the behavior sufficiently to be able to claim innocence in any specific instance and avoid a fight. But even a spouse who felt clearly legitimate anger often did not express it. The partners tried desperately to avoid arguments and seemed constantly on edge, lest violent arguments erupt. Both would go to great lengths to keep secrets which, if discovered, might lead to arguments. One who discovered such a secret would sometimes pretend ignorance of it so as to avoid an argument. The discoverer seemed somewhat relieved if not accused of knowing the secret, which would have impelled an argument. The implicit fear in these disturbed families seemed to be that arguments might lead to drastic action: violence, separation, or divorce. And these constant fears made the truce an uneasy one.

In the nondisturbed families, arguments could be very real and involve considerable hostility, but without the frantic fear of the possible consequences. These parents seemed to have basic understandings between them which provided a layer of fundamental agreement that was not threatened by disputes (4). The couples could tease each other and laugh at each other's jokes. They would wink at or smilingly pinch each other. When the disturbed partners poked fun at each other, the recipient did not laugh because the bitter cutting edge of the joke was too real and too thinly disguised.

The disappointment which the disturbed spouses felt with each other corresponded very closely to their perception that they were very different from each other. Indeed, there seemed to be an equilibration between the amount of disappointment the spouses felt in each other and the amount of difference they perceived between themselves (5). The parents most disappointed with each other also felt that they had attitudes most different from their

(4) This is analogous to Durkheim's noncontractual agreements which serve as the basis of the formal contract. Emile Durkheim, *On the Division of Labor in Society,* translated by George Simpson; New York, MacMillan, 1933.
(5) This corresponds to the finding that in couples that regard themselves as happily married, the partners say they have many common interests, even if objective lists of their interests indicate the contrary. Purnell Benson, "The Common Interests Myth in Marriage," *Social Problems* (1955) *3*:27-34.

spouses, while the nondisturbed parents felt that they had relatively similar attitudes. And for a given couple, various changes in this equilibration could be observed. When a mother and father, through treatment, became more optimistic about the possibility of getting along well, they began to think that their underlying attitudes were actually very similar. But when they became pessimistic about their relationships, they tended to emphasize the disparity between their basic attitudes.

At first, the differences which spouses perceived in each other seemed to be based simply on the extent of real differences. However, in analyzing the value-orientation patterns of each spouse, the staff soon realized that value-orientation differences between disturbed spouses were not very great when compared with the possible range of value-orientation differences (6). In fact, the spouses had fairly similar value-orientations, but both had severe internal value-orientation conflicts.

The pattern between spouses was completely reciprocal. A husband, for example, might recognize certain characteristics in himself but not in his wife, and not recognize other characteristics in himself that he could see very clearly in her (7). His perceptions, though based on reality, would distort reality considerably. The perceptual distortion in turn was 'verified' by the wife, who responded as if she, in fact, had only those characteristics assigned by her husband and he had only those characteristics which he consciously espoused. This reciprocal recognition served to confirm and stabilize the perceptual distortions.

The perceptual distortion is in part a solution to problems

---

(6) The value-orientations were analyzed according to the categories of Florence Kluckhohn, "Dominant and Variant Value Orientations," pp. 342-357; in *Personality in Nature, Society and Culture* (2nd ed.), edited by Clyde Kluckhohn, Henry Murray, and David Schneider; New York, Knopf, 1953. This is further developed in her forthcoming book on variations in value orientations.

The couples were not consciously aware of value-orientations as such, but only of concrete behavior which they felt to be right or wrong. The standards or the concrete behavior which they consciously perceived were representations of their underlying value-orientations.

(7) In his analysis of perception, Ichheiser has termed this the mote-beam-mechanism. Gustav Ichheiser, "Projection and the Mote-Beam-Mechanism," *J. Abnormal and Social Psychol.* (1947) *42*:131-133.

arising from the value-orientation conflicts. Many of the disturbed spouses could not conform to the two conflicting sets of values they actually held, and because these values were highly internalized and involved very strong feelings of right and wrong, the failure to conform to both led to considerable frustration and negative affect (8). There were several possible ways such negative affect might be channeled. Self-criticism, a painful solution, was rarely used in these families (9). Nor was projection on to some object outside the family successful for discharging chronic and pressing strains (10). Instead, the marital partner was the object chosen for projection of internal difficulties. The marital relationship is an intensely personal kind of relationship in which one can constantly validate the correctness of one's projections (11). The spouse continually acts as if he held certain beliefs, and because the marital partners share precisely the same conflicts, the partner is a cognitively appropriate object for projection. In addition, feelings of hostility are felt to be less dangerous when expressed toward the spouse rather than toward outside persons since the negative affect can be counteracted by positive ties (12).

Each disturbed partner contended that his own standards were

---

(8) This is the same sort of phenomenon that Kurt Lewin called attention to in his discussion of self-hatred among Jews, which arises from partial internalization of gentile standards. Kurt Lewin, "Self-Hatred Among Jews." pp. 186-200; in *Resolving Social Conflicts,* edited by Gertrud Weiss Lewin; New York, Harper, 1948.

(9) It is possible that the absence of this solution was a by-product of the use of only cases with emotionally disturbed children. If one of the parents could accept the hostility generated by the conflict, then perhaps it would not be necessary to utilize a child as a scapegoat.

(10) These spouses did express prejudice against certain ethnic groups, but this did not serve as an effective drain for their fundamental and omnipresent frustrations. Perhaps use of an object as a focus for such continuous hostility requires constant interaction with the object or else constant validation by group norms. Probably other ethnic groups were also not cognitively appropriate objects for the most intense hostility.

(11) Projection between spouses is a pervasive and fundamental mechanism as has been shown, for example, in the research of Dicks. Henry V. Dicks, "Clinical Studies in Marriage and the Family: A Symposium on Methods. 1. Experiences with Marital Tensions Seen in the Psychological Clinic," *Brit. J. Med. Psychol.* (1953) *26*:181-196.

(12) Indeed, this is one of the striking characteristics of the marital bond. The positive attractions can bind the negative affect which might disrupt other types of relationships. See *The Sociology of Georg Simmel* edited and translated by Kurt Wolff; Glendale, Ill., Free Press, 1950; and Robert F. Bales, *Interaction Process Analysis;* Cambridge, Mass., Addison-Wesley, 1950.

the right ones and those held by his spouse were the wrong ones. This had a double effect. First, in criticizing the behavior which he observed in his partner, a spouse could direct the negative affect for that side of his own internal conflict toward his partner. He could say that it was not he who held these attitudes which deserved negative sanctions, but his spouse. Second, whenever he could not fully live up to the standards which he consciously favored, he could say that his failure was the fault of his spouse; the fact that the spouse did not accept the standards made this seem particularly appropriate.

Projection of internal difficulties on to a partner not only produced satisfaction from the displacement of negative affect and enhancement of self-esteem, but also yielded a feeling of self-consistency or ego-identity (13). Just as people are generally reluctant to recognize their ambivalence toward objects, so, too, they apparently need to achieve conscious consistency of attitudes, and derive cognitive satisfaction from its orderliness. Thus a spouse was able to behave as if he were consistently following certain standards, and to deny all conflicting standards in himself by constantly projecting them on to and perceiving them in his partner. This served to prevent the ego boundaries from the disintegration that might result if an awareness of conflicting standards diffused the spouse's self-concepts.

Choosing one side of a conflict with relative consistency also enabled the spouse to act, for if both sides of the conflict had been constantly present, he would have been immobilized.

Although a spouse sometimes complained about the attitudes held by his partner, even asking his spouse to change, he did not really seem to expect results and seemed indifferent when the spouse did not change (14). He could maintain his consistent,

---

(13) Erik H. Erikson, "The Problem of Ego Identity," *J. Amer. Psychoanal. Ass.* (1956) *4:*56-121. Gustav Ichheiser has discussed the common perceptual distortion of perceiving oneself and others as being more consistent than the facts indicate, in "Misunderstandings in Human Relations," *Amer. J. Sociol.* (1949) *55:* Part 2 [monograph supplement]. Parsons and his associates have dealt with this problem in a general way. All systems have boundary-maintaining mechanisms which are used to prevent the disintegration of the system. Talcott Parsons, Robert F. Bales, and Edward A. Shils, *Working Papers in the Theory of Action;* Glencoe, Ill., Free Press, 1953.

(14) This is in striking contrast to Spiegel's description of the various ways partners may attempt reequilibration. See footnote †.

extreme position, knowing that he probably would not be required to act on it, since the spouse would provide some balance (15). Accordingly, the protests and hostility to the spouse did not really reflect a desire for change. Explicitly, each complained about the other's attitudes, but implicitly, both accepted the role system very much as it was. In a few instances in which one responded by changing his behavior, the other quickly changed his position so that the old equilibrium could be restored.

RECURRING THEMES OF DISPUTE

The content of the polarization was closely related to underlying value-orientations conflicts of the spouses. The precise conflict varied from case to case, but two of the problems noted were so common that they are especially good illustrations of the stable, balanced polarization. These conflicts were found to some extent in the nondisturbed families but were much more severe in the disturbed families.

One of these problems in the Irish-American and Italo-American families was the relative speed of the spouses in the transition to American value-orientations. In the disturbed families, in general, the wife was closer to the dominant American value-orientations than her husband. She came to stand for things American, and the husband came to stand for things as "they used to be." In all of these cases, the husband and wife had reached similar levels of acculturation, but they had tended to become polarized in relationship to each other. An example of the closeness of their value-orientations can be drawn from the case of Mr. and Mrs. M.

Mrs. M continually criticized her husband for being old-fashioned. One of her most persistent criticisms was that he did not let her out of the house enough. At one time, however, Mr. M was so concerned about being able to pay all his bills that in his anxiety he suggested that his wife should go out to work. Mrs. M was completely surprised at this idea, and, though flustered, she pointed out that she ought to be home for the sake of the children — an argument which her husband always used in urging her to stay home. After the excitement was over, Mr. M again told her to stay home, and she in turn gradually began to complain that she should have a chance to go out.

(15) This analysis may help explain why two people who feel so hostile toward each other are willing to continue their marital relationship.

Thus, although in their usual interaction she appeared much more Americanized, it was clear that their underlying attitudes were very similar and that she had been implicitly giving him permission and perhaps even encouragement to hold the position which he usually held in arguments with her.

Another general source of conflict centered around value-orientations regarding independence from relatives, particularly parents. As psychoanalysts have shown, negative attitudes toward parents and often separated out from positive ones and displaced on to other objects (16). In many of these families there was still relatively close contact with the extended family, in contrast to the more isolated middle-class American nuclear family. Consciously, each spouse generally favored remaining closer, either emotionally or physically, to his own parents. In relation to each other, the husband and wife argued about how close they should be to their parents. The husband generally argued that they should be closer to his parents and do more things for them, and the wife took the opposite position. When they discussed the wife's parents, the wife generally argued that they should be closer to them (17). At a deeper level, each spouse was conflicted about how close to be to his parents, and derived many satisfactions from increased distance. He could contend that he would have been closer to his parents if it wery not for his spouse, while being secretly happy that the spouse's demands resulted in the greater distance. Thus, in relation to each other, the spouses were again polarized.

THE MAINTENANCE OF THE TRUCE

The armed truce that was ordinarily maintained between the disturbed conjugal partners imposed a severe strain on the integrity of the marital system since the hostility constantly

---

(16) See, for example, Flugel, footnote 3.

(17) This generalization should be modified in accordance with the important cross-cutting variable that women in general have somewhat more involvement in relationships to the extended family. See, for example, Mirra Komarovsky, "Continuities in Family Research: A Case Study," *Amer. J. Sociology* (1956) *62:*42-47.

threatened to disrupt it. Considerable energy had to be expended in the solution of integrative problems in order to avoid any situations which might result in explosions and destruction of the relationship.

When relationships with factors outside the family threatened the integration of the marital pair, it was necessary for the family to maintain a very rigid defense against the outsiders. Two of the families which were seen therapeutically as a part of this research program discontinued treatment against the advice of their therapists. In both families there were unusually strong conflicts between husband and wife which became more overt during the course of therapy. In one of these families, the decision to discontinue treatment came immediately after the most severe outbreak of hostility between the spouses, which almost meant the end of the marriage. The outbreak of hostility was closely related to the changes in therapy, and discontinuing therapy made it possible for them to preserve the integrity of the marital bond. Such drastic action was required because the marital bond was so tenuous.

Similarly, it was often necessary for the parents to prevent the attachment between a child and a parent from becoming so strong that it threatened to disrupt the husband-wife relationship. Typically, the strongest parent-child ties followed Oedipal lines, with one parent and the opposite-sex child in a coalition against the other parent. When this parent-child relationship became unusually strong and threatened to upset the marital equilibrium, the child had to be severely restricted. At such times, even the favored parent participated in punishing the child or, at a minimum, gave clear approval for the other parent to punish the child.

In addition to these defenses against outside threats, a variety of mechanisms were used to minimize the disruption that might come from within the marriage itself. Most of them involved increasing the distance between the spouses (18).

---

(18) The importance of the optimal distance in maintaining an equilibrium in a social system has been recognized by many sociologists, but is perhaps best represented in the work of Georg Simmel and Leopold von Wiese. Simmel pointed out, for example, that if a couple has an equilibrium involving a very close relationship, the arrival of a child may

The simplest way of keeping the distance of physical separation. In all the conjugal pairs with disturbances, there was an unusual amount of physical separation between the husband and wife. Many of the men worked odd hours and had extra part-time jobs which kept them away from home during the wife's waking hours so that there was little opportunity for them to have contact with each other. But in addition to having long work hours, many husbands liked to leave the house early, and either sit at a snack bar and have a cigarette or listen to the radio before beginning work. Many liked to stop off someplace on the way home. The men protested about how hard they worked, but were often indifferent to being separated from their wives for such a long period of time each day. While the wives sometimes felt that their husbands should be helping them more and doing more things around the house, they also were often indifferent to the husband's being away so many hours.

Even if the husband was home several hours a day, the husband and wife had little contact. If he worked late, the wife generally would not stay awake to greet him when he came home, nor would the husband wake his wife as he came in. If the husband got up early in the morning to go to work, the wife typically would not awaken before he left, and he would fix his own breakfast and pack his own lunch. In one extreme case, the husband and wife saw each other only on week ends even though they slept in the same room. In another case, the husband left home before the wife was up, took a nap when he returned from the first job, went to the second job after the nap, and usually came home from the second job after his wife was asleep.

Even if the husband and wife were home and awake at the same time, they had relatively little contact with each other. Often the husband had a special province, such as the basement, where he stayed while the wife stayed someplace else in the house. Or else

---

create demands that would separate them more than the equilibrium could tolerate and lead to serious problems. Similarly, if a couple had an equilibrium in which they were very far apart, the birth of a child might require them to be so close that this would seriously disturb the equilibrium. See Wolff, footnote 12; and Leopold von Wiese, *Systematic Sociology,* adapted and amplified by Howard Becker; New York, J. Wiley, 1932.

the husband worked on the house, the car, or the yard so that he had little opportunity to be with his wife.

The physical separation was not simply a result of economic conditions since among the nondisturbed families of the same economic level there was not nearly so much separation. In two nondisturbed families the men did sometimes work long hours, but the spouses disliked the long separation, and still managed to spend a considerable amount of time with each other.

Not only was there greater physical separation between the husband and wife in disturbed couples than in control couples of the same ethnic and class backgrounds, but there was also a relatively rigid differentiation of husband and wife roles (19). The differences in the amount of role segregation were most striking in the areas of child care and child management. In most of the nondisturbed families, the fathers spent a great deal of time with the children, took them places, and joined with their wives in discussing things that involved the children (20). This was generally not true for the disturbed families. In the disturbed families, even if the husband took part, usually either the husband or the wife was responsible for the children at a given time and there was little overlap in their contacts with the children. Often one parent knew little about what the other did while with the children. In addition, management problems were left to the wife,

---

(19) There were variations in the average amount of segregation of conjugal roles among different ethnic or class groups, regardless of the amount of disturbance in the husband-wife relationship. For example, the traditional Italian conjugal roles were much more segregated than those of middle-class American conjugal roles. But when one compares the disturbed families of a given ethnic and class background with the control families of the same ethnic and class background, one notices differences in the amount of role segregation.

It may be suggested that, in general, when the nuclear family is relatively isolated, the social system demands greater flexibility in role assignment between husband and wife since there may be times when one person is not available to perform the usual requirements of his or her role. When more closely interwoven with the surrounding social system, the nuclear family can more easily find substitutes from outside the nucleus − for example, aunts, cousins − to fulfill family roles in emergencies, so that the roles can remain relatively segregated.

(20) In two of the disturbed families, the fathers did spend considerable time with their children, but, in general the decisions about what the children should or should not do, and the responsibilities for child management and child control were left entirely up to their wives.

and the husband participated only in what they considered an emergency.

The extent of role segregation can also be seen in their methods of handling finances. The typical pattern in the disturbed families was that the husband was given an "allowance" each week to buy the things that he was expected to be responsible for and the wife kept an amount of money with which she bought the things she was responsible for. Often one spouse had relatively little idea of what the other spouse was doing with the money, and there was little flexibility in how the money was allocated. If one ran short of money, that was his problem and he could not turn to the other spouse for more money. In the control families, however, there was much more sharing and flexibility in the handling of money. Typically there was some spending money available which either the husband or wife could use.

Although only in the areas of child care and handling of finances were consistent differences observed between the disturbed and control couples, there was a general pattern of difference, regardless of area of activity. In the disturbed couples, generally one person performed any given activity. There was little flexibility in who performed the activity, and amost no activities were carried on jointly by the spouses at the same time. Each spouse's spheres of activity were kept clearly separate from those of the partner. This meant that they did not have to consult with each other about the tasks they performed, but that each could carry out his own activities without interfering with the other. In the nondisturbed families, more activities were carried on jointly, and there was also considerable flexibility in who performed which activities. For example, husband and wife sometimes participated together in cooking, serving, or cleaning. Some husbands in the disturbed families did participate in the housework, but generally by means of inflexible assignments and alone rather than in cooperation with the wives.

As mentioned, even if the disturbed husband and wife were physically together, they talked very little to each other about important matters, particularly about topics which might be disruptive. Often both partners confessed to their therapists that they could not talk to their partners about important things. All of them expressed the view that it was best to keep things to oneself and that talking only led to arguments. Some of the couples, like Mr. and Mrs. D of the illustrative case, had agreed not to talk about certain topics which they regarded as particularly explosive. While the nondisturbed families often did not talk about certain topics for a period of time, the restriction of communication was not nearly so severe.

In comparing the disturbed and control families, some of the general characteristics of the nondisturbed couples should be emphasized. As indicated, value-orientation conflicts were not so severe. Although the value-orientation of some of these couples bridged the gap between the American and the Italian or Irish value-orientations, the couples did not have extremely positive or negative attitudes toward the two different value-orientation patterns. They were more on a plateau in their particular combination of value-orientations and were not suffering from value confusion. Generally their respective parents had expected that they would move some distance closer to American standards, and had not attempted either to keep them in line with the old patterns or to push them completely to American patterns. They moved to new values only after they had acquired some acquaintance with them, and they left the old values not when intensely angry at them, but only when they had neutralized their affect toward the old values.

The control families also had polarized certain elements in their relationships, but this polarization did not involve the extremes of negative valuation that it did in the disturbed families (21). The

---

(21) It may be suggested that such polarization is a common feature in diadic relationships in which the participants are oriented primarily to each other. The contrasting instances, in which persons tend to act out the same role, seem to involve common orientation to an outside object — for example, a leader or other focal person. See, for example, Sigmund Freud, *Group Psychology and the Analysis of the Ego;* London, Hogarth, 1948; Fritz Redl, "Group Emotion and Leadership," *Psychiatry* (1942) *5:*573-596; W. R. Bion, "Experiences in Groups: V," *Human Relations* (1950) *3:*3-14.

The same kind of polarization in the marital relationship has been described by A. T. M. Wilson and his associates at Tavistock Clinic in terms of the internalization of bisexuality. A person derives gratification from acting out his own sex role and seeing elements of his internalized bisexuality acted out by the other person. This is also consistent with the analysis of Parsons (footnote 1), regarding the internalization of

spouses were able to take complementary roles, but these roles did not involve great hostility. Hence their relationship was not so threatened that it necessitated mechanisms of isolation to avoid possible explosions.

DYSFUNCTIONS OF POLARIZATION AND ISOLATION

The mechanisms of isolation utilized by the disturbed couples did operate to minimize disruption, but were not entirely successful in preserving the marital bond. The lack of communication meant that coordination of activities which required contact between husband and wife was extremely difficult. For example, such simple problems as the wife's preparing supper for a certain time or the father's driving the car to meet his family required considerable coordination between husband and wife. Misunderstandings inevitably resulted from inadequate or partial communication. Indeed, the same mechanisms of isolation that made it possible to preserve the marital relationship also led to further tensions.

Because there was relatively little interaction between the husband and wife, particularly on critical problems involving intense affect, there was little opportunity for developing new ways of adjustment and growth. Avoiding discussion of sensitive issues meant that the partners did not discuss even those issues on which they might have reached an agreement. As a result, tensions continued to accumulate from dissatisfactions which might have been prevented. Lack of communication tended to rigidify the relationship between husband and wife at a given equilibrium since

various roles from the nuclear family while acting out only one of these roles.

This kind of polarization also seems to occur in diadic systems of other types. For example, Parsons and Clifford Geertz have noted that although the value systems of Indonesia and the West have fundamental similarities, polarization of attitudes occurs in the contact between them. The same type of polarization seems to occur in countries with two major political parties, even though there is a considerable measure of fundamental agreement between the two parties; the agreement between American political parties has been described in an unpublished manuscript by Parsons. The phenomenon can also be seen in rivalries between kin groups, traditional college rivals, business rivals, and the like. The amount of conflict between the two parties related to the severity of internal tensions and conflict within one party.

there was no opportunity of exploring possible changes (22).

Because problems could not be resolved as they arose, the tensions often built up until there was an explosion which was very disruptive to the relationship, at least for a period of time. Such explosions occurred in a number of the disturbed families during the period of contact with the research team. Even if an attempt was made to avoid the explosion as tensions increased, the severity of the tensions created a sense of urgency which demanded immediate action. This usually led to unilateral attempts to induce change quickly rather than mutual efforts to develop a new relationship based on modification of the roles of both spouses. Spiegel has termed these processes respectively "role induction" and "role modification" (23). Attempts to induce change quickly involved coercing, coaxing, evaluating, masking, and postponing, and required that alter change his position while ego did not. The hostility the disturbed spouses had toward each other very often made them suspicious of such attempts, and a partner was likely to try to neutralize attempts to manipulate him. This led either to a stalemate or to further attempts at role induction that in turn led to further explosions.

Another dysfunction of isolation as a solution to the integrative problems of the marriage stemmed from the constant comparison of the couple's pattern of relationships with the normative standards of their reference groups (24). In all the disturbed cases, for example, there was constant pressure from relatives or friends of the wife who told her that her husband should be participating more in helping her around the house or in child-care responsibilities. This pressure was not simply against the husband, but also

---

(22) See Nelson Foote, "Matching of Husband and Wife in Phases of Development," *Transactions of the Third World Congress of Sociology*, 4:23-24; London, Internat. Sociological Assn., 1956.

(23) See footnote †.

(24) Such comparison is inevitably made in a society in which deviant groups have constant contact with other segments of the society. Redl, for example, had exposed the myth of the well-adjusted delinquent who is simply acting out norms of his group. The delinquent in America inevitably comes into contact with norms other than those of his subgroup and incorporates these other norms into his own standards, at least in part. While the ties to his subgroup may be much stronger this does not necessarily mean that conflict is avoided. Similarly, a deviant family at least partially incorporates the standards of other families with which it constantly interacts.

affected the wife because she had a vested interest in and gained satisfaction from the present role allocation in the family. Although the couple may have reached the most stable equilibrium compatible with the polarization of their attitudes, their relationship was inherently somewhat unstable because of the accumulating internal tensions and the constant pressure from people outside the nuclear family.

One suspected that many of these marriages would have been dissolved except for one fact — a child had become the scapegoat for the tensions of his parents' marriage. Instead of the parents' discharging the full force of their affect on each other, they discharged much of it on to the child. One of the several determinants of the emergence of an emotionally disturbed child appears to be that the child is being used as a means of preserving his parents' marriage (25). The parents have succeeded in preserving the marital bond, but perhaps at the cost of the impairment of the child's personality development.

---

(25) The ways in which the child is used as a scapegoat will be the subject of forthcoming publications by Spiegel and members of the staff.

Chapter 2

Family Interaction in the Therapy
of Adolescent Patients*

DEREK H. MILLER

AMID the turbulence that exists in the patient-family interaction when a severely ill adolescent requires psychiatric treatment, the mutual provocation of disturbed behavior is often evident. If, as is generally considered desirable, contacts with the family are kept as free and open as possible during treatment when a patient is hospitalized, the problem of the deleterious aspects of the continuing interaction is not solved by the patient's temporary removal to the hospital. Unless the specific nature of the interaction is considered and dealt with, contacts between the patient and his family may be to the detriment of the treatment process. This paper describes the steps which were taken to minimize the effects of the undesirable aspects of family interaction on a group of adolescents who were hospitalized. The research was designed to demonstrate, in particular, the significance for the etiology and treatment of psychiatric illness of the often unconscious mutually provocative interaction between the patient and his family. Although adolescent patients and their families show more clearly some of the typical problems, these also exist in all age groups and social classes.

Several authors have discussed the relationship of the family to the treatment of patients of various ages and types (1). In the

Note: Reprinted by permission of the author and *Psychiatry, 21*:277-284, 1958.

(1) See, for example, for children: Bruno Bettelheim, *Truants from Life;* Glencoe, Ill., Free Press, 1955; pp. 479-481. Nathan W. Ackerman and Peter B. Neubauer, "Failures in the Psychotherapy of Children," pp. 82-102, in *Failures in Psychiatric Treatment,* edited by P. H. Hoch; New York, Grune & Stratton, 1948. Anna Freud, *The Psychoanalytic Treatment of Children;* London, Imago Publishing Co., 1946; p. 36. Dorothy T.

therapy of the hospitalized adolescent, Anabel Maxwell points out that if the treatment plan is not the parents', there is a grave question about the quality of the parents' participation and whether they can sustain the child's treatment (2).

The need to have the families recognize the necessity for hospitalization is, however, important to all age levels. Because of the feeling that many families have who send their relatives to state hospitals — that this represents being "put away" — there is a distinct risk that the families of adult patients may abandon them in the treatment situation; in private hospitalization the family may, because of their extreme anxiety, remove the patient before treatment is complete. This is likely to be a more acute problem in adolescent treatment, because parents have not as yet developed substitutes for their children and still need them a great deal. They face a physiological as well as a psychological maturation in the patient, who may still remain dependent on them. Because of this, they need to know about the significant events of their child's life during <u>treatment</u>, although they cannot, of course, receive

Burlingham, "Present Trends in Handling the Mother-Child Relationship during the Therapeutic Process," pp. 31-37; in *Psychoanalytic Study of the Child,* Vol. 6; New York, International Univ. Press, 1951. Rose Green, "Treatment of Parent-Child Relationship," *Amer. J. Orthopsychiatry* (1948) *18:*442-446. Berta Bornstein, "On Latency," pp. 279-285; in *Psychoanalytic Study of the Child,* Vol. 6; New York, International Univ. Press, 1951. For adolescents, see: Adelaide M. Johnson, "Causation of Juvenile Delinquency." *Pediatrics* (Springfield, Ill.) (1956) *17:*934-939. Anabel Maxwell, "The Parents' Role in Resident Treatment." *Amer. Assn. Psychiatric Social Workers Newsletter* (1945) *15:*37-43. For adults, see: Henrietta B. DeWitt, "The Function of the Social Worker in the Total Treatment Program in a State Mental Hospital," *Amer. J. Psychiatry* (1948) *105:*298-303. Harry S. Moore, "Hospitalization as a Dynamic for Use in Casework with Relatives," *J. Psychiatric Social Work* (1956) *19:*141-146. John A. Rockmore, "Casework Today in a Psychiatric Setting," *J. Psychiatric Social Work.* (1951) *24:*26-33. Henry Freeman, "Casework with Families of Mental Hospital Patients," *J. Social Casework* (1947) *28:*107-113. Derek H. Miller. "Treatment of Adolescents in an Adult Hospital: A Preliminary Report." *Bull Menninger Clinic* (1957) *21:*189-198. For homosexuals of all ages see: Adelaide M. Johnson and S. A. Szurek, "The Genesis of Antisocial Acting Out in Children and Adults." *Psychoanalytic Quart.* (1952) *21:*323-343. For unselected schizophrenics, see: J. Kasanin, E. Knight, and P. Sage. "The Parent-Child Relationship in Schizophrenia," *J. N. and M. Disease* (1934) *79:*249-263.

(2) Maxwell, reference footnote 1.

information as to the details of the psychotherapeutic process.

THE PATIENTS AND THEIR PARENTS

Over a two-year period, a group of 25 adolescents, including males and females, varying in age from 13 to 18, was treated at the C. F. Menninger Memorial Hospital. All of these patients were severely ill, over half of them had had delinquent histories, all had had previous treatment, and 15 had been hospitalized elsewhere. The patients were from the higher economic groups, and some of the general treatment techniques employed are discussed elsewhere (3).

Many of the patients were brought to treatment because of external pressure on the parents from legal authorities or schools. Thus, the family came for help with distressing feelings of failure, inadequacy, guilt, and — since in many cases previous outpatient and inpatient treatment had failed — doubt about the helpfulness of treatment. Perhaps also as a result of past experiences, the parents often felt that the hospital would be threatening, censoring, or quick to criticize them for their "failure." Stanton and Schwartz discuss the blame of relatives by hospital staff for the patient's illness, and remark that on occasion they are the victims of a tacit collaboration between staff and patient against them (4).

When the patient had been overtly delinquent, the parents often tended to see the hospitalization as a type of punishment which would help limit expressions of rebellion. The expectation was that the child would be made "good" and then returned to the family situation. For the more disorganized schizophrenic patients, the attitude was more complex. Although the parents sometimes felt angry with their child, in many cases one or the

---

(3) Miller, reference footnote 1.

(4) Alfred H. Stanton and Morris S. Schwartz, *The Mental Hospital;* New York, Basic Books, 1954; p. 99. This was confirmed by our own experience. The failure of a resident psychiatrist to keep the parents of a 15-year-old patient informed about his progress could quite clearly be understood as an identification with the boy's negative feeling about his family — that they had "deprived him of all the things he needed."

other of them was unable to see the patient as being really ill and hopes the hospital would reassure them that there was nothing wrong, and that what had been seen as sick behavior by many people was in fact merely an idiosyncratic quirk. This parental attitude often was associated with a denial of illness on the part of the patient.

TREATMENT GOALS FOR THE FAMILY

The patient's situation in the family constellation was not automatically improved as his individual therapy progressed. Some parents needed to be helped to recognize the adolescent's need to become a mature, independent human being. Other parents demonstrated a degree of emotional disturbance which might have justified a recommendation that they, themselves, enter therapy. None of them showed any motivation for this, and thus it was unhelpful to tell them directly that they were considered to be in need of psychiatric treatment. Even if such a recommendation had been possible, it would have been no solution, since it would not have helped in the crucial initial stages of the patient's hospital treatment. The parents often saw only those aspects of their problems resulting from difficulties with the patient, or such situational problems in their own lives as marital strife.

The following significant parental attitudes and feelings had to be mitigated in order to make treatment possible: Initially, it was necessary to help the parents to deal with the fear, guilt, and anger which the patient's illness precipitated, and also to interrupt the parental stimulation of disturbed behavior in the patient. As treatment progressed, the parents needed to be helped to handle the anxiety produced both by the independent decisions which their children made and by the mistakes inevitable in the maturation process. Finally, they needed to be helped to convey to the adolescent child their expectations as to what was acceptable and to set firm limits to allowances and behavior during visits, and so forth. A subsidiary but important goal of working with the parents was to help them develop more satisfying and positive relationships with each other.

INITIAL PARENTAL PROBLEMS

The parents who had responded with anger to the pain inflicted upon them by the illness of the patient could convey unwittingly to their adolescent child the image of the hospital as a punitive agent. In an institution requiring payment of fees, this reinforces the patient's almost invariably expressed initial distrust and his belief that the physician is not really interested in him, but is someone hired by his parents to make him over into the image of what they think he ought to be. Yet as the staff by their actions dissipate this distrust, the parent may become convinced that they are oriented only toward meeting the patient's needs. To deal with such problems, the parents were reassured by the social worker's recognition with them of the inevitability of their negative feelings under the circumstances, and by a realistic discussion of how these feelings got in the way of treatment and prevented a better relationship with their child from developing.

Excessive parental anxiety was to some extent diminished by using the authority of the physician. In an early interview, the physician discussed the etiology of the patient's illness, and an attempt was made to show the family those areas in which it was impossible for it to be the result of their failures. For example, the basic needs of a person were discussed in relation to what can possibly be provided by a family. The family were told that most parents felt as they themselves did about their errors, and that the responses of an ill child cannot be met by the average person. No effort was made to defend the child's reactions to the parents. They were told that even if they had made mistakes, so had all parents, and the fact was that their child had continued, albeit unwittingly, to perpetuate attitudes for which the parents were not totally responsible.

The social worker then kept the focus on the stressful situation to which the parents were exposed, particularly as this related to the development of the child into adolescence, and on the child's treatment itself as a precipitating factor for parental anxiety. Misconceptions about treatment and the roles of the physician and social worker were frankly discussed. The social worker's meetings with the family were oriented toward the reality situation, and explanations were made to show where parental responses were not realistic. An attempt was made to maintain a positive relationship between parents and the social worker.

PARENTAL STIMULATION OF DISTURBED BEHAVIOR

As is illustrated by the following example, the relationship between the actions of the parents and the behavior of the children was often clear to the examiner, even in the case of delinquencies:

> A 15-year-old boy who had as a presenting complaint that he carried loaded revolvers around with him, had been given the guns by his father. In addition, he had been given money by his father to "soup up" his high-powered automobile, and many times had been arrested for driving at speeds of over 100 miles an hour in 30-mile zones. The father had told the patient — and also the social worker — how much he, himself, enjoyed high-powered cars, and he encouraged his son's interest in them by sending him "hot-rod" magazines and offering to buy him a sports car when he left the hospital.

At times the patients seemed to identify themselves with the expressed behavior of their parents, as well as to gratify their unconscious wishes.

> A delinquent boy of 17 had never been able to use previous attempts at psychiatric help because he felt he could not possibly talk intimately about himself. He was having great difficulty continuing his psychotherapy, because "it goes too deep," and his mother talked to him during a visit of the fact that she used her psychiatrist only for "support," telling him, "I cannot envisage really talking about myself."
>
> Another father boasted to his son on many occasions of his own youthful destructive delinquencies. He told of attempting to derail a train at the age of 16; treatment for the son was precipitated by his arrest for wanton destruction of a large amount of property.

Overt schizophrenic symptoms occasionally seemed related to previous parental actions.

> A boy, age 17, diagnosed at age 7 as suffering from childhood schizophrenia, presented feminine mannerisms and, under stressful situations, used high-pitched baby talk. Until the patient was 10, the mother would hold his hand as they crossed the road and would feed him at the table, and during the initial interviews with the social worker she referred to him as "my baby." On admission he spent two to three hours daily making up his face, after shaving, with powders

and lotions. In his childhood and early adolescence he was encouraged by his mother to watch her in her two- to three-hour toilettes.

An 18-year-old boy became acutely disturbed while hospitalized, expressing incestuous fantasies about his mother. This followed an episode in which she had visited him and, although his extreme illness was evident, asked him what he would think of her divorcing his stepfather.

The parents were unaware of the significance of their actions, and sometimes these tended to continue throughout most of the patient's treatment, particularly when the parents found themselves in uncomfortable, stressful situations.

A delinquent 17-year-old boy who was progressing well began psychotherapy, with the parents' knowledge, with a French woman analyst. This was an intensely difficult situation for him, since he regarded women with fear and distrust. Despite her stated approval of his starting therapy, his mother, who had expressed her feeling to the social worker that she was losing her son, wrote in a letter to her son that she considered the French "charming but unreliable." The patient always had felt that his mother had taken from him the things he needed, and he felt powerless to resist this.

An initial goal was to prevent the stimulation of disturbed behavior in the patient by the parent, and this letter, therefore, was returned to the mother. Had the letter arrived later in the treatment process, when the patient had an ego strong enough not to respond, the letter would not have been withheld, since it expressed an attitude which the patient was bound to meet sooner or later from his mother.

All parents were kept informed of the patients' progress by semimonthly letters from the physician, and they visited at intervals of approximately two months, usually remaining for two or three days. They would be seen initially by the physician and social worker together, and at this time the patient's clinical situation would be reviewed. The timing of the visits and their duration and location were arranged as follows: before and after each visit, the physician saw the patient and the social worker saw the family. Then plans would be made with the patient as to what would be appropriate for the next visit, whether it should be off the grounds, and if so, when the patient should return to the hospital, and so on. One of the aims of the relationship established by the social worker with the family was to help them in their responses to the patient's actions so that a mutually provocative interaction would not develop.

Early in the treatment process, the patients were helped to realize that the parents probably would change their attitudes and actions only insofar as there was change in the patients themselves. As treatment progressed, their response to the parents' wishes and actions, and, when appropriate, the parents' provocation of these responses, were interpreted. The patients seemed to go through three stages in relation to their families. At first they would both provoke and act on the unconscious parental provocation, and would not recognize this as such. Then they would be disturbed by the unconscious provocation which was recognized, but take no overt action. Finally, they became more understanding of themselves and of their parents and were relatively unaffected by what previously had been disturbing parental actions.

> For example, when one 17-year-old patient left the hospital to become a day-hospital patient, he asked that his shotgun be sent, so that sometime in the future he might be able to go hunting. Asked only to send the gun, the father included shells with the patient's package. The patient felt very angry because his father had ignored his wishes, but felt inclined to take the shells and use them. Later, the patient became eager to learn to live on a budget, to have a limited amount of money and manage it himself; but his father continued to offer him monetary gifts. The patient felt angry that his father was "trying to sabotage" his budget and did not want him to manage his own affairs. Therefore, he refused the gifts. At a later date, talking of the fact that his father kept offering him special coaching in school, he said: "I really feel from the way my father keeps offering me tutors, which he knows I used to resent, that although he means well, somehow he wants me to fail. I don't need to."

This demonstrates the problem of the timing of the psychiatrist's intervention. The patient was asking for the gun at a time when he felt particularly helpless; just prior to the request, he reported a dream in which his house was set on fire by a gang of men, and he had tried to ward off the incendiarists with a gun which would not fire. The patient should have been prevented from asking for the gun, or the father should have been told not to send it. In the later events there was no indication that the psychiatrist should have intervened directly with the parent or the patient.

Early in the treatment process, when parental anxiety was great, the families on occasion did unconsciously stimulate delinquent behavior in their children. When this occurred, the physician discussed with the parents the effect of their actions. For example, on the second visit made by the family of a 17-year-old patient, just as he had begun to be more friendly with them, they took him out for an evening, and he returned to the hospital drunk. The parents had taken their son to a motel for a "nightcap," and despite their awareness of his history of the excessive use of alcohol, they had offered him liquor, and during dinner the father had offered him brandy. The physician told the parents that they were harming the treatment process and that if treatment were to be successful, they would have to recognize how unacceptable this behavior was. In talking with the social worker afterward, the parents were able to recognize that, they unwittingly had tried to "corrupt" their son in an attempt to get closer to him.

It was not unusual for the patients to try to provoke from their parents the response which might in turn lead to greater delinquent behavior. A 15-year-old girl, a drug addict, felt that she had started on drugs because her father, a physician, had given her amphetamine two years earlier to "pep her up." When the father visited the patient, she felt sleepy, complained of hay fever, and hoped that the father would give her the pill her psychiatrist refused to prescribe. The father in fact gave her an aspirin, and the patient angrily felt that this proved that he wanted her on drugs. Prior to the visit, the father had been asked by the patient's psychiatrist not to give the patient any medication, and afterward the father was able to recognize how he had been trapped into this action by his daughter.

The physician intervened actively, in order to try to prevent the transmission from the parent to the child of the unconscious provocation which disturbed the treatment situation. The social worker's task was then to meet the parents' emotional needs and support them.

PARENTAL ANXIETY

Apart from the threat to the "intrafamilial libidinal

equilibrium" (5) posed by therapeutic success with the patient, some parents responded with feelings of fear, anxiety, and deprivation to the independent decisions their children made during the treatment process. As patients left the hospital, the parents expressed concern that perhaps previous delinquent symptoms might reappear. This was a request by the parents for reassurance that it would not happen, and possibly for confirmation of both a hope and an unconscious fear that perhaps the child might really be getting better. This posed a dilemma for the physician and the social worker. It was impossible to promise the parents that there would be no symptoms or that ultimate cure was a certainty, but there were discussions with the parents as to what might be realistic expectations about their child's behavior.

Those families who were placed in stressful, anxiety-producing situations by their children were encouraged to ask for help. They were urged, initially, not to make independent decisions about which they had doubts. Later they were encouraged to do freely what they thought would be best.

One of the difficulties which the families faced was that they felt they had lost touch with their children, and they seemed not to know what might be expected from a reasonably normal adolescent. With the feeling of loss which developed, the parents could experience a feeling of competition with the physician. Worth-while decisions mutually arrived at by the doctor and the patient might then be angrily questioned by the parents. In a few cases, the parents would ask whether senior consultants within the hospital were involved in their child's treatment; and, on occasion, parents would write to the hospital and demand that certain attitudes or behavior of their child should be changed immediately.

It was considered important that all patients recognize that the real world outside of the hospital could not be changed to meet their needs, and that any modification in the way their parents behaved toward them would be largely a function of change in themselves. To help the patients recognize the realistic demands of

---

(5) Communication from A. Aichhorn to Ruth S. Eissler; Ruth S. Eissler, "Scapegoats of Society," pp. 288-305; in *Searchlights on Delinquency,* edited by Kurt R. Eissler; New York, International Univ. Press, 1949.

their families, the parents were encouraged to state what their attitudes and expectations might be. For example, one young patient met his mother at a hotel, dressed in dirty jeans and a T-shirt. The patient was well aware that he was doing this because of his anger directed toward her. The mother felt very uncomfortable as to whether she should comment on this sort of behavior, wished very much to do so, but was afraid of "doing the wrong thing." She was encouraged to tell her son frankly her feelings and her opinions.

Another patient ostentatiously ate in a crude manner when his family were present, but did not do this when they were not there. When the parents mentioned this to the social worker, they were told they could feel perfectly free to talk to the patient about his behavior and ask him to change it.

Most of the patients visited their homes during their treatment. This was likely to be a time of considerable anxiety for the family, for they justifiably could be concerned about the possibility that their children would return to the same gangs they had left or that the behavior which had existed in the past would be repeated. Visits were discussed with the parents beforehand; if they felt any concern or anxiety during the visit, they were encouraged to call the social worker. The interaction which occurred during the visit was later reviewed with the family by the physician and the social worker, and with the patient by the physician.

Both the parents and the children often needed to be helped to recognize each other's feelings directly. The patients tended to see their fathers or mothers in an unrealistic way, and they found it quite difficult to appreciate them as persons. In addition to work in this area in formal psychotherapy, talks with the hospital physician, and discussions with the parents, both the patient and his parents might be seen by the physician together.

A 17-year-old boy saw his father as being "bossy, demanding, and always pushing me around." The father, on the other hand, complained to the social worker that his son tended to try to boss him and push him around. Each regarded the other as being cold and unfeeling and having no concern for the other's needs. An attempt was made to work with each of them individually around this problem without success; finally, it was suggested to the patient by his therapist that it might be desirable if the father, the patient, and the therapist talked together. The patient was somewhat concerned about this, feeling frightened that perhaps the therapist would reveal some of his confidences; but since he recognized the need and wished to get along with his father, he consented to the joint interview. The father, similarly, felt that he was quite likely to be humiliated in front of his son, and he talked about this as a possibility with the social worker before the three met. During the interview, the two of them were able to convey to each other their similar feelings. The therapist discussed with them this similarity, and the father then was able to say that he missed his son very much and that he greatly regretted the whole treatment process, because he did not have, as other fathers had, the pleasure and satisfaction of seeing his son grow up in the family situation. The boy was touched by this remark and commented afterward that for the first time in his life he appreciated his father as a "real person." On the next visit home, the patient and his father were able to go off on a trip together for the first time in their lives, a visit which they mutually enjoyed. They had one day in which they quarreled, but, nevertheless, the father was able to feel that this was something which might happen with any 17-year-old. The boy was able to say that his father had not become too angry with him and had seemed to appreciate how he felt.

This realistic appreciation of his father as a person did not solve the patient's neurotic conflict, and he still continued to see the father as a dangerously powerful person who could control him with his displeasure and who frightened him in certain situations; but these feelings were not so evident to the father in the real-life situation. When writing about his trip, he showed real understanding of his son for the first time. "I think when he got quiet in social situations, I tended to take over too much, which made him pretty mad at me. On the other hand, if I did nothing, he got very troubled, but I think I understood by the end of the trip what was needed."

COMPARISON BETWEEN THE RELATIVES OF ADULTS AND OF ADOLESCENTS

The interactions which occur between relatives and hospitalized patients are therapeutically significant in all age groups. The focus of work with the parents depends not only on the expected results of treatment, but also on the age of the patient. For example, if the goal of the treatment process is a social adjustment, then certain expectations of the family must be considered in planning for the patient's future. If the patient is expected to be able to live more independently, then the goal is to help the family keep their relative in treatment and to assist them with the situational problems created by treatment and other factors. The families of both adolescents and adults can stimulate disturbed behavior in their sick relatives. The alcoholic's spouse often unconsciously encourages the alcoholism of the patient, the mothers of schizophrenic patients unwittingly encourage regressed behavior, and the parents of adults suffering from character problems often have highly corruptible superegos, themselves. In adolescent patients these factors often are more dramatically evidenced, but for both adolescents and adults this type of interaction has to be controlled if treatment is to be successful.

The relatives of adult patients often become distressed and angry when the patient improves, because of their unconscious wish to have him remain sick and dependent (6). The same is true for the adolescent, although it would seem that all the parental responses are more intense, the interactions between parent and child are more overt, and the results are less disguised than with adults.

For the younger patient, who is likely to return to the family, an attempt to deal with the pathology in the home situation is an essential part of the discharge planning, which begins when the patient is admitted. Once the severely sick member of the family is removed, parents often seem less disturbed, but early in the course of hospitalization it is necessary to decide what can be expected from the family situation.

One 13-year-old patient had a father, a stepmother, a half-sister, and two sisters, all of whom quarreled violently with each other. Here it was necessary to help the parents improve their relationship and to send two of their daughters away to school, at the same time arranging psychiatric treatment for them; only then was it possible to envisage returning the patient to the home. Although the patient realized there was much pathology in her home about

(6) Marcia A. Leader and L. L. Robbins, "Psychiatric Social Work in a Small Psychiatric Hospital," *Bull. Menninger Clinic* (1952) *15*:85-90.

which she could do nothing, she was not equipped to deal maturely with such a situation. Such planning is particularly necessary with young adolescent patients, for alternatives to returning to the home situation are often not desirable for them, as may be the case with older adolescents or adults. With older adolescents the problem is less intense, since they are likely to go to school or college, or to work; yet they still need the parents for economic and moral support and as a source of continuing social and cultural identification. This is of particular importance, since when the patients are well enough, they may have to make a conscious choice as to the cultural identity they want.

Work with the family in the treatment of the hospitalized patient is needed not only to help provide an optimal environment to which the patient can return, but also to expedite the treatment process itself. None of the principles discussed here is applicable only to adolescents, although the specific problems of physiological and social maturation within this age group create an additional stress. The intensity of a patient's reaction to his family is a function of his age and clinical situation and of the degree of illness from which he suffers. One of the most important determinants of the appearance of symptomatic manifestations of illness is interaction with the family, and during the course of therapy, it is important in the initial phase to control this relationship in an individualized way. The length of visits, the circumstances under which they occur, and their frequency should depend upon the patient's degree of illness and upon their effect on him. Routine visiting hours are necessary in a state hospital because of staff limitation, but even here the same principles apply. Communication between the patient and his family should be supervised by the treating physician; and this means that he has a responsibility for reporting the patient's progress to the family at frequent intervals, either directly or through the social worker, particularly if the patient's illness dictates relatively infrequent visits during the initial stages of treatment. When the patients are sufficiently recovered to be able to cope with the actions and wishes of their families without causing undue distress to either, free and open communication becomes desirable and necessary. The time at which the psychiatrist should refrain from intervening directly in the family interaction depends upon the following factors: the extent to which the family equilibrium needs the illness of the patient, the ego strength of the patient, and the amount of support the patient obtains from his relationship with his psychiatrist and his healthy environment. Finally, intervention is necessary if the patient needs to use the parents to justify his own superego lacunae. Correct judgment as to when these direct interventions should cease is as necessary as the accurate timing of an interpretation in psychotheray.

The Menninger Foundation
Topeka, Kansas

Chapter 3

The Role of the Parent in Psychotherapy with Children*

HILDE BRUCH

ONE of the outstanding differences of psychotherapy with children as distinguished from the treatment of
adults is the fact that one's activity is not restricted to just one
patient, the sick child, but that one has to deal with the parents
and other significant people of the child's environment as well.
Without undue exaggeration one might say that in many cases it is
the parents who constitute the real problem in child psychiatry.
They often seek help for their own difficulties in rearing their
children, for their anxiety and guilt, and for their own annoyance
and disappointment about the child's symptoms and shortcomings. I intend to discuss in this chapter some problems in the
handling of parents which I have encountered in the private
practice of child psychiatry. I shall focus on those aspects which I
personally have found difficult and many of which have remained
unsolved problems in my daily work. I wish to apologize for
presenting a chapter which raises new questions instead of
answering them. But I do hope to stimulate further thought by
raising these questions and to clarify at least some of the issues
involved.

This problem of how to handle the parent has been recognized
as a serious difficulty since psychotherapy was first extended to
the treatment of children. The first psychoanalytic treatment of a
child — that of a 5-year-old boy who suffered from a phobia, the
famous "Little Hans" — was carried out through the father, who
transmitted Freud's interpretations to this son. This early method

---

*Note: Reprinted by permission of the author and *Psychiatry, 11:*169-175, 1948.

of treatment has been largely abandoned. In contrast to the early harmony between parent and therapist, there developed later the conviction that a strong conflict would necessarily develop between the two, and that the parent's anxieties and jealousies would interfere with the success of treatment. It was necessary to maintain a friendly contact with the parents in order to obtain information about the child's behavior at home, and they were kept informed as far as was absolutely necessary of the progress of the analysis; but the main emphasis was on the insistence that they refrain from all interference. During the last decade, or somewhat earlier, a more tolerant attitude toward parents has been expressed. More and more it was recognized that the inadequacies of the parents were not due to willful malice or ignorance but were often the expression of unresolved personality conflicts of their own. Instead of giving them instructions as to what to do and not to do, the emphasis shifted more toward giving psychotherapeutic help to the parents themselves. Since it was assumed that difficulties would arise in the handling of the transference situation, the parent was usually referred for treatment to another analyst.

A similar approach, that of separating treatment of the child and the parent, was developed in the child guidance clinics which made psychotherapy available to a wider group of the population. Treatment was carried out as teamwork. The child was seen by one therapist, usually a psychiatrist, and the mother was usually treated by a social worker. The practice varied in different clinics, but treatment of the mother has come to be considered as a necessary auxiliary procedure.

Despite the danger of appearing naive, I must confess that when I first went into the private practice of child psychiatry I labored under the conviction that dealing with the parent when the child was under treatment was not quite right. There was, of course, the practical necessity of obtaining a detailed history from the parent and of being kept informed about the child's progress. Yet the need to approach detrimental and faulty attitudes of the parents caused me uneasiness, because "that *should* be handled by someone else." There were many practical objections against sending parents away for their treatment; an outstanding one during the war years was the fact that nobody else had time.

Under the pressure of circumstances I began to see the parents for psychotherapeutic interviews and found that it worked very well in some instances; but that in others all kinds of puzzling situations arose which might even lead to discontinuation of treatment. I began to notice that this happened when I had been uneasy in my relations to the parents. It gradually became clear to me that the unfavorable result was not due to having broken a technical rule but to the fact that I had failed to understand the irrational nature of some of the parents' demands or of my reactions to them. For example: One reason for becoming uneasy was the feeling that I could not live up to the parents' expectations, namely, that of transforming their child on short order into a model of perfection. After this interrelationship had become clear to me, I felt comfortable in dealing with both the parent and the child and, I might add, obtained much better results for both with less conflict and frustration for myself.

I have given special attention to these personal aspects because it seems that quite often people with good training in child psychiatry give up its practice. I have inquired into the reasons and usually received the answer that the parents were impossible to deal with. I do not know what personal difficulties others have experienced in relation to the parents. It seems to me that in this question of how to handle parents in child psychiatry the personal attitudes and reactions of the psychiatrist have not received sufficient attention. It is my impression that anxiety over problems which seem to be completely resolved in one's everyday living and in dealing with adult analytic patients may become aroused again in these contacts, probably due to the very fact that one is dealing with *parents.* There exists also the danger of excessively identifying with the child and thereby becoming less perceptive of problems in the relationship; or even of competing with a parent for the child's affection and loyalty.

My new awareness has led me to change my approach in handling the initial contact with parents. As before, I try to evaluate the leading conflicts between the parent and the child and in which way the symptoms are related to the parents. In addition, I try to obtain as clear a picture as possible of the parents' psychological orientation to treatment; what had led them to seek psychiatric help; why they had come to me; and, most of all, what they expected from the treatment of their child. A detailed assessment of the parents' psychological situation at the beginning of treatment has become for me an indispensable part of evaluating the possibilities of treatment, necessary for determining how much work has to be done with the parents – quite often even before seeing the child.

There exists, of course, a wide range of variations in parents' awareness of their children's difficulties and of their role in these difficulties; in their readiness to accept a diagnostic formulation; and, even more, in their capacity and willingness to cooperate in a treatment program. There are certain common factors which probably apply to all parents who seek our help. For one thing, there is the fact that they are people who seek help – for something which is painful and, we might add, often shameful to them. It is part of our cultural tradition that one should be able to handle one's own affairs; therefore to ask help for raising one's children may mean a declaration of personal failure. Whatever the averred attitude of the parents, whether they are glaringly hostile and accusing in relating their problems with the child or aggressive and demanding in their attitude to us, I think this basic fact needs to be kept in mind, that coming to us in itself is an expression of seeking help, and should be met with understanding and respect. It is important to realize that the decision to ask for help, the psychological processes which precede it, often represent a crucial change in the parents' attitude toward a troublesome child. The amazing successes which one often observes following a few interviews, even sometimes a single consultation, seem to be related to this changed attitude toward the child's difficulties.

The evaluation of a parent's attitude toward psychiatric treatment does not, of course, remove all treatment difficulties. I might confess here that the subtitle that kept flashing through my mind while preparing this chapter was, "Troubles I Have Known." There remain many situations which I have found inaccessible to treatment, and I should be very grateful for constructive advice on how to handle such problems. There are parents who frankly object to psychiatric treatment – who consult us only under outside pressure, for instance, from the school or some relative. Usually the children are quite sick and there is crying need for help; but no way of achieving it. Sometimes it is only one parent who objects to treatment and the other is more than eager. I have found it unwise if not impossible to treat a child against the expressed opposition of one parent. Occasionally one succeeds in convincing such a reluctant parent of the need for treatment. I recall the father of a 15-year-old girl who stormed into the office, inquiring, "What are you doing, breaking up the sanctity of my home?" I reviewed with him his method of dealing with the girl and he gradually admitted that he himself was not happy with this regime and he finally pleaded with me to accept his daughter for treatment. However, the mutual hostility between father and daughter was so great that subsequently the girl refused to come.

Another form of resistance to treatment is denial of the existence of difficulties, thereby removing the need for treatment. These parents, too, only come under outside pressure. They come with the expectation of finding an ally against the school or whoever had suggested that the child was in need of help. They resent any inquiry into their family problems and, most of all, reject the diagnosis and may become quite violent in the expression of their dissatisfaction; often this takes the form of being indignant about paying a fee. The question of how to deal with these parents has puzzled me. If the child's difficulties are not too urgent, a wait-and-see attitude has been a help. It may happen that the child's difficulties had been exaggerated by an overzealous teacher or a new convert to psychiatry, and that the parents were correct that no need for psychiatric interference existed. Usually, however, the children are very disturbed and quite often it is the diagnosis of schizophrenic development or feeble-mindedness which the parents so vehemently reject.

Another group of parents who express a hostile attitude have recognized the abnormality of the child for quite some time but, again, come for treatment only under outside pressure or because they are conscientious and certainly would not miss any opportunity, even though they do not "believe in psychiatry." It is this group in which the direct analysis of the parental attitude may lead to a successful, constructive cooperation. If this contemptuous attitude is silently accepted and left untouched or, worse, leads to counterresentment in the therapist, not much can be accomplished with either the parent or the child. Sooner or later the parent will feel that he was right in the first place, that there is no help for his child, and treatment will be discontinued.

I wish to illustrate this point with a case history. Mr. and Mrs. R came for help for their 10-year-old daughter because the school felt that the girl's eccentric behavior made her too conspicuous. The parents had been aware of the difficulties for quite some time but felt they could handle things themselves. There were numerous phobic and compulsive symptoms which showed frequent changes, and each change was interpreted as improvement. Both parents gave detailed descriptions of the child's symptoms. The father focused on the fears and the mother gave an amazingly accurate picture of the child's interpersonal difficulties, particularly of her great self-absorption and selfishness. The mother was cold and detached in giving her account. In discussing a treatment plan the need for frequent interviews with the mother was stressed so that she might understand her own attitude toward the child.

In subsequent visits the mother's behavior remained strictly obedient: Here I am and I am cooperative. Changes in the child's symptoms were reported as, "I have good (or bad) news for you." An undercurrent of reproach became apparent: she, the mother, did not receive sufficient instructions as to how to handle the child. She spent much time pointing out contradictions between what I was supposed to have said last time and this time. She offered an impenetrable wall of resistance against any inquiry into her personal life. The same condescension and even rudeness-in-a-superior-way was expressed in her behavior toward the secretary or in the way she answered the telephone or in the urgency with which she ordered certain teachers to have conferences with me. After five or six visits she insisted on staying away, there was nothing to discuss that she could not communicate just as well in a written note.

In summarizing the interviews, her own behavior was described to her, particularly the undermining condescension with which she treated everyone whom she seemed to consider as not on a level equal to her own social standing and upbringing; that, indeed, it was the outstanding interpersonal attitude that she had revealed thus far, except for a literal-minded obedience which she used to prove the other person wrong. Since these traits were so pronounced, it might appear justified to assume that they had had a profound influence on the development of her own daughter. Treatment of the child without a change in the mother's attitude might be possible although it would involve much more time than we had assumed and the child would have to receive the affection and warmth which she craved from outsiders. The mother was willing to accept this as long as she was not forced to expose herself to the indignity of psychiatric interviews. One more point was mentioned to her, that not only would the child grow up without having enjoyed warmth and affection from her mother but that she, the mother, would miss the experience of receiving love from her own child. It was at this point that she suddenly wavered and, for the first time, made a personal remark. She addressed to me the question, "What would you do if you had to choose between your husband and your child; I certainly would not sacrifice my husband." The question was interpreted as representing an important problem in her life and as implying that she considered the child to be "expendable" — to which she replied, "Exactly, that is what she was always been." She left the office somewhat shaken but still determined that treatment should continue without her. Within an hour she phoned, apparently weeping, and begged to allowed to return for further treatment. This interview was followed by an amazing change in her attitude toward the child. Her husband, whose selfish demands had dominated the household, was more cooperative than she had dared to expect. At first she was just determined to be a good mother but very soon, in a number of rather touching episodes, she came to the awareness that she really could enjoy her child, that she was not punished with "the most clumsy, awkward and dopey child anyone could imagine," but that this child of hers was lovable and responsive to her efforts. There was also considerable change in the child's response to direct therapy.

I have described this case in some detail in order to illustrate how this approach to the parent's attitude to psychotherapy can and should be used as an entering wedge to an understanding of the mother's own problems, her significant relations within the family and to the sick child in particular.

I have discussed thus far problems in which the parents expressed a negative attitude toward psychiatry. They are not too numerous nowadays. It is much more common for parents to express verbally great confidence in psychiatry — and the expectation that a miracle will be performed. Many parents have acquired all kinds of psychological information and have applied it in bringing up their children — only it did not work. They now come to the expert to find out whether there is anything new for them to learn.

One could devote a great deal of time to a discussion of what modern psychiatry and its popularization has done to and for the family and in what way it has influenced the raising of children. My experiences are such that I sometimes doubt the value of so-called parent education; what one observes as a psychiatrist is so often a state of pathetic confusion. The old-fashioned, rigid, dominating, hostile parent offered at least a definite attitude and a matter-of-fact conviction of being correct. Many modern parents have acquired along with a psychological vocabulary an inner conviction of their not being able to know the "right method" and they are burdened by the guilt of always doing the "wrong thing."

It is quite a task to obtain information — and not so-called psychological interpretations — from such parents. One mother came just to find out "whether I have a problem or not." Gradually we could narrow down the statement to the fact that "a problem" referred to her 12-year-old son, an unhappy and forlorn boy, one of whose difficulties was bed-wetting. When the mother was questioned about the early training she gave the classic answer, "I don't know — I forgot. I'm sure it was whatever was the thing to do in those days."

Certain misconceptions have become so widespread that one finds some evidence of it in the life histories of most of our young patients whose parents "apply" modern psychology. I am referring to the opinion that training and discipline, per se, are harmful, that the ideal way to raise a child is to permit him to develop *all* his creative possibilities and never to frustrate *any* of his impulses; to praise him for any achievement and never to show anything but love and tolerant acceptance no matter how aggressive and disturbing the child's behavior becomes. Under extreme conditions where the parents are consistent and even try to outdo each other in permissiveness and tolerance, the child will develop into a demanding, aggressive, uncivilized pest. Need for treatment occurs when the child becomes anxious and guilty about his unbridled aggressiveness or when the parents, in spite of the best intentions, can no longer tolerate the unbearable situation.

Handling of such super-psychological parents is no less of a problem than that of the antagonistic and doubting ones. The competitive striving for perfection needs to be dealt with in the beginning lest the treatment· situation become one more experience for intellectualizing and avoidance of spontaneous emotional expression.

As I mentioned before, one encounters some evidence of such misinterpretation of psychiatric concepts in many modern parents. I have seen the more severe manifestations in parents who had been or were under analysis and who had not worked through the conflict in relation to their own parents. It seems that a constructive and accepting attitude toward one's own past is not achieved by many patients until they are well along in their analyses; until this stage is reached, the tendency to raise one's own child by *avoiding all* the mistakes of one's own upbringing seems to be rather compelling. Another difficulty encountered in parents who are under analysis is that they may become so wrapped up in their own problems that it is difficult, if not impossible, to effect a constructive change in their relationship to the child. My experiences with children of parents under analysis has been by and large so discouraging that I prefer – unless a real urgency exists – to postpone treatment of the child until a certain stabilization in the parent has taken place. This does not apply to all cases, and there are situations in which constructive collaboration with a parent under analysis is possible.

Modern parents with all their psychological knowledge show, of course, just as many variations in their basic attitudes in relation to the child as the old-fashioned parents. It is a necessary aspect of treatment to help them to come to an awareness of their true attitudes – without further undermining the parents' confidence in their capacity to be good parents. Hidden behind this anxious quest for psychological knowledge is often a fundamental doubt about one's own adequacy. The therapeutic task is to help such parents discover their capacities for love and a genuine relationship with their child so that they can throw off the facade of expert knowledge.

Another group of parents who also come full of confidence that all will be well once they see a psychiatrist are those I am in the habit of calling "doorstep" cases. They themselves are not experts — as a matter of fact, they are more than ready to admit that they know nothing at all about children. They have raised their children by hiring experts and the child psychiatrist is the last in a thus far disappointing series. Such parents are apt literally to drop the child at one's doorstep, expecting one to do the job for them. An essential part of treatment is to convince them that they too have something to give to their child; the success of treatment will depend on whether or not one can get the parents to take part in the child's life. If one can reach the parent at the point where he experiences this self-doubt, progress can be made. I wish to add here that the type of mother who has been labeled by the unlovely term of "rejecting mother" often can be helped to a considerable degree at the same point: namely when one approaches not her hostility but her sense of inadequacy and failure in her role as a mother.

I have emphasized here the importance of evaluating the attitudes which parents bring to psychiatry. This emphasis on the initial contact does not imply that the working through of the interpersonal attitudes and difficulties is not equally important: it is indeed the essence of treatment in child psychiatry. This initial evaluation has proven helpful in many cases in making long-term treatment possible. Treatment of parents has to be as diversified as the attitudes with which they come to treatment and the problems they have experienced in relation to their children. I have spoken throughout of "parents," thereby indicating that both the father and the mother need help, although usually the mother is more intimately involved and needs considerably more assistance.

I have encountered amazingly few difficulties which might have arisen from the fact that I see both the parents and the child. I make a statement to the effect that the secrecy of personal confidences will be guarded and repeat it if and when necessary. If there is persistent mistrust or hostility and rivalry then they need to be treated as symptoms and manifestations of an unhealthy relationship. If the basic hostility is so severe that it cannot be handled by one person, it will be advisable to refer the parents to someone else for treatment. Quite often, however, it will become necessary under such circumstances to arrange for a change of environment and for treatment of the child away from home.

In dealing with parents I try to limit treatment to the areas which significantly enter into the relationship to and the handling of the child. It is not uncommon that in the process of disentangling the parents' involvement with the child, their basic neurotic patterns become apparent. Whenever possible, I try to postpone treatment of the parent until a clarification of the child's conflict has been achieved, so that treatment of the parent is clearly recognized as something he needs for his own sake and not something he does "to help the psychiatrist to help the child."

I have focused in this paper on some problems which the child psychiatrist is likely to encounter in relation to parents whose children come for treatment. A marked change has occurred in the attitude of child psychiatrists towards parents. This attitude of respectful understanding of the parents' problem has proven itself useful in making more lasting collaboration possible. It is also of utmost importance for the direct treatment of the child. One cannot treat a child successfully if one does not respect his parents. Whatever the child's fears and hates and uncertainties are in relation to his parents, he needs to gain from treatment the conviction that his parents, in spite of their shortcomings and errors, are fundamentally good people (unless the parents' attitude is so detrimental that the child must learn to accept this as a reality of his life and to recognize his personal worth in spite of it). A good relationship with the parents cannot be accomplished when the therapist acts as if the parents were hateful and bad people. Not only will the child be burdened by the additional fear that he, too, is not "good" because he comes from "bad" stock, but one will fail in one's goal of treatment: to make it possible for a child to find love and affection in relation to his own parents and thus to become secure enough to develop along the line of personality growth and maturity.

Chapter 4

Theoretical and Clinical Aspects of Short-Term Parent-Child Psychotherapy

E. LAKIN PHILLIPS and MARGARET S. H. JOHNSTON

N EARLY everyone who has thought seriously about psychotherapy has entertained notions of how to shorten it. In the outpatient child guidance clinic the interest in short-term treatment and flexible treatment methods is usually heightened because of public demands on the time and skill of professional clinicians. At a meeting of the association of clinics in the metropolitan area of Washington, it was reported that waiting lists for child treatment vary from a few months to over two years in various parts of the United States. In the Washington, D. C. area, waiting lists range from a few months to over one year.

Two factors contribute to the feasibility of flexible treatment methods and short-term treatment in child guidance clinics[†]. First, children are highly amenable to psychological treatment; because they are growing and changing, the forward surge can be made use of to heighten participation, to lessen pathology, and to shorten treatment. Second, parents probably respond better *as parents* than they do simply as adults seeking help. Since a child's

---

Note: Reprinted by permission of the authors and *Psychiatry, 17:*267-275, 1954.

† The data for this paper were collected at the Arlington County Guidance Center and the Fairfax County Child Guidance Clinic which are conducted by the State Department of Mental Hygiene and Hospitals, Richmond, Va. The ideas and practices expressed herein are the authors' and do not necessarily represent those of the Department.

The authors are indebted to Drs. David McK. Rioch, Ardie Lubin, and Harold M. Skeels for their helpful comments during the preparation of this report. Mrs. Gloria B. Gelfand worked with many of the parent-child cases at the Arlington County Guidance Center.

problems tend to reflect in various ways the problems of the parents (1), the child's need for help means in most instances that the parent, too needs help.

This chapter reports an experience with the use of short-term therapy at two child guidance clinics, and it attempts to compare the results with those obtained at the same clinics by conventional therapy. Short-term therapy in this instance consisted of a stated number of interviews — subject, in some cases, to extension which was also of defined length. This plan was based on a somewhat different rationale than that of conventional therapy and, in turn, brought about a somewhat different type of therapy. In general, therapy was directed, not at retrospective self-examination, but at the child's pattern of interaction in current situations.

We have been encouraged to explore short-term treatment by the experience which has been reported from the general field of social psychology. It has, in certain situations, been amply demonstrated that improvements in human relations, and the subsiding of internal stresses in schools, factories, neighborhoods, and so on, can be brought about by short-term contacts with the persons concerned, by group opinions and pressures, and by a general atmosphere of interpersonal acceptance (2). Thus this experience has led us to stress, as a part of short-term treatment, group and situational factors. Such approaches have sometimes been dismissed scornfully on the basis that they bring about only superficial attitude changes, leaving the deep wellsprings of human motivation untapped. But while the exploration of deep motivation undoubtedly has its place, those who work in clinical settings

---

(1) See, for instance C. M. Loutitt, *Clinical Psychology:* New York, Harper, 1947. E. L. Phillips, "Parent-Child Similarities in Personality Disturbances," *J. Clin. Psychol.* (1951) *7:*188-190. Merrill Roff, "Inter-Family Resemblances in Personality Characteristics," *J. Psychol.* (1950) *30:*199-228. P. M. Symonds, *The Dynamics of Parent-Child Relationships;* New York, Columbia Univ. Press, 1949.

(2) See, for instance, D. Cartwright and Alvin Zander, *Group Dynamics: Research and Theory;* Evanston, Ill., Roe, Peterson, 1953. A. W. Gouldner (ed.), *Studies in Leadership;* New York, Harper, 1950. Kurt Lewin, *Resolving Social Conflicts;* New York, Harper, 1948. Lewin, *Field Theory in Social Science;* New York, Harper, 1951. Elton Mayo, *The Social Problems of an Industrial Civilization;* Cambridge, Harvard Univ. Press, 1945. Mayo, *The Human Problems of an Industrial Civilization;* New York, Macmillan, 1946.

cannot afford to overlook the realistic benefits which have been obtained by social psychologists with alternative treatment practices stressing group interaction.

Allport, in a discussion of motivation theory, has commented on this question as follows:

> This prevailing atmosphere of theory has engendered a kind of contempt for the "psychic surface" of life. The individual's conscious report is rejected as untrustworthy, and the contemporary thrust of his motives is disregarded in favor of a backward tracing of his conduct to earlier formative stages. The individual loses his right to be believed. And while he is busy leading his life in the present with a forward thrust into the future, *most psychologists have become busy tracing it backward into the past* [italics added] (3).

Cameron in a discussion of modern methods of therapy says the following:

> The newer approach to therapy is relativistic, elastic, and plastic. The old is doctrinaire, essentially fundamentalistic and deterministic. . . . In dealing with the living organism you are dealing with a continually emergent situation and, as often as not and sometimes oftener, the newly established conception has, within a short period of time, developed sufficient powers of inhibition, to prevent the reestablishment of the less-effective blueprints which previously governed his behavior (4).

SETTING OF THE STUDY

The experience with short-term therapy described here took place in two outpatient child guidance clinics in the Washington, D. C., area — Fairfax and Arlington (5). At the Fairfax clinic, short-term therapy has been in use for about two years, and a follow-up study of 16 parent-child pairs treated at this clinic has been included in the data presented in this paper. Fourteen

---

(3) Gordon W. Allport, "The Trend in Motivational Theory," *Amer. J. Orthopsychiatry* (1953) *23:*107-119; p. 108.

(4) D. C. Cameron, "Unorthodox Working Concepts for Psychotherapy," *Med. Ann. D. C,* (1953) *22* (May):226-234, 278; see especially pp. 228-229.

(5) The type of short-term therapy described here was begun at the Fairfax clinic by Dr. Thomas A. Harris, who calls it the "block" method. It has been adopted at the Arlington clinic at the instigation of the senior author, on the stimulus of Dr. Harris' work.

conventional cases have also been included. During one period of time, the conventional method was used by all therapists for all cases; and during another period, the short-term method was used exclusively. Thus there was no selection of method for any particular case. In short-term therapy, treatment has usually terminated at the tenth interview.

At the Arlington clinic, short-term parent-child treatment has not been in progress long enough to provide follow-up data. Thus while many of our general statements on short-term treatment are based on experience at both clinics, we have included no data on this method from the Arlington clinic. Data on the conventional method at this clinic have been included. Short-term therapy has not at any time been mandatory for all cases at the Arlington clinic, but it has usually been accepted when offered. Following the tenth interview, the clinic has adopted the practice of extending another block of treatment in those few cases where more help is required.

In considering setting a limit for therapy, we first explored the experiences of other outpatient clinics in the Washington area and found the average number of contacts for parent-child pairs to be between 12 and 18 interviews. This average, however, included extreme variation, from two or three interviews in aborted cases up toward a hundred interviews in other cases. In essence, there was no correlation between the length of therapy and its success. Therapy might be short either because it was abortive or because it was incisive; and therapy might be long either because the problems were formidable or because the therapy failed to be incisive.

THEORETICAL ORIENTATION AND METHODS

In attempting explicit statements of our rationale, we are confronted with a difficulty which has been noted by Ruesch and Bateson:

> For the present we observe that psychiatry is predominantly concerned with the perception and description of the abnormal and undesirable and that the technical vocabulary is almost entirely focused upon the pathological aspects. ... It is a science rather

inarticulate about its operations and with its theoretical focus concentrated upon the diagnosis of abnormality and the analysis of normal dynamics in abnormal circumstances. The dynamics of normal circumstances and the methods of implementing the therapeutic process are comparatively little studied (6).

To Whom Does Short-term Therapy Apply? In our experience, most of the children who come to the outpatient child guidance clinic present no problems of a deep nature. Moreover, when such problems do occur, we feel that the outpatient clinic is not the place to provide the intensive treatment which is required. The common core of the problems brought to the clinic is a too loose structure of interpersonal relations, seen most clearly in disciplinary and management difficulties encountered by the parent or teacher. The child is at odds with significant adults, largely because these adults do not set appropriate limits for the child. The recognition that many parent-child problems are those of management entails the adoption of different goals from those of therapies which require retrospective self-examination, the uncovering of severely repressed feelings, and so on. The therapist is concerned with the structure of the child's interpersonal relations and the setting of appropriate limits for him, and he endeavors to obtain clarity about this in a concrete way with the child and also with the parent. It is because these problems are amenable to help, without requiring exhaustive exploration, that short-term therapy is applicable and helpful. Moreover, this viewpoint affords an opportunity for flexible arrangements, for example, either parent or child can be treated alone.

The Notion of Structure and the Importance of Limits. We use the term, structure, in the sense that Lewin uses it in referring to the shaping-up, forming, and delineating of experience as it progresses from a vague and undifferentiated condition to a more highly articulate one. Seemingly, man finds it necessary to structure vague, formless, rootless experiences, so that he is better able to cope with them. Theoretical support for this notion of structure can be drawn from Sherif's findings (7) in his study of

(6) J. Ruesch and G. Bateson, *Communication: The Social Matrix of Psychiatry;* New York, Norton, 1951; pp. 234-235.

(7) Muzafer Sherif, "A Study of Some Social Factors in Perception," *Arch. Psychol.* (1935) no. 187.

the autokinetic phenomenon, showing the social influences of perceived motion, and from the electrical study of the brain showing the seeking for structure by means of "scanning operations":

> ... the alpha rhythms are a process of scanning — searching for a pattern — which relaxes when a pattern is found. It is as if you were looking for one particular word in a page of print; you scan the page, line by line, until you come to the word; then the scanning movement ceases; anyone watching your eyes could tell when you had found what you were looking for (8).

The parallel in the parent-child situation is that the parent fails to structure the relationship with the child in emotionally acceptable ways: the parent is inconsistent, expects too much or too little, vacillates, is too easily cajoled, and so on. The child's scanning of the behavioral and interpersonal field yields a different pattern from that which the parent's scanning yields, and hence conflict and emotional involvement ensue. In this relative inter-personal chaos, the child seeks clearer structure and more validity for his pattern; but since he is a child he cannot seek it in the most mature and productive ways. Nor can the parent, who, by the time the child begins testing everyone, is herself beginning to wonder if there is or ever can be any order in the universe of children. The mother often reports that the child seems to take advantage of her inability to say yes or no, her inability to stick by her guns on disciplinary matters, and her inability to follow through on a restriction, regulation, or expectation, and to resist giving in to the nagging, whining child. In these instances, she characteristically presents a picture of exhaustion, or being at the end of her rope, of having "tried everything," and of feeling victimized by an unscrupulous child (in the most perplexing cases). Often she has grossly overexercised a rational, persuasive, reasoned, verbal approach to the child, until the point is reached where words and threats mean nothing and both the parent and the child are gripped by emotion. From the child's point of view, he is faced with a parent who cannot maintain a stable position, wrong or right, and who cannot offer him security and safety. The child

---

(8) W. G. Walter, *The Living Brain;* New York, Norton, 1953; p. 109.

keeps pushing, seeking to delimit his areas of operation, seeking to find out what is related to what. He learns that the parent's words do not mean what they are supposed to mean, that there is always a way of getting around them on an impulse of the moment. But the child is also made anxious by the indefiniteness and the insecurity of the relationship; he feels cast adrift, and he may experience the parent's feeble stand as disinterest, as license, or as simple confusion and inadequacy, all of which are far from comforting to the child.

Thus a basic idea in our approach to short-term therapy is the importance of the firmness of the interpersonal structure — or, in other words, the importance of limits. This view of the nature of the parent-child problem is also the core of the treatment practices. Confusion for both the clinician and the parent arises when these testing episodes are interpreted as wholly id-dominated, as signifying deep, underlying problems, as entirely representing hostility and belligerence, or something of the sort. What they signify, from our viewpoint, is clumsy, inarticulate, and immature ways of wanting to know where one stands, of wanting to have a dependable relationship to an adult. Such acting out is a self-system characteristic, not a matter of the alleged id (9).

This, then, is roughly the theme of the therapy hours with the parent, characteristically pursued in verbal and other symbolic ways. The child learns more mature ways of relating to people in the therapeutic exchange by means of the limits set in verbal, physical, and other activities; depending upon the child's age and other particulars, he may act out his problems.

Structuring the Treatment Situation. Just as a certain firmness of structure is needed in the child's other interpersonal relations, so it is needed in the treatment situation itself. This conception is one of the most important contributions which the use of

(9) The theoretical question can be raised as to *why* the parents are unable to set appropriate limits, with the implication that this question requires extensive answering, thus forcing the therapist outside the position promulgated here. Questions asking *what* (the parent does or does not do that leads to difficulties) and *how* (the parent perceives the parent-child impasse) are relevant and answerable in the clinic treatment, whereas *why* questions are not; the former are heuristic, the latter is not.

short-term therapy has made to our clinical approach. While treatment usually consisted of a block of 10 interviews, it would have been equally valid to set the interview limit at 8, 12, 15, or some other number; for the actual number, within reason, is not the important matter. What is important is that the interview series has a beginning, an end, and other discernible features — in other words, that the treatment experience itself has a structure. While at first the sheer time limits of short-term therapy were uppermost, this same consideration is now fitted into a larger theoretical framework. Time is still important, but it now fits into its proper place in the total treatment setting. It is as if time considerations forced the issue; the issue, then, receives at least a temporary solution in the terms outlined in this paper. The structure has now been made larger; the time element, as such, is not given as close attention, yet the result is that treatment remains short-term although the load is carried by the *total* treatment milieu rather than by and through time limits alone.

The Child's Patterns of Interaction. We regard the child as a shifting point in an interaction matrix, in accordance with Sullivan's comments on personal individuality (10). The child is part of the interpersonal system of family, neighborhood, school, and so on. *Change the system* (as one does in therapy with varying degrees of success) *and you change the child.* Thus we consider the child's patterns of interactions with others to be the key to his problems and to be more important, in understanding his difficulties, than his areas of repression. The child is not a historical or developmental capsule that has to be explored for its own sake. His relationship with others is the important facet of the therapeutic enterprise — not extraction, not recovery of repressed materials or of the lost past. The child in our experience — Klein (11), to the contrary notwithstanding — is largely incapable of such historical, retrospective self-examination and is developmentally unable to comprehend it when it is carried on in monologue form by the therapist.

Children like adults, suffer more from what they *affirm* (or

---

(10) H. S. Sullivan, "The Illusion of Personal Individuality," *Psychiatry* (1950) *13:*317-332.
(11) Melanie Klein, *The Psycho-Analysis of Children;* London, Hogarth Press, 1932.

assert) than from what they deny. The role of affirmation in anyone's psychological space is clearly seen in his relationships; the role of denial derives from psychic isolation and psychic autonomy. The notion of interaction places emphasis on the child's ability to relate and on his growth capacities, both of which are important in treatment.

Relatedness is not a one-way street, but depends upon reciprocal capacities in the therapist, as Sullivan (12), Rogers (13) and Allen (14) have stressed. Treatment is "reflexive" in the sense that Ruesch and Bateson have described it (15); that is, it includes therapist as well as patient, and even includes the theorist. There is feedback to patient and therapist as each talks, gestures, and so on. The feedback from patient to therapist has affected our attitudes, practices, and theory. In general, replacing assumptions about repression and denial with assumptions about relationships helps to free the therapist to work more realistically with parent and child and helps to establish working relationships in therapy without placing all the burden of readiness on the client.

The Starting of a Self-healing Process. Emphasis is placed on the patient's own forward direction in treatment. The criticism which has sometimes been made that short-term therapy is perforce superficial and evasive we find to be unsubstantial and to be in conflict with the idea of the part played by self-healing processes. The person "is not passive, but a participant in his own universe," as Ruesch and Bateson have said in developing the idea of "negative entropy" (16). Therapy is a continuous exchange between client and therapist — an open system of codification, evaluation, hypothesis formation, and so on — making possible the development of new or alternative attitudes or hypotheses on the client's part. The fact that a person is not a closed energy system, but an open, ongoing one, gives the therapeutic interaction its

(12) H. S. Sullivan, *Conceptions of Modern Psychiatry;* Washington, D. C., William Alanson White Psychiatric Foundation, 1947. Sullivan, "The Theory of Anxiety and the Nature of Psychotherapy," *Psychiatry* (1949) *12:*3-12.
(13) Carl R. Rogers, *Client-Centered Therapy;* Boston, Houghton Mifflin, 1951.
(14) Frederick Allen, *Psychotherapy with Children;* New York, Norton, 1942.
(15) Reference footnote 6; pp. 253-256.
(16) Reference footnote 6; p. 250; see also pp. 177-183.

opportunity to effect behavioral and attitudinal changes. This ongoing exchange is another way of talking about such clinical notions as growth potential, forward surge, and so on. Casting thoughts into quasi communication theory helps to make more explicit the seemingly esoteric clinical notions and helps to point up the interpersonal processes of therapy in their more constructive modes.

Concurrent Stimulation Versus Serial Causation. We feel that the child in therapy is placed in the context of what might be termed concurrent stimulation from all sides; although we expect a degree of change, we are willing to let changes come as they will, when they will. We do not feel that our patients "must see their hostility before they can relax," "must recover the past before they can control the present," and so on. There is no necessity to "get at this before tackling that," because the total relationship is the focus. If the relationship is near optimal, then the child will change at the rate and in the ways he finds available to him. Many changes occur concurrently or in nondiscernible ways; the patient and therapist are not running up and down a psychic ladder which has incontrovertible steps in an incontrovertible order, nor are they dealing with a psychic filing system in which everything has a specific place. *Whatever is basic gets tested out in living; it does not have to be pursued for its own sakes.*

TABLE 4-I

OUTCOMES OF SHORT-TERM AND CONVENTIONAL THERAPY
FOR THREE TREATMENT SAMPLES IN TWO CLINICS

| | Fairfax Clinic | | | | Arlington Clinic | |
| | Short-Term Cases | | Conventional Cases | | Conventional Cases | |
Judged Results	No.	Percent	No.	Percent	No.	Percent
Successful	2	13	1	7	4	13
Improved	14	87	8	57	19	64
Failure	0	0	5	36	7	23
TOTAL	16	100	14	100	30	100

DATA

Outcomes of Cases Treated by Short-term Therapy. This study included 16 short-term parent-child cases and 14 conventionally treated cases at the Fairfax clinic, making a total of 30 pairs (17). Thirty conventionally treated cases at the Arlington clinic were used as a second control group (18). Table 4-I presents three categories of outcome for these cases — *successful, improved,* and *failure* — giving the number and percentage of cases falling within each category. These evaluations of outcomes were made on an overall basis, including the written case records, consultation with the psychiatrists, psychologists, or social workers, and follow-up interviews with the mothers about one year after termination of treatment. As far as possible, all cases were treated alike in the judgment process; bias, if any, was more apt to be against short-term treatment because of its newness and its challenge to old assumptions.

When the frequencies of the short-term and conventional cases falling within the three categories are compared with those frequencies which would be expected by chance, a Chi Square of 5.546 results. For two degrees of freedom, this figure is just short of significance at the .05 level (.05 level = 5.991). In other words, the difference in outcome between the short-term and conventional methods would be, by chance, as great as shown in Table 4-I only 5 to 6 times in a hundred. This level of significance is high enough to warrant further study.

Types of Endings. The types of endings associated with the two treatment methods are shown in Figure 4-1. The classification of types of endings was the following: *Mutually agreed* (that is, the ending of the therapy was mutually planned and agreed upon by parent and therapist); *return for more therapy* (that is, the therapy was considered successful to a point, but it was agreed that more

(17) Mean ages of the children were 8 years 4 months for the 16 short-term cases, and 8 years 3 months for the 14 conventional cases; in both groups the age ranges were from preschool age up to adolescence.

(18) While short-term treatment is now being used at the Arlington clinic, it has not been in progress sufficiently long enough to provide follow-up data. The 30 conventional Arlington cases used here as a second control group were treated before the advent of short-term practices.

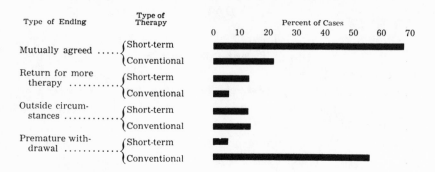

Figure 4-1. Types of endings for short-term and conventional parent-child treatment cases. (Fairfax sample only.)

help was required); endings brought about by *outside circum-stances;* and *premature withdrawal* (that is, the therapy was abortive because of premature withdrawal of either the therapist or the parent and child).

It may seem obvious that in short-term therapy, where a block of ten interviews was planned from the beginning, mutually agreed endings would be much more frequent than in conventional therapy, as shown in Figure 4-1. The significance of the number of mutually agreed endings is more apparent when one compares it with the number of premature withdrawals. In other words, it was presumably more feasible for all concerned to carry through a limited, planned program to some kind of goal without discourage-ment and withdrawal, than it was to carry through an indefinite program to some unspecified point where it could be agreed that some goal had been reached.

Number of Interviews and Use of Staff Time. While short-term therapy was based on the block of 10 interviews, the actual mean number of interviews for the 16 Fairfax short-term cases was 11.43, because of the inclusion of four cases which continued beyond the tenth interview or returned for more help. The Fairfax conventional group showed a mean of 12.1 interviews, but this figure includes four failures, one coming for 9 interviews and three for 6 or fewer interviews. Thus the difference between these two means is unreliable. However, among the successful and improved cases, the mean of 11.43 visits for the short-term group is to be compared with a mean of 14.10 visits for the conventional treated cases, netting a t value of 1.15 (P = .04). The difference is great enough to have arisen only 4 times in 100 by chance (19).

Two examples of short-term therapy drawn from our case material are presented below to give some qualitative idea of the nature of the work. Case 1 is abstracted from a series of 10 interviews with a mother-child pair. Case 2 is abstracted from 5 interviews with a mother whose three preschool children were not seen.

Case 1

When Frank, age 4, was first brought to the clinic, his mother reported that he was aggressive and "seems to feel the need to hit or push children without warning and without provocation − same at home and at school." He was reluctant to leave his mother on the first visit, broke away from the therapist who was interviewing him, and interrupted his mother's interview with another thera-pist. He had been in and out of three nursery schools, and the parents were at that time considering placing him in an all-day treatment home. The clinic approved this plan, and the case was closed at the clinic. These plans did not materalize, and a year later the parents reapplied to the clinic for help. We gave the child psychological tests, reinterviewed the mother, and offered them a series of 10 interviews, which was accepted.

Interview 1, with child. Frank was hyperactive, overly verbal, restless, and interested in various play material for short periods but tired quickly. After 20 to 25 minutes in the playroom, he began to cry and to yell that he wanted to leave; he finally left the playroom and interrupted his mother's interview with her therapist.

(19) Durham's study, carried out on a similar outpatient child guidance population, shows how varied treatment practices may be within the conventional framework. Although the mean number of visits in her study was 13.74, the standard deviation was 13.38 visits, and the range varied from 2 to 67 visits. The short-term structure permits as good if not better results concerning treatment outcomes without incurring the limitations of conventional practices. Mary S. Durham, "Some Observations Concerning External Criteria of Success in Psychotherapy," *J. Psychol.* (1952) *33:*175-181.

Interviews 2, 3, 4 (weekly intervals). During these interviews, Frank became less obstreperous and more conversational; the therapist anticipated emotional storms, but these were truncated at each interview by a firm refusal to let Frank leave the playroom before the time was up, although Frank would contest this several times.

Interview 5 (one-week interval). Frank began to express his aggression with toys and did not spread himself out emotionally as much as before. After one bout of acting out with his toys, he said, "Whew, there I feel better," then sat down in the chair as if to recuperate from strenuous physical and emotional exertion. The therapist reported that the child was "over the hump."

Interviews 6, 7 (weekly intervals). Frank played more quietly and seemed more conversational and matter-of-fact. Compared to earlier hours, Frank was contented, happy, and self-contained. He discussed his feelings and relationships with others in a more considered, less emotional and bombastic way than before. He no longer converted his feelings into immediate, impulsive demands or aggressive action.

Interview 8 (two-week interval). The child brought his own games along today to share with the therapist; he invited the therapist to play checkers and other games with him, and played with finger paints some. He was conversational and matter-of-fact.

Interview 9 (one-week interval). Frank brought some more games today and again wanted to play checkers and to paint. He talked about an impending vacation trip. His conversation was matter-of-fact.

Interview 10 (nine-week interval). Frank came back today, tanned and exuberant about his trip and his new experiences. He appeared very normal, outgoing, comfortable, and conversational. He obviously enjoyed his "visit" to the therapist and felt no need to release tension or work off anything. He reported that he liked school now.

Interviews with mother (same dates as child's interviews). During the period of the interviews, the mother moved from a position of guilty, self-accusing attitudes — in which she felt that she had "rejected" and mistreated Frank — to a feeling that she had greatly overindulged him and had let him be "cock of the walk" without any bounds or limits. This insight gave her a new view of the boy's needs and made it possible for her to exercise more judgment and more control over emotionally provocative situations. In this way she could overcome her exhaustion, her bewilderment, and her lack of resourcefulness in respect to Frank's demandingness.

At the last interview, the mother reported that she was very pleased with Frank's progress and with her own newly found ability to enjoy the boy and relax with him; she reported that Frank was doing well at school and that he no longer struggled so much with members of the family or with his peers.

Case 2

Mrs. D's initial contact with the clinic was over the telephone. During this conversation with the therapist, she complained of her plight, despaired of doing anything about it, and cursed. She had three children, ages 5, 3, and 1.

Interview 1. Mrs. D clenched her fists and pounded on the arms of the chair during this interview. Although she admitted that her problem with her two oldest children, ages 5 and 3, was her own, she continued to express exasperation and despair. They would not mind her, she said, and they never took no for an answer. They kept her breathless from morning to night, and she wondered if they would not turn out to be "real problems as adults."

Interviews 2, 3 (weekly intervals). The nature of the parent-child involvements became more manifest in these interviews. The children would contest the mother's discipline and involve her in a tug-of-war; she would become exhausted, act childish herself, hate herself for this, and fail to follow through on her requests and admonitions; and in this way a cyclic pattern in interaction was maintained. We discussed her failure to follow through and her fear of hurting the children by making them do something after they had protested.

Interview 4 (two-week interval). Mrs. D seemed more relaxed today and reported that she was beginning to "get my point over to the boys and to get them to do *some* of the things I request."

She began to see how she could "mean 'no' when I say 'no.' " In discussing problems about child rearing and her own remaining problems, she seemed much less pushed, less angry, and less urgent.

Interview 5 (two-week interval). Mrs. D came in and said, "My problem is over — I've solved it. Stevie is really much better because I'm better, and Jon is really a darling — he's so little trouble now." She reviewed her behavior with the children over the past four or five weeks and the changes in her attitude. She had seen some signs of jealousy in the older child over the baby, but she understood this and felt it was temporary, and she gave additional evidence of being on the way toward solving her practical difficulties as they arose with the children.

CONCLUSION

The evaluations of the results and the types of endings of the two therapy procedures suggest a reasonably clear advantage for the short-term practice, within the limits specified herein. The suggestion is evident that the short-term structure helps to create a more clear-cut and decisive treatment milieu and to bring about more favorable treatment outcomes. Although conventional treatment may often be short, the very feebleness of its structure and its lack of self-consciousness, as it were, often obfuscates the results, and the clinician often fails to know wherein he succeeded or failed. When short-term mehtods are used, the associated firmness and clarity of structure allow each person concerned to know where he is most of the time, and the whole process has more tonus. It is this aspect of short-term therapy which we believe is beneficial to the patient and which is an aid in his assimilating help from the therapeutic relationship, rather than the number of interviews.

Our case material shows many instances of, for example, children who had been dismissed from school because of the seeming enormity of their problems, but who were able to return to school within two or three months after beginning treatment and have since been able to adjust satisfactorily. In many cases, parents who were at the end of their ropes were able to see what the child's lack of being properly controlled was doing to them and to the child, and were able, sometimes within a very few interviews, to gain new perspective and to give firmness, assurance, and dependability to the disciplinary situation. In general, we have found that the kind of help most usually required is the setting of limits for the child and the firming-up of parent-child relationships.

We do not wish to give the impression that results comparable to these could not be duplicated by other therapists using different methods based on different philosophies. The point is that our findings illustrate, in part, the results of a set of attitudes or expectancies that the persons concerned can handle their own difficulties with a small amount of judicious help. When such cases occur in more conventional therapy practice, their real significance is lost, because current problems and attitudes of the parent-child pair are regarded as resistance, or as examples of repression, or are otherwise dismissed from scrutiny; and the improvement of management and current relationships is viewed as superficial.

The approach which we have described fits into the public health framework of helping many people gain better mental health rather than spending inordinately long periods of time treating a very few. By relying on self-corrective processes, aided and abetted by a few interviews, the child guidance clinic can permit and foster a wider service to the general population.

Chapter 5

Psychotherapy with Parents of
Maladjusted Children*

VICTOR SZYRYNSKI

INTRODUCTION

T HIS paper is concerned with observations on psychotherapeutic work with parents of emotionally disturbed children, with special emphasis on a treatment period for the parents *preceding* therapeutic contact with the child. For the purpose of this study 38 families were selected and the parents advised to attend the psychiatrist's office on a regular basis before their children were assigned for direct therapy.

The children referred to the psychiatric clinic were first evaluated by the clinical psychologist, and the social work service collected data concerning the family. Then the child and the parents were seen by a psychiatrist for diagnostic contact and some other techniques were employed with the special purpose of determining the interfamilial dynamics. In this respect the "Two Houses Technique" (9, 10) was found to be of particular value. After such preliminary contact a psychodynamic working hypothesis about the existing problems was advanced and in the absence of any psychiatric emergency the parents were invited to attend the psychiatrist's office for about six to ten regular interviews before their child was accepted for therapy. After such a preliminary period further planning for assisting the family, including the child, was elaborated. At this point some parents reported satisfactory improvement in their child and either discontinued treatment or remained under therapy themselves, but

*Note: Reprinted by permission of the author and the *Canadian Psychiatric Association Journal, 10:*350-357, 1965.

not the child. In the other cases treatment was continued with the parents and child as well.

The advisability of including the parents in psychiatric management of children has been recognized for a long time and its importance is becoming progressively more and more evident. In various neurotic and psychosomatic conditions of children, parents were advised to undergo intensive psychiatric therapy. As an example, the work of Peshkin (8) and Abramson (1) with parents of children suffering from bronchial asthma, may be quoted. Special publications such as *Parent's Guide to Child Psychotherapy* (2) and other orientational texts have been published. The most progressive development of such an approach has probably taken place in England where at Ipswich child psychiatry was almost fully integrated with the psychiatric services for the families (3, 7, 4, 5).

SIGNIFICANCE OF PARENTAL ATTITUDES

The basic premise for such an approach is that children's general behavior depends primarily on their social learning taking place between themselves and the other significant people in the parental home. Through a continuous learning process, based largely on trial and error with introjection of the parental system of values, children are developing preferred patterns of behavior which they find satisfactory in enabling them to control their environment. This may be referred to as a "style of life" of a child acquired through such learning experience. This works actually both ways since the parents usually respond unconsciously to such established patterns of behavior in a child by modifying their own habits, and eventually a firmly crystallized pattern of give and take begins to prevail in the family. Of course, this may be different between the parents and each one of their children. In some cases such patterns acquire a neurotic character and underlie the clinical picture of an emotionally disturbed and behaviorally troublesome child. The most efficient way to modify such socially defective patterns is by changing the customary responses of each of the parents. This is accomplished by helping the latter to recognize the origin and nature of their habitual responses and to relieve various underlying emotional factors which basically determine or further aggravate such mechanisms. Through psychotherapy therefore, such parents learn to understand themselves, to rectify their own neurotic responses, and to gain better understanding of the nature of their children's style of life.

Our basic psychotherapeutic philosophy in working with all the patients has always been that the psychiatrists should hardly ever treat the symptoms but the underlying basic disturbance of the whole personality. The symptoms are looked upon as nothing more than the signals signifying some basic disturbance of the adjustive mechanisms within the personality or the dangerous weakness of the ego strength. The only exception admissible to this principle is in cases when we are dealing with the dire psychiatric emergencies, requiring the immediate control of the presenting symptoms. By the same token our basic approach to the parents of emotionally disturbed children, as discussed in this paper, was obviously carried on in the absence of direct psychiatric emergency.

Working with the parents is particularly important in respect to the younger children. It has been well knwon that the contact of a small child with the therapist encounters serious difficulty. Many years ago Susan Isaaks was stressing difficulty in transference when the therapist has to "compete" with the parents who are usually very distinctly evident and functional in the child's everyday existence. Still more, some of the psychotherapeutic systems, like the theories of Carl Rogers, would require reasonably satisfactory independence of the patient from his social environment in order to achieve good psychotherapeutic results. Considering the above factors and the fundamentally powerful influence of parents on the child's adjustment, which has been discussed above and in some other papers (11), working through the parents has always been considered the most desirable approach whenever feasible. It is only in adolescence that the therapist may attempt to help his young patients in gaining insight into their psychological relationship with the parents. When a young boy or girl is assisted in understanding the nature of parental behavior they may develop greater understanding and achieve better maturity in handling their own problems. This may further relieve the neurotic guilt feeling and alleviate the intra-psychic conflict so frequently responsible for neurotic or psycho-somatic symptoms. Such a process, which may be called "turning the table," diminishes hostility and eventually assists in disrupting the vicious circle of hostility towards the parents, leading to guilt for such hostility and subsequent hostility towards people who are producing guilt feelings. Such therapy towards production of insight is rarely feasible when working with younger children and, as mentioned above, the main emphasis would here be on parental behavior patterns and their modification through treatment of the parents.

The second very important purpose in our approach is to change the erroneous attitude of the parents who bring their child for psychiatric assistance. In keeping with the prevailing tradition of attending medical offices, the parents expect the child to be "fixed" by a psychiatrist and returned in an improved condition. Facetiously we like to call this attitude "the garage syndrome" by comparing it to depositing a damaged car in a garage and calling for it when the expert finishes his job. Such an attitude, of course, is entirely contrary to the above discussed role of child psychiatry. Inviting the parents to participate in the first stage of therapy without their child and before the child is assigned for treatment, usually corrects such an erroneous orientation and helps them to appreciate their own role in rehabilitation of a disturbed child. This not only assists individual families but also results in slowly changing the attitudes of the whole community towards the nature of psychiatric treatment. It is not only highly economical with respect to a particular situation of a child brought for treatment, but it may have a far-reaching effect in rehabilitating the climate of the whole family and stretching the psychiatric influence on the other children, who are either already present in the household or may arrive in the future. This approach, however, should not be identified with parental education. It is based in the first place on a thorough dynamic psychotherapy of individuals responsible for the mental health of their children. This obviously depends on the proper motivation of such parents. In our psychotherapeutic approach, we take this into consideration and attempt to modify the degree of such motivation and of parental attitude by a suitable technique which will be discussed later in this chapter.

The third reason, therefore, for this selective approach is to help the parents to understand their own hidden problems and unconscious processes which may consistently frustrate and hinder their most eager attempt to assist the child. Such situations are very well known to all psychiatrists so we may just briefly enumerate some of the most typical psychodynamic patterns found among the parents. The common attitude of rejecting the child may often be disguised and modified by blaming it on the child's aggressive and provocative behavior, by a fault-finding attitude, by a withdrawing and evasive role of the parents, by indifference and passivity, or eventually an overconcerned and excessively overprotective display of parental management. The parents who superficially display guilt and self-accusation may actually be asking for reassurance and acceptance of their attitudes. We may also find parents with more severe emotional disturbance and even those who are quite unable to handle their children except after undergoing very intensive therapy, being mentally ill or severely socially disturbed, not to mention alcoholics, mental defectives, etc. In working with the parents, they are helped here to understand that by modifying their own behavior they are capable of changing the behavioral responses of the child. They are helped to see how a certain stereotype has developed in their family when a certain action of a child brings about regularly the same customary responses from the parents. It is often possible to point out to the parents that their persistent responses tend to reappear as if in a "push button" manner when the child presses a button and the parents react with nearly mechanical regularity. Many parents develop a keen interest in verifying such assumptions and in experimenting in their relations with their own children. Some of them soon report amazing observations when they attempt to "surprise" the child by withholding the anticipated response and replacing it with a deliberately new and unexpected reaction. A mother who responds with growing anger to the child's slow eating habits attempts to disregard this behavior and finds to her surprise that the child's habits change quite rapidly. This in turn may help the mother to see the reason for her lack of patience and lead to a relaxed attitude at the family table.

SOME TYPICAL PROBLEMS AND ILLUSTRATIVE CASES

A few illustrative cases will probably prove our point in a more vivid manner.

We had a few cases when parents required treatment even before their first child was born. They usually turn up at the social agencies with the strange request to get assistance in giving up their first child for adoption. Often such couples present the outward appearance of the most suitable parents intellectually, socially, and economically.

One such couple was in their early twenties, their health was good and appearance very pleasant. Both had a high school education, the husband was employed as a successful mechanic, the wife worked in an office. They had been married for three years and claimed to enjoy regular sexual relations which, even if not very exciting, was apparently acceptable to both of them. They had been dating each other since high school days for about four years. They insisted that they never planned to have children and they were very annoyed with the pregnancy of the wife, already in her sixth month when asking for her baby to be adopted. They were accepted for psychotherapy and their ambivalent attitude was the most conspicuous. Both complained at first that the only purpose of seeing a psychiatrist was compliance with the request of a social agency. On the other hand, they kept their appointments very regularly and soon developed good contact with the therapist. It became quite obvious that their resentment against accepting the child was just a presenting symptom of a deep-rooted emotional maladjustment in this family. The husband was found to have been exposed through his childhood and adolescence to the influence of a very overprotective, seductive and neurotic mother who was attempting to baby him quite persistently. His notion was that tenderness and attention to girls are attitudes unsuitable for an independent grown-up man. His wife carried into their marriage the even more severe trauma of being sexually accosted by an elderly member of the family who took advantage of her for a few years since the age of six. This strongly implanted fear of pregnancy and severe guilt for the situation, and most likely for some pleasurable aspects of such a contact. This girl never played with dolls and was very happy in finding a boy with whom they could mutually condemn most of the emotional aspects of the marital life. Obviously, both of them were emotionally unprepared to accept a child and to provide for a baby the necessary climate of a warm mature home. During psychotherapy it became obvious that the girl was already undergoing a significant emotional growth but this had been repressed for fear of antagonizing her husband with any evidence of emotional display. She was helped to recognize and to accept her normal maturation into full femininity. On the other hand, the husband was also assisted to understand and accept his wife as something more than an insecure and restrained adolescent, and at the same time to gain insight into the nature of his neurotic attitude towards marriage and domestic life. A characteristic development in this case was that even before they had made any decision and still insisted on rejecting the baby, they recognized the seriousness of their problem and requested their therapy to be continued even after the mother delivered the child, whether the child be accepted or adopted out.

An attitude of the parents, present before the child is born, may be illustrated by a few other cases.

In one of them, a girl of 17 married a man who was 35. During her pregnancy she did not make any preparations for the baby. When questioned by a public health nurse, her answer was that she expected the baby either to die at birth or to be crippled and until she saw the baby in good health there was not much point in wasting money on preparations since it might not be necessary. Psychodynamically it was evident that this young girl suffered from severe neurotic guilt feelings about marrying a man twice her age, particularly as it had been done against her parents' will. She was expecting, therefore, that her child should be either dead or crippled as a punishment for her disobedience and acting against parental advice. This is still more deeply related to the built-in idea of sexual guilt which has not been alleviated even by the fact of a legitimate marriage.

An even more involved psychodynamic situation was found in another case when a healthy young woman, pregnant with her second child, was slightly jolted and fell down while riding in a streetcar, and when taken to the hospital developed paralysis of both legs. With negative neurological examination it was obvious that her paraplegia was of a hysterical nature. She remained for a few weeks in hospital and during the first few nights suffered from terrifying nightmares. Dynamic psychotherapy was undertaken and after a few days her nightmares disappeared, her anxiety subsided, and she started walking but had to watch her legs all the time as no feeling returned to her extremities. She described her experience as "floating in the air from the waist down." Such condition remained unchanged for another few weeks until the day of delivery. After delivering a healthy baby boy she inspected her child very carefully and when she found that his legs were normal she promptly regained full motor power and sensation in *her* legs. The possible psychodynamic factor responsible for this condition was suspected to be her resentment of having her second pregnancy right after the first one and within the first two years of her marriage. She was a person of rather strict religious principles and considered her resentment toward pregnancy unacceptable to her cultural pattern. Severe guilt feelings for such an attitude resulted in fear of punishment manifested by the anticipated birth of a crippled child. Consequently, the symptoms were based on the mechanism of identification with an interjected object, a rather interesting mechanism in such a hysterial manifestation.

The most straightforward psychodynamics were present in the following case:

A lady of 45 arrived in the psychiatrist's office complaining of severe obsessive-ruminative ideas. She could not let her four-year-old boy out of her sight, expecting all the time that he would be badly injured, run over by a car, mutilated, or murdered. Her neurotic condition was so severe that even when the boy was invited to some neighborhood children's party under the care of adults, she experienced a compulsion to telephone them practically every five or ten minutes to get assurance that the child was in good health. Such an attitude resulted in the boy being rejected by the neighborhood, who found it difficult to cope with the neurotic behavior of the mother. The child in question was the third boy in an apparently well-adjusted middle class family. Two older youngsters were very happy, popular, and all around well-adjusted teenagers. In their case the mother never manifested any overly protective or overly solicitous attitudes; just the contrary — easily allowed them to attend summer camp, participate in sports, and in fact display more independence than average for their age. However, during dynamic psychotherapy, clear-cut reasons for neurotic symptoms were revealed. During the second part of her family life, marital adjustment became somewhat more precarious and some domestic tension resulted. The third pregnancy came up quite unexpectedly and it was bitterly resented by the woman who was already past her 40's. Still more, her physical health was at a low ebb. She felt tired, run down, and was losing weight. She was strongly considering abortion but it was entirely against her ethical and religious principles. Still, she doubled her physical efforts, hoping tacitly that a spontaneous miscarriage would take place. However, the sturdy little infant held his own and a very healthy boy was delivered, who soon became the full joy of his parents. In this new situation our patient developed severe neurotic guilt manifested by anxiety that her initial murderous wishes might become true in a "magic" way and result in injury to her little boy. (Such "magic thinking" described by Piaget in children is also quite common, even markedly exaggerated in some neurotic conditions.)

Another typical pattern was found in three families who were referred to the clinic on account of alleged mental deficiency of their children. In all three households the parents were highly respected in the community. There was one child with borderline intelligence who was, however, quite capable of benefitting from parental care and grade school education. However, the overly critical and demanding attitude of the parents resulted in all three cases in placement of the children in institutions for mental defectives after they failed to benefit from teaching, even at the special education level. The basic reason for this situation, however, was found to be severe insecurity in the children caused by the neurotic, overly demanding, rigid, intolerant, and basically hostile and rejecting attitude of the parents. While in one case the inflexible attitude of the parents necessitated transferring the child eventually to a foster home, in two other cases intensive therapy with both parents resulted in considerable modification of their own neurotic style of life.

The Adlerian concept that every child develops individually his or her own methods and techniques to "control the world" has been made full use of in helping the parents to understand some patterns of behavior in their children.

It was probably best illustrated by the case of a girl of ten of good intelligence and satisfactory scholastic adjustment, who was brought to the clinic by the exasperated parents who could not rectify in any possible way her unusually slow eating habits. It was found that the girl was spending considerably more time at the table and in particular liked to chew her food indefinitely before swallowing at infrequent intervals. The seriously neurotic background of the situation rapidly unfolded itself during psychiatric investigation. In cooperation with the family physician both parents have been found to be suffering from numerous psychosomatic disturbances. Both were college graduates, very highly strung, demanding, compulsive, and utterly rigid. Their control of the child's behavior was excessive and inflexible. They fully controlled her manners, dress, and overall behavior according to their strict preconceived ideas. There was only one situation where the girl could retaliate and punish her parents by successful resistance and this was chewing and swallowing of her food.

Most obviously this case required prolonged and meticulous therapy of both parents to change their lifelong neurotic patterns, while the child could easily be left alone with the simple advice to spend more time away from home with relatives or family friends, where her presenting symptoms were actually never displayed for the simple reason that nobody was interested enough to react to them.

In two cases the external circumstances found out in the family history helped the parents to understand their difficulties with their children with the assistance of a simple explanation.

In one case a child was born to the parents who were both still studying at the post-graduate level. They were forced to live in an apartment house and their main concern was to keep the child quiet. Consequently they indulged the child for the first two years of life, allowing themselves to be blackmailed by his threats of crying or the raving temper tantrums, into complete neurotic passivity. In the other case the girl, the first in the family, was brought up in a house where her father, a church minister, also had his office and the mother was attempting to bribe the child into being quiet, since her cry would disturb her father's work and his contact with visitors. Both children were seen at the clinic from the age of ten and both presented themselves as fully unmanageable. In both cases the first concern of the therapeutic planning was to take care of a considerable amount of repressed hostility which displayed itself under the disguise of the apparently tender and devoted behavior of parents.

Promoting insight in the parents is not an easy undertaking. Many of them cling to their neurotic patterns and consciously or unconsciously resist their uncovering. Perhaps one of the most typical attitudes in this category would be the people who at every visit to a psychiatrist display their gratitude and appreciation for his guidance and assistance. However, when their handling of the child is described it is most evident that they have been behaving just the oppsite to the patterns suggested during psycho-therapeutic contact. This obviously requires lengthy and patient management to change their pattern of defending inner hostility with a superficial pseudo-cooperative and submissive attitude.

A very special group of parents requiring intensive psycho-therapy are the families where the children are suffering from school phobia. In such cases, the parental attitude is usually characterized by indecisiveness, a very soft approach to the child and also the unconscious desire for the child to stay at home or to remain sick in order to provide the parents with an opportunity to display their overprotective and overaffectionate attitude toward the child to gratify their "need to be needed." This may occur equally as well in the mothers and fathers of such children, but in some cases we are dealing with the frustrated mothers who are not fully accepted by their husbands and who use their children as substitute love objects. Such situations provide perhaps the best examples when psychotherapy of the whole family is seriously indicated.

> In one of our cases a boy of seven-and-a-half, the last child in a family of eight, had been brought for psychiatric consultation on account of persistent refusal to stay at school. This child of average intelligence and reasonably good health remained practically for the whole hour of the interview seated in the lap of his overattentive mother and sucking his thumb. Any attempt to separate this excessively symbiotic relationship, even for a short while, were quite unsuccessful. A history of a long-standing serious marital frustration was easily obtained.

MOTIVATING THE PARENTS FOR PSYCHOTHERAPY

One of the most fundamental problems in our "garage syndrome" is inadequate motivation of some parents to get involved in the therapeutic process. In all such cases a very special approach is indicated. In particular it is important to remain nonaccusatory and noncondemning in respect to such parents. They are usually quite aware of their inadequacy and pointing their errors out to them results in increasing their insecurity. Consequently, at the first stage of our approach we ask such parents to help the psychiatrist in understanding their child. They are not subjected to his criticism or reprimanded but are invited to assist the doctor in analyzing the behavior of the child. Their guilt feelings are always played down by the ego-supporting approach where their concern about the child and their devotion to parental responsibilities are praised. Then with their full cooperation we usually discuss the characteristic "style of life" of such a child and, going further, attempt to reveal the possible reasons for his psychodynamic development. In this way the parents become increasingly interested in their child's mental mechanisms and begin to look for some corresponding factors in their own life adjustment and their personalities. In this way they drift away very gradually and imperceptibly from the child's problems to analyzing their own adjustment and behavioral responses in relationship with the child. Such an ego-supportive approach is often particularly important in dealing with the fathers who have a tendency to leave the child's problem to their wives and withdraw from contact with the clinic. Again many of them feel somewhat guilty for their lack of constructive contribution to bringing up their children and they prefer to stay away, not to be blamed by the figure of authority represented by a psychiatrist. They would dodge their appointments and avoid any contact. However, the attitude of such a man changes when a psychiatrist calls him and reverses his position by stressing his own difficulty in under-standing the problems of the child or of the mother and asking the father for assistance and help. Seeing that the approach of the psychiatrist is changed from a threatening authority figure to a friendly modest individual who is only asking for assistance, usually protects and adequately boosts the ego of the father to produce prompt response of cooperation.

In working with the parents various psychotherapeutic tech-niques are used, depending upon the needs of such patients. In this respect we are using the individual dynamic psychotherapy when each parent is seen individually. Sometimes they may be treated as a couple and it is also beneficial to organize group therapy when a few couples are working with the psychiatrist. So far we have not tried the therapy of the whole family in more than a few cases, but Howells (6) describes very good results with this approach. In addition, the general enlightenment and educational program, with assitance of such adjunct material as books, pamphlets and films for a group of parents, are also used.

THE GENERAL RESULTS

The most significant finding with application of this technique was that in a number of cases, after the preliminary contacts of the parents with the psychiatrist, the behavior of the child has so improved during the stage of parental therapy that no further psychiatric assistance for the child was actually necessary. In still other cases, the length of therapeutic contact with the child was markedly shortened with change in his behavior enthusiastically reported by the parents. In all the cases the therapeutic emphasis was moved from the clinical contact with the child to the changing of the parental handling of the patient, with the parents abandoning the idea of depositing the child "in the garage for fixing" and developing an interest in their own role and relationship with the child.

From among 38 in our experimental group of families, in 11 cases no further treatment with the child was carried on after the parents had gone through the six to ten therapeutic sessions themselves; in 14 other cases therapy with the child did not extend beyond six therapeutic sessions; in the remaining 12 cases longer treatment with the child and maintaining of therapeutic contact with the parents was necessary. All the children in the experimental group ranged from 6 to 13 years. Obviously it should be mentioned that in addition to the child patient the other children in the same family were often discussed with the parents who learned to understand and respond to their individual patterns of adjustment and to their favorite way of controlling the world.

REFERENCES

1. Abramson, H. A., and Peshkin, M. Murray: Group psychotherapy of the parents of intractably asthmatic children, *J. Child Asthma Res. Inst. Hosp., 1:*77-91, 1961.
2. Halpern, H. M.: *A Parent's Guide to Child Psychotherapy.* New York, A. S. Barnes and Company, 1963.
3. Howells, J. G.: *Family Psychiatry.* Edinburgh and London. Oliver & Boyd, 1963.
4. Howells, J. G.: *The nuclear family as the functional unit in psychiatry. Brit. J. Psychiat. 108:*675-684, 1962.
5. Howells, J. G.: Family psychiatry and the family doctor, *Practitioner, 188:*370-376, 1962.
6. Howells, J. G.: Child psychiatry as an aspect of family psychiatry, *II Congresso Europeo di Pedopsichiatria,* Reports and Contributing Papers, 256, Rome, 1963.
7. Howells, J. G., and Lickorish, J. T.: A projective technique for

investigating intra-family relationships designed for use with emotionally disturbed children, *Brit J. Psychol, 33:*286-296, 1963.

8. Peshkin, Murray, and Abramson, Harold A.: Screening procedures for admission to the children's asthma research institute and hospital, *J. Child Asthma Res. Inst. Hosp, 1:*221-288, 1961.

9. Szyrynski, Victor: A new technique to investigate family dynamics in child psychiatry, *Canad. Psychiat. Ass. J., 8:*94-103, 1963.

10. Szyrynski, Victor: Investigation of family dynamics with the "Two Houses Technique. *Psychosomatics, 4:*68-72, 1963.

11. Szyrynski, Victor: Parents and children in the light of dynamic psychology, *Psychosomatics, 3:*33-36, 1962.

Chapter 6

Involving Parents in
Children's Treatment*

J. R. WILKES

PARENT participation in treatment programs is not new to child psychiatry. The evolution of the child guidance movement was characterized by a realization that parents must often receive help concurrently. It is generally accepted that disorders which subside when the child is treated alone, as in a residential treatment center, often reassert themselves when he returns home, unless his parents have also been successfully engaged in treatment. Despite this, few clinics, hospitals or children's residential centers adequately involve parents in their treatment programs. There may be regular meetings with a social worker, or the parents may be seen occasionally by the psychiatrist. Meetings between nurses or child-care staff with parents are also infrequent and tend to take place during visiting hours, or when the child is taken home for a weekend visit. In short, sessions between the child-care staff and parents are few and those which do occur are generally kept 'safe,' superficial, and social.

In our Service, we became convinced that a valuable treatment opportunity takes place when parents meet with the staff person responsible for the day-to-day care of their child. Consequently, we decided to maximize its usefulness. Instead of avoiding some difficult situation with a parent, perhaps by referring him (or them) to the social worker or the psychiatrist, the child staff were encouraged and helped to deal with the parents directly and by themselves. This article will examine ways in which child-care staff can involve parents and help in the treatment of their hospitalized, emotionally disturbed children.

Note: Reprinted by permission of the author and *Canada's Mental Health*, Bi-Monthly Journal of the Department of National Health and Welfare, Ottawa, *118:*10-14, 1970.

TREATMENT PRINCIPLES

The Children's Unit at the Clarke Institute contains five bedrooms and a living-dining room. It has the use of an outdoor play-roof and access to community facilities. The staff consists of a psychiatrist, social worker and 12 nurses. In addition, there are two part-time school teachers and an occupational therapist. Children from three to 12 are admitted for short periods in time of crisis. No diagnostic category is excluded. Psychoneurotic, autistic, constricted, and acting-out children have all been admitted.

Four major principles underlie treatment. First, the presence of parents in the unit gives the staff a chance to see at first hand the quality of parent-child interaction. Second, on observing maladaptive interaction, the staff openly bring it to the attention of parents and, if at all possible, discuss it with them. Third, the presence of the parents in the unit provides the opportunity for all the professional staff to be involved in this observation and to discuss it with the parents. Finally, this kind of confrontation with reality is held to be an important therapeutic concept. Every attempt is made to strip off the often frightening and mystical aura and stigma of the psychiatric facility and bring parents face to face with the people working with their child.

ADMISSIONS

In the preadmission procedure, after the child and his parents have been assessed and it has been decided that the child requires hospitalization, a visit to the unit is arranged for the parents. The social worker lets them know that during their visit all matters concerning their responsibility regarding the child's admission will be fully discussed. This discussion, however, occurs after the parents have had a tour of the unit, conducted by the head nurse, but without the psychiatrist or social worker being present. It seems wise that the parents meet with the nurse alone because we feel the presence of the already familiar psychiatrist or social worker may detract from developing the crucial nurse-patient relationship. It is also important for the parents to meet with the person who will have the day-to-day care of their child. It is involvement of this kind in visiting the unit which really helps parents to make meaningful and responsible decisions about their child's admission and the part they must play in it.

A typical admission day will be something like this: The parents accompany their child to his room where they help him unpack and get settled in. The nurse also takes the child's "home life inventory." This is a way of involving the parents in giving the staff personal details about the child's daily life. It includes, for example, details about special words he uses for favorite toys, or dolls, any bedtime rituals, whether he says prayers at night, and so on. Taking this "inventory" also gives the parents an opportunity to talk about how they feel about the management of their child and about his hospital stay. This helps to relieve the guilt they can have about abandoning him. All this helps to lay the groundwork for a future rapport with nursing staff.

NEXT STEPS

In the first two weeks after admission the child undergoes various psychiatric, neurological, and psychological assessments. Other than at visiting hours, contact with the parents is maintained through the social worker and no additional integrating steps are taken during this period. At the end of the two weeks a "family diagnostic session" is held by the psychiatrist, following which the whole family visits the child in his unit so that his brothers and sisters can see where "they are keeping" him.

At this point, sufficient information and understanding has been exchanged and the staff are ready to proceed to the next steps of parent integration by inviting them to spend a morning or afternoon with the child. They will be with him at meals, playtime, special outings, and organized activities. If it is not possible to be with and observe the child in occupational therapy or at school, then arrangements are made to do this at some other time.

Then there are other visits designed to involve the parents in the treatment program. The staff purposely select "difficult" situations of child management for the parents to deal with, observe, and discuss. These are usually such things as mealtime, bedtime, playtime, outings, and the like. It is not necessary, of course, for staff to be able to "manage" the child easily. In fact it is helpful to parents to see that the "professional" also has difficulties for this helps to relieve guilt and encourage greater self-confidence. In discussing these difficulties afterwards with the nurse, there is the opportunity to release considerable anxiety and tension. Parents are encouraged to talk about how they felt about a similar situation at home and to explore how the nurse managed not to become upset. Slowly the staff begin to turn over to, or at least to share with, the parents more responsibility for coping with various crises that arise.

STAFF-PARENT CONFRONTATION

In working with the parents, ward staff foster clear and direct communication, since this kind of open communication is therapeutic. However, at first there was a real reluctance by the staff to confront parents in an open and direct way. After a number of parents had complained that they were not sure just what to do, or that they felt uncomfortable, it became clear that the staff had been dodging issues and hiding their real feelings. This had prevented free communication in potentially therapeutic situations. But when the staff learned to risk themselves and became more direct, not only did the parents become more responsive, they also learned to become more direct themselves.

Generally speaking, the nurse promotes discussion in areas where parents seem to be experiencing the greatest anxiety. For example, if when they enter the unit and their child ignores them by only paying attention to the nurse, she will refer to this if the parents fail to do so. She may then ask the parents if they feel left out, and ask in such a way that implies that this would be a very healthy and natural thing in such a situation. The point is that she is dealing with "here and now" situations in a therapeutic way. Or again, if the parents are present at a particularly disruptive meal, the nurse will not ignore or dismiss it, but say something like, "I guess you must have found things pretty chaotic in there today. So did we." Here again, the problem has been brought out and not ignored, and the way has been opened for the parents to voice their attitudes, feelings, and expectations.

PARENTS ASSIST IN ASSESSMENT

Assessment involves the collection and consideration of all relevant information for the use of those responsible for the patient's care and treatment. In child psychiatry an important part of assessment is to discuss the findings with the parents in such a way that is meaningful and helpful to them. Our program of parent involvement, we find, assists assessment in two essential ways: it provides clear, on-the-spot data, and it helps parents to better accept and deal with the assessment.

In the case of the former, it is obvious that observation of parent-child interaction can be helpful in assessing the healthy and unhealthy aspects of the relationship. The greater the variety of situations in which these observations take place, the richer the assessment, and the less likely it is to be based on subjective parental opinions and descriptions. In regard to the latter, i.e. parents' acceptance of an assessment, seeing what really goes on helps to prevent them from forming distorted fantasies which interfere with an accurate understanding, and acceptance of, the assessment. Furthermore, they can understand various treatment methods much more easily. They know, for example, what occupational therapy is. They have seen it, have seen their child involved in it, and they have talked with the occupational therapist. All of this tends to minimize defensive reactions and parents to begin to appreciate the source and meaning of their child's behavior.

PARENTAL PRESENCE ASSISTS IN TREATMENT

In residential treatment, close and intimate ties can be established between the child and his ward nurse, sometimes to the point where the attachment develops at the expense of the parents. This appeal of the child, while understandable, can blind the staff to the problems being faced by the parents. Levy (1)

(1) E. Z. Levy: The importance of the children's needs in residential treatment, *Bull. Menninger Clinic, 31*, No. 1, Jan., 1967, pp. 18-31.

writes, for example, that because of the nature of the work with disturbed children, staff possessiveness often develops. This can lead to competition with, or unrecognized hostility to the parents, as well as to "rescue" fantasies or other emotional attitudes that block the treatment program. For example:

> R. K., a 6-year-old adopted boy, presented as a pathetic child who spoke very little and who relied on the adults around him to initiate conversation. He showed a number of signs of early deprivation. From his history it was apparent that both parents tended to be strict and somewhat compulsive about neatness and daily routines. The staff tended to see the parents in a negative way and, in compensation, were lenient and did things for him. This approach tended to reinforce the boy's dependency and passivity. But when his mother came to the unit and the staff were able to see that she was not as strict or compulsive as they had imagined, they stopped "feeling sorry" for the boy and put more demands on him to be independent.

Bell and Zucker (2) have discussed the incompatibility of the stereotyped expectations of a family, on the one hand, and of the hospital on the other. This incompatibility often causes frustrations and dissatisfactions on both sides. The point made is that these differing expectations are ordinarily brought sufficiently into the open to lead to confrontation, followed by cooperation. Consequently, the situation moves through phases of puzzling nonengagement, mutual complaining, mutual withdrawal, and mutual manipulation. Clearly, if child and parent are to gain from the hospital experience, these kinds of relationships must be avoided and confrontation is required to prevent them.

Involving the family in treatment keeps the child within the family orbit. It is a well-recognized principle of rehabilitation that the patient's place in his family and community must be maintained lest he become "forgotten" in the hospital and subsequently, on discharge, suffer a loss of treatment gains because in the meantime, the patient and family had grown away from each other.

Then, too, because there is a constant reaching out by the staff to the parents for their reactions and opinions, the parents feel a sense of significance and their self-esteem is maintained. Too often

(2) Bell, N. W., and Zucker, R. A.: Family-Hospital Relationships in a State Hospital. Paper presented at the First International Congress of Social Psychiatry, London, Eng., August 7-12, 1964.

when a disturbed child is admitted to hospital the parents are used merely as a source of information and are never really involved in the treatment program. When parents have been left out in the cold and are not responsibly involved, they are likely to feel that they have abandoned their child. This only compounds existing guilt and makes them feel even less worthy as parents. Maintaining parent esteem is crucial to the child's future relations with his parents.

There are other important advantages to a parent program. Improvement of parenting skills is one. Having to more or less objectively observe their child's behavior, discuss it with the staff, and practice coping with it, helps parents to develop skills of parenting that many of them need. We have found that the continuing flow of new parents through the unit tends to prevent the sort of narcissistic satisfaction and lack of self-criticism that can develop in some hospitals. Parents serve as a built-in corrective to staff complacency and self-satisfaction. The question by a parent about procedures often results in a reexamination of the value and function of these procedures, either by two or three staff or at a unit conference.

The involvement of parents in the program can also be a valuable aid to the child's individual psychotherapy, particularly when their presence evokes material in therapy which might otherwise remain dormant:

> S. B., an 8-year-old boy, had suffered maternal bereavement several months before admission. Making matters worse, was the father's opinion that the boy was responsible for his wife's death. He felt that she had exhausted herself with the time and effort she spent dealing with S. B.'s acting-out behavior at home and school. Father had never spoken to S. B. about his mother's death. When S. B. was admitted, it was not surprising that his mother's death was well repressed and strongly defended. The theme did not seem to come up in his play therapy. Through the integration program he managed to develop a relationship with the mother of another boy from the unit. It was after this that he began to talk openly about his own mother and her death. His therapist was then able to help him work through a number of feelings he had about his own mother's death.

The purpose of this article was to illustrate the importance and process of parental involvement when their children are hospitalized for psychiatric reasons. In a sense, its development at the Clarke Institute is part of a general trend in mental health toward a family-centered approach. If it does anything else, we hope this report on our own experience with this technique will stimulate colleagues working with disturbed children and their parents to think along similar lines.

Chapter 7

Clinical Work with Parents
of Child Patients*

WILLIAM S. LANGFORD and ELMA OLSON

A CHILD rarely comes to a physician for help alone or of his own accord, whether his problem is one of physical illness or of emotional disorder. Physicians who care for children in clinical psychiatric settings or in more general medical settings find it difficult to escape an awareness of the importance of parental attitudes and parent-child relationships. The emotional climate of the home and the personality development of a child are affected by a parent's attitudes, his ways of feeling, of thinking, of acting, or of doing for a child. Disturbances in parent-child relationships are not only highlighted in behavior and personality symptoms in the child but also may be reflected in the child's reactions to illness, surgical procedures, hospitalizations, convalescence or immunizations. Pediatricians have noted that the attitudes of parents affect the way in which they are able to give information about their children or to carry out instructions. The course of even a purely physical disorder may be influenced by the quality of the parent-child relationship. Pediatricians and other physicians engaged in child care seek contributions from child psychiatry to help them in this aspect of their practice. Child psychiatry has developed methods and principles of working with parents which are applicable in nonpsychiatric medical practice with children.

Such methods and principles of work with parents are, of course, based on a desire to understand their behavior and to be helpful to them. Unfortunately, today there is a common

*Note: Reprinted by permission of the authors and *Quarterly Journal of Child Behavior*, 3:240-249, 1951.

tendency to blame parents for all of the difficulties of their children. Not so long ago a newspaper headline blared, above the report of a talk on parent-child relationships, "Doctor Flays Parents"; this headline did not properly describe the content of the talk which was summarized quite accurately below it. Even some psychiatrists, though in their practice they accept unconscious and uncontrollable motivations as part and parcel of their patients' overt behavior, take the attitude that parents ought to know better, or at least change their attitudes and actions when it is suggested to them. Too often parents are regarded as inevitable but unnecessary appendages to children. Terms used to describe parents or parental attitudes toward children have tended to become one word "diagnoses." Some of these as rejecting, overprotecting, dominating or coercive, and compulsive have achieved quasi-official standing; other, less learned, are doting, impossible, stupid, hopeless, hypertonic, and occasionally good, nice, or solid. Most of these appellations merely express irritation with the parent whose attitudes are interfering with the physician's attempts to help the child. As Dr. Fred Allen once quipped, "These days it almost seems as if parenthood is a disease." The attitude of blaming parents or calling them names adds nothing to a basic understanding of parent-child relationships and their why's and wherefore's.

The current principles and methods of working with parents in clinical psychiatric services for children have evolved gradually as a better understanding of the dynamics of parent-child relationships has developed. American child psychiatry, as developed in child guidance clinic practice, was concerned with inter-personal-relationships of children and their parents. Work with parents has almost always been a part of all efforts to help a child. Our knowledge about disturbances in parent-child relationships and the factors responsible for those disturbances has emerged out of attempts to develop effective techniques of helping emotionally disturbed children. The greatest contributions have come from the collaborative work of child psychiatrists and psychiatric social workers.

The early efforts to influence parental behavior were through the giving of advice, suggestions, or explanations. It was hoped that through these educational approaches parents would be able to alter their behavior and that "faulty attitudes" or methods of child-rearing could be "corrected." A basic supposition was that ignorance about children's needs and of the proper child-rearing techniques was an important factor in the parent's misbehavior. When patient persuasion failed to be effective the parent might be dogmatically "instructed" or warned about what might happen if he failed to heed the advice. At other times authoritarian lectures and exhortations to be better parents were omitted and a friendly, noncritical, nonblaming, noncoercive understanding approach was substituted. Attempts to interpret the meaning of the child's behavior often seemed to work better than specific suggestions about how to handle this or that situation or what to say when the child does this. A slithering up sideways on the source of the parent's pet notions was more effective than a direct frontal attack. A general discussion of mental health principles worked out better than ready-made cookbook recipes on what should be done to get rid of tics, enuresis, thumb-sucking or what not.

Some parents were able to utilize the new information given them effectively and for the benefit of the child. Some were able to accept it intellectually but used it in such a manner that the opposite of the desired effects was obtained. Their own underlying attitudes were unchanged even though consciously they might be able to alter their external behavior. Other parents might meet the educative efforts with arguments or reject them completely. It became clear that the educative approach was most useful where the parent felt reasonably adequate as a parent and was relatively free from emotional conflicts interfering with satisfactions in the parental role. The failure to be able to put sound information into effective action was seen to be related to the parent's own deep-seated emotional needs and conflicts which were involving the child. It was also seen that even with some of the more tense, uncertain, emotionally-involved parents pedagogical efforts could be effective when a good relationship had been established between the parent and the professional person working with him.

The need to develop effective methods of helping parents who were unable to utilize educative or supportive approaches led to experimentation in working with them around their own emotional needs and conflicts. Some of these intensive treatment programs were focused on the parent-child relationship, others developed around the intrinsic psychopathology of the parent as a person. Although time consuming, the methods developed were effective in ameliorating untoward parental attitudes in many instances. From these experiences a great deal was learned about the dynamics of parental attitudes and parent-child relationship functioning.

It was learned that in most cases aberrant parental behavior was not due to ignorance, stupidity, stubbornness, or pernicketiness but that it was related to the parent's own personality structure, his emotional conflicts, his past experiences. The position of a child in the psychic economy of his parent was bound up with the parent's own earlier relationships with his own parents, his brothers and sisters and other significant people, including the spouse. Conflicts in feelings in early relationships and also in other current relationships are reflected in a parent's contacts with his child. Patterns of a parent's behavior with a child — his attitudes toward obedience, concerns about feeding, preoccupations with education, worries about social behavior — are related to patterns which were important earlier in the parent's own home. The head of steam behind a parent's undue, and at times almost irrational, concerns and tensions in day by day living with a child is related to unresolved conflicts from the past. The child is caught in the backwash of emotional disturbance properly belonging elsewhere in the parent's total life experience. Unresolved hostilities and resentments from the past seem to have a special importance in a parent's relationship with the child in the present.

It was found that, as a parent could understand and resolve the emotional conflicts in earlier relationships, there was a concomitant decrease in pressures on the child, a lessening of tension and concern in his dealings with the child and greater consistency in behavior toward the child. Greater freedom in the expression of positive feelings accompanies acceptance of and decrease in guilt about hostile feelings. Along with this there is often an increased sureness and deftness in the parental role which leads to greater satisfactions from it.

Although this understanding of parent-child relationships

developed out of clinical practice in psychiatric settings similar factors operate in general medical practice with children. Most physicians who deal with children have been frustrated by their inability to allay the fears of an overconcerned parent about a trivial abdominal pain or minor illness with reassurance or rational explanation. The mother who is convinced that her child is not eating enough is untouched by the evidence of the scales or growth charts which may show that the child is actually overweight.

One such parent brought her robust 3-year-old son to the pediatric clinic for help with his small appetite. Although his nutritional state was much more than adequate she stated that she was so ashamed of his scrawniness that she could not take him out on the street or to the park. A careful physical examination and painstaking explanation of the facts failed to convince her that she had no cause for concern. The student who had worked up the case was sure that she was a mother who needed much psychiatric work. It was learned that the father, a night club waiter, was away from home from 5:00 PM until 6:00 AM each night. After sleeping he would go out with the two older adolescent boys. The mother resented the lack of time with her husband and justified her remaining at home with her unrealistic concerns about the younger child. As she discussed these things she wondered if her husband could not give up some of his afternoons to her. On the return visit her concern about the child's food intake and poor nutrition had evaporated. She spoke of the improved relationship with her husband as being like a "second honeymoon." Here the somewhat irrational concern about the child was related to the mother's current dissatisfactions in marriage.

Another mother brought in her 4-year-old child with complaints of "sadistic" behavior. This consisted of occasionally shoving other children in the playground although he usually played quite well with them. She, too, could not accept a statement that there seemed to be little to be concerned about. Her overconcern about the child was found to be based on her conflicted feelings about her husband who used to abuse her when drunk. Her overconcern about the child disappeared when she was able to differentiate between the two relationships.

A 6-year-old boy was being coddled and protected by his hovering mother for months after he had recovered from pneumonia. Her behavior came out of her fear that he would develop pulmonary tuberculosis as her father had done following a similar illness. She felt responsible for the developments in her father since his nursing care had been in her hands.

Concerns and anxieties basically related to other aspects of a parent's own life problems are carried over into his reactions to illness or defect in the child. Such untoward parental attitudes may seriously interfere with medical management of the child or may contribute to general behavioral disturbance in the child. The mother of a child with a minimal hypospadias shopped from one physician to another in her search for a magical cure. She was helped only after she became aware of and accepted the connection between her concern about the child and her own sexual conflicts which were related to her parent's reactions to her sexual interests in her childhood.

The parents of John, ten years old, had been unable to talk with him about his artificial eye since the enucleation two and a half years before. They attributed this attitude to a statement by the surgeon (this could not be verified) that it might be best not to talk about it. They also said that the boy never mentioned it. Even in the care of the eye, the parents rather pointedly avoided referring to the injury, the operation or the artificial eye. For the period following the operation the boy had had almost nightly frightening dreams, only some of which he could recall in the morning. In addition, his school work had been poor after the operation. His left eye had been removed as a result of an injury at six years when, during a scuffle with his four year old sister, she punctured his eye with a fountain pen. The injury had led to an immediate loss of vision.

The boy during our contacts with him was at first very reluctant to speak of his eye. He did, however, say that if he mentioned it to his mother she would look "crumpled." During the first two visits the father, too, wanted to limit conversation to the school difficulty. By the fifth visit the boy was talking freely about his eye with the pediatric resident who was working with the case under supervision. The sleep disturbances, which had been about a man in a green robe chasing him with a knife had cleared greatly, he was feeling encouraged about his school, and there was less resentment of teasing about his eyes by his schoolmates. He was still unable to speak to his parents or sister about his eye.

On this occasion his mother came for the second time; John had been brought in twice by his father and once by an older brother. In discussing her feelings about the loss of the eye and the preceding injury the mother revealed much self-blame and guilt. When the resident attempted to show her that the accident could not have been the fault of anyone she brought out material which made the parental attitudes understandable. The night of the accident, John's sixth birthday, the father was out with a woman with whom he had been having an affair for some years. The mother felt that he should have been at home on that night especially and that, had he been there, four eyes could have watched the children more closely and the accident prevented. When he arrived home and learned of the injury the father upbraided her for neglect, called her names and threw the keys at her. Each blamed the other for the accident. Subsequently the father gave up his girl friend and had become a model husband, attentive to his wife's needs and interested in the children. Although he could not talk of the eye difficulty with John he helped him with his homework and tried to be a good father in other ways. The mother went on to point out that her husband might have had trouble in settling down as he was only twenty when he was married. She now felt reasonably sure that he loved her. He had not wanted her to come to the clinic since he did not want her to reveal the marital difficulty. In some way he had seemed to recognize that it was intimately tied up with the reluctance of both parents to talk about the eye situation in the boy. In fact, they both tried to avoid the topic of the infidelity at home just as they did the eye.

On a visit a month later the mother reported that things at home were relaxed. She and her husband were able to talk more freely of the boy's accident and artificial eye with each other and with him and had a more relaxed attitude about the care of the eye and socket. The boy was comfortable in bringing it up with her and the father. There were no further sleep disturbances. The father's infidelity was forgiven and the marriage seemed to be on a firmer footing. Two months later the emotional climate of the home was still relaxed and the parents were enjoying their son. There were eight visits over a six-month period. A striking change was seen in the boy's responses to the Rorschach ink blots.

Not only were both parents helped to be less tense, and preoccupied in their relationship with each other but the parent-child relationships were also helped when the two problems, the eye and the marital difficulties, were separated. Even if the marital situation had not worked out to the good, one can feel sure that the relationship with the boy would have been helped and that the parents' distorted attitudes about the eye would have cleared.

These few illustrations from a pediatric setting show that the basic underlying factors in disturbed parent-child relationships are the same whether the problem is one of emotional or of physical disorder. The basic principles involved in helping such parents around their children are the same in both psychiatric and pediatric settings. In clinical psychiatric services for children, the degree of emotional disturbance in the child and parent is apt to be more severe and fewer situations seem to respond to other than intensive methods of working with parents. Such specialized intensive methods are not applicable in pediatric practice. Many parents can be helped to become more effective, less tense or preoccupied, with a clinical approach which falls short of a program designed to clear up most of their personal problems. Such a clinical approach is utilizable in the pediatric setting. A larger proportion of parents seen in pediatric practice can be influenced favorably by an educative approach than is the case in clinical child psychiatry.

In medical practice with children the center of clinical interest is in the child; this may lead to a preoccupation, in the physician, with the child and his needs. In any clinical work with parents, which is aimed at influencing attitudes and parent-child relationships, there must also be an expressed interest in the parent, his concerns about the child and his problems in relation to the child's disorder. The physician who devotes his interests to the child and has little interest in the parent except as someone to give information and to carry out directions is not apt to be too helpful to most parents. A tolerant, nonblaming, noncritical attitude which accepts the parent as the child's parent and assumes that the parent is interested in helping the child is the starting point for successful work with parents. While objectivity, in the sense of not getting the physician's feelings involved in the relationship with the parent, is important, such objectivity should not connote aloofness or detachment. The physician is looked on by most parents as someone who knows a great deal about scientific child care, as someone in a position of professional authority, and as someone who is able to judge them as parents. Actually, the parent is often being judged but progress in helping him is affected as these attitudes are taken into account by the physician.

Many present-day parents feel quite insecure in their roles as parents. This feeling of insecurity in parenthood is related to the current widespread attitude of blaming parents for children's difficulties and also to the conflicting and changing customs in child rearing practices. Many young parents are confused by the cultural pressure to raise perfect children and need encouragement to assume their own responsibilities and prerogatives as parents. The young mother who combined the best features of the old and new schools of infant care by feeding her baby whenever he was hungry but only after he had cried for fifteen minutes by the clock, was trying not only to keep both of the grandmothers contented but also was reflecting this general cultural pattern. Anything which the physician can do to increase the parent's self-confidence, self-esteem, and courage to try again is helpful in increasing the feeling of security in parenthood. Attention to the worries and anxieties, no matter how trivial, in the job of being a parent, praise and encouragement when justified, and any means the physician can use to show his own confidence in the parent's ability, all contribute to the development of competency in parenthood. The pediatrician who sees the parent and child at intervals for health supervisory visits is in a strategic position to strengthen the parent's feelings of adequacy and to help him to react spontaneously to the child's changing needs. If, in his on-going relationship with the parent, the child's physician is aware of the importance of these things outlined above he can help the parent to see his job as something more than an intellectual learning of certain rules of child rearing and carrying out orders. Any advice or counsel which is given to parents is apt to be more effective and more meaningful to parents when the relationship with the physician is one of genuine interest in the parent and one in which he is attempting to promote feelings of competency, of security in parenthood.

Although an encouraging supportive relationship with a parent can be helpful in improving parent-child relationships and in enabling the parent to make effective use of new information, advice or suggestions, at times he needs to be encouraged to verbalize his frustrations, feelings of deprivation, resentments, hostility for which he has felt guilt and elaborate his earlier and current relationships with other significant persons. If the physician has indicated his interest in the parent, in his concerns about the child and in his problems related to the child's disorder, most parents will talk freely with little further encouragement and reveal the significant aspects of their own life problems. This is helpful in understanding the dynamics of the particular parent-child relationship and in helping the parent to separate his problems about the child from those related to other aspects of his life. In such discussions the parent often spontaneously associates the ways in which he was handled as a child and how he felt about it with the ways he is handling his own child. He is often able to see the connection between his attitudes toward the child and those related to his own parents, his spouse or other important people in his life. Frequently in these discussions one is able to help a parent to become aware of those attitudes carried over onto the child and to deflect such attitudes to some extent away from the child. Thus the untoward attitudes do not interfere so much with the handling of the child even though the basic attitudes of the parent are largely unchanged. With parents presenting symptoms indicative of clinical psychopathology, who have a fatalistic attitude about changes in the child, or who fail to recognize a problem in their relationship with the child, a more intensive treatment program will probably be necessary before the parent can disentangle his relationship with the child from his other life problems. It would seem, however, that most of the children seen in pediatric practice can be materially helped short of such intensive treatment programs with their parents, to become relatively free from complicating emotion properly belonging elsewhere in their parents' life experiences. Then the child's parents are more able to accept him as an individual in his own right; they are more able to evaluate his potentialities correctly and to permit him to grow and develop according to his own unique patterns.

Chapter 8

Extending a Hand to Parents of
Disturbed Children*

JOYCE EDWARD

Now that the right of the emotionally disturbed child to education is firmly established, those of us who work in special education can direct our efforts toward the challenge of insuring that every emotionally disturbed child likely to profit from special education receives it. To meet this challenge is not as easy as it may appear. Parental resistance can sometimes limit the child's opportunities for therapeutic programming. Some parents resist accepting a reliable diagnosis of their children's disorder as disturbed and are unable to follow recommendations for special class placement.

Ten years of experience as a psychiatric social worker in the elementary school division of the Luther E. Woodward School for Emotionally Disturbed Children, Inc. (LEW), in Freeport, N. Y., which takes children aged 4 through 16 years, has made me much aware of the problems of the parents of disturbed children and of the measures an agency can take to help these parents accept their children's special needs. At LEW, casework with families is an integral part of the program from intake to discharge. We have found that, though placement of the child in a special class is usually painful for parents, it is a process through which they can be helped to reach a better understanding not only of their child and his needs but also of themselves. What the professional worker does can have a great deal to do with whether the parents' adjustment to the child's placement improves as the child improves or whether it disintegrates, leaving the parents even less

---

Note: Reprinted by permission of the author and *Children, 14:238-243, 1967.*

effective than before in helping their child.

Basic to the professional worker's efforts is the recognition of both the conscious and unconscious effects the disturbed child has on his family. The problems parents expose to professional workers reflect their individual personalities, the interactions of the entire family, and the actual difficulties they face in rearing a disturbed child.

The severity of the symptoms of such a child can make even healthy, stable families anxious and defensive. The child's hyper-activity, impulsiveness, bizarreness, regression, and obsessiveness, to mention only a few characteristics that may occur singly or in combination, place an inordinately heavy strain on family life. The behavior that makes a child unmanageable in a regular school class makes him no less so at home. His care is taxing; his behavior is incomprehensible; his conduct can be embarrassing; the medical attention he requires is costly; the social services he requires are difficult to secure; and the time his care requires is excessive. His illness is a severe blow to the parents' self-esteem, and their feeling of guilt for having produced such a child is accentuated by the hostility and anger the child provokes. It is difficult for them to air their feelings or to separate themselves from him. Even the most mature parents worry about how to handle an emotionally disturbed child without harming him further. They worry not only about the present but also about the future.

In addition to having problems directly related to the child's disorder, parents may be beset by other kinds as well. Some have serious psychiatric disorders themselves. Complicated pathological relationships may exist in the family, of which the child's illness may have become an integral part. Some parents cannot view their child's disorder realistically because they identify themselves with his behavior. Others are so limited intellectually that they cannot understand what professional people tell them about their children. Social and cultural deprivation hinder others from understanding. Or daily problems stemming from economic want, bad health, or poor marital relations may contribute to the parents' inability to act wisely for their child.

Of course, the school is not responsible for helping parents solve all their problems, but unless the school recognizes that many influences affect the ability of the parents to come to grips with their child's disorder, attempts to secure their cooperation will not succeed. There is an important difference, for example, between a parent who fails to keep an appointment because he has no transportation or can get no one to care for other children and a parent who fails because he fears the school or is hostile toward his child. There is also an important difference between a father who in momentary anxiety and defensiveness denies that the acting-out behavior of his son represents a serious problem and a father who denies the existance of the problem because he himself is psychotic and sees his son's actions as justifiable retaliation for an imagined insult to the family. What we as professional people do to enlist the parents' support is determined by the degree to which we recognize that their actions are as symptomatic of their needs as are the child's of his.

Sometimes parents are unable to comprehend the explanation we offer them about their child's illness or, if they do, they cannot act positively on the information for various reasons. The emotionally depressed father who is told his son needs more attention may never have been able to form a meaningful relationship with another person and certainly does not know how to form one with his disturbed child. The disorganized, perhaps mentally retarded, mother who is told that her child could benefit from sound eating and sleeping habits may be completely unable to put this suggestion into practice without a great deal of support.

It is not enough for the helping person to be aware of the parents' feelings, however. As professional persons, we must be cognizant of the kinds of feelings parents arouse in us. Our reactions to parents contribute as much to the climate of interchange as the parents' reactions to us. We all have feelings about parents as such, for we have all been children. We may transfer either positive or negative feelings, depending on our own experience. To work successfully with parents, we have to control our own unsound reactions. We may, for example, react to the parents of disturbed children with hostility because we think they are responsible for their children's troubles. We may have a feeling that if we could only rid the child of his noxious parents and have him to ourselves we could effect a "cure."

Unfortunately, such feelings are often communicated to parents, and their recognition of these feelings may account for some of their resistance and hostility. When we realize that mental illness in childhood is the result of a complex interplay of biological and environmental forces, we will no longer assume that all parents of disturbed children are alike. Whatever contribution the parents make to the child's problem are most likely unconscious reflections of their own psychic difficulties. Our anger at the parent only increases his anxiety and impedes even more his ability to improve the quality of the care he gives his child. To control our own reactions to these parents is no easy task. for their behavior is often provocative and productive of irritation.

PARENTAL CARE

It has been my experience that where the parents' anxiety is primarily a reaction to the child's disorder and not symptomatic of pathology, an understanding attitude on the part of the professional person promotes the development of a positive relation between family and school. In time, this relation becomes the cornerstone for the work between the family and the school and enables the parents to trust the school's judgment and to accept the educational plan the school's recommends as a logical outcome of a joint endeavor. This is never an easy process, however. When the child enters school, parents must face the child's problems squarely. The school must be prepared to work with families in a crisis and to give even healthy parents the support they need to resolve their problems and enough time in which to do it. Accepting the fact that one's child does not fit into the public school, one of the most basic institutions in society, cannot be worked through in one session. We must be prepared to help parents through a painful time when their thinking may be muddled by pain. We must remind ourselves that some conditions in life are never really accepted, but are only tolerated by those who must face them, and that for most families of chronically handicapped children sorrow persists throughout life.

For mature families the process of working with persons from the school to secure the right educational plan is in itself helpful, for it tends to lessen anxiety. The knowledge we share with the family about the nature of the child's disorder, the educational plan recommended, and the childs development help them learn to control their anxiety through intellectualization. It also gives them enough time and experience to correct distortions about the child through consistent opportunities to test reality. Regular, planned meetings with parents are basic to a good special education program, and they can be as important to mature parents as to immature.

Parents who, despite the sensitive professional effort extended to them by the school, continue to deny the problem and project their difficulties onto the school cause great concern in professional workers. If the diagnosis of the child's condition is accurate, the parents' reaction to it often indicate the degree of disturbance in the family. The parents may themselves require special help. However, whatever blocks their ability to accept assistance for their child is also likely to block their willingness to seek help for themselves. Nevertheless, schools must work with these parents to the best of their ability if the right educational plan is to be made for the child.

Two cases of work with parents of children sent to LEW back up my points. In these cases, each couple's problems were reflected in the difficulty they had in accurately sizing up and solving their sons' problems. Both members of the first couple, Mr. and Mrs. G, have emotional problems of long standing that have resulted in marital discord. They are intelligent and are sophisticated about psychological problems. The other couple, Mr. and Mrs. L, are both paranoid and extremely withdrawn, hostile, and suspicious. They are not intelligent and are economically and culturally deprived. Despite difficulties, however, their family is intact and self-supporting. Both families are concerned about their children and their education.

FRED'S PARENTS

Mr. and Mrs. G at first greatly resisted the idea of placing their 10-year-old schizophrenic son Fred in a special program for mentally disturbed children and had difficulty tolerating the placement for a long time. Psychiatric and school reports indicated that the school had tried to help Fred and had kept him in regular class as long as possible. When the parents came to LEW, they were agitated and quarrelsome, accused each other of being at fault, and showed the resentment they felt against the school for recommending special placement. Mrs. G soon took over the interview. Although Mr. G seemed more realistic than his wife, he only contributed to the interview when questioned directly. But as Mrs. G always contradicted whatever he said, he gradually grew silent.

Mrs. G, while admitting there was something wrong with Fred, said he was not so ill as the children in our classes. As the interview progressed it became apparent that Mrs. G hoped the caseworker would, on the basis of the referral material, confirm her belief that the school had failed the boy and that all he needed was a regular class of higher quality.

The caseworker acknowledged that it was difficult to accept a special class like ours but said she felt that, despite their doubts, Mr. and Mrs. G knew that Fred needed something more than a regular class or they would not have kept the appointment. Because the caseworker felt that they were afraid of our program, she tried to help them learn something about the program while she tried to learn something about them.

The caseworker said she knew from the referral material that they had already spent time and money on psychiatric help for Fred and counseling for themselves. She told them she inferred from this that they felt great concern for Fred and that he had a serious problem. "Was his difficulty only something that manifested itself in relation to a poor school situation?" she asked.

After this question, Mrs. G relaxed a little and both parents described in detail Fred's sickness and the great problems he imposed on family life.

The caseworker pointed out that their observations confirmed the reports. She then said that she wondered if it were possible for a child like Fred to learn in a group of 28 children in a regular school. Both parents agreed that he had not, although the teacher had tried to help him. The caseworker said that Fred's school seemed to have tried its utmost and that it was unlikely that Fred's needs could be met in an ordinary school.

The caseworker then pointed out that, from the description they had given, Fred's case sounded like those of some of the children at LEW, and she described some of them. "How did you feel he might differ from the pupils described?" she asked. Mrs. G said she was afraid that neither the other children nor academic program would stimulate Fred. "What," the caseworker asked, "has happened in the last 4 years while he was with children who performed adequately?" He had either withdrawn completely or acted out in an extremely disruptive way, the parents admitted. Mrs. G felt Fred was bright and that with proper handling he could be brought up to grade level in a short time. The caseworker described LEW's academic program and said with emphasis that, while the school offered stimulation, it was impossible to predict how a child would progress and that disappointment was often inevitable. This statement seemed to free Mr. and Mrs. G to discuss their disappointment. Mrs. G cried; Mr. G looked into space.

By the end of the interview, their fear was somewhat allayed but they still had doubts. The caseworker told them that she felt they should come in again to observe the classes and to discuss the matter once more before bringing Fred in for an interview with the psychiatrist. She pointed out, however, that on the basis of their description and the referral material she was sure Fred needed special schooling. Whether our program was suitable remained to be seen. She also told them that she realized they were full of doubts and were disappointed, but she stressed how important it was to go slowly because much of the success of any program would be their feeling that it was right to try it. They did return for another interview, and after we worked slowly with them, they decided to place Fred with us.

When Mrs. G brought Fred to school for the first day, she was upset. She wept during the interview and said that the other children "looked sick but not her son." The caseworker told her she understood the anxiety she was going through and that other parents were also anxious. The caseworker held to the belief, however, that Fred did belong in the program. The caseworker made plain to her that the school believed that Fred could be helped. She said that in time, after Fred had begun to adjust to the school and Mrs. G could see improvement, she would find it easier to accept the placement. The caseworker reminded her that she had had similar feelings when Fred had had other services and that she had come through the experience all right. The caseworker made another appointment for her a week later and told her to telephone if she had questions before then. At the next appointment, Mrs. G said she had gotten through the week and that while she still did not like our program, her concern had lessened and the children looked better. The caseworker continued to see her once every 3 weeks for several months, and she gradually became more accepting. Mrs. G still does not like Fred's being at LEW, but she has been able to support the placement for 3 years in a constructive, meaningful way. From time to time the caseworker must reinterpret Fred's needs to her, give her an opportunity to air her disappointment that he is still ill, and answer her questions.

The personal and marital problems in this family have not changed because of our efforts, but our efforts were influenced by the knowledge of these problems. If we had not understood what was behind the parents' behavior, we could have easily become annoyed with them, particularly with the mother, because Mrs. G displayed her anxiety through excessive talkativeness, hostility, and projection. Our basic attempt to help was focused on using the family's positive characteristics — their concern for the child and their intellectual awareness. We gave them an opportunity to express their disappointment and pain and to raise their doubts and fears about what a special class might do to their son. We always focused our efforts on reality: their son could not be provided for in a regular class despite all reasonable attempts to help him adjust. We did not attempt to get them to like the placement, only to face it with tolerance. And we gave them the continuing support they required. Ultimately, the boy's gains enabled them to accept the placement with less pain.

DARREN'S PARENTS

Mr. and Mrs. L were referred to a special program for their

10-year-old son Darren because of his destructive behavior and failure to learn throughout 4 years in school. One year before referral, he had drawn a knife on another student and as a consequence had been excluded from school. The parents regarded this exclusion as a plot by the school to get rid of Darren, whom to them was a quite, respectful son. To a quiet, withdrawn family, his silence seemed a virtue. The parents considered Darren's flareup in school as a justifiable response to provocation. They resisted special placement, disagreed angrily with psychiatric reports, and threatened to secure legal counsel. When referred to a special program for emotionally disturbed persons, they refused to apply. Darren was out of school a year. Diligent efforts by the school psychologist and the social worker for the special program, coupled with the family's concern for Darren, finally brought the parents to LEW for an interview.

All of the problems already described were evident in the interview. Both parents appeared withdrawn, hostile, and suspicious. The caseworker made clear to them that she shared their concern about Darren's being out of school. "What has happened since we spoke to you on the telephone last year?" the caseworker asked. Mrs. L answered by recounting all of Darren's virtues and placing special emphasis on how helpful he was with the family ironing. The only problem he faced, she said, was not being able to go to school. The caseworker agreed that this was a serious problem. She said their keeping this appointment was a positive step on Darren's behalf, whether or not they found LEW's program suitable. Mr. and Mrs. L quickly launched into an angry discourse on Darren's former school. The caseworker, after listening for a few minutes, said that she understood their anger but, as they had gone over this many times before without Darren's getting into school, it would perhaps be more helpful to consider the kind of schooling Darren required now.

"You have spent a lot of time with him in the last year; what do you think of his ability to learn? How did he do at school until excluded?" the caseworker asked.

Mrs. L said that she was surprised that he had not learned to read. Even when she taught him, he did not grasp things, she admitted. When the caseworker asked her if she felt he might need special handling, Mrs. L said, "Yes." The caseworker then asked if she had ever felt that a large class might confuse him. "I guess it could," Mrs. L admitted. At this point her hostility seemed to lessen, and she began to ask questions about the special school. The caseworker answered her questions by citing facts about LEW and indicated that the program was for children with problems, some similar to Darren's.

Later when they visited classes, Mr. and Mrs. L said that some children looked different or "spoke funny." The caseworker agreed that the children were troubled, but she pointed out that she thought Darren had some problems, too. They replied that they did not think he was like the other children, but Mrs. L felt he should go to school and perhaps it would be best to place him in LEW.

The caseworker, moving slowly, in some ways mirrored their resistance. She said she could not say immediately whether this was a good plan for Darren; the school psychiatrist and psychologist would have to see him and give a lot of thought to the matter. Perhaps home teaching was best. At this the parents immediately suggested that the intake study be conducted.

Darren was accepted, and his parents were willing for him to go to LEW by the time he was placed. In the first interview after placement, Mrs. L came alone; she said that her husband would not be able to come. As she saw it, the family's problems with the school were really her responsibility. We did not insist upon the father's coming, although we usually try to work with both parents.

Mrs. L immediately complained that Darren's sweater had been torn in class, and she asked whether the teacher was supervising the class properly. The caseworker told Mrs. L she knew how hard it must be for her to have Darren's clothing torn, with prices as high as they are and a large family to clothe. Mrs. L then related in detail the concern her many bills gave her. The caseworker let Mrs. L know that she felt her concern was realistic and her management on a small income, competent. After this, Mrs. L seemed less hostile. Darren had made a good start, and the caseworker gave her examples of what he was doing. She admitted that he appeared pleased about school, which was unusual for him. Mrs. L said she guessed that with boys one had to expect a tear or two. The caseworker agreed, but told her she would bring the matter of the tear to the attention of the teacher. The caseworker then asked her if she would like to meet the teacher and see Darren's class. She said, "Yes." The visit delighted her, especially Darren's pleasure in introducing her to his class.

Mrs. L now has appointments monthly with us, which she always keeps. During these interviews the caseworker shares with her information about Darren's progress in school, which has been slow but consistent. Darren no longer acts out as he used to. A change that has confirmed his need for the program to the parents. Mrs. L has been gratified by the academic gains, too. The causes of some of Darren's problems come to light now and then in what she says. We asked her once about Darren's laughing at times when nothing seems to be happening. Mrs. L said that she had noticed this and thought she laughed the same way. Often she has funny thoughts that caused her to laugh and she thought everyone else did too. We did not pursue this matter, nor did we deal with other obvious indications of pathology. Mrs. L developed a friendly feeling for the school. She told us how much it meant to her that there were no complaints about Darren. Although she continued to feel he was not like other children, she thought that he was learning and that since we were not making him angry he should remain another year.

We never attempted to help Mrs. L to understood Darren's real problem. All previous efforts in this direction had only stimulated her anxiety and tendency to act out. We worked with her as she was and tried to make the most of her concern for Darren's education. As he improved her anxiety lessened.

A FOCUS ON RESPONSIBILITY

There still are and will continue to be many problems in these families. No basic alteration in the personalities of the parents have been made, nor have we touched the core of their relation with their children. We have, instead, tried to enable them to allow their children to take advantage of an opportunity for special education without interference. We have focused our efforts on stimulating feelings of responsibility rather than stirring feelings of guilt. We believe that through this process some of the parents' anxiety was diminished and that a more pleasant atmosphere was created at home, thus lessening the strain that builds up when tension between home and school is strong.

When we assume responsibility for the education of the emotionally disturbed child, we assume an imposing task. It is not placing a child in a "special" class that makes his education "special" however; rather it is the recognition of his many complex needs and an interweaving of the insight and skill of various professions to meet these needs. To do this, we must have concern for many aspects of the child's life, including the role his family plays in relation to his schooling. The most capable teacher, the finest curriculum, the most expert clinical service will be of little avail if the child's family refuses to accept a program for him or, in placing him, sabotages the school's efforts.

ADDITIONAL READING LIST

Family Life Education — A Cause For Action. American Social Health Association, 1740 Broadway, New York, N.Y. 10019, November, 1966, 64 pp., $2.00

Reports on a demonstration project conducted over 9 years by the American Social Health Association in 23 States and the District of Columbia through which family life education programs were incorporated in the curriculums of public schools and teacher training institutions.

Child Life Programs in 91 Pediatric Hospitals in the United States and Canada. Robert H. Dombro, Child Life Program, Children's Medical and Surgical Center, John Hopkins Hospital, Baltimore, Md. 21205, 1966, 18 pp., 50 cents (mimeographed).

Reports the findings of a survey of the characteristics of recreational and educational programs for children in 91 children's hospitals.

Listen Everybody! Youth Participation in Community Action: Report of a Demonstration Training Project. California

Department of the Youth Authority, 401 State Building No. 1, Sacramento, Calif. 95814, 1967, 66 pp. Copies free on request from the Department.

Reports on a 1-year demonstration project in which 182 young people from impoverished areas in California were trained to work in community improvement programs. Sponsored by the Governor's Advisory Committee on Children and Youth and financed by the Office of Economic Opportunity, the project was administered by the California Department of the Youth Authority.

Understanding the Disadvantaged: A Source Book. School of Home Economics and Extension Division, University of Missouri. Available from the Technical Education Services, University of Missouri, 417 South 15th Street, Columbia, Mo. 65201, 1966, 187 pp., $1.

The proceedings of a short, inter-agency, interdisciplinary course in studying the disadvantaged held at the university of Missouri, July 13-15, 1965.

Chapter 9

The Fate of Advice: Examples of
Distortion in Parental Counseling*

MORTON LEVITT and BEN O. RUBENSTEIN

T HE tremendous growth of the mental hygiene movement in the last twenty years has resulted in the wide dissemination of psychological advice to the general public. University classes, adult education programs, parent-teacher meetings and child study-groups have all made positive contributions to this end. Inherent has been the belief that parents who have been exposed to mental hygiene principles would become more effective and more secure in the educational handling of their children (1). That the state of affairs described above has proved something of a mixed blessing could be seen as far back as 1946 when an editorial [1] in the *Child Study Quarterly* as well as articles by Stone [2] and Gruenberg [3] in the same periodical called attention to the fact that emphasis upon "problem parents" was proving an onerous burden to parents in general. More recently such perceptive observers of the contemporary psychological scene as Spock and Bruche have taken a similar position. It should be recalled, however, that Freud in two articles [4] written as early as 1907 and 1908 suggested exerting some caution in efforts to accomplish educational tasks, warning specifically against "the unwisdom of putting new wine into old bottles."

This paper concerns itself with the fate of advice given to parents whose children are in treatment. The forced intimacy of the therapeutic task makes for close relationships with parents and

Note: Reprinted by permission of the authors and *Mental Hygiene, 41:*213-216, 1957.
(1) A paper by M. L. Falick, M. Peters, M. Levitt and Ben Rubenstein entitled, "Some Observations on the Psychological Education of Teachers" in the July 1954 issue of *Mental Hygiene* discussed related problems in the education of teachers.

the need for frequent consultation leads to efforts to make parents literally "partners" in treatment by offering educational suggestions. Observation of the fact that some parents could do little with such advice brought the present authors to the realization that unconscious elements in the personality structures of parents often cause the distortion, nullification and even on occasion, the reversal of well-intended service. It is important to be aware that the treatment relationship between therapist, child, and family provides a unique opportunity to observe the vicissitudes of advice, for the child analyst has a three-sided observation booth, as it were, speaking to and hearing from the child as well as each parent.

In the four brief case studies that follow efforts will be made to indicate what advice was given and what actually was its fate in the exchange between the parent and child.

Sam, a 9-year-old, had been completely toilet-trained by the age of 3. Shortly after the birth of another child, training broke down and Sam wet nightly from then on and also began occasional soiling episodes. Interviews with his parents established the fact that they had never made the patient consciously aware that they disapproved of his defections. Sam's reality, as he saw it, provided *carte blanche* for symptom continuation; he exploited this fact defensively in treatment. Since a continuation of the *status quo* at home threatened therapeutic success, his parents were advised to express some irritation and annoyance regarding his problems. The parents agreed, with some reluctance, to try to be firm with Sam. Results were forthcoming immediately. Sam came to his next appointment in full resistance and threatened never to come again. What had happened? His father had told him that he would now have to be treated more firmly because the therapist had so directed.

Ted, an 8-year-old was placed in treatment because of un-controlled behavior. His father's interest in the process could be characterized as a "tell-us-what-to-do" attitude. He invited the therapist to come into the home in order to do a "time study" of the family to "reorganize" the household along more "economic lines." (All quotes are the father's exact expressions.) His persistent demands for advice led to a cautious suggestion that he try to spend a little more time with his son under pleasant circumstances. In this endeavor the father took his son to the family business, a tool shop, and assigned him impossible tasks such as cleaning expensive tools with kerosene. When Ted broke some of the tools and fled the father spent several hours looking for him and then called the therapist to report how poorly the treatment was going.

Gary's mother complained of his stealing money and candy, of his tantrums, and his refusal to eat. She pleaded for help with her 6-year-old son. The suggestion that she pay less attention to the eating problem and avoid open exposure of money and candy brought no relief. The unhappy mother continued to complain that the suggestions were of no avail and attempted to enlist the therapist's aid in detecting the whereabouts of the loot. When it was pointed out to her that she was nullifying the suggestion she could only describe her impotent rage at Gary's denial of ownership of the stolen money and candy in his drawer. She concluded by saying that she would be satisfied with nothing but a complete confession of his guilt.

Stuart, an 8-year-old soiler, had revealed during treatment his unqualified belief in the omnipotence of women. His intelligent, smiling, cooperative mother, carried the complete burden of the treatment plan, his father being resistive and threatened. At one point when Stuart became difficult to manage in the home the mother asked for help. It was suggested that her husband assume the responsibility for discipline. She returned with a smile but indicated failure of the plan, for Stuart persisted in behavior which required his physical removal from the scene when the father was not present. She was then advised to tell Stuart that she could not physically control him but would report his behavior to his father. The now unsmiling mother responded vehemently that she could never accept the implication that women were in any way inferior to men. In was apparent that this women could neither involve her husband in discipline nor depreciate her own power in the eyes of her son.

DISCUSSION

Gary's and Ted's circumstances bear certain familial similarities.

The parents of these children are characteristic of a group who are persistent in their pleas for advice and yet are unable to utilize it when it is offered. They admit the failure of their own methods and are seemingly desperate in their need for help. "Tell us what to do" is their cry. Our relationship with them, however, convinces us that our advice will be gratuitous. The probability exists that the desperation of these parents is based upon an unconscious awareness that they are forced to support the child's symptoms because these represent their own unresolved conflicts. We feel that in those instances where attempts are made to alter the balance of psychic forces between parent and child the parent is compelled to regress and to re-establish the original neurotic involvement with the child. It appears that the child responds to parental regression and the resultant behavior of the child provides the parent with the opportunity to righteously vent his feelings in defensive fashion against the representation of his own conflicts. As this circular current mounts in intensity so does the unconscious guilt of the parent. It is at this time that he asks for help but if we understand him clearly he is saying, "I want you to relieve my guilt." Concurrent with this is the unconscious hope that the advice will inevitably fail. Psychic economy is thus maintained by the thought, "The expert has failed; therefore I cannot be so bad." The initial unquestioning acceptance of advice is now clear, for the complete confidence in the therapist prepares the way for the preordained hostility when the advice, by necessity, fails. The connections between self-perpetuating conflict and preverbal symbiosis is most marked in those instances where the child is inordinately sensitive to the parents' unconscious. The child responds to the parents' repressed wishes but immediately becomes the victim of their defensive reaction. By the same token the therapist's activities fall into the identical orbit. Suggestions that aim to free the child must be denied. The correctness of the above formulation can be verified in part by the poorly concealed eagerness of Gary's mother to enlist the therapist as an ally in her desperate effort to stamp out every vestige of disguised impulse-expression as objectified in her child by the stealing of money and candy.

The fate of advice in the instance of Stuart, whose mother

could not tell him that women were weaker than men, reveals another concatenation of psychic forces. We are here dealing with the mother's unconscious denial of the anatomical distinction between the sexes. Her defensive reaction was of such intensity that her son's masculinity hung in the balance. The mother was cooperative and positive in her wish to aid her son against all odds. All suggestions were completely acceptable and were carried out until they ran counter to her own specific difficulty. Considerable experience and sensitivity are required to correctly assess such situations. Earlier perception of this mother's phallic aspirations could have forewarned us that any advice to restore Stuart's masculinity would activate the kernel of her own neurotic conflict.

Sam's parents, who were completely accepting of his problems, are typical of another group. These are the parents who have drawn considerable intellectual support from their specialized interest in the permissive aspects of mental hygiene literature. Great strength underlies the apparent passive acceptance of Sam's symptoms by his parents. We feel that their support can be explained by the need to maintain a positive relationship with their child. For such parents, to be negative, firm or aggressive has a specific ontogenetic meaning. Sam's mother had been enuretic until the onset of menstruation; Sam's father had reacted strongly to his own father's punitive handling of an older brother who wet his bed. Here again we find parents identified with the child's symptoms but the defensive alignment differs from that in the previous example. Sam represented a truly emasculated child for he wet and soiled at age 9. The resulting guilt of the parents was the touchstone of their resistance. They felt unconsciously responsible for the child's disorder and therefore could not be firm. We would suspect that there are strong elements standing in the way of identification with their own parents. In this sense the therapist may well represent a bad father in the minds of such parents.

CONCLUSIONS

Advice that runs counter to the unconscious defenses of parents and that threatens their own psychological adjustment is likely to be rejected.

Such advice must be defended against because it threatens the neurotically-continuing nature of the symbiotic attachment between child and parents.

The peculiar significance of symptoms to parents often precludes the giving of any advice until the therapist is aware of the unconscious meaning of the child to each parent.

REFERENCES

1. Wolf, Anna W. M.: Problem parents, *Child Study, 24* (Winter, 1946-47), 35.
2. Stone, L. Joseph: The earliest years, *Child Study, 24* (Winter, 1946-47), 38.
3. Gruenberg, Sidonie Matsner: The modern mother's dilemma, *Child Study, 24* (Summer-Fall, 1947), 100-103.
4. Freud, Sigmund: The sexual enlightenment of children and On the sexual theories of children, *Collected Papers,* Vol. 2 London, Hogarth Press, 1948.

Chapter 10

The Family in Psychosomatic Process*

A Case Report Illustrating a Method of Psychosomatic Research

JAMES L. TITCHENER, JULES RISKIN,
and RICHARD EMERSON

T HIS paper is the report of a study of an entire family in which one son developed ulcerative colitis. It has been written to point out a method by which one of the conditions specific to the etiology of psychosomatic processes may be further understood. In setting forth this method we propose an expansion of current hypotheses regarding the object relations factors in the causes of and predisposition to psychosomatic illness.

In his thorough review of the ulcerative colitis syndrome Dr. George Engel writes the following: "Elucidation of the specific aspects of the object relations constitutes a most important problem for further research" (1). This comment seems appropriate for the whole field of psychosomatic investigation. From his own research and from his extensive review of the work of others, Engel has formulated the recurrent patterns of significant relationships in ulcerative colitis patients and he has pointed out how these rigid and confining patterns predispose these individuals to psychosomatic illness. This formulation is part of a theory of the etiology of ulcerative colitis.

Dr. Engel views ulcerative colitis as a response of the whole organism with a particular locus in the lining of the large bowel. The effective and healthy bowel lining serves as a selective barrier against penetration of organisms and other substances from the "outside" i.e. the lumen of the colon. In ulcerative colitis the

Note: Reprinted by permission of the authors and *Psychosomatic Medicine,* *22:*127-142, 1960.

Research reported in this paper was supported by research grants M999 and M2534 from the National Institute for Mental Health, U.S. Public Health Service, Bethesda, Md.

physiologic function of the bowel lining quite probably becomes affected in such a way that organisms in the lumen can penetrate and are, thereafter, no longer innocuous, but pathogenic. It is considered likely that a constitutional predisposition is necessary for this situation. Among the other possible factors, some still unknown, is the psychophysiologic factor; there is imposing clinical evidence to support the significance of a psychosomatic relationship.

The reports of Engel and others reviewed by him are persuasive that the essential psychological condition operating with somatic factors towards the onset of ulcerative colitis is an affective state characterized by helplessness and despair arising from a deep disturbance in a key object relation which is lost or threatened, or whose loss is imagined. The ulcerative colitis patient is unable to accomplish the grief work nor any other adjustment to object loss and so suffers a deep disruption of previous adaptation, with consequent development of a state of helplessness. It is probable that this drastic change in psychological systems breaks through to affect the operation of somatic systems, particularly if they are predisposed to dysfunction.

This unfortunate lack of adaptive capacity, combined with incessant need, develops, in Engel's view, from the early, very much prolonged symbiosis between mother and child. In very brief summary, the mother-infant and mother-child relationship are conditional ones in which mother will give love if she can control. The necessary submission of the child lays the groundwork for uninterrupted need for similar relationships throughout life. Such relationships in adolescence and adulthood, when society rules against the maintenance of a symbiosis with mother, are very difficult to find and to maintain with potential substitutes. Usually the patient-to-be manages to find someone who will fill the bill at least partially. But almost always this chosen person, who perhaps unwittingly finds himself or herself a "key" person, cannot stand the strain and the interpersonal needs of the potential patient are frustrated or threatened. Such individuals are so sensitive to the vicissitudes of the mutually controlling relationship that almost any occurrence may upset the tenuous equilibrium.

THE FAMILY IN A PSYCHOSOMATIC PROCESS

In launching our study we have assumed the conditions for the onset of ulcerative colitis as Engel has hypothesized them. Our contribution toward a new look at this hypothesis is confined to the object relation aspects of the formulation.

Our investigative approach may be likened to the one used by cultural anthropologists who, if interested in the psychodynamics of a relationship in a culture would study not one but both persons involved and, further, would seek any others who could offer intimate observations upon the relationship in question.

Our methods of study of whole families provide us with corroborating and contrasting observations by each family member, including comments upon individual feelings, upon the feelings and behavior of others, and upon their own and other relationships. We are enabled to derive a stereoscopic view of the family as a field and of the individual's functions in this field. In addition, we can develop concepts of the family's working as a whole system — a social unit with a structure and a dynamic pattern.

We assume that, as with personality, there are patterns of adaptation for a family too. A particular person or a particular relationship — for example, mother and child — are involved continually in mutually influencing transactions with the whole family, as a social system. Let us now return to Engel's hypotheses about the prolonged mother-child symbiosis which becomes a mutually controlling relationship, pathogenic, in some cases, of ulcerative colitis. We would add that this relationship is, from the beginning and during its later vicissitudes, conditioned by the milieu in which it exists — the family. The mother-child axis turns in a social field of which the family constitutes a large and important segment.

To put our case more strongly, our approach would seem to obviate a concept of a colitigenic mother, as it would also the schizophrenogenic mother, for the relationship is not one in which the mother *per se* forces herself in a pathogenic way upon a child, but one made by the mother and conditioned by the dynamics of the family in which she and her child live. The significant element is not simply the mother's personality, but the way she acts in a particular relationship with the particular child in a particular period — all in the context of the *whole* family's psychodynamic patterns.

Let us imagine a study in which personality assessments of 20,000 mothers of ulcerative colitis patients were compared with those of 20,000 mothers of children without colitis. We would surmise that, though there would be a contrast in the groups, the correlation of colitis patients with mothers having certain traits of personality at the time of assessment would *not* be especially high. We are of the opinion that colitigenic mothers are not born nor even made in their own childhood. Their ways of relating to their children come into being *in a family situation* and their special relationships with future ulcerative colitis patients are largely determined by the dynamics of the family environment. The figure of the mother obtained in the anamnestic data from the patient is not reality, nor totally a mythical figment of the patient's psychopathology. Truly, the mother figure, like other figures in the family, is largely *a family legend* created by the relationships of all the individuals in the family with a central figure. The patient, then, presents us this image compounded of reality, of his own distortions, and of the family's idea of mother. One thing is probably true, however: Whatever the mother "really" is beneath the figure and the role and the image represented in the family, she is this way most of all with the patient. We can speculate that the deeper, intrapsychic conflicts, emerge most strongly in the relationship with the patient-to-be. This selection of the patient for the focus of family conflict is determined by a number of factors — environmental, individual, and constitutional. For a real understanding of the forces which motivate object choice and which bring about sensitivity to object loss we need to examine early and late object relations from this multidimensional point of view, rather than being concerned only with the binary relationship in a vacuum.

A study correlating mothers' personalities with a psychosomatic illness is, in our theory, likely to produce unimpressive results because of the existence of so many other factors crucial in the moulding of the object relations which are the really essential aspects of pathogenesis. More important, studies of this kind fail to provide us with much information about *how* the mother's relations with a patient have influenced him.

In the following case study we wish to demonstrate how object relations can be seen in depth. We shall attempt to illustrate our opinion that the mother's attitudes and behavior alone are not etiologically responsible for the predisposition and onset of the illness. If her characteristics were so responsible, might she not have started a small epidemic of ulcerative colitis in this family? Instead, the theoretically pathogenic object relations are moulded by the whole interlocking set of relations, although the mother is the central figure. We shall further try to demonstrate how the affected member of the family becomes a focus of conflict for the parents and his siblings.

The case report was assembled as part of a larger and more general research on family dynamics (2), which is related to the expanding interest in the dynamics of the individual and his family. Ackerman (3), Chance (4), and Kluckhohn and Spiegel (5) have provided extensive review and bibliography in this area.

The methods of our research included an observed interaction session including all family members, a number of interviews with each member individually, and a family relations inventory designed by our research team. For the purposes of this report we shall include only the individual interviews, although we learned about some aspects of the family inadvertently in some informal sessions with several of the family members. The individual interviews have a sequence which lends them some extra value. One member (J. T.) of the research team does all of the interviewing with a family, seeing its members in sequence. Then, when a series has been completed, it is repeated. In the family studied, the series was repeated four times with the exception of the patient's brother who could be interviewed only once for somewhat more than a hour. In this case we also have notes from a course of psychotherapy undergone by the patient. The interlocking or revolving sequence of interviewing tends to bring out some aspects of a family's characteristic transactions. The interviewer's ear soon becomes very sensitively tuned to the communication of the family group he is seeing, and the material covered in the associative anamnesis interviewing is directed somewhat by what the interviewer hears from all the family members. For example, in this family there was a surprising tendency for all to comment upon some early memories first reported by the patient. This tendency was encouraged by the interviewer. The fact that several people involved in a fairly intimate situation comment upon the same current issues is also extremely helpful in seeing, almost *in vivo,* what characteristically transpires in a family.

CASE HISTORY

Our acquaintance with the Neal family (pseudonym) began in early 1957 when Bob, Jr. was admitted to our psychosomatic study service upon the urgent recommendation of an internist and a psychiatric consultant. By that time Bob had lived through more than 12 months of discouraging battle with his ulcerative colitis. The anniversary of onset had passed just before Christmas without signs of improvement and, in fact, it had seemed to be marked by a moderate relapse. His self-respect had suffered with the suggestion of psychiatric treatment and his reluctant agreement to the hospital admission had carried some degree of last-resort submission on his part.

As far as we know, the illness began about the middle of December, 1955 with twelve watery and bloody stools per day, diffuse abdominal pain, and nausea. Through December and January, 1955-6 the diagnosis of ulcerative colitis was confirmed by proctosigmoidoscope and x-ray. He improved slowly with antibiotics and supportive care although there was a gradual decline in weight from his original 170 lb., and an anemia that stabilized at medium-low levels. A psychiatrist had one brief contact in February, 1956, but his interview and the suggestion of hospitalization in a Veterans Administration psychiatric service resulted only in a petulant change of physicians. After Bob left the hospital, his condition improved a little, then relapsed a little, each setback shaking further his hope of final relief. By the fall of 1956 the relapses were more severe and enduring than the remissions, while home medical care became less effective and less resourceful.

When we first met him, Bob was a long, thin young man of 24, usually huddled and curled in his bed with a stool-chair close by. He weighed about 115 lb. Any conversation of more than 10 minutes had to be interrupted by a rush from the bed and a burst of diarrhea. He had long, dark-blond hair falling over a pale, strained, and thin face. Talking with others was painful for him, not so much because it was fatiguing and he was ill, but more because it was emotionally difficult. Medically he was toxic and psychiatrically he was helpless and hopeless. The alternate sides of Bob's character can, even at this point, be illustrated by the contrasting picture of him 12 months later, after treatment, surgery, and steroids. Then we see him standing, emerged from the cocoon of bed clothes and psychic withdrawal, with a full, heavy face and air of complacent, assured stiffness.

Mrs. Neal was seen the day of admission. She is a moderately obese woman of slightly more than average height. She seemed relaxed, accessible, and poised. She talked easily, gave quick assurance of understanding our methods, and promised cooperation. She appeared to be empathic towards her son's recent ordeal, although first impressions could have been mistaken. She never showed much tension in response to the course of Bob's illness. Nevertheless, even a researcher oriented to the subtleties of family dynamics was surprised by the occurrence that took place immediately after this first interview, when the mother went from the office to her son's room and burst in saying, "Your father is in an agony of stomach pain from worrying about you." This drastic double-bind (6) and conflictful expression of common family problems, which will be explained more completely below, expresses the divided pity of the mother and forces Bob, in a loving way, to accept the responsibility for the father's illness. It would be impossible to say whether the occurrence had a physiological effect, since the bowel was already operating at near maximum speed of contraction, secretion, and hemorrhage. Soon thereafter, Bob was seen in his room. He was tightly huddled, sometimes trembling and almost unable to talk except to emit short bursts of anger at his father for not taking care of himself and his stomach. The conversation was strategically directed towards introductory small-talk. A little anxious himself, the interviewer strayed to the window and there spoke aimlessly of promises to bring magazines and of the hospital's need for new buildings to replace the old, dreary ones. While the interviewer was looking away, the patient hurried from his bed and had a torrential bowel movement. With the decision, then, that the patient needed a nurse more than a doctor, the interviewer ended the first contact.

Mr. Neal (Bob, Sr.) is a stout, full-faced man of about 50, with silver hair and moustache. He leaned back in his chair in a posture of confidence, but sometimes would tilt forward on his elbows to make a point. With a few exceptions his manner was that of a man of straightforward half sincerity. He exuded a confidential and friendly air which is useful in business and was usual in his interviews, although he spoke meaningfully of personal feelings and of his observations of others in the family. Several brief times in each interview the impact of events would change his voice a little to an imploring tone.

There were three other children: Doris, 29, and Dottie, 22, were not available, although we know something of them. Ken, 27, is a trim Air Force officer with a quiet, friendly, but noncommittal manner.

PRECIPITATION OF THE ILLNESS

The precipitating events of a serious illness seem to gather in one period linking and joining forces to upset a psychosomatic equilibrium. Bob Neal's difficulties were preceded by a set of associated occurrences, some of which were probably not truly separate precipitating factors, but rather representations or subordinates of the more significant ones.

By the fall of 1955 Bob was out of the Navy 2 years and in a business college, where his work was deteriorating. He seemed distracted, while his parents were urging him on and demanding to know why he could not do better. He partially supported himself, feeling a little angry that he had to but, at the same time, ashamed and guilty that he was being helped by his parents. It was impossible for him to know whether it was proper to be dependent upon his father while attending college, since it was never decided whether he appreciated the financial strain on his parents. His younger sister was being sent to the same college at the same time; was this reason to pay his own way or justification for expecting more?

These circumstances further affected object relations. The mother, by her own report and from those of others, had entered menopause in early 1955. She seemed less attracted by previous interests, was more likely to be irritated, and withdrew from her previous maternal attitudes. She was subject to crying spells, manifesting less energy, more complaints, and increased expectations of others.

About the same time (and also related to the uncertainties regarding college) Bob became puritanically angry at his younger sister, although they had previously had a close and sympathetic relationship. He felt she was "running with the wrong crowd," that she had involved herself with the "wrong" man and, worst of all, was behaving in a disrespectful, irresponsible, and impudent manner. He knew, and said, that he could not have escaped censure had he acted that way. But, most important, his criticism and bitterness, openly expressed, brought about resentful quarrels and a subsequent break with his sister. Coincident with Bob's near failure in college and the financial complications arising from his attendance, his father began to show, in the form of gastro-intestinal symptoms, the effects of strain. However, these symptoms did not deter him from his exhausting work, but rather forced an even more frenzied and hard-driving application to business interests. The father's response to the mother's emotional change was that of strenuous work over long hours while, as an executive, he took on complex tasks that promised one crisis after another. Mother and son shared the worry over the father's alleged foolhardiness; in Bob's case it turned to exasperation. Perhaps realistically, he wondered how necessary it was for his father to exert and punish himself so much when the return of a peptic ulcer threatened. The father's ways of dealing with his illness affected Bob's relations with both parents, adding to his problems of self-respect and feelings of inadequacy. While the father strove mightily and while he obviously had pain, he urged his son as he always had, to fear not and to perform better. At what price, the son might ask. Bob must have known the frustrations his father suffered in his self-incurred struggles. Perhaps as a parable of his attitudes to his father, Bob reported an incident that occurred in the fall of 1955 and involved his relations with a part-time employer. As assistant to a bartender, he was caused anguish by the demands of the latter that he have the courage to throw out unruly customers. Bob knew that at the same time this same man was stealing from the cash drawer.

For several years Bob had been courting a girl, with whom there was an informal understanding about marriage. This girl, named Dottie, as was his younger sister, we know little about, except that the state of his relationship with her heavily affected our patient's equilibrium. In very gross summary it seems to be true that by the fall of 1955 the courtship had gotten to the point where he felt pressed to commit himself, yet he did not feel secure enough to set a date for marriage. In early 1955, he thought he was involved in a pregnancy case as a result of a presumed interval of dalliance with another girl. The latter had married by that time out of malice toward Bob, but claimed to be pregnant by him. This episode threatened scandal, but proved a false alarm and taught him a stern lesson in fidelity. Bob thought he wanted to marry late in 1955, while his father, particularly, thought it a good idea that Bob become a "family man" and show his independence. The couple tacitly agreed upon the spring of 1956. In the midst of this excitement and during some celebrating at college, where he had very recently acquired a new habit of taking some alcohol every night, he found himself on edge about the coming holidays and the trip home. He vaguely remembers having some diarrhea before the vacation, but this symptom dims in importance relative to the acute onset of his illness soon after coming home for Christmas.

From this account three main currents stand out, yet even these cannot be clearly disentangled.

First, there is evidence concerning the change in Bob's mother in the direction of withdrawal, depression, irritability, and less maternal dependability.

Secondly, perhaps as consequence of the change in Mrs. Neal, the father began to manifest a recurrence of his gastrointestinal illness and, at the same time, an increase in the overcompensating drive expressed through the search for business crises. He doubted more the advantages of supporting his son in college, urging better performance and more independence upon him, and advising incessantly that fear of the future should be shunned. Meanwhile, Bob did poorly in school and became dreadfully uncertain that he would have the funds to finish.

Thirdly, there was the commitment to marry, which seemed something thrust upon him rather than being sought and desired. He wondered whether he had dealt with another girl cruelly, and was partially relieved to find that he had not. In spite of insecurity about marriage, he felt he was obliged to marry and hoped that he would find someone dependable. His troubles with his sister seemed to represent the conflicts involving his fiancee and his mother, as well as the malice of an old rivalry that added to his guilt and shame. He felt an ambivalence involving anger and a wish to break from all three of these women, but this wish was opposed by his continuing needs. We know from both Bob and mother that very shortly after the onset of the disease the older brother and sister petitioned the mother by letter (since Bob was then home and ill) that she not "baby" him as she always had.

The force of these trends in the year that preceded the onset of illness is made more evident from what we learned about the patient's life history and from his reactions during the months of psychotherapy that followed admission.

FAMILY HISTORY

The Neal family had two children by 1932. The father tells us that he left home early in his life and fought hard to protect his family during the depression. Though the Neals always had an income, the father's early experience warned him that he must be industrious if poverty were not to overtake him. The arrival of Bob, Jr., in the depth of the depression in 1932 undoubtedly posed some threat to the family security, although we have no way of really knowing how much. The Neals tell a story about Bob's birth that may reflect upon the significance to them of his arrival in the family. Mr. Neal tells it most dramatically:

But Bob was a little bit different than the rest of them. Did she tell

you the way he was born? Well the children had the mumps when she
was carrying Bob — or the whooping cough, that's what it was. So I
took them up to my folks and left them and I went up to see them
one night a week. When I got back, my gosh, the police was swarming
all over the place. I went in there thinking, "What in the world is
wrong!" Well, her and this woman were sitting out on the front porch
and my wife got up to go in the house to do something and a nigger
came running out of the bedroom around the bed and jumped out the
window. It liked to scare her to death. So she run out — we didn't
have a telephone — she ran out the front door and started over to the
neighbors and the neighbor's dog jumped off the porch and scared
her. She was a nervous wreck! Well, the next morning Bob was born.
That was on a Friday night 'cause Saturday I had to get the payroll
out. I don't know whether that could affect a child or whether it
would have made her feel any different towards him, but he was a
good child, he slept good, and had very little sickness or anything else.

We have little doubt of the truth of this story with respect to
the essentials of its plot. We have interpreted the story for its
current significance as a kind of family legend to explain to the
rest of the family why Bob is "different." The way that the
parents tell the tale and the portentous meaning they attach to it
make this episode a family legend with symbolic significance.
They seem to speak of the anxiety Bob's birth signified. Each
parent attributes the main fright to the other. Most evident is the
indication of an intruder entering the home. Several times we have
been asked for our opinion on the effect of this incident upon
Bob's later development. In other words, they ask what effect
their feelings had upon the intruder.

We know from the comments of everyone in the family that
this child, with his father's name, was given extra care and
protection by the mother. The mother admits to some of it, but
denies that the term baby is descriptive of her attitudes. She
claims to have sensed that his boy needed more, particularly in
rivalrous situations with his siblings.

Some of Bob's memories constitute comments upon the effects
of early childhood. He recalls the financial strain of buying a new
house shortly after the birth of his younger sister, and that this
house was endangered by the flooding river. The mother
comments that actually the new house had been a step forward for
the family, and that this same house was one of those most safe

from the floods threatening their community. This memory at once depreciates the father and adopts his feeling of threat and insecurity. Bob relates another memory of childhood as though it were an episode of childish rebellion. He recalls collecting Christmas trees from the neighborhood and piling them in the driveway to the extent that they blocked the father's entrance to the garage. Mother tells of the incident as though it was a bit of a sportive behavior on the part of her son. Bob also tells — with some of the original terror — of being cornered in the back yard by rats and of being rescued by his mother. No one else remembers this incident, but there is little wonder that his mother felt he needed help in relations with his siblings. We know little of his later childhood, except that after the age of five or six, Bob was an appealing and outgoing boy according to the reports of both parents. By the time he entered high school he had acquired a severe form of examination anxiety, although he did his best to conceal his fear. This hiding was reinforced by his father's incessant and particular advice to stifle all recognition and expression of anxiety. "When it came to butting his head against a wall, when he *had* to do something, he had a psychological fear of it," his father said.

Nevertheless, Bob became a reasonably successful athlete as a high school varsity football and basketball player. This activity had his mother's enthusiastic sponsorship, an attitude she had acquired from her brothers. She was a spectator at all of his games, although the father never could find the time to attend even one of them. Although he had been more successful in these activities than in anything else in his life, Bob never talked of his athletic experience with any pride or pleasure.

He finished high school at the start of the Korean conflict and, managing to overcome his mother's stout resistance, entered the Navy, as had his brother before him. His recollection of the service career is characterized by a feeling of isolation and loneliness in relation to his fellow sailors. He recoiled from the language commonly used by the others, but he felt ashamed when he found himself speaking it. His ship was hit off the Korean coast by shore batteries. When his mother read the news, she became distraught, expecting to receive the announcement of his death. Bob was disgusted when he heard of his mother's reaction. This event had none of the terror for him that he felt when caught with a soiled uniform during the admiral's inspection.

THERAPY

It can be appreciated that the doctor (J. R.) responsible for the psychotherapeutic part of the total treatment faced some difficult tasks. However, anyone experienced in such matters will know that the coordination and balance of the three methods of treatment (psychiatric, medical, and surgical) in a complicated case is difficult to maintain. Try as the psychotherapist may to coordinate the efforts of the internist and the surgeon with his own work, at times the collaboration becomes imperfect. Occasionally the psychiatrist will find himself making surgical and medical decisions certain to influence his relationship with the patient; at other times he will find that a decision has been made without his consultation and with which he would not have agreed. His treatment goals, his comprehension, his therapeutic anxieties, and his countertransference are all complicated by the delicate imbalances inevitably occurring in a three-way collaborative treatment. Although these were factors influencing the treatment of Bob Neal, they never completely upset his progress. Over the approximately 16 months of Bob's treatment on our service, his principal therapies consisted of steroids, two operations (an ileostomy and a colectomy, 10 and 13 months after hospital admission), and his work with the psychotherapist. To describe the nuances of the interactions between these approaches would require another study. In fact, it will be necessary to be cautious in interpreting the occurences of relapse and remission as responses to psychotherapy. In this study we can hope only to learn more about the patient's conflicts and defenses, leaving aside the question of the absolute value of psychotherapy for ulcerative colitis.

Analysis of the purely verbal interaction of the first month of psychotherapy is of little use. In the interviews there was a halting and stereotyped expression of thought and feeling. He really doubted the value of this work, but tried to conform. Certainly, the acute phase of his physical illness affected his participation, and he slowly made some adjustment to the ward, the nurses, and other patients. Rorschach tests done shortly after admission and then repeated a month later show some change. In the beginning he was seen as an outwardly adjusted and conforming person with underlying detached and depreciative attitudes toward others. At a still deeper level there was evidence of angry frustration — of an individual who wanted much but expected only husks of things or token gratifications. He seemed regressed to an infantile level, but even there he was depressed. A month later, after improvement on steroids, Rorschach tests found him much the same, although there were increased indications of hostility and other signs of an enhanced willingness for emotional expression.

After this very halting, difficult beginning, Bob began to express some material relevant to his suspicion of the frightening power of his needs and feelings. He noted that he was worse when home on pass or when the psychotherapist was away. A struggle for power and control began to emerge as a feature of his relationship with his fiancee: "She is the one who can relax me." However, it was necessary that she be there at the right time and do the right things or she would disturb him more than anyone else. Meanwhile, he worried about the drain of the hospital expenses upon his father. Following one interview in which these problems with father and fiancee became associated, he suddenly acquired a sensitivity to one of his medicines and developed a distressing and massive urticaria. "Amazingly," the observer's notes state, the diarrhea and cramps disappeared for the duration of his skin disorder. Prior to this anxiety occurrence the therapist had decided to facilitate the relationship through a bit of role playing in which he became the "good doctor," on the patient's side against the "bad doctors" who unfeelingly prescribed things to make him uncomfortable. We cannot say whether this maneuver was necessary, but it appeared to raise the question of the trust the patient could have in the relationship. He first doubted the therapist's reliability, then relaxed with him and hinted, shamefully, that he found himself at the apex of a triangle involving his doctor and the head nurse. However, at the same time, the therapist's role of siding with the patient led to expressions indicating that the doctor would bend to the patient's will, which produced tension in both Bob and the therapist. Bob could not find the relationship really gratifying and the doctor found Bob "demanding" and "oral-aggressive" — both irritating qualities. But then, for reasons no longer manifest, the psychotherapist began to take control enough to balance some of the patient's drives and, at that point, Bob seemed more a master of his own feelings and less fearful of abandonment. The therapy could by no means settle on this plateau, for there were other forces to contend with: problems with the family and fiancee, and difficult issues concerning the ulcerative colitis. However, Bob tried to hold the relationship at this mutually controlled level. He feared the anger that might break it and he resented the therapist when a decrease in his defensiveness was urged. He wondered how much was demanded of him in terms of psychiatric performance in therapy. The latter has a realistic basis, since it appeared that with physiological improvement the expectations of everyone — therapist, family, fiancee, and nurses — increased.

These trends in therapy brought from him memories of submission to his mother's urging during the year of illness before admission to our hospital. She would cheerfully suggest that he "go out" and enjoy himself to prove his strength, and that he widen his shrinking perspective. Although he had no enthusiasm at all for such activity, he would be afraid not to humor her. He also submitted, despite his own opinions, to her repeated suggestion that he ignore the doctor's advice and eat foods not on his prescribed diet. In fact, he was not tempted by these foods, but his mother thought he should be. Her urging seemed to say: "I am offering you signs of love, but you won't accept them." He felt guilty about resisting the foods that he thought it wrong to eat. These memories were associated with a description of the tenseness that had been present in the relationship with the mother since his return from the service. The "change of life" previously noted required more energy and more appeasement from the patient in order to maintain the old equilibrium. His father had warned that the mother had changed while Bob was away. He recalled ruefully in the same interview the closeness with his mother when he had been a successful athlete. It is possible that he longed for the days when the mother-son relationship had been mutually most gratifying.

Meanwhile, there seemed to be little chance for relaxation in the psychotherapy. This was never a relationship which permitted some quiet and rewarding reflection upon thoughts and feelings. There was a tautness, difficult to analyze at the time, which represented a push and pull in the interaction between doctor and patient. There could be no sharing, no peaceful discussion. Remarks had to be expressed or shamefully withheld while the patient expected to be pushed and pulled in the same manner. He tested repeatedly to see what would be required from him and what he could safely resist without the danger of severing the relationship. It was difficult as a therapist to see beyond the patient's stubbornness and his tendency to deal with every event in strictly literal terms. Although we see now that he wanted a dependent relation with the therapist, he wanted it to be without intrusion into emotions on the verbal level and without danger of anything unexpected. He said once, "You're just like my mother: you asked me if I wanted another appointment; I said, 'No,' and you came anyway." He went on to say that he could not understand why the therapy had to concern itself with such irritating matters as his worry over finances (father), dreams, and the idea "that I'm trying to hang on to some feelings." He could talk somewhat about his irritation towards his mother, since he felt at fault for that.

Thereafter, the more open hostility towards the therapist increased until headaches replaced bowel symptoms. This phase, in which the therapist was becoming pessimistic and shifting to the viewpoint that the patient needed surgery, seemed to be preparation for the next phase in the treatment. A more frankly dependent move occurred in which, in Bob's mind, the therapist became a clearly reliable person who made decisions, commiserated with the patient over his need for surgery and, in general, had taken or had been given the control of the relationship. Most likely this mutually controlled relationship repeated in an assuring way the early mother-child relationship. With very little trouble Bob provoked his fiancee to defy him and thus to give him reason for breaking the engagement. His reaction to this break was not intense. It seemed to have meaning only in the context of his new and more reliable symbiosis. He could afford to give up the fiancee at this point.

However, by this time surgery did seem indicated. The patient had had steriods so long and in such doses that it did not seem that he could soon relinguish them. Hence, rather than serving as a start for a long process of psychiatric treatment, the relationship was instead an aid in helping the patient through surgery.

For the purposes of this study the events in psychotherapy demonstrate for us the type of object relations our patient tends to form. We can see the push and pull, arduous for both Bob and his therapist, and how the interaction finally settled to some form of equilibrium in which the stronger member of the symbiosis has control but is also controlled.

In the following section, the causes of Bob's need for this kind of situation are sought in the milieu in which such habits were made necessary the network of relationships within which Bob's personality developed — his family.

THE NEAL FAMILY

Throughout the worst of Bob's illness, Mrs. Neal had been his faithful though often insistent, nurse. During some of the most difficult times at home Bob was close to morphine addiction, and the prevention of this was arduous for mother and son. His sleep pattern reversed, and his mother sat with Bob through the hours from midnight to day talking endlessly of his childhood. She commented: "I think it's been rough on me, since on top of it I'm going through the change of life. I said to a friend that maybe it's been a blessing in disguise, since maybe I would have given up to my own feelings had I not had him to worry about this year." In discussing this remark she explains at length that she "swallowed my own feelings." Anger, her disappointment regarding the lack of financial and social success, and depression were diverted into maternal care, pity, and worry over the adversities of another. Bob's illness revived, in many of its essentials, the guilt-appeasing, controlling, emotionally expensive symbiotic relationship of earlier days — but not quite!

In talking of herself Mrs. Neal was the most guarded of all. Although immensely voluble and indirect in telling of her life, she dealt with her own feelings and her personal history on a chatty and bland level. She was an only girl with three brothers, one of whom — the youngest — died when she was about seven. She had no memory of feelings about his death. She recalls a tiny and sickly mother, some kindly brothers, and a strong, authoritarian, and distant father. Family solidarity and respectability, without sign of emotional disturbance, was her ideal and a treasured memory of her childhood experience. She revealed slightly the feelings of insecurity imparted by her husband and reinforced by the realities of the economic depression, but these emotions were not nearly as intense as her perception of other's needs, particularly those of her husband and her third child, Bob. As mentioned above, she has no doubt that Bob required her special attention during childhood; she also knows that her husband has always disagreed and even resented this tendency. She said that the rest of the family thought she "favored" the third child, but she knows that it was simply that he needed her more.

Mr. Neal (Bob, Sr.) was far more open in talking of himself, at least in so far as he reveals his character. We see more clearly in him the nature of the equilibrium between needs and reactions to them, and between conflicts and adaptive techniques to quiet the anxiety arising from them.

In addition, Mr. Neal's personality stands out in his relations with Bob, Jr. He spoke first, and with affect, of his perception of an inability to speak effectively and comfortably to his children and particularly to the one who bore his name. He could see that his lifelong absorption in his work, and his consistently long hours had deprived him of the feelings of closeness and other gratifications his family might have afforded him. But, more self-righteously, he repeatedly told of how he had tried to convey a belief in fearlessness and independent strength. He felt he had demonstrated to his son what hard work could do for a man, and he emphasized hard work because he had known poverty in a large family as a boy, because it had been necessary that he support himself when he was 16, and because his mother had died shortly before he left home. The evidence is clear that the hard driving suited his angry fight against material insecurity, that it helped withdraw him from his need for love, that it reassured him that he could overcome his difficulties — in a word, overcompensation. In later years when economic adversity was not so threatening, Mr. Neal sought out and obtained executive positions which were not so financially rewarding as they were filled with unending crises and laced with complicated troubles. He is known in his business circles as one whom employers have given the thankless, troublesome tasks that require much worry and a 70-hour week. Mr. Neal enjoyed voicing his unconvincing complaints and he was genuinely proud that he had almost never had a vacation except for sick leaves.

The woman he left at home through all this — Mrs. Neal — was allowed to respond to his wishes for loving care only when he was troubled by his ulcer. He knew that he was unusually too tired, too headachy, and too preoccupied to ask from her or give to her. When he wanted to yield a bit to his needs he had to "shove off" his wife's sympathy and affection. Currently he sometimes feels that even when he is ill his wife has lost her ways of approaching him, presumably because she had been held off so often.

There are indications that Mr. Neal permitted some warmth between himself and his older son and two daughters; but he was alienated from Bob somehow. He thinks that perhaps it was because of the protectiveness Mrs. Neal lavished on the boy, making it necessary for him to strengthen the child by the opposite treatment; it also seems that the special attitude of the mother towards Bob may further have shut out the father. The latter idea neatly rationalizes the father's own participation in frustration of his own needs.

He explains his conviction that his son needed to cultivate independence and fearlessness with an incident from Bob's boyhood: One evening, Bob was out when supper was served. His father went to fetch him and, finding him, called his name. The boy retreated further into the shadows. The father called again and walked towards him, but Bob ran again. Ignominiously he called and called into the silence, but had to go back without his son. He was deeply hurt and the question he never could face was, had he, the father, caused fear in his son? From that time on he sought often to extinguish signs of anxiety in Bob and, in doing so, warned him repeatedly of the things feared by himself. His rivalry with his namesake could not help but emerge. When the mother was overprotective, father was "rough." It was this offspring who had to do the most to get his college education. İt was Bob who, by implication, was the greatest drain on finances even before his illness. When young Bob was home long his father forcefully suggested marriage and a job elsewhere. When the mother worried about the son's illness, the father reassured her that death too could be tolerated; for after all, he had known the death of both parents and two siblings.

Mr. Neal had a recurrence of his ulcer just before Bob's admission to our hospital. Then, when the events in the hospital were most acute, Mr. Neal decided that, for the first time in more than 10 years, a vacation and rest were in order. Mrs. Neal agreed that her husband needed this trip with her; for once he seemed to be submitting to her wish to care for him. Near the end of Bob's hospitalization when plans were being made, Mr. Neal again put forth his idea that his son would be better alone in a distant city. As we reflect on the problem the father, of course, seems to be wrong — but he was also right.

Ken Neal, 27, and Bob's older brother is, in many respects, a model of his father. He has the self-assurance and complacent ease, but his exterior is not quite so brittle. He has rather successfully adopted the themes of independence and strength and he does not find it necessary to struggle quite so much to compensate for his need for some emotional attachment. He is a successful career officer in the Air Force, risen from the ranks. He moved from post to post, always seeking another technical school and cheerfully taking the distant assignment, claiming he needed no place to "light." In his relationships he was outwardly noncommittal and nonchalant. He was matter-of-fact about his mother's forceful attitudes. He recognized her needs and put distance between himself and her. He was sympathetic, but not especially worried or stirred emotionally by his brother's illness. In fact, he seemed not at all surprised that an illness would bind his mother and brother. He agreed with the father's idea that Bob should depart from his parents' home. In our contacts with Ken he revealed the conflictful side of himself in only two ways; one of these was characteristic, and the other surprise. First, he told us with little affect that he had been twice engaged. He had drifted rather easily from the first relationship and the second was near a break at the time of our interviews. About a week before, he had planned a marriage after his fiancee had proposed it; a law suit involving the girl had then intervened. He rather dispassionately accepted the interruption and seemed little concerned whether the marriage would ever take place.

Near the end of our last talk, Ken was asked if he had any questions. Without change in facial expression he said, "Well, I get lonely sometimes." Then he halted and floundered a little before adding, "I have one thing that bothers me. I can't express any emotion. I have a terrible time with it. I want to stay just as far away from emotion as I can. I hate to get emotionally involved, even with my family. It hurts me . . . it hurts them sometimes, I know." This sudden expression is surprising from a taciturn young man who joins the rest of his family in the unity of dampening feeling, and in upholding the family ideal that emotional quiet and a respectable calm must be maintained in family life.

We are not at all certain of our data concerning the two sisters, since we have not seen them. However, from the corroborating comments of the others we have strong hints that Doris, 29, the oldest, is a slightly more rigid and imperious version of her mother. Dottie, 22, must have been — in the view of the family — "spoiled," since she is more truly independent and boisterous than the rest. She was obviously a rugged competitor with her brother.

AN ATTEMPT AT FAMILY ANALYSIS

Remaining is the goal of demonstrating from the above account that, in Bob's case, the rigid and confining patterns of object relations were not only formed in the binary mother-child symbiosis, but were conditioned by the multidimensional matrix of object relations constituting the field in which his personality developed. When we attempt, in studies of human behavior, to analyze events occurring in multidimensional fields rather than in simple binary systems, we compound our difficulties. However it is the argument of this chapter that the ways of forming and selecting object relations are shaped in a complex system such as the family.

We have chosen to simplify this task for ourselves and the reader in the following paragraphs by describing a number of interpersonal cycles which, in time, fixed the type of interpersonal relations Bob would have to make in adolescence and maturity. These cycles are conceptually designed to depict the flow of feelings and conflicts among family members. It is possible to construct an almost endless number of these cycles. Their schematic nature allows only a summary of the complexity of incessantly interacting systems. We hypothesize that most of these cycles operate simultaneously, and that the one on which we concentrate at any moment is determined by our point of view at the time. However, one or more may predominate in particular aspects of the family transactions and also at one time in the family's history. It is our thesis that the whole field — that is, all the individuals — is involved and influenced by each of the cycles. For the sake of convenience and simplicity in this paper the field will be limited to the mother, father, and patient — a system complex enough for a first attempt. The others, nevertheless, influence this three-person system in many ways.*

The basic cycle operating in the relationship of these three began before Bob was born. It had its overt impact briefly and then was deeply buried, although it made the succeeding family adaptations necessary. The following is a graphic representation of the cycle (Fig. 10-1).

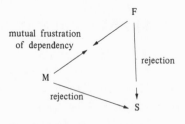

Figure 10-1.

---

*Lindemann (7) has used a similar conceptual scheme in the explanation of his hypotheses concerning the key object relation in the pathogenesis of ulcerative colitis.

In this and subsequent representations, *M, F,* and *S* signify mother, father, and son, respectively.

The mutual frustration of dependency needs in a mother who needed more than she seemed and a father who, for a long time greatly feared poverty, led to the unconscious wish that they could exclude an additional burden from their family and home. Maintenance of equilibrium in a system functioning like this cycle is impossible. It is potentially explosive, and each of the three family members must be driven off.

Hence, two more cycles come into almost immediate operation (Fig. 10-2).

In the first of these two cycles the mother compensates partially for her dependency needs and counteracts her guilt by maternalizing the new son. In a sense, the mother obtains an opportunity for expression of her own needs, but the father gets only a rival. Later, the son adopts the style of his mother's angry feelings toward the husband and father. In the second cycle the mother's "babying" of her son intensifies the father's competitive feelings.

The father's defensiveness is the main impetus for another set of cycles in which we can use the almost identical terms given us by father and son for their feelings towards the mother: shoving her off when they perceive any need for her (Fig. 10-3).

Father has to ward off mother as part of his overcompensation, but still feels the rivalry towards his son as the mother is pushed into expressing maternal love to him. However, to help balance the system, the son identifies with the father, and does his own

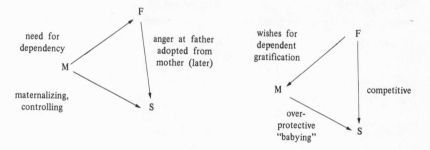

Figure 10-2.

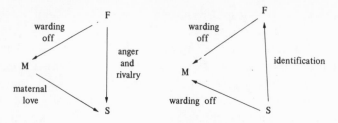

Figure 10-3.

warding off.

The situations which most probably was significant in the precipitation of Bob's illness is as follows (Fig. 10-4).

Essentially the above cycle is initiated by the mother's withdrawal from both father and son as a result of menopausal depression. The father reacts in his usual manner (with over-compensation) and competitively demands that his son show the same alleged courage. But Bob's defenses are not so well developed, and thus his father's attitudes towards him only intensify the reactions to the relative loss of the mother. An attempt at renewal of the old symbiosis leads to a cycle which involves the whole family (Fig. 10-5).

The siblings' and father's feelings in response to the mother's withdrawal stimulates rivalry toward the one who has supposedly enjoyed the most maternalizing in this family. There are not many possibilities for achieving an equilibrium in this cycle unless the illness causes a major shift in the total family adaptation. An escape was needed, and it was most likely that this would involve sickness.

Several other reconstructions are possible to conceptualize the dynamics of this family as a history and as a factor in the precipitation of our patient's ulcerative colitis. Our motive is

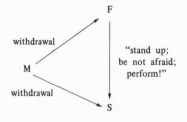

Figure 10-4.

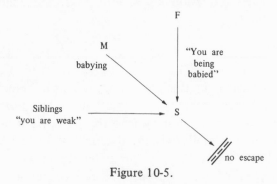

Figure 10-5.

primarily illustrative: to show that reconstructions can be made — by our schematic cycles or by some other evaluative system which attempts to span the entire field of family relations.

The family's adaptation involved resolution of a conflict between frustrated needs for dependency and the family ideal of independence, respectability, and avoidance of allegedly selfish desires. To do this, the members of the family must remain, for as long as possible, deeply committed to each other. In the process of this devotion to common needs there must be no overt demonstration of individual needs, since such an eruption would compromise the family ideals. There can not be the slightest hint of the emotions which arise from frustration of needs. Our methods of study of this family revealed that, to accomplish this resolution, a definite organization of family life is required. Essentially, the organization in the Neal family consists of the maintenance of a rigid system from which the unexpected and the uncertain are eliminated. Roles within this organization are carefully prescribed and rigidly adhered to. For the maintenance of emotional tranquillity this family requires that communication be confined largely to the matter-of-fact; vagueness, excitement, or disturbance are shunned. Nevertheless, there must be some breakthrough and when this occurrs it can be extreme. The stereotyped form of communication can not permit much perception of another's inner feelings. In our summarizing phrase — anxious cohesion — for a family of this kind, we refer to a quality of family life in which the individuals maintain almost desperately their cohesion as a group at the high cost of *underlying* anxiety.

SUMMARY

We have suggested in this case study that the object relations aspects of psychosomatic hypotheses may be more comprehensively investigated by inquiry into the patterns of interlocking relationships in the family. Use of the field study method of the anthropologist in observing the whole family provides a view in depth of important relationships, instead of reports from the individual patient.

We have proposed an expansion of current hypotheses concerning the object relations aspects of predisposition and etiology in psychosomatic research. In the case discussed we have attempted to show that the patient's adaptation was conditioned by an interlocking set of relationships within the family. The crucial mother-child relationship was itself conditioned by the family setting as a transacting field of object relations between its members. In our opinion it is not the *mother* who affects the child, but the *family's mother,* whose relationship with the child is a product of the dynamics operating within the family as a social system.

REFERENCES

1. Engel, G. L.: Studies of ulcerative colitis III. The nature of the psychological processes. *Amer. J. Med., 19:*231, 1955.
2. Titchener, J., and Emerson, R.: Some methods for the study of family interaction in personality development. *Psychiat. Res. Rep., 10:*72, 1958.
3. Ackerman, N. W.: *The Psychodynamics of Family Life.* New York, Basic Books, 1958.
4. Chance, E.: *Families in Treatment.* New York, Basic Books, 1959.
5. Kluckhohn, F., and Spiegel, J. (Eds.): Integration and conflict in family behavior; a report of the Committee of the Group for the Advancement of Psychiatry. Report #27, 1954.
6. Bateson, G., Jackson, D., Haley, D., and Weakland, J.: Toward a theory of schizophrenia. *Behavioral Science, 1:*4, 1956.
7. Lindemann, E.: Modifications in the course of ulcerative colitis in relationship to changes in life situations and reaction patterns. Life stress and bodily disease. *Proc. A. Res. Nerv. Ment. Dis., 29:*706, 1950.

Chapter 11

Psychotherapy with Families of
Allergic Patients*

VICTOR SZYRYNSKI

BASIC CONCEPTS

FROM the psychosomatic point of view, many allergic conditions may be understood as faulty types of adjustment to environmental stress (1, 2). We assume that the living organism is constantly subjected to stimuli arriving from the surroundings, particularly from the most changeable and the least predictable part of the environment which is the social milieu in which an individual exists. Here again, the most significant elements of the social environment appear to be the individuals who primarily gratify our emotional needs; in respect to the child one will find here the parents, among whom most commonly we consider a mother to be the more significant person, then the siblings, the grandparents, and in some cases even the domestic animals (3). In respect to the grown-ups, it is usually the marital partner who acquires the primary significance, although the parents, the in-laws, and the children should be considered. In some cases, the influence of domestic servants may also be important, especially for the children (4).

The process of visceral adjustment takes place through the autonomic nervous system in preference to the voluntary one which is involved in the hysterical conversion phenomena (5). Such primary involvement of the autonomic nervous system signifies also that these responses are primarily of a regressive and primitive nature resembling typical reactions of very young

---

Note: Reprinted by permission of the author and *Annals of Allergy, 22:*165-172, 1964.

children. This, in addition, makes them ordinarily inaccessible to any voluntary control.

Such a responsiveness of an organism to the environment implies communication. Stress is communicated to the individual through various signal systems. The two most important ways of communication are the verbal and the nonverbal (6). The influence of the two systems on an individual is responsible for his security or may create a situation of stress of varying degree. Messages conveyed by these two systems may be similar or contradictory. They may also be consistent or inconsistent, whether arriving from the same individual who changes his behavior or when coming from the two or more members of the "significant environment."

All types of communication from the parental figures, in respect to a child, are of particular significance because of the following:

1. They usually take place very early, with a young, poorly protected and rapidly developing organism which is probably much more responsive to stress created by inconsistency in the content of communication.
2. Such stimuli create patterns of responses which often become firmly established in the organism.
3. Such early crystallized behavioral patterns have a tendency to return later on in some future situations resembling the initial experience when, for instance, a response acquired in relation to the mother is transferred to the individual's wife who in some situations may be recognized or rather "felt" as a maternal figure.

It has been postulated some years ago, and pertinent material seems to accumulate, that some allergic conditions should be understood along with the other psychosomatic disorders as characteristic responses of the organism to stressful influences from the environment. Some stress-producing signals are communicated to the organism from the significant persons in the environment in a verbal, or, more frequently, a non-verbal manner. This in turn creates an emotional tension state which again, through the autonomic nervous system, is discharged through what we may call some "specific behavior of the tissues." An attempt to link some psychosomatic disorders in a more specific manner with particular stressful situations has been ordinarily somewhat less convincing. This is particularly due to the very important complexity of the whole situation which would involve the general pattern of adjustment of a particular individual: the intensity of his needs and expectations based on the organic factors and on the previous learning, relative resistance or sensitivity of the special organ systems to stress, and the current psychobiological level of general health. All of the above results in a specific pattern of responsiveness which we like to call "personality."

THE PATIENT'S ENVIRONMENT

Conspicuous inconsistency between the verbal and nonverbal communication is often observed in the environment of our allergic patients. Two general patterns may be found here:

1. A significant person in the patient's environment, usually his mother, verbally claims her love and acceptance for the child. In a similar manner, the patient's wife may talk about her devotion and loyalty to her husband. However, even during the preliminary contact with such significant individuals we may often observe the underlying climate of hostility, resentment, and rejection; The mother of an allergic child displays her exasperation and annoyance leading to impatience and hostility in respect to the child's illness. A wife of an asthmatic is considerably upset and irritated that in spite of her "perfect" attitude, her husband's condition is not improving, and there are even some people who try to blame her for aggravation of his illness. There is obviously little doubt that such underlying feelings are very easily communicated in a nonverbal fashion to the patients themselves.

2. The second pattern is usually related to basically unstable personalities of significant individuals in the patient's environment. Here we find that considerable inconsistency in the emotional stimuli produced by such significant people is due primarily to their own distorted personalities.

Occasionally, such individuals are actually psychotics. In many cases their personalities are characterized by inability to cope with their own emotional problems with frequent escape into various neurotic conditions. In general, we may call them emotionally immature or victimized by various neurotogenic patterns of maladjustment.

Whenever we find, therefore, a patient whose condition may be linked to such a disturbing relationship with his environment, two ways of management may be considered:

1. His stressful and traumatic environment may be changed by removing the patient to other surroundings.
2. Significant individuals in the patient's environment may be treated in order to change their personalities and enable them to create a different emotional climate for the patient (7).

A combination of the above two methods would consist of removing the patient temporarily while his family is subjected to intensive psychotherapeutic handling.

The most important point in such treatment with significant members of the family, whether handled individually or as a group, is the necessary awareness that not only their attitudes but also their basic feelings should be influenced by treatment. Considering that nonverbal communication, which is probably the more important of the two in respect to the family climate, depends primarily on the deeply repressed and primitive emotional responses, no superficial change of attitude is usually sufficient. Such parents or marital partners cannot simply attempt to behave differently, nor even is a considerable degree of insight into the nature of their faulty behavior usually sufficient to influence their allergic children. Above all, they should be helped to feel differently about themselves, their family, and the patient. This is obviously pointing out the necessity of a quite thorough dynamically-oriented psychotherapy which would help an individual reorganize his own personality. In this way, not only the parent's conscious attitudes, communicated verbally, but his or her whole system of feelings conveyed nonverbally to the patient would be positively altered.

The above emphasis on nonverbal communication based on

actual feelings applies also to the physician who handles allergic patients. In his strenuous efforts to improve the patient's condition, the doctor is not always free from frustration and unconscious guilt feelings, which naturally give rise to some repressed hostility and resentment. This is again communicated to the patient and his family in spite of an honest effort to display apparently perfect "bed-side manners." In this way the physician may become imperceptibly included in the vicious circle of the disturbing hostile signals system already operating in the domestic environment of such patients.

SOME TYPICAL MODELS

Asthma, eczema, ulcerative colitis, or neurodermatitis may be taken here as our typical operational models (8). The faulty mother-child relationship has been often stressed in analyzing many cases of asthma (9), with the underlying pattern of maternal rejection resulting in the child "sobbing" for warmer acceptance (10). At face value, this was very often apparently denied by an exceptionally tender and over-solicited attitude of such parents. At closer scrutiny, however, the pattern of maternal inconsistency with swinging moods or ambivalent feelings were eventually uncovered. Not infrequently some secondary repressed hostility in the mother could be found, which resulted from irritation and annoyance with the severe and recurrent condition of her child. Such feelings communicated nonverbally to the patient would usually aggravate the situation still further. On the other hand, however, through reaction-formation, such mothers may become, on the surface, even more attentive and solicitious toward the child.

A somewhat different pattern was observed in the household of patients who were developing asthma in the fourth or fifth decade of their life. Quite often their wives appeared on the surface as very efficient, dedicated, and matter-of-factly administrators and life companions. However, in our experience they were found to be quite often cold, rigid, and rejecting under the surface. One of the patients described his wife in a characteristic way. "For my wife, the most important thing to take care of is our house, then comes the garden, the furniture, our car, our cat, and after a long while, myself." (In this case, a cat was nothing more than a "red herring" as the patient was not allergic to it and markedly improved with psychotherapy.) Many such patients find it difficult to discuss anything with their wives which may involve criticism or a difference of opinions. They are expected to submit themselves to domestic routine which is after all observed rigorously only "for their own good." One is tempted to formulate this as a situation in which a patient is "hardly allowed to breathe." This very obviously points out to the underlying hostility in such women, whom their husbands are afraid of touching for fear of producing a flare of aggression. Still more, very little of warm and tender feelings is nonverbally communicated to such patients, although they are frequently referred to in conversation with such wives. It is no wonder that under such circumstances an individual is regressing psychodynamically to an early infantile level and feels himself rejected by a rigid and forbidding maternal figure of his "friendly and efficient" wife. Accepting both partners for intensive psychotherapy, in some of our cases, have very satisfactorily resolved the difficult situation with remarkable improvement in the asthmatic symptoms.

DIAGNOSTIC CONSIDERATIONS

Just a few words about the diagnostic approach to the families of allergic patients. We are basically interested, of course, in evaluating their general pattern of life adjustment and their specific attitude towards the patient. This may be primarily based upon the clinical impression of an experienced psychiatrist or a nonpsychiatric physician interested in psychosomatic approach, but it may be also supplemented by certain batteries of psychological tests, questionnaires or check lists, just to mention, as an example, one developed at the Children's Asthma Research Institute and Hospital (11). More recently, seeing the patient together with his family or particularly with the most significant members of it has been stressed and found quite valuable by revealing the actual emotional interchange which takes place before the eyes of a physician. Still more, some new diagnostic devices aimed at uncovering psychological dynamics within the family have been advanced, just to mention as an example the Family Relations Indicator of Dr. J. G. Howells (12) or the Two Houses Technique of the present author (13). Such additional techniques may be applied either by the physician himself, who in such case would need some additional specialized training,or by a clinical psychologist cooperating in his diagnostic work.

It may be of special interest to mention a new diagnostic approach based on the phenomenological orientation (14). In this respect, a diagnostician, most commonly an experienced psychiatrist, attempts to observe not only the patient but also his own personal reactions to the patient. It simply means, in terms of our previous discussion, he attempts to become aware of messages arriving to his personality from the patient both in the verbal and nonverbal manner, the latter being conveyed by the patient's general behavior. In this way, it is quite interesting to notice how various individuals affect us by producing a certain amount of tension or hostility or annoyance or insecurity or impatience or an excessive amount of sympathy, emotional tenderness, attachment, or enthusiasm. By watching oneself, a diagnostician is very often able to observe those interesting phenomena which may very markedly help him in understanding the influence of such an individual on his immediate environment which obviously includes the patient who is the primary object of our interest. Still more, we may mention here the team approach when diagnostic impressions are discussed by the physician with his clinical psychologists and social workers who may independently study the emotional interactions within the patient's family.

AN APPROACH TO SIGNIFICANT FAMILY MEMBERS

The five goals for psychotherapeutic approach to the significant members of the family of an allergic patient may be enumerated here:

1. To help them understand the patient's emotional responses, his unhealthy patterns of adjustment and their influence on his allergic condition.
2. To help them understand their own behavior, their "style of

life," and how it is communicated to the patient.

3. To develop a more mature, accepting, and relaxed attitude towards themselves and the patient.
4. To modify, eventually, their own attitudes and feelings.
5. To modify in this way the patient's pattern of adjustive behavior, the allergic symptoms being here included.

Basically, we may start such therapy by asking those individuals to describe for the therapist their understanding of the patient's personality. This, of course, will reveal their objective observations, but on the other hand also their projected and often distorted ideas, which give an important clue to their own personalities. Gradually, their own attitudes and responses to the child's or an adult allergic patient's general life pattern, which includes the symptoms, are discussed, the focus of attention being very gently directed to their role in the patient's overall adjustment to life. At this stage, most commonly, such people begin to turn attention to themselves and discuss their own problems, pattern of adjustment, and their feelings about the patient. This process is also modifying their attitudes towards the patient, whereby a confused and not infrequently hostile orientation is replaced by the more objective interest in his emotional problems.

With progress of such therapy, we observe how the parents or marital partners would gradually relax, in respect to the patient. To say it more correctly, they will relax in respect to themselves and their own life adjustment, which naturally involves their relationship with the patient.

The final effect of the therapeutic approach to the family members results in changing the patient's patterns of adjustment. This takes place on the conscious and unconscious levels, again the second one probably being the more important. At first, some parents and other relatives gradually learn to modify their behavior towards the patient. This, of course, remains largely as a conscious effort. The unconscious result, however, is probably best expressed by saying that the patient simply begins to live with different people, with the people changed by psychotherapy and in this way replaces the unhealthy adjustment patterns with the more wholesome ones.

A few further points are important in psychotherapeutic approach to the relatives of an allergic patient. Many of them have a considerable amount of guilt feelings and they anticipate condemnation and criticism from the physician. Instead of criticizing their behavior, pointing out their errors, and instructing them in better ways of managing the patient, it is much more profitable to display a noncondemning and nonaccusatory attitude. Such people, being the parents or marital partners of the patient, are invited by the physician to help him towards better understanding of the patient's personality. They are not the object of criticism but the respected allies in the doctor's attempt to help the patient. The second point would suggest down-playing such guilt feelings by what we call in psychiatry the "ego-supporting" approach. Such family members are commended for their interest in the patient, for their efforts to help him, for their cooperation with the physician, and for their interest in adjunctive psychotherapy. As we see, the positive values are picked up and stressed while their mistakes and negative feelings for quite a while are rather ignored. This builds up better self-confidence, promotes closer cooperation, and results in a more relaxed general attitude, which most likely will soon communicate itself to the patient.

Still further, their anxiety, which is usually quite considerable and results from the experience of helplessness in handling the patient, gradually would be alleviated by helping them to understand the patient's problem more clearly, the patient's mental mechanisms, their own role in the patient's adjustment, and the best way to cooperate with the physician towards the patient's improvement.

PSYCHOTHERAPEUTIC MODALITIES

Before special psychotherapeutic technique is selected in dealing with the family members of the patient, two basic points should be stressed once again: first, that a thorough psychodynamic evaluation leading to a psychodynamic working hypothesis should always precede such therapeutic intervention; second, that in every psychotherapy, with exception of emergency measures, we do not aim at the removal of symptoms but at the treatment of the whole personality. (From that point of view, parents of patients suffering from allergic conditions should consider such symptoms as a situation resulting from some disturbances in the personalities of interacting individuals.) Fundamentally, no psychotherapy is aimed at removal of the symptoms, which are simply considered a by-product of emotional maladaptation. When health is returned to the personality, symptoms usually take care of themselves. An allergic manifestation is often just a presenting symptom, a red flag waving for help. With intensive psychotherapy the focus of attention soon drifts away from this signal to management of total life adjustment, not only of the patient, but of his whole family.

Among the psychotherapeutic techniques, very many may be selected and used individually or in combination. Here we may use the individual psychodynamic therapy or more classical psychoanalysis (15). If a patient is psychodynamically treated himself, his significant family members may be handled by different therapists. For example, the patient and his wife may see two different psychiatrists, a child and the parents may have again two different therapists. Occasionally, we may prefer to treat the parents as a couple, still further, the entire remaining family including the parents and the other members may be treated as a therapeutic unit. This has been recently stressed in the interesting work in England (16) and by some other workers in America (17). Group therapy may be instituted for parents or relatives of allergic patients (18). Still further, general enlightenment and information programs may be organized for such audiences. As we have mentioned before, this last approach usually succeeds in alleviating anxiety by increasing information and developing skill in handling life problems.

SUMMARY

In this chapter, we have reviewed the basic principles, psychodynamic mechanisms, and some fundamental techniques of psychotherapeutic approach to family members of allergic patients. It has been assumed that intrafamilial emotional tension states are based on the mutual influence of various family members, which is communicated in a verbal and nonverbal manner. In some individuals, such an intrafamilial climate may produce or aggravate allergic reactions patterns. Psychodynamic treatment of significant family members may produce for an allergic patient a markedly changed environment resulting in improvement of his allergic condition.

REFERENCES

1. Abramson, H. A.: *Psychodynamics and the Allergic Patient.* Saint Paul, Bruce, 1948.
2. Weiss, Edward, and English, O.: *Spurgeon: Psychosomatic Medicine − A Clinical Study of Psychophysiologic Reactions.* Philadelphia & London, 1957, pp. 486-494.
3. Szyrynski, Victor: Investigation of family dynamics with the "two houses technique." *Psychosomatics, 4:*68, 1963.
4. Abramson, H. A.: Psychodynamics of the intractably asthmatic state. *J. Child Asthma. Res. Inst. Hosp., 1:*18, 1961.
5. Noyes, Arthur P., and Kolb, Lawrence C.: *Modern Clinical Psychiatry,* Philadelphia & London, Saunders Co., 1963, pp. 413-414.
6. Mirsky, I., Arthur, Miller, Robert E., Banks, James H., Jr., Ogawa, Nobuy: The communication of affects. *Proc. Third World Congress Psychiatry,* Montreal, Canada, 1961. University of Toronto Press, 1:88, 1961.
7. Szyrynski, Victor: Psychotherapy with Parents of Maladjusted Children. Presented at the 10th Annual Meeting of the Academy of Psychomatic Medicine, San Francisco, 1961.
8. Wittkower, Eric D., and Cleghorn, R. A.: *Recent Developments in Psychosomatic Medicine.* Philadelphia & Montreal, Lippincott, 1954.
9. Tuft, H. S.: The development and management of intractable asthma of childhood. *J. Dis. Child., 93:*251, 1957.
10. Alexander, Franz: *Psychosomatic Medicine − Its Principles and Applications,* New York, 1950, pp. 132-141.
11. Peshkin, Murray, and Abramson, Harold A.: Screening procedures for admission to the children's asthma research institute and hospital. *J. Child Asthma. Res. Inst. Hosp., 1:*221, 1961.
12. Howells, J. G., and Lickorish, J. T.: A projective technique for investigating intra-family relationships designed for use with emotionally disturbed children. *Brit. J. Educ. Psychol., 33:*286, 1963.
13. Szyrynski, Victor: A new technique to investigate family dynamics in child psychiatry. *Canad. Psychiat. Ass. J., 8:*94, 1963.
14. Rumke, H. C.: Phenomenological and Descriptive Aspects of Psychiatry. *Proc. Third World Congress Psychiatry,* Montreal, Canada, 1961.

University of Toronto Press, 1:17, 1961.
15. Sperling, Melitta: Psychotherapeutic techniques in psychosomatic medicine. In, Bychowski, Gustav, and Despert, J. Louise: *Specialized Techniques in Psychotherapy*. New York, Basic Books, Inc., 1952, pp. 270-301.
16. Howells, J. G.: *Family Psychiatry*. Edinburgh & London, Oliver & Boyd, 1963,
17. Greenberg, J. M., Glick, I., Match S., Riback, S. S.: Family therapy: Indications and rationale. *Arch. Gen. Psychiat., 10:*7, 1964.
18. Abramson, H. A., and Peshkin, M. Murray: Group psychotherapy of the parents of intractably asthmatic children. *J. Child. Asthma. Res. Inst. Hosp. 1:*77, 1961.

PART II

THE MOTHER IN THERAPY

Chapter 12

Simultaneous Treatment of a Child and His Mother*

PAULA ELKISCH

T HIS chapter deals with the treatment of a child in which the mother-child relationship was the focus of my therapeutic efforts. Subsequently, the child as well as the mother were in individual psychotherapy for, in the beginning, individual therapy could not be considered since the child was too disturbed − a disturbance which expressed itself in his partly autistic and partly symbiotic behavior to his mother. Hence mother and child were treated simultaneously.

It is the aim of this presentation to describe this simultaneous treatment which may be considered a preparatory stage of individual psychotherapy, because this study may be of value in similar cases. I think in particular of cases where a young child and his mother represent a pathological unit that cannot and should not be broken, but can be treated as a unit − until the child may be able to live on his own and the mother be able to let him do so.

The preparatory phase in the case of George and his mother lasted four months. Of these four months I will describe more specifically only what happened during the first month of treatment. I knew the boy from the age of two and a half until he was eight. Unfortunately I have lost track of the case in the last five years.

George was brought for treatment for the following reasons: He had violent temper tantrums during which he threw himself on the floor, kicking and screaming. Frequently, and apparently without any provocation, he would spit and bite wildly. This behavior was

Note: Reprinted by permission of the author and *American Journal of Psychotherapy*, 7:105-130, 1953.

the more exasperating to his environment as the reasons for it were inexplicable because the little boy did not talk except for three or four "words," or rather sounds, which he shouted inarticulately and explosively. His sleep was restless and disturbed by nightmares; when he was lying in bed he used to rock, and constantly suck his thumb. During the day he was extremely restless. He displayed great jealously toward his two older brothers. He had no regular habits in regard to eating or toilet function. He could never be made to eat at regular meal times — and as for bowel movements, it was claimed that from birth he had never had a normal evacuation, but had always to be given a suppository or an enema. Thus the child was conditioned to defecate only by force and struggle.

With strangers, George was timid to the point of complete withdrawal. This withdrawal the child displayed by means of a very expressive bodily movement or gesture, that is, he hid his face, or head, encircling it with his arm, at the same time turning himself away from either person or any other object he apparently avoided to be con-"fronted" with. At a symposium on childhood schizophrenia, Escalona described a child who used to display the same gesture [4]. When I saw Spitz's film illustrating the behavior of children who had been deserted by their mothers, I was reminded of little George who might have been one of them. Those deserted children in the film behaved and looked as do adults in deep depression. So did George at times.

I met George in his immediate family circle in his home before he was brought to my office for treatment. His mother to whom he clung anxiously, handled him oversolicitously, and with compulsive artificiality. She vainly tried to make him say a word. She herself was verbose and eloquent; but her language was rather highbrow and seemed to lack simple words — the words of direct human communication.

George was the youngest of three boys. His two older brothers were twelve and six when George was two and a half. He was what is currently called a "planned child," but when he was born, he was so "very ugly," according to his mother, in contrast to his two "beautiful" older brothers, at the time of their birth, that it was difficult for his parents to accept him. The delivery was "too fast." Mrs. L. was not able to nurse George for more than a week though she had breast-fed her two older boys for several months. George was such a "fretful, jumpy baby and never relaxed" that the mother felt she could not manage him by herself, and got a nurse for him when he was three weeks old. The nurse, a rather domineering person, stayed two weeks. At four months, George fell seriously ill with pneumonia. The nurse was recalled and took over for two months during which time she had tried to toilet-train the baby. The mother complained that the nurse had tried to teach her how to handle the child, but by doing so Mrs. L felt that the little self-confidence she had had, had been completely undermined; so that she felt more helpless than ever, after the nurse had left their home.

At one and a half years, George was taken ill with a second attack of pneumonia, and this time was put into a hospital where he was confined for three weeks. When Mrs. L visited George, she could not decide whether or not she was recognized by the child. After George had returned from the hospital "he could't let us out of his sight," according to his mother's report. About six weeks after he had recovered from this second pneumonia, he was forcibly weaned from the bottle through the unfortunate fact that his mother had "forgotten" to take his bottles to the place where the family spent the summer, a remote village in the Scottish Highlands.

During the following winter — he was then two years old — George developed the alarming symtomatic behavior previously described.

When George was born, Mrs. L was near the climacterium. The family was English. They lived in London where Mrs. L had a reputable career as a singer. She was a gifted woman and had even composed a number of songs which had been recognized for their exquisiteness. Her religious background and upbringing to which she was strongly tied, was strictly puritan. Her longing and ability for artistic expression, as well as her craving for an unconventional form of life in contrast to her background, had caused a long-standing conflict. She was the fourth of five children; the oldest, a brother, had had several schizophrenic episodes of the paranoid type. Her father was said to have suffered from paranoid schizophrenia. He had died before George was born.

Shortly after George's birth, and particularly in connection with the fact that Mrs. L felt at a loss in handling her baby, she had again taken up music with intensified interest and devotion.

The father, a college professor, seemed, superficially, a much better adjusted person than his wife. Actually, however, he was emotionally very unstable and extremely ambivalent. He had a history of severe asthma. In his immediate ancestry there was also mental disease.

George's parents had become more and more estranged from each other. I could reconstruct later that their marriage had reached a climax of unhappiness at the time of George's birth.

DIAGNOSIS

A diagnostic evaluation was attempted in two areas: (A) Concerning the child's personality development; (B) Concerning the mother-child relationship.

(A) Spitz has listed six sectors of the personality pertaining to the organization of the ego which may be observed during the first year of life [13]. These sectors are the following: (a) Perceptive Mastery, (b) Body Mastery, (c) Social Relations, (d) Mastery of Memory and Imitation, (e) Manipulative Ability, (f) Intelligence. At the age of two and half, when I met him, George functioned in some of the sectors of the ego not at all, and in some sectors in a disturbed way. He had no social relations. His body mastery was greatly arrested. The circumference of his chest was far below normal, with a conspicuously decreased muscular tonus, and the other areas of his personality also showed distortion, as we shall see later.

In addition to disturbances which pertain to the organization of the ego, George displayed severe somatic symptoms such as constipation, unusually frequent and prolonged colds, anorexia, and sleep disturbances.

(B) With regard to the diagnosis of the mother-child relationship, Mahler's concept of autism versus symbiosis seems to be applicable to George's relationship to his mother and vice versa [6] (1). Mahler's theory has particularly helped me to clarify the

(1) The autistic behavior to which Mahler refers was described by L. Kanner in 1942, 1944 and 1949.

dynamics of George's case. Both mechanisms, the autistic as well as the symbiotic one, were present at times, alternating with each other. Yet, all in all, in the beginning of treatment, autism prevailed. However, in the measure that autism prevailed, the child craved symbiosis.

Mahler's concepts of autism versus symbiosis are concepts which she used in describing infantile psychosis. Clinically, George's behavior, his facial and gestural expressions, were strikingly reminiscent of the children described by Escalona [4], Bender [1], Spitz [14], Mahler, and others. These children were considered by those authors psychotic, schizophrenic, or severely disturbed in terms of anaclitic depression.

However, I want to stress that my aim in this chapter is not to discuss whether or not George's case belonged to the category of child psychosis. As I said in the beginning, my aim is to describe the treatment and how the consideration of the mother-child relationship effected therapeutic results in this severely disturbed small child (2).

PLAN FOR TREATMENT

Three major points were considered in the treatment plan:
1. Mother and child should be treated by the same therapist, and be treated simultaneously, i.e. in the same session, twice a week.
2. In addition, Mrs. L and I were to meet before these joint sessions of mother and child.
3. Occasionally, that is, whenever George's treatment necessitated such contacts, his two older brothers as well as the father were to be seen by the therapist (3).

I should like to add a word about my reasons for adopting this plan of treatment for both practical as well as theoretical considerations led me to this procedure.

---

(2) In her paper on Early Developmental Stages, Mahler further developed her ideas about the autistic-symbiotic relationship, pointing out particularly that certain degrees of either or both of these mechanisms may be found in less severe disturbances than psychosis [7].

(3) Schwarz described a similar approach. However similar, it is different from the approach I describe here, since Schwarz merely had the mother present during the sessions but did not treat the mother-child relationship [11].

The Practical Aspect

The practical consideration was that *time* was of the essence. Since the relationship that existed between George and his mother was of an autistic-symbiotic nature, every day counted in the attempt, or struggle, to free their relationship from such distortion.

It goes without saying that once such an autistic-symbiotic interplay had been established, it would have been the most difficult and even mistaken plan to attempt to separate the child from his mother and treat him individually.

Whereas, on the one hand a severe disturbance in the elemental relationship between the mother and a young child constitutes a grave problem, it seems possible in certain cases to establish a treatment situation in which the mother may be exposed to the experience of forming a different relationship to her child through the presence and emotional participation of a therapist; at the same time, the child can be made to react in a new way to the changed and changing relationship of the mother toward him.

This last consideration leads us to the theoretical aspect of the treatment plan.

The Theoretical Aspect

The establishment of the object relationship between mother and child depends upon the ability to have spontaneous experiences. This implies creating conditions which will facilitate such experiences. How can this be done? Though I am discussing here the specific case of George and his mother, nevertheless the specific description of their case and situation may be looked at as a paradigm, potentially representative of cases similar to theirs.

Conditions favorable to the producing of such spontaneous experience between Mrs. L and George were brought about in the following manner.

1. The triangular situation — child, mother, and therapist — presented to each of the participants a configuration which, in its special significance, they had not experienced before. Within this framework both child and mother were given

the opportunity of reacting toward each other in a new way.

2. The mother's interviews with the therapist preceding the triangular sessions were undertaken with the idea of preparing Mrs. L, so that she would enter into the "group" experience with the reassurance that not only little George but she herself and her own needs were being considered. The developing relationship between Mrs. L and myself played a decisive role in the ensuing therapeutic process. The mother's transference to me became the vehicle that paved the way for her to reach her child. It furthermore enabled her to give up her defensive rigidity by alleviating her guilt-laden fear of the child and her anxiety in her role as a mother. It could be assumed that Mrs. L would soon want to imitate my handling of the child — and not merely "imitate," but want to participate in my unconditional acceptance of George to which she was exposed without feeling undue competition on my part. Thus, the emotional experience of her personal hour with me was a condition without which Mrs. L would not have been able to become an integral part of our little group.

3. The attempt to establish conditions in such a way that a spontaneous relationship between mother and child may emerge, needs a clarification of the role and the attitude of the therapist as a member of the triangular situation. Being a member, an integral part of this group, a "participant observer" — to use Frieda Fromm-Reichmann's descriptive term [5] — meant to be aware of my feelings toward both mother and child as well as of their relationship to each other and to myself.

During our sessions of three I tacitly focused all my attention on the child. With a child like George who tended to withdraw entirely from any new situation, encircling his head with his arm, face down, and turning his whole little body away, who first would not touch anything or let himself be touched or spoken to, one had to be completely passive and quiet, simply waiting — but this waiting had to be free from expectancy.

The description of a few "sessions of three" which I shall

attempt to give now can hardly convey the feeling-tone and the atmosphere that pervaded those hours.

The Treatment Proper

When George came to my office he was carried by his mother. After a quick and frightened glance at me, he encircled his head with his arm, so that he could not see anyone, nor could his face be seen. The small child made himself appear still smaller (4). He clung frantically to his mother. When George finally gave up his hiding and clinging position, he would resort to it, again and again, while Mrs. L held the child. Then George climbed down from his mother's arms. Some toys were lying around, trains and cars, which the child tried to smash by stamping on them wildly, sticking out his tongue at his mother and me. He did not touch the toys with his hands. In fact, he shrank from touching anything. During these activities he seemed to be anxious not to loose sight of his mother, even for a second, and many times took refuge in her arms. Simultaneously, he kept repeating his habitual autistic gesture of withdrawal as if to ward off everybody and everything from the outside world; at other times he would dart toward his mother as though he wanted to crawl into her and to be incorporated in her body. In this hour Mrs. L responded to George's behavior and aggressively clinging motions with awkward embarrassment. Her arms and legs seemed stiff and as though they were made of wood, her movements abrupt, staccato, her lap entirely unyielding, while her speech was intense, compulsive and overly articulate. No contact between George and myself was made in this first hour. He was completely autistic as far as I was concerned.

When George and his mother came for their second hour, I greeted them in the bathroom. It was my feeling that the medium of water might facilitate acceptance of bodily contact with the

---

(4) Paul Schilder speaks of the "shrinking" and "expanding" body image [9]. It was interesting to see how unambigously George expressed the "shrinking" in his abundant production of drawings and paintings throughout two years; later on, in conjunction with his growing outgoingness, his art work expressed more and more an expanding body image [3].

therapist of which George was afraid as of any bodily contact.

While the water was running into the tub I casually played with it. Little George who this time soon climbed down from his mother's arms, stood beside the tub watching what was going on — but with a very unhappy look on his face and without taking any part. Instead, he hid his face with his arm in his habitual gesture. I went on playing by myself for a while, thus inviting the others to join me in this play. Mrs. L responded hesitatingly, waiting for George to join first, but again he turned away. Mrs. L and I played very gently, no "real" waterplay, no splashing. Everybody was quiet. All of a sudden, George put one of his fingers in the running water but immediately withdrew his hand. He looked at me and, very timidly, smiled. He did not enter into the play between his mother and myself which continued for a while. However, the contact between George and myself had been made in this hour.

As I had expected, playing with water became the major medium during the initial phase of the treatment. Water seemed to help to overcome the child's fear of touching things, it drew him out of himself without arousing his need to protect or defend himself.

Playing with water suggested making inarticulate noises, imitating its special sounds of splashing, babbling, and gurgling. Since it was imperative that little George learn to use the muscles and innervations needed for the articulation of speech, the imitation of less articulate and more primitive sounds seemed a comparatively easy achievement. But in order to imitate sounds, one first had to listen — and so listening played a great role in our early sessions. The child was induced to listen to sounds or noises or voices around him that he perhaps might want to imitate. Sometimes we would just listen to the running water — or we would sit on the floor, or at the children's table and listen to whatever was audible around us and, perhaps, participate in what we heard by responding to it, falling into its "talk." The learning of "how to listen" was as important an experience for Mrs. L as it was for George. For it made the mother aware of her own voice and of her abundant talk, mostly consisting of a highbrow vocabulary that, as she soon expressed it herself, must have been like an "overwhelming force" to the child, powerful enough to "shut him up completely."

Just as he had been overwhelmed by his mother's vocabulary, he had been overwhelmed with suppositories and enemas. To this forceful, robbing attack on his little body the child had responded with the most obstinate constipation. After I had conferred with George's pediatrician I suggested that all enemas, suppositories or any other laxatives be discarded and the possibility be faced that the child might not have any bowel movement for several days. Three days after this suggestion had been put in effect George had his "first bowel movement" without artificial help. From then on his constipation gradually decreased. However, during the time that followed we sometimes had to go back to using some laxative, particularly at times of acute distress or illness and, all in all, it took slightly over a year before George could manage his bowels. He stopped wetting his bed during the fourth month of treatment. Enuresis had never been a problem. But George's most startling progress was in regard to speech. The boy who could say not even "yes" and "no" with distinct articulation, and who only made a few inarticulate animal-like sounds, which were completely unintelligible – came forth with two single words in the sixth session, words which he articulated distinctly, and two days later he spoke six words in succession, this being his first real achievement of speaking. After one month of treatment George had a vocabulary of 117 words.

In my opinion such progress was possible only because I participated in all of the child's reactions. For instance, during this first month, three of his sessions were conducted at their home while George, who was so frequently ill, had to stay in bed.

Mrs. L kept a conscientious record of George's speaking performance over four months, and I have analyzed the child's "117 words" of the first month, considering their meaning and their grammatical potentialities. My study of the 117 words revealed that, potentially, the child would have been able to form full sentences. However, for three months he spoke only single words, almost all of them in imitation of what he had just heard. To connect the words, that is, to make something that is not "just words" but a meaningful construction, seemed to be difficult for him. Furthermore, George had striking difficulty in enunciating.

For two and a half years one could note him struggle when speaking. And he struggled all the more since he developed a great interest in words, or language. In fact, he had an affinity to language that was unusual and showed up in his superior verbal IQ. (At five years his binet was 135.)

It seems important to me to mention in detail these features of George's language behavior. His language not only lacked the quality of object-related communication, the flow of speech, but was used in an introverted way. The boy's interest in words was far beyond that of a child of his chronological age, and yet this interest was expressed frequently through an autistic playing with words, which naturally was not object-related and adapted to reality.

Now I should like to give a description of another session, namely, the hour when George spoke his "first word."

After some waterplay, the three of us had settled around the children's table on which stood a doll house. George, as usual, first encircled his head and then sat there, just looking unhappy and not making any move. No one said a word. At last I took the baby doll out of its crib and put it in the arms of the mother doll. Then George moved. He took a piece of furniture out of the house and put in on the table. He continued this performance for some time, taking one piece of furniture after the other out of the house, apparently in a deliberate manner, as though he wanted to organize, or reorganize, the "household." His mother and I participated in what George was doing just by being with him and perhaps trying to understand his play. George did not touch or pay any attention to the dolls, only to the furniture which he set up in an extremely orderly fashion. The way he touched each piece was overly cautious, timid, ritualistic. It was utterly characteristic of the behavior of autistic children — first putting out their feelers, as it were, toward the outside world. Moreover, it was characteristic of the mode in which these children who seek contact with inanimate objects even avoid the representatives of animate objects, such as dolls (5). He never used his whole hand, only the tips of two fingers — and even these two little fingers

---

(5) Personal communication with Margaret Mahler. Also see Mahler [8].

barely touched the object. After some time of silent observation, I named one piece of furniture after the other, while George was taking them out of the house. I said, slowly and distinctly, "This is a seat — this is another seat." A little later, appraising what George had been doing, I expressed affectionate admiration, saying to him, "My — you are very neat." Whereupon, very softly, George said, "neat" — and he repeated this word again and again looking at both his mother and myself. During the same hour he also spoke the word "seat." (Note the Klang association which is reminiscent of schizophrenic or organic disturbances.)

In order to understand more fully how George's reactions came about, it is necessary to interpolate something about the collateral circumstances, or changes in the environment since the beginning of psychotherapy, particularly in regard to my interviews with Mrs. L.

Concerning the content of my sessions with her I must confine myself to such information as is pertinent to the understanding of the mother-child relationship and my treatment of this relationship during the first four months. Mrs. L's dependency was extreme. This need apparently never had been fulfilled in proportion to her demands, and had always caused her suffering and frustrations which she had tried to sublimate in her artistic productions and career. During her pregnancy with George she had felt threatened by the anticipation of being tied down once more by maternal duties, and in her objection to such duties she became a woman who was unable to give herself to her newborn child. She was a mother who needed a mother — but a mother different from the one she had in reality. Under the emergency situation in which therapy of mother and child was undertaken here, certain gratifications were given to Mrs. L at the beginning, gratifications which under less critical circumstances would have been withheld. Such necessary gratification was represented, for instance, by the very direct personal contact with the therapist — a relationship which was not analyzed until much later. Moreover, Mrs. L was given advice and direction, and the reassurance that the responsibility for George's growing up was intimately shared. While on the whole Mrs. L accepted in a most dependent and overconscientious way whatever was suggested to her — with regard to sharing the responsibility for George's growing up, her competitiveness as a mother (and woman) was aroused and also this reaction of hers was used for the immediate purpose of treatment.

The following are examples of such suggestions: Mrs. L, who was very unhappy about George's obviously disturbed and arrested development, was told to disregard completely her child's chronological age and try to go along with the therapist in regarding the situation as if it were that of a very small baby. George thus was to be treated with the permissiveness one would bestow only upon a baby — no matter how he behaved. George's rhythm of eating and elimination — disturbed as his rhythm was — had to be observed and taken into consideration, as fully as possible, in regard to his feeding and voiding, rather than demanding that he adjust himself to any artificial schedule. Likewise, he was to be indulged regarding his sleep. Bedtime was loaded with anxiety for him — and it remained this way for years, despite the fact that, once therapy was begun, his mother, or sometimes his father would sit by George until he had falled asleep. His mother would sing to him, or just gently hum a lullaby using few words. And whenever she used words, she would use only those which George had mastered and used himself. Mrs. L was creative my making rhymes for George, and many of them she fitted into familiar nursery tunes, or she made a tune herself. Her response to this particular suggestion was so enthusiastic that, as she told me one day, she was no longer eager to think of herself as a professional singer, in fact, she wanted· to divorce herself from her career-life, at least until George had outgrown his babyhood. Soon little George, who proved to be highly gifted in music too, started to hum and sing, first at home with his mother, later also in his hours with me. (Music and water are akin. They both flow. "Flow" — Greek "rheo" — etymologically, is the root of "rhythm.") From these suggestions, and the way they were carried out one may infer that, naturally, some modifications had been made with regard to our "baby-approach" for, actually, George was no longer an infant, but a boy of two and a half. Mrs. L's developing relationship with me seemed to have an almost visible immediate effect on her relationship with George. One could notice this change in the way she spoke to him or would look at him. Her speech was less stilted and highbrow, her voice warmer; at times it became almost "musical." Her look which before had expressed frightened curiosity mixed with an impulse to devour her child, now seemed to include him affectionately. After about three months she even was holding the child differently. Whereas, before, she had been stiff and unyielding, gradually she understood that, where the child has a protrusion, or makes one, the mother should have a groove. And so, at last, little George did find a lap in his mother to sit on (6).

There is no doubt that the mother's changing relationship to George, to a great extent, was responsible for the changing attitudes of the entire family toward their youngest member. However, according to the treatment plan, I had individual interviews with Mr. L as well as with George's two older brothers with the aim of making each of them realize the trouble little George was in, so that they would want to participate in the assignment of improving George's condition. For about three months the cooperation of the whole family was exceptional. I consider this radical immediate change in his environment a major factor in the result of my initial treatment of George. That later such an unusual cooperation was not consistently maintained, had no disastrous effect on him. For he had been accepted by his family at a time when it was still most vital for him and his development during treatment made him reasonably invulnerable to the ups and downs in the family. Anyway, this new attitude toward the little brother continued to be carried through, at least in the conscious efforts of the family members.

Before I go on with my account of the treatment, I would like first to go back and explain somewhat more specifically what I mean by "visible change" in this mother-child-relationship. I said before that "autism prevailed," and that, in the measure that it prevailed, the child craved symbiosis. This craving of his found a

---

(6) Schilder has made an observation that pertains to this experience: "Whenever there are disturbances in the postural model of the body, the patients also have difficulty in recognizing the different parts of the bodies of others" [10]. Silberpfennig-Kestenberg has described the subtle perceptiveness of the young child with regard to his being handled by his mother [12].

response in his mother. One may say that the first reaction which treatment brought about, was a shift of emphasis from autism to symbiosis. Let me give an example. One of George's most disturbing symptoms was his biting. In the autistic phase his biting connoted a defense against everyone and everything, a warding off of any object relationship. In the symbiotic phase this very biting became an expression of the wish to possess, to retain, to devour; an aggression that was libidinized; an urge to incorporate, as well as to be incorporated. To the degree to which the symbiotic character of their relationship came to the fore, the boundaries between child and mother seemed to become blurred. However, in speaking of these two phases, it should be understood that each of them, very distinctly, also contained the characteristics of the opposite, i.e. the autistic phase had elements of symbiosis, and the symbiotic phase had elements of autism. Only the emphasis had been shifted.

After four months of simultaneous treatment I decided to treat George and his mother individually. What were the criteria for my decision? A definite change had taken place in the relationship between mother and child. I may say, the situation seemed such that I could attempt to further disentangle, or try to dissolve the autistic-symbiotic involvement of the two. George's postural behavior had changed; so had his mother's. The child had completely stopped his habitual gesture of withdrawal. His symptomatic behavior had greatly improved in all six sectors that Spitz has pointed out as indicators of ego organization. Likewise, the change in the mother-child relationship expressed itself in our "sessions of three." Whereas, in the beginning, mother and child were a "unit" and were treated as such, they became individuals each of whom then was a member of a "group." In other words a change in the Gestalt, in the configuration of the triangular situation had emerged.

George loved to come to his personal sessions and very proudly climbed the last part of the stairs to my office all by himself. He was treated for three more years, twice a week. After that time he came for occasional visits. From the time of his individual treatment I would like to relate a few incidents which stand out in my memory as particularly significant. One day when we were playing on the floor he crawled into my lap saying, "me – your baby." One day when we played "water," he asked me to undress him and then wanted to be put into the bathtub. Symbolically, George thus expressed the desire to go back into "mother's womb." This desire obviously was connected with his first real contact with me in the bathroom – when he had touched the water. I recalled this incident to him when I followed his request and put him in the tub.

Throughout these years of psychotherapy, George became much stronger physically. At the age of four the circumference of his chest was above average. This fact was all the more amazing since, all in all, he still was a rather frail, delicate child; yet he had developed a good and joyous mastery of his body.

At times his facial expression was almost radiant. In his social adjustment, George made enormous strides. He became very popular with his contemporaries. I have felt, from the beginning of treatment, that George's high native intelligence which, however, also had a definitely precocious quality, was unfolding with the release of his emotional difficulties. Learning, therefore, has always been a source of excitement and adventure to him. He was one of the best students in school. I should not omit mentioning the artwork George did during and for his therapeutic hours. This artwork is unusual both with regard to quality and quantity.

CONCLUSION

In conclusion, I will try to explain what, in my opinion, happened in the case of George and that of the mother-child relationship. Actually, in order to understand George's response to treatment – as severely disturbed as the little boy was – one cannot even pose the question the way I did; for, what happened to him seemed to have happened mainly through the treatment of the mother-child relationship. The treatment of that relationship was approached in two ways: (a) through the triangular situation; (b) through Mrs. L's individual session with me preceding the "sessions of three."

Mrs. L's relationship to me was one of the potent dynamic factors in the therapeutic process of the case. Her need for dependence made her at once a "good child" that wanted to please mother – please and imitate her. As the transference relationship developed, her imitative behavior grew into a more real identification with me. But since George was the actual center of my therapeutic endeavors, it was he on whom I focused. Thus, Mrs. L's identification with me necessarily developed into an identification with her own child. In addition, Mrs. L's transference relationship to me also influenced her relationship to George in another way. While on the one hand, she was the "obedient," "good child" to her mother-therapist, she was also a mother herself and a woman who "competed" with another woman (the therapist) for the love of her son. One can imagine how stirred up, and sometimes confused, Mrs. L's feelings became in and through the triangular situation. The handling of such feelings requires both experience and great empathy with the patient if they are to be used and directed constructively.

There was another potent factor that I would hold responsible for the therapeutic results. It was the opportunity for George to experience a normal babyhood that was created through the therapy, an important stage of development which this child had lacked, and to which his whole family contributed in the most generous and intelligent way. This experience however, also hinged on the treatment of the mother-child-relationship and, besides, on the treatment of the whole family situation.

With regard to the dynamics of the case, I would like to make a few final comments on the procedure presented in this chapter.

Potentially, a "simultaneous treatment" situation implies, dynamics not unlike those we find in group therapy (as *"tres faciunt collegium,"* three make a group); so it implies dynamics like cross-transferences and counter transferences, or a certain amount of "drama" that may be acted out. The therapist therefore has to be aware of such forces. However, "group dynamics" are at work only inasmuch as the triangular situation *is* a "group." For, if mother and child represent a unit, as was true of Mrs. L and George in the beginning of treatment, the therapeutic focus is a different one, namely on the mother-child-relationship, with the child as the actual center. In my description of this case I have pointed out that the change from the unit to the becoming of separate individuals was one of the criteria, perhaps the major one, for my decision to terminate the preparatory phase of treatment; and it seems to me that this is a criterion which would be applicable to any such situation. Therefore, it also may be a preliminary "goal" to work toward, during the phase of simultaneous treatment of the child and his mother.

However, speaking of a "goal to work toward," I feel I must correct myself. For such a "device" does not fully take into account a condition or presupposition, indispensable for the carrying out of such treatment. Subjectively expressed, this condition refers to the high degree of flexibility that is required on the part of the therapist; objectively expressed, to the focusing on the ever-transitory quality of the therapeutic process. While flexibility is desirable in any therapeutic situation, it seems indispensable in this particular procedure. For, the "ever-transitory quality" in the simultaneous treatment that I have described here, pertains to the preparatory, preliminary phase that this treatment represents. Perhaps not just by "accident" the matrix of water, that flexible element, had to be introduced into this treatment situation. As Laotse put it, "There is nothing weaker, nor more yielding than water, yet it effortlessly overcomes that which resists it." And more specifically even, "Water is recognized as the symbol of the mother or refers to aspects of birth" [2] – and rebirth. In this respect it was not "by accident" either that George during one of his individual sessions had asked me to put him in the bathtub.

Through this request he connected me with his mother, he merged his two mothers, as it were – and, at the same time, I became the "midwife" who eventually was able to deliver the child to his real mother.

DISCUSSION

Judith S. Kestenberg, M.D. It is not unusual for a child psychiatrist to be gentle and patient with children. But it is the patient and understanding approach to the mother which is so often lacking and so sorely needed in child treatment. The session in which mother and child participate can be the most revealing and most gratifying to all concerned.

Some two years ago, in a panel on "Transference in Child Analysis," Bornstein and I reported on such sessions with mother and child. Those who first applied analysis to the treatment of small children, visited them in their home, in their natural setting. The presence of the mother, at least in the initial contact, substituted for familiarity; it offered the child the security of its own home. Also, if necessary, one could confront the third person, in case of strong resistance in the child. It depends on the age and mental state of the child how long such triangle situations are necessary.

I should like to discuss the two cases* Dr. Elkisch presented separately: a) Group sessions plus individual consultations with the mother (which I shall call *group sessions*) and, b) the subsequent simultaneous treatment of child and mother in separate sessions (which I shall call *treatment sessions*). What goes on in child therapy has most certainly a therapeutic effect on the mother; but this is true in some measure, also of such situations where treatment is not intended. A mother watching the examination by a pediatrician or the work of a good nursery school teacher, learns. She identifies with them, imitates them, and she learns a better approach to the child. Of course, she may not always be as competitive as Dr. Elkisch's mother became. She might, in extreme cases, tell Johnny that she will tell the teacher of his bad behavior or ask the doctor to give him an injection as a punishment for his bad behavior. Johnny will then fear or dislike the doctor or teacher, and there will not be any need for further therapy. The mother may, on the other hand, feel uncomfortable in her role of a mother, may perhaps discuss Johnny's masturbation in front of the nursery teacher and greatly embarrass the boy.

One cannot expect a parent to have pediatric or deep psychological education. Parents may fail in the training of their child not only because of their own personality disturbances, but also simply because they are not well equipped for this difficult educational task. Except, of course, for the one fundamental

---

*The case of Johnny was not included in this book.

factor of love and affection which may somehow guide them, for better or for worse, despite the lack of a degree in child rearing.

The mother's love and care give the child a powerful incentive for his development. But it is rather fortunate for the child that the mother's love is not inexhaustible. An always patient and always loving mother — there are such pathological, masochistic mothers — will not bring up a child that is capable of adjusting to the hardships of reality.

Usually, by the time the mother brings her child for treatment, she has partially given up her role as a "good mother," and her relation to the child has become disturbed. However, I have never seen a mother who had no object relationship to her child. Withdrawal from an autistic child in babyhood does not necessarily constitute complete withdrawal of object relationship. Forgetting the bottle of a child, as in the case of Dr. Elkisch, may be an expression of ambivalence in the mother's relation to this child. When a little baby, in the first year of life, is really "impossible," one does not immediately know that this conduct is pathological. Many children, for example, will suddenly change their position, which the mother does not expect; or assume a position in which treating the child becomes impossible; they may become completely stiff; or the babies may have temper tantrums; but here we have a baby who suddenly spits in his mother's face, in a rage-like reaction, so that the mother does not know when she has to be on guard.

There is an interdependence of reactions between mother and child. It is very difficult to be specific. One has to learn more satisfactory methods and better ways of understanding the child's communications and manifestations.

Dr. Elkisch has shown us here a model example of tact and skill in teaching the mother how to approach the child. She did it unobtrusively and almost without expecting it to succeed. This is psychiatric adult education at its best. Great improvement in the parent-child relationship was accomplished by it. The transference reactions on the part of the parent and of the child proved equally constructive. The parent gained insight indirectly into her own difficulty, apart from the problem of the child. But whether or not the primary etiological factor in the child's problem was the parental neurosis, the parent used the insights she obtained in her own treatment to foster the recovery of her child. I think it is wrong to take a parent into treatment with the sole aim of improving her relation toward her child.

This brings us to the second case of Dr. Elkisch, and the question of an individual treatment of mother and child. Is it desirable that mother and child be treated by the same therapist? Melitta Sperling has done this. Ordinarily, in situations where one family member has the physical power over the other, as the mother over the child, it might be dangerous to have in therapy also an acting-out mother who, at the same time, may be herself feeling toward the therapist like a little girl toward her mother.

It seems to me that Dr. Elkisch had remarkable success with this child. I should therefore, like to close my remarks with the hopeful note that Dr. Elkisch's paper proves that experimentation is a valuable help to all theoretical knowledge. It may lead us to a better understanding of the mother-child relation, even if it should contradict some of our established principles.

Wilfred C. Hulse, M.D.: I consider Dr. Elkisch's paper a landmark in the treatment of the severely disturbed young child with psychotic behavior. I am glad that Dr. Elkisch avoids the term "childhood schizophrenia," because this clinical picture is basically different from that described by E. Bleuler for the schizophrenic illness of the adolescent and adult. She follows very correctly also Margaret Mahler's observation that these children do not suffer only from autism, but also from a severe disturbance of the symbiotic relationship between mother and child.

Because of the persistent symbiosis, these young children (and unfortunately many others with the same syndrome who are brought to us at a much more advanced age) cannot be treated separately from their mothers. On the other hand, it is very difficult at the present time to find the right therapist for them, i.e. a therapist who, like Dr. Elkisch, is well trained, sensitive, imaginative, and last, not least, sufficiently devoted to the task before him.

There is very little a discussant can add to this excellent chapter which should be used in teaching, because in this specific type of therapy (as in other new branches of psychotherapy) we need the development of teachable standard procedures. Dr. Elkisch has described the sick child, his mother, and the specific treatment procedure with classical clarity, and we should like to see the chapter enlarged for publication so that we could learn still more of the details. There are number of therapeutic aspects in this chapter which would deserve analysis and discussion in separate papers and I can enumerate only a few of them here: (a) The communication of sound without words; (b) sessions with mother and child at the bedside, while the child is acutely ill physically; (c) treatment and handling of a child according to its developmental age instead of its chronological age; (d) the meaning of the water play; (c) interpretation of the child's behavior to the mother in the individual session preceding the "group session."

The use of the words "group session" and "group psychotherapy" in this specific situation are, I think, quite applicable, if we establish a clear distinction between the common treatment of an artificially composed therapeutic group and the treatment of a natural family group. I have tried in a previous chapter to establish a clear distinction between these two very different branches of group psychotherapy. The threesome described by Dr. Elkisch is acceptable only in the family group session. In the classical procedure of group psychotherapy with the artificial group, the old Latin saying of *tres faciunt collegium* does not hold true.

In closing these remarks, I should like to thank Dr. Elkisch for having formulated three sentences (aside from all her other achievements) which merit to be part of our teaching armament in child psychiatry and child psychotherapy, and which should become so popular that Dr. Elkisch is likely to experience the highest reward of a successful author, namely the kind of plagiarism in which the originator's name is "forgotten" while his formulation becomes a common slogan. Her three formulations are the following:

Where the child has a "protrusion" or makes one, the mother should have a "groove."

The (rejected) child finally found a lap on his mother to sit on.

Finally, her description of the child psychotherapist as *a midwife who delivers the child to his real mother.*

Simon I. Wenkart, M.D. I was intrigued and gratified by Dr.

Elkisch's paper. I think that this is the first time in a psychiatric or psychoanalytic meeting that I encountered a therapist who in her approach discarded all rigmarole and treated her patient with humanity. I am one of the fortunate ones who have treated many children while in general practice. At the present time I limit my work to adults and treat children through their parents, in an indirect way. I analyze their mothers and fathers. What disturbs me in cases where the family situation as such remains unaltered, is that the child, even after a successful therapy, has to go back to the same family situation.

Dr. Elkisch realized that in order to have a child derive maximum benefit from his treatment, the entire family must not only accept the child, but must understand their own problems and the role which they impose on each other. In her case, there was not only a disturbed mother-child relationship, but also a disturbed husband-wife relationship. Dr. Elkisch did not mention what the disturbed father-mother relationship entailed. It may have its psychologic merits to know about it.

One of the discussants said tonight that the mother is necessarily confused when her child behaves in this way. I have yet to see a child that would develop neurosis unless his mother is neurotic. Emotionally adjusted, mature mothers do not produce neuroses in their children. This holds true even in pediatrics. Some mothers are given wrong instructions: she must not disturb the child, and so on. If she is emotionally well adjusted and completely accepts her child, she will disregard the instructions of an overanxious pediatrician.

I think that the contribution which Dr. Elkisch has made here is the flexibility in treating the family situation, a situation where the presenting symptom was a disturbed child. But that was only one major sympton of a disease, which must be treated in its entirety.

Maria Brick, Ed.D. It seems to me that most of the discussants have been trying to make both diagnosis and therapy fit into their particular theoretical and methodological ideology. At the same time, I have the impression that all of the discussants realize that the successful therapy reported by Dr. Elkisch was brought about by a human factor which is beyond the "textbook knowhow."

Did this discovery cause the speakers anxiety and hostility?

Harry Stack Sullivan once said that "better results could have been achieved with much less wear and tear if the dynamics of the group, the shifting pattern of interpersonal field forces *making for or obstructing collaboration,* had been better understood."

The significance of interpersonal attitudes as a causative factor in the etiology of personality and character warpings, i.e. neuroses, as well as in the "getting-well" process, i.e. therapy, is fully appreciated by only a minority of workers in our profession. More often than not, this factor seems to be blotted out by what may well be "selective inattention."

In regard to psychotherapy, I am referring to what lies beyond the dynamics of transference and countertransference, namely, the importance of the therapist as "a person." F. Fromm-Reichmann stressed this issue in her book, *Principles of Intensive Psychotherapy.* Sullivan consistently referred to the significance of a "benign person" in the development of human beings, both within the environment and in therapy. Erich Fromm, in discussing the professional qualifications of psychoanalysts, mentioned as "most important, but difficult to define," the analyst's "gift and character."

These and other structural factors all too often may be sacrificed for the sake of fitting what happens in a patient's life and his psychotherapy into static categories, concepts, and nomenclature. I should like to use some of the data from Dr. Elkisch's report to illustrate my point:

1. The water play in the bathtub, without talking to the child. Categorical definition might label it as "anal." As an interpersonal experience it may well have been the first opportunity for this child to be with an adult "other person," who did not coerce him, nor make demands of him.

2. When the child asked Dr. Elkisch to undress him and to lift him into the water. This was labelled as the child's wish to return to the womb. But when we consider it in terms of an interpersonal relationship, we note that is previous sessions the child had experienced a "togetherness" with Dr. Elkisch, in contrast to the "againstness" of his experiences with people in the family prior to meeting Dr. Elkisch. Thus, the child was able to express his own wishes to Dr. Elkisch, and possibly to test whether her benignity was genuine and, also, whether his own power was genuine, the power "to make things come about" rather than being the object of what happened to him.

3. The initial absence of talking to the child etc. The term "indirect" method was used. Even without the use of language, communication takes place between human beings. Without words, Dr. Elkisch probably conveyed to the child that she genuinely respected him, even his wish to stay in the non-communicative, defensive, "shell." It reminds me of the work of Sullivan and Fromm-Reichmann with schizophrenics, in which a similar technique was applied.

Emil A. Gutheil, M.D. I should like to refer to that part in Dr. Elkisch's therapy which was played by "indirection." I have noticed that a favorable influence on the patient can be obtained by an indirect approach. I have treated patients whom I was able to influence constructively by talking to their wives, parents or other relatives in the patients' presence. In some cases I did not even look at the patient. I could feel, however, that the patient was responding. Indirect education is a powerful education, although we may sometimes be inclined to underestimate it. Indirect criticism often proves to be more effective than the direct approach. Such criticism does not tend to provoke strong negative reactions, such as defiance or resentment. It is absorbed by the patient's own assimilatory effort.

In Dr. Elkisch's case we also see a sort of magic influence utilized as a therapeutic force. Speech, the verbal contact, did not seem to play as great a part in this case as in other cases. We heard that in the beginning Dr. Elkisch spoke almost-nothing. She met her patient, who was in a state of emotional disorganization, who, therefore, was susceptible to magic gestures more than he was to verbalization, on the patient's own magic level. Much of the identification, so important for the success in therapy, took place not because of what Dr. Elkisch said, but because of what she did. Both mother and child identified with Dr. Elkisch. This identification brought about emotional growth in the mother, and the child then identified with a gradually improving image of his mother. Such an operation which is conducted on a nonverbal, magic level has a definite place in the therapeutic process. As long as we know that it exists, and also why it is indicated, we need no excuse for using it.

A word about the influence of music. I have been interested in this influence for a long time; it is also generally known that music has an influence on human emotions. What seems particularly important, however, is the fact that music which reaches our sensory organs in form of sound waves, does not have to be "understood" to have its emotional effect. Other forms of art have mostly some literary content, and — except, perhaps, for some nonobjective art — have to be "understood" to be impressive. Of all the arts, music is one which is most direct, one that may perhaps reach our subcortical centers without having to be first decoded by our cortex. Ingrained as a peculiar force in the minds of mankind, it has been used by mothers of all countries at all times for definitely sedative purposes in putting their infants to sleep. These mothers have instinctively felt the soporific value of their little cradle songs, which did not have to be understood to be effective. The scientist may wonder whether in such cases the effect is due to the melody, the rhythmic pattern of the lullaby or to the fact that it derives from the person of a mother, a source of protection and security; but there is no doubt that whatever the active agent, it reaches the unconscious of the child, the level on which it can be most effective. In Dr. Elkisch's case it was as though "on the wings of the song" the unconscious of the mother was speaking to the unconscious of her child: an example of a therapy on a nonverbal level.

To summarize, the success obtained in Dr. Elkisch's case was initiated and brought to an advanced stage, first by the use of magic gestures — rather than of words, and — then — by the use of another nonverbal medium, namely, music.

Camille K. Cayley, M.D. The neurotic child is just one part of the neurotic network of the family. What does this mean practically? It means that one should not choose to treat children in a vacuum but, under ideal conditions, one should attempt to treat children in a vacuum but, under ideal conditions, one should attempt to treat every neurotic member of the household where the maladjusted child lives, including the child itself.

According to the classical freudian concept, each member of a family should be treated by a separate psychiatrist. However, within the framework of our economic system this cannot always be realized.

Some psychiatrists practice by choice individual therapy for the child alone, without including the nosogenic key-parent. Some must do this because they are lacking the double training required to include both parent and child in therapy. Others feel so much stronger an identification with the child than with the parent that they are unable to establish the right transference with the adult.

There are child analysts who treat the child analytically and offer to the parents only guidance on a purely conscious level at regular or irregular intervals.

Then we find therapists who treat patients and children concomitantly, but in different sessions.

Dr. Elkisch's method — treating mother and child simultaneously in the same sessions — represents a novel form of psychotherapy.

In addition to the above described four direct treatment methods, there is a fifth group of therapists who believe in an indirect treatment of the child, where all the analysis is given to the parent alone, and the child is not treated at all. (Freud used this method in one of his cases.) In this case, the parent becomes a sort of assistant to the analyst, using everyday living with the child as a prolonged therapeutic session. The parent's therapist becomes a modified control analyst for the treatment of the child.

The $64-question is — Which of the above-mentioned five treatment methods is the best? Unfortunately, there is no clear-cut answer to this difficult question. Even the Utopia of having a separate analyst for each sick member of the family cannot be considered as ideal. Psychoanalysis represents such an individualized skill that I cannot visualize three or four analysts all engaged in curing the various members of the same family. Such a family, undoubtedly, would be confused by the various approaches of the individual analysts. Furthermore, psychotherapists are human beings also. It would be hard for them to eliminate their competitive drives for therapeutic success within the same family.

My criticism of the superficial guidance of the parents is that by this method no real character change can be achieved.

The concomitant analytic treatment of parent and child in different sessions requires an unusually skilled and well-trained therapist, an individual who is equally capable of handling parents and children. Such therapists are rare, and Dr. Elkisch's method requires even a more unusual therapist, namely, one with the best emotional balance, the greatest talent and the most heterogeneous training.

It would be a mistake to believe that even an indirect treatment of the parent alone — without therapy of the child — can be successful in the hands of a therapist who has no training in child psychiatry, as the core of the problem is a faulty parent-child *relationship,* and not the neurosis of the parent alone. If the child happens to have psychosomatic problems, then pediatric knowledge is also desirable. Only proper pediatric training can give the security to dare disregard sometimes alarming somatic symptoms and handle them on a psychological level.

Finally, the therapist has another difficult task. He has to handle his double counter-transference in a very healthy and skilled way. Because of the emotional appeal that children have on most of us, we have to be constantly on guard in order not to over identify ourselves with the child at the expense of the parent.

It is obvious that the training and attitude of the therapist will determine the choice of the technique. I think that with a mildly maladjusted child, where one feels that neither the child nor the mother is ready for a long therapeutic program, or where there are economic, geographical or time obstacles in the way, guidance is the choice technique. Not all analysts agree with me here.

If the child is more severely disturbed and the treatment of the mother and child is not feasible for some reason, either by one or two psychiatrists, one should choose the sicker member of the family for intensive individual therapy. Sometimes this is the mother, sometimes the child. The other member receives only infrequent and superficial guidance. If the child is less than five or six years old, very often indirect therapy is just as successful as combined therapy of mother and child.

Finally, in case of adolescence or pre-adolescence, one can have success even when one disregards the more sick parent and concentrates on the adolescent alone with minimum guidance to the adults involved.

Dr. Elkisch's work is a shining example of the present trend in psychotherapy to improve our techniques. There is a general tendency now to retain the original concepts of Freud and to modify his original techniques in the hope of achieving equally good results in a shorter time, with a greater number of patients. Dr. Elkisch's departure from the original technique is certainly a worthwhile addition to our psychiatric armamentarium.

Paula Elkisch, Ph.D. (concluding remarks): First of all, I should like to thank all the discussants for their generous acceptance of my paper. I realize that the topic itself which suggests an experiment with a new approach has stimulated your thoughts in a productive way. In turn your thoughts have stimulated my thinking again — so I feel very grateful for the "give-and-take" that has been going on between us.

To answer the many and pertinent questions that have been asked, or to respond to the suggestions I have received, would mean writing another paper, or actually more than one. I certainly will keep these questions in mind and hope to be able to respond to them at some later date.

Some of you, it seems to me, have taken the material I presented and put it into a different context, as it were, thus shedding new light on the subject. I should like to respond to at least some of those comments. To Dr. Gutheil I must confess that I have not been conscious of using "magic" in my approach other than meeting the child on the level on which he happened to be and, it is true, on that level "magic" was still operating magic in terms of Ferenczi's descriptive conceptuology. Through his elaboration on that concept here and now, Dr. Gutheil has opened a new vista for therapy on a nonverbal or preverbal level. Also Dr. Hulse's specific suggestions represent a stimulus for further and more detailed elaborations, suggestions for which I am very grateful.

I wish I had the time to formulate my thoughts that have been stimulated by all the speakers. However, instead, I have come to an end, once more assuring each of you of my gratitude.

REFERENCES

[1.] Bender, L.: "Schizophrenia in Childhood." Paper read at the Symposium on Childhood Schizophrenia, at the Midwinter Meeting of the American Psychoanalytic Association, New York City, 1951.

[2.] Brody, M. W.: The symbolic significance of twins in dreams." *The Psychoanalytic Quarterly,* Vol. XXI, No. 2, April 1952, pp. 172-180.

[3.] Elkisch, P.: Children's drawings in a projective technique. *Psychological Monographs,* Vol. 58, No. 1, 1945, pp. 12-15.

[4.] Escalona, S. K.: Paper read at the Symposium on Childhood Schizophrenia at the Midwinter Meeting of the American Psychoanalytic Association, New York City, 1951.

[5.] Fromm-Reichmann, F.: *Principles of Intensive Psychotherapy.* The University of Chicago Press, 1950.

[6.] Mahler, M. S.: On child psychosis and schizophrenia: Autistic and symbiotic infantile psychoses. Paper read at the 17th International Psychoanalytic Congress, Amsterdam, 1951. *The Psychoanalytic Study of the Child,* Vol. VII, 1952.

[7.] Mahler, M.S.: "Early Developmental Stages of the Ego (with Special Emphasis on the Mother-Child Primary Unit)." Unpublished paper read in Philadelphia, November, 1951.

[8.] Mahler, M. S., Ross, J. R. and De Fries, Z.: Clinical studies in benign and malignant cases of childhood psychosis (schizophrenia-like), *American Journal of Orthopsychiatry,* Vol. XIX, 2, April, 1949, pp. 295-305.

[9.] Schilder, P.: *The Image and Appearance of the Human Body,* Psyche Monograph, No. 4, Kegan, Paul, Trench, Trubner, London, 1935, p. 202.

[10.] Schilder, P.: *The Image and Appearance of the Human Body,* Psyche Monograph, No. 4, Kegan, Paul, Trench, Trubner, London, 1935, p. 43.

[11.] Schwarz, H.: The mother in the consulting room: Notes on the psychoanalytic treatment of two young children. *The Psychoanalytic Study of the Child,* Vol. V, 1950.

[12.] Silberpfenning-Kestenberg, J.: Early fears and early defenses. Selected problems. *The Nervous Child,* Vol. 5, No. 1, 1946, pp. 56-70.

[13.] Spitz, R. A.: Psychiatric therapy in infancy. *Amer. J. Orthopsychiatry,* Vol. XX, 3, July, 1950, pp. 623-33.

[14.] Spitz, R. A.: Anaclitic depression. *The Psychoanalytic Study of the Child,* Vol. II, 1947.

Chapter 13

The Simultaneous Treatment of a Mother and Child: The Mother's Side*

EILEEN BERRYMAN-SIMPSON

THE importance of the mother in the treatment of young children has been stressed more and more in recent years and increasing efforts are being made to include her in her child's therapy. In clinics a social worker frequently sees her. In private practice the child's therapist may see her once a month. She may become more intimately involved, as described by Elkish (1), when mother and child are seen at the same time. An adaptation of Elkisch's method by the author was reported in *Amer. J. Psychother.* (2.) In that case, the tie between mother and child was pathologic and had to be dealt with delicately in order to ensure the successful treatment of the child and essential modification of the mother-child relationship. Since then, mothers have been invited to listen in on sessions of young children — always of course with the child's knowledge — and many do so once or twice in the beginning, and from time to time during treatment. Occasionally there is a mother who, while seemingly free to let the child move separately, is more closely tied to him than appears at first — for example, in most cases of school phobia in young children (3) — and therefore becomes more deeply involved in the child's treatment.

When it was routinely suggested to Mrs. T that she might want to listen in on her daughter's sessions, because she, like many mothers, would find it hard to turn her child over to a stranger and might feel uneasy about what was going on in the playroom, she promptly rejected the idea and says in retrospect:

Note: Reprinted by permission of the author and the *American Journal of Psychotherapy, 17:*266-274, 1963.

I was struck by this notion. I, at least, couldn't have cared less. So great was my relief at the sharing of responsibility for her that I would have turned her over to the milkman if he'd asked.

But her attitude changed abruptly at the end of one month and she became intensely eager to be involved in each of her daughter's sessions.

Because it is difficult to know how mothers feel when their child is in treatment, how they feel about the therapist, what mistakes were made either from their point of view or in actual fact, and because it is so important to know these things to secure their cooperation, especially through difficult periods, and to insure the best possible therapeutic results, I considered sending a questionnaire to each of them after termination. I thought that formulating the questions would be easier if one case was explored in detail first.

When this was suggested to her, Mrs. T seemed interested and willing to cooperate. She had once been a writer and it was hoped that writing such a report would not be the burden for her it would be most mothers; rather, it was felt writing was perhaps the only way she could freely express her feelings because, although not inarticulate, she was extremely introverted and shy and found it painful to talk about herself. Her intelligence, honesty, and the fact that the newly terminated treatment was still fresh in her mind made her eminently suitable.

CASE HISTORY

To understand Mrs. T's comments better, a brief review of her daughter's treatment is in order. Penny was brought for testing when she was five years and two months old at the urgent, not to say hysterical, suggestion of the headmistress of the school where she was in kindergarten. Her teacher found her unmanageable. She was unwilling to take direction, behaved peculiarly (hiding under desks, taking off her clothes, screaming, laughing inappropriately) and was a disruptive influence in the class. Mrs. T said that at home she was all of this and more — that she was "odd," remote, behaved strangely, and was excessively dependent on her sister who was two years older. By the end of the history-taking session it was clear that Mrs. T thought she was schizophrenic and Mr. T regarded her as retarded.

Penny, when tested, was clearly neither. She had an IQ of 135 and although extremely restless was friendly, moderately cooperative, and basically attractive looking. The Rorschach suggested that her major problem was intense hostility (toward whom was not clear) which she was trying to disguise, less and less successfully, by passivity and docility. She thought of herself as "an ugly little bird" and had an ego and ego defenses about as strong as one. Her sister seemed to be the dominant and maternal figure. The tentative plan for treatment was to investigate this hostility, her relationship to her sister, and to change her self-concept

Mr. and Mrs. T are extremely well-endowed parents, attractive, gifted, sportive, and well off. Early in his career Mr. T had been recognized as an outstanding research scientist. His wife was equally intelligent and talented. Sally, Penny's older sister, was the first in her class, extroverted, athletic, and very popular. In this household Penny was a freak — small, timid, unathletic, friendless, slow in school, and capable of making herself unattractive and even seemingly dull-witted.

Treatment lasted two years, during which time Penny was seen twice a week. Mrs. T after the first month, had one interview a week and in the last six months of treatment one every two weeks. After the first three months the child's bizarre behavior disappeared. Learning how to express and control hostility was indeed the major problem as the Rorschach suggested. In a year she was behaving normally but was still timid and while she had, after great difficulty, learned to read, to ride a bike, to assert herself from time to time, it took another six months to get her to function as well as she is able. She is now at the top of the class and happily in this family, is not afraid of riding, swimming, skating — all the things she used to hate. Since she has a very attractive and charming manner, she is a great success with her teachers and has, as she said in a recent follow-up session, "millions of friends."

MRS. T'S REPORT

In the initial letter Mrs. T was asked if she would write a detailed account of what, for her, had occurred in the course of Penny's treatment; to recall what she could of her feelings before she brought Penny and at various stages of treatment; how she felt about the therapist, what had pleased and what had disturbed her most, at what times she wanted to terminate before treatment was finished, and how she feels now. In reply she wrote the following:

> Let me say now that I will do my best to cooperate to the extent of writing the detailed and candid account you require — but also that I'm afraid I expect to find the assignment more unsettling than interesting.

Mrs. T was urged not to continue if it turned out, in fact, to be unsettling; but if she felt she could go on with it to do so with no sense of haste, and if she found anything particularly painful, to leave it out with just a note that she had done so.

In less than a month an 11-page report arrived, which both moved and astonished me. If there were sufficient space, it would be worth publishing *in toto*. Since there is not, I will quote directly what seems most useful.

Feelings Before Treatment

> I find that the outstanding thing about my state of mind for the first five years is that I had no feeling about her (Penny) at all. I used to forget her. A number of times I put her outside in her carriage and left her there — in the rain, or dark.

Going even further back, Mrs. T talks about the time before her pregnancies. Her husband was reluctant to have children because he was very much afraid he would make no better father than his own had been and because he and Mrs. T had a very close relationship which he did not want interfered with.

> I reassured him by telling him that the children would be in the nature of a hobby for me and would make no change in our personal relationship or way of life.

Although Mrs. T says, "I never enjoyed such prolonged periods of both physical and mental well-being as during both pregnancies" — as soon as Sally, the older girl, was born, Mrs. T set about concealing the love she felt for her from her husband because she felt that somehow she was being disloyal to him. Despite the anxiety this deception caused her, they decided to have another child as soon as possible so that "a closeness in age would make the children companionable and leave us freer." This pregnancy temporarily restored mother's sense of well-being. Penny was born prematurely and her mother did not see her at all until she came home from the hospital a month later.

> During this time I felt exceedingly depressed. I worried about her, but not as much as I ought to have. I kept thinking when she came home I'd find that I loved her. But instead I found that there was barely enough love to go around between the other two and when I tried to give more it seemed to deplete the very source. So I gave Penny the mechanical attentions and motherliness that I had given spontaneously, though furtively, to her older sister.

Despite all this, for the first four years, "Penny seemed calm and jolly and self-sufficient." The onset of her difficulties occurred when Penny was about four and a half years old; at that time she began to be withdrawn, behaved inappropriately, and often cried almost inconsolably at bedtime.

> We discovered that Sally could comfort her much more quickly than I could and we encouraged her to do so as it left me free to give attention to my husband. But by this time, my husband was having a pretty thin time of it too as the attention I gave to anyone was strictly phony. I became more and more tightly wound until I had spells of trembling. During the day I brooded over the children. Penny appeared to be slipping back into babyhood. The two girls grew closer together into a little dark, sly, unwholesome world where I was shut out. Their relationship seemed to be almost incestuous with its vague erotic overtones. I worried about Penny's being retarded, and Sally unprincipled. The atmosphere was on the one hand feeble-minded, on the other corrupt.

More and more desperate, she found she needed a barbiturate and a drink to get through the day, and this was followed by headaches and attacks of asthma with "terrifying anxiety and fear of suffocation." Attempts to distract herself, to go back to the writing she had done before marriage, all failed. She began to feel trapped and to daydream of running away. It was therefore a great relief to her when the principal of the school suggested that Penny needed "outside help."

Many child therapists, I think, may find it typical that most of the facts about Penny were known to the therapist before her treatment had been going on very long, but almost none of those about Mrs. T. Her intense anxiety, asthma attacks, desire to run away were all hidden behind a facade of competence, cooperativeness, punctuality, and willingness to talk about Penny.

Treatment Proper

As so often happens, there was a crisis at the end of the first month. Penny had had some superficial relief of symptoms and then abruptly regressed. Mr. T called and clearly needed reassurance. Neither he nor Mrs. T had any insight into the fact that her regression was caused by Mrs. T's panic (a panic we later discovered she always felt under these circumstances) at leaving Penny to go with her husband on a ten-day vacation. As she remembers it:

> My husband was perturbed because you did not have an M.D. or a Ph.D. at least and while I felt that experience might be worth more than the Ph.D., at least I did think that you might have made an error, that Penny might slip through our fingers and have to be institutionalized.

During the first month it had become clear that Mrs. T must not be allowed to turn Penny over to the therapist as she had turned her over first to the nurse, then to Sally, and as she would have to the milkman. Mrs. T became very resentful of the therapist to the point where treatment was threatened. Sally had to be replaced by Mrs. T as mother, and Mrs. T had to be helped to accept, and eventually it was hoped, to enjoy this role. But for the first time it was dramatically clear that her lack of interest in Penny and in the treatment were part of a facade and that actually she and Penny were so deeply tied together, so identified, that she suffered enormous separation anxiety when she had to go off with her husband.

After this first crisis, when asked if she would like to come more frequently, say once a week, Mrs. T readily agreed and she also began listening in on Penny's sessions. Although she says:

> At no time, incidently, did I feel any jealously of you over Penny. I felt jealous, as you know, of Sally regarding Penny and also of my husband regarding you — particularly when I seemed to myself the great All-American Flop. But throughout the treatment, I felt a kind of steadfastness in Penny's pursuit of me that never really wavered. At the time — which lasted so long — when I couldn't respond to her, I found this tenacity irritating. Later, when I could and did respond, I found it tremendously moving. . . .

She does admit to very complicated feelings about what I was doing to her child.

> It wasn't long after that I did start listening in on Penny's sessions and after I'd overcome some aversion to "spying" that I began to fear you were suggesting — implanting, actually, preoccupations of a murkiness and sophistication which her mind could not possibly have held before and might even "drive her crazy" if she were not so to begin with. . . . I then became very vigilant. . . . I listened with the greatest care for any sign of deviousness. I don't mean for anything I might consider unethical but rather for any moral obtuseness in your character. Reassurance cannot be said to come at any specific point but emerges over a period of time and exposure. I cannot over-emphasize the importance of this, however, as until such a trust is established no real commitment is made — and once it is, a continuity is felt and one is willing to go along with almost any technique or emotion however incomprehensible at the time. To this end I was much impressed by your willingness to let me listen. . . .

Mrs. T. then went on to say,

> I was concerned that you be honest and straightforward without slyness or deceit or tricks. If this seems fantastic to you, remember that to the layman a psychologist seems armed with very special knowledge which the layman holds in almost supernatural dread. . . . I believe I simply required that you be a kind of worldly boy scout.

From this one might suppose that she was particularly disturbed by hearing the working out of Penny's oedipal problems, particularly since the child's resistance to this subject was enormous. One would expect a mother to react strongly to such sessions and in fact most therapists would say that it would cause more harm than good to have the mother hear them, and that it might be dangerous. In this case, despite the above, I do not think it was true. Mrs. T, like other mothers before her, had been carefully prepared for this part of the treatment. What would be said had been gone over in her private sessions, and in any case her fantasies about Penny's fantasies always far exceeded the repugnant notion of the child's attachment to her father. No, what she was really guarding against was the theft of her child by the therapist — by changing Penny so that she would be un-recognizable (if we only had half the power we're supposed to have!) or by taking Sally's place and excluding her when now she was eager to be the mother.

> There were a number of times throughout treatment . . . when I thought Penny seemed so much improved that she was ready to stop. I was leery of too much psychologizing; I was worried about her becoming too dependent on you, becoming too absorbed in herself or even in a kind of brain-washing effect which would leave her too well adjusted; happy but sappy.

Getting her to discuss this aspect was by far the most difficult part of therapy, not because she was afraid of hurting my feelings, but because she was afraid to recognize the strength of her feelings for Penny and her fear of the therapist as a rival. If the threat to break treatment came at the usual times — after vacation, or in a plateau — and the need for continuing was explained to Mrs. T, she readily agreed. But when it concerned Penny's relationship to me or Mrs. T's to me, it was far more difficult.

> Some time toward the end of the first year the treatment seemed to me to become bogged down. It occurred to me that it was your fault, that you might have become emotionally attached to Penny and be unconsciously prolonging treatment. Alternatively I thought I might be doing the same thing with regard to you since some of our sessions appeared to me as little more than pleasant chats which I enjoyed.

These "pleasant chats" occurred when this mother was unable and unwilling to use her sessions as so many mothers do, to talk about themselves. An effort was being made not to talk about Penny but to get her to express her feelings, her anxieties, to talk about her childhood.

> I felt a number of breakthroughs, however, invariably after either Penny or I had been pushed to bring up painful material. In my case this amounted to my being very specific about those times in my own childhood which I feared to re-live through Penny, or those characteristics which I found most unattractive in myself and believe

Penny shared. At these times I had to force myself to return to your office. It seemed to me that once this was all hauled out of me (and the necessity explained) and the information relayed to Penny, she lost little time in extricating herself and presenting herself purposively in a more attractive light. Everything moved very swiftly after this.

That Mrs. T was deeply identified with Penny and that this treatment was very much hers as well as the child's, the therapist felt, but the degree to which this was true was only clear later!

> ... the high point came near the end when Penny cut loose with the paint jars and clay. Ah those were happy days. Since you were generous enough to share the details, the entire family was able to join in — our pleasure lessened only by envy at the hand that wielded the goo.

Later Mrs. T continued.

> Throughout the treatment I also experienced an overwhelming surge of what I guess is called libido ... I became as oversensitized (to all but Penny) as a spiritualist ... I started writing again. I wrote furiously, against time, haunted by the fear that when the treatment was finished my creativity would turn out to have been spurious.

At first Mrs. T mentioned her writing in a very oblique way and was reassured more than once that it would be good for her to go back to it. Typically she never volunteered any information about what she wrote, and when asked how it was going always changed the subject.

The most surprising and unpredictable revelation was the depth of her transference to the therapist and how greatly it resembled that of an adult directly in treatment (quite unlike what occurred with Mrs. M [2]). But not only did it never come up directly in our sessions but also the first report only hinted at it by saying, "Much of the time my own involvement overshadowed my concern for Penny. I was altogether dazzled and often dismayed by the parts being played by me, or, if particularly unacceptable, by you." When pressed for more details she wrote the following.

> As to the roles you played. . . . those of mother, sister, friend and lover. I should like to say father, as that seems to me to make good psychological sense, but if this was so I wasn't conscious of it. I'm sorry too because perhaps it would have cleared up my feelings about my father and even more his feelings toward me which *so* baffled me.

Perhaps the most difficult period for her and the one least

comprehensible at the time was when it became clear that Penny was near the end of treatment. Before I prepared Penny, Mrs. T and I discussed it. She agreed and said her husband also had been thinking that Penny was really well. But two weeks later she came for her session very much depressed (she had long since stopped listening to Penny's sessions and was only seen once every two weeks) and immediately announced that Penny had completely regressed and was worse than ever. Surprised since I had not yet discussed termination with Penny, I tried to reassure Mrs. T that somehow the child must have sensed what was planned and was reacting as many children do in the last few weeks. This regression was spurious. It was a last attempt to hold on to the departing neurosis and to convince everyone that she was not well enough to stop. How little Mrs. T was reassured I did not know until. . .

> Toward the end I recall one particularly bad time . . . Penny made a last ditch stand. All the worst symptoms reappeared at once and I was unprepared. I collapsed into the deepest depression I ever felt. And there I sat, with all the fight gone out of me, feeling indifferent and suicidal for several days. For the first time since I'd taken Penny for treatment I had trouble again in breathing. I had no memory of when or how this ended. I suppose that when Penny's symptoms subsided so did mine.

What happened here is that Mrs. T was reacting to termination, not Penny, who didn't know about it and who was fine, and I think we see this clearly here:

> After termination, I found I had to break the habit of thinking and remembering what I had to say to you — resulting in long conversations held with myself. There were times when undecided and panicky over some problem, I wanted to rush to the telephone . . . but mostly I felt a sense of loss — and I felt nostalgia not for the roles you played with such virtuosity but for the person I'd caught a glimpse of whom I liked.

The actual end of treatment, the period I'd been preparing for when the mother and daughter would have a month together without the older sister before Penny's last session, was like this:

> The month that Sally was away, which was also toward the very end of treatment, was a wonderful climax. In the beginning Penny and I were able to discuss and share our sadness instead of withdrawing to nurse it separately — and it soon went away. Then, after eyeing each other with a certain weariness, we began to draw closer together. It

was all rather formal, like a dance begun tentatively while we learned the steps and finished fast with great fun and bravura. It was a very touching experience and my husband shared in it with pleasure and ease.

This pace was slowed, naturally, since termination. At times it stops altogether, at others it slips backwards. We both get discouraged and tired. It's a constant struggle for Penny to maintain her sense of identity against the stronger personality of her older sister, and for me to see that she gets the opportunity. But Penny and I have faith in our relationship now, and a perspective on its fluctuations.

Mrs. T has given an extraordinarily useful and illuminating account of one case of a mother and child therapy — corroborating and correcting, solving problems and raising others. Despite its uniqueness and idiosyncracy, it is hoped that this account will be useful to anyone treating children and struggling to improve and perfect the method.

SUMMARY

Because there is considerable speculation and little direct evidence about a mother's feelings when her child is in treatment, an attempt was made to investigate this problem in detail. The case of one mother, who had been intimately involved in her child's therapy, was selected because the mother was willing and able, at termination, to give a detailed account of her feelings before therapy began, at the various stages while it was going on, and immediately after it was over.

Following a brief history of the child's treatment, quotations, taken from the mother's 11-page report, are commented on and analyzed by the therapist in the hope that the insights so gained will be useful to other therapists, and will be helpful in improving techniques in handling mothers whose children are in treatment.

REFERENCES

1. Elkisch, P.: Simultaneous treatment of a mother and her child, *Amer. J. Psychother.*, 7:105, 1953.
2. Berryman, E.: Simultaneous treatment of mother and child, *Amer. J. Psychother.*, 9:821, 1957.
3. Berryman, E.: School phobias: Management problems in private practice, *Psychol. Rep.*, 5:19, 1959.

Chapter 14

An Approach to Childhood Psychosis: Simultaneous Treatment of Mother and Child*

KENNETH H. GORDON, JR.

W ITH simultaneous treatment of mother and child, one can examine their relationship to each other and the disturbances that exist in it. In childhood psychoses the relationship is usually disturbed, and simultaneous treatment can be of use in understanding and modifying it. This approach can illuminate powerful forces which tie the mother and child together and which foster the development and continuation of psychopathology. Through observing the circumstances under which this occurs, one can learn how to act as an insulator between mother and child by helping them to see what has been going on and to see each other as separate, individual human beings. The following cases were chosen to demonstrate this technical approach and to show some of the dynamic forces at work in childhood psychoses.

CASE REPORTS

Stanley

Stanley S was referred at six and a half years of age. He had had several months of treatment by a previous therapist who was leaving the city. The chief complaints were negativistic behavior, lack of friends, inability to get along with anyone, treating inanimate objects as if they were animate and animate as if they

Note: Reprinted by permission of the author and the Journal of the American Academy of Child Psychiatry, 2:711-724, 1961.

were inanimate, enuresis and encopresis. These symptoms had been present since the age of three when his brother was born. Stanley's conception six weeks after his parents' marriage was unplanned. During her pregnancy Mrs. S had vomited frequently. Stanley was described as a happy, cuddly baby who enjoyed his bottles. At six months he weighed 26 pounds. Mother had started a vigorous program of toilet training at that time because Stanley had severe diaper rash and could not wear rubber pants. This effort was not successful. At the age of one and a half he developed coeliac syndrome with diarrhea, swollen abdomen, and weight loss. This condition required a great deal of medical care. Following the birth of his brother, Stanley became increasingly disorganized. His mother then entered psychotherapy, seeking help because she could not manage the confusion at home.

When I first saw Stanley he was crestfallen about his doctor having left him. He continued to be quite disorganized, manifested bizarre behavior, drooled, and used many neologisms. His mother complained that he was impossible, never did anything she told him to do, and was always soiled and wet. He made constant demands for toys from his mother, but when they were given to him he soon broke or lost them. She interpreted to him that he was wishing for love and not toys; when her interpretations proved ineffectual she was upset because she could not be a good psychiatrist for him.

During four months in which I utilized the common techniques for dealing with very disturbed children such as siding with what healthy ego there was, operating as auxiliary ego, and permitting certain regressive satisfactions, the overall situation went from bad to worse. After consultation with the mother's therapist I finally asked the mother of this dirty and very miserable little boy to join us in our treatment sessions, explaining that there might be something going on between her and the child which was preventing progress in treatment. Mrs. S was described by her therapist as a borderline schizophrenic, a diagnosis that on superficial observation was difficult to accept. She wore tasteful clothing and makeup like a glamorous movie queen and appeared to be most poised and sophisticated. Her doctor suspected that she saw Stanley as her own psychotic self.

We worked together for several weeks. When at Stanley's suggestion we played Hansel and Gretel he insisted that mother was the witch. This upset her a great deal. She said that she did not want to be a bad witch and get killed and she very reluctantly played that part in the game. She participated much more actively if allowed to be Gretel or Hansel.

Stanley later turned to playing the game "Sorry" and other board games with us. I noticed that whenever Stanley counted his moves he would drool, expel flatus and feces, say that the flatus was machine gun fire or an explosion that killed us all, and talked about eating B.M. bombs; he acted as if he were not counting properly. In spite of the latter, he usually ended up on the right space on the board. Mother would then pick up his token, berate him for his stupid sloppiness, and do the counting over again for him. I pointed out to her that it seemed that she had to have Stanley wrong even when he was right. Perhaps she needed him to be wrong in other ways as well, unable to get along with people, always messy and dirty. She seemed startled, and said slowly, "You are right. Somehow, and I don't know why, I have been expecting him to be sick for me." I was quite impressed by this response to my pointing out their pathogenic interaction. However, when I saw them four days later, Mrs. S had not combed her hair or taken a bath since previous session and appeared to be quite disorganized. Stanley, on the other hand, looked like a normal American boy, chipper, not drooling, clean, full of life, and asking to play games. His mother thereupon said that she refused to go along with any more of this kind of treatment; that I could see Stanley as much as I wanted to by myself, but she would not participate because it was just upsetting to her and was making her "come apart at the seams." Thereupon she dismissed herself.

I went back to working with Stanley. He arrived at the next session dirty, had soiled his pants, was drooling, and was the picture of the completely disorganized child. However, with continued separate treatment during the following two years, his mother was more and more able to allow Stanley to be himself. He progressed to the point where he became able to go to the appropriate grade in a public school instead of the private school for disturbed children he previously attended and he had stopped wetting and soiling. He was most pleased about growing up. Psychological studies two years later showed no evidence of a psychotic disturbance. Five-year follow-up revealed solid personality development.

Simultaneous treatment in this case led to a clarification of the interrelationships between mother and child; it revealed that this child was psychotic for his disturbed mother. Although the experience was extremely upsetting to the mother, the understanding she gained through observation of her own behavior apparently enabled her to make an important giant step in her own treatment so that she could allow Stanley to live his own life instead of being a part of her, her dirty self. This mutual acting as one person I regard as indicative of a continuation of the oneness of the symbiotic relationship of the child and mother during the first year of life. Until the changes effected by treatment, the mother appeared to be unable to give up the closeness or let the boy individuate; this had led to the development of psychosis in the boy.

Lois

Lois L was brought to the clinic at the age of two and three-quarter years because her mother thought she was psychotic. She was "acting like a baby," had bowel movements in her pants, and had many fears, especially a phobia of trucks. She would not play with other children. Lois had a sister one year younger. The maternal grandmother and aunt both had chronic schizophrenic conditions. Mrs. L had been in psychotherapy for some years; she had many emotional problems including "kleptomaniac tendencies." Her treatment had not improved her relationship with Lois whom she thought of as her "feeble-minded sister" or psychotic mother.

Lois, a lovely little girl with platinum-blonde hair, and her mother came to the playroom together. She painted "a crying boy in bed. His mother socked him on the tussy and he felt better. He got socked for wee-wee-ing." Mother looked uncomfortable and interrupted, saying "That story is typical of Lois. She has a problem with a primitive conscience." Lois became angry with me for talking with her mother and asked to leave the room. I said that running away was one way to try and handle her worries, but it would be better to find out what was going on. She asked me to draw pictures for her, which I did and which she appreciated.

In the next session Mrs. L reported that the night before Lois used the toilet for her B.M. for the first time. The mother then indicated that she felt very uncomfortable about talking about the child in her presence. I encouraged her to talk, "because the problem is between the two of you and here's where we can figure it out. Lois is a real person and wants to figure this problem out too." They both appeared to enjoy the session.

The following week Lois arrived with mother and small sister, Lynne. Lois made a show of being affectionate to her sister. Lynne, a very pretty child, was quite aggressive toward Lois and her mother. Mrs. L said that Lois's passivity distressed her. Lois reminded Mrs. L of her weak sister, her weak mother who was in a state psychiatric hospital, and her own weak self. I said, "Yes, it does seem that you see Lois as your mother." She was surprised and said that she did not understand how I could think such a thing. I said that she had just told me this. She reflected on this, seemed amazed at what she had said, then agreed that it was so. While we were talking this way Lois made a picture of trucks. Mother and Lois together told me how Lois "protects" her sister from trucks. At that moment her sister started painting, whereupon Lois held onto her mother's breast. Mother frowned but nestled Lois and appeared to be treating her as if she were a baby. I said that perhaps Lois thought that the only thing to do was to be a baby for mother when mother expected her to be a baby. She stopped clinging to her mother and again the mother was amazed. When I was able to see what these people were doing, confront them with it while they were doing it so that there was no doubt in anybody's mind about the situation, they were able to pull away from each other and be more objective about what was going on.

Several weeks later, after a family vacation, Lois struggled to dress and undress her doll. Mrs. L said that at home Lois would ask her mother to do this for her. I commented on the difference and told them that I knew that Lois really did want to grow up.

Mrs. L said that at home Lois insisted on playing baby and the mother played along with her, even used diapers, because she always thought that Lois was cheated out of her babyhood by having a new baby come so soon. In response to this talk, Lois held onto her mother's breast and smirked. I suggested that perhaps Lois thought that her mother wanted her to act this way, to be a baby. I said that Lois really wanted to be allowed to grow up and not have to follow what she was taking as commands from her mother to be a baby and dirty and messy all the time. Mother said that she wanted Lois to grow up, and was coming here to get help to help her grow up. Following this, Lois went to nursery school and did well there. Mother was able to allow the child to separate from her and Lois stopped clinging to her mother all of the time. Mrs. L arranged for herself to so some part-time teaching.

Lois was apparently seen by her mother and expected by her to act as her own dirty self and as her own psychotic mother and sister. Lois responded to this by being dirty and infantile, clinging to mother's breast, and insisting on mother's constant presence even though she was more comfortable and performed quite adequately when away from her. When this was pointed out to them at the moment they were living it out, mother and child were subsequently able to separate from each other and the child was able to resume her normal ego and libidinal development. Her mother was able to seek out and obtain some sublimated gratifications instead of maintaining a precarious balance by perceiving and manipulating the child as a part of herself. It is my impression that children who give up ego functions to play an infantile part for a parent become trapped or fixed in this role and thus can end up permanently psychotic.

Jim

Jim J was referred at age fifteen because of bizarre bahavior after having had dozens of medical studies. As an infant, he had not appeared to be using his eyes; this led to repeated ophthalmologic examinations under anesthesia. Optic atrophy was diagnosed at age three and a half; this only partially interfered with his watching television and learning to read. Until the age of two years he was happy only if he was cuddled and rocked by his mother. He then became most interested in music. He did not talk until the age of three at which time "he started to sing and he has not been quiet since." When he began to talk it was to quote others, especially phonograph recordings; this persisted. He had often been diagnosed either as mentally defective or else as having superior intelligence. He once spent several months in a school for the blind. In the three years prior to treatment he had been described by various experts as suffering from childhood schizophrenia. Inasmuch as he always showed a desire to be close to and cuddle with his mother, it would appear that he was suffering from the symbiotic type of childhood psychosis. He had an unusual capacity at rote memory, apparently due to an inability to repress. There was in some examinations suggestive evidence of brain damage. He had a grand mal seizure at age twelve and since that time had been taking anticonvulsants.

When I first saw Jim he acted in a most bizarre fashion. At times he looked spastic, at other times defective, and appeared to be blind. He assumed odd postures such as putting his feet behind his neck; his speech was rambling and full of clang associations; he imitated recordings including applause and needle scratch. During an effort to perform a psychiatric examination I asked him his three wishes. He said, "You, you, and you," and kissed me. He wiped his nose on my Unabridged Webster while reading definitions aloud. When asked to copy a geometric figure, he not only turned it around but put his nose in the center of it and walked around it. When residential treatment could not be arranged, I agreed to see him in an effort at outpatient psychotherapy.

During several months of treatment I learned a great deal about how the unconscious part of the mind operates but was unable to get near Jim. He would do everything from spouting neologisms to making up new and very personal lyrics to "My Heart at Thy Sweet Voice" from "Samson and Delilah." Due to previous experience with simultaneous therapy I finally asked his mother to join us. She appeared to be trying so hard to be a good mother that she could hardly stand it. Jim put her on the spot whenever he could, either through making broadside accusations which led her to defending him as a sick child or through getting her to do things for him. Once he appeared to be in danger of tripping over a heater on the floor and Mrs. J and I both anxiously started to grab at him to prevent this. Our eyes met. We did not touch him and he skillfully avoided the heater by himself. Soon I realized and was able to point out to them that Jim was acting like a baby and expecting his mother to baby him. She said with surprise, "That is so. I've been doing this for sixteen years." She went on to say that this was the first time she had realized what was going on and now had hope that I would help her and her son to get out of an impossible situation. Jim said that he did not want to be a baby because it was too dangerous: "I would rather be crazy. Nonsense is better than nothing." I agreed with him but went on to say that I thought he had more choices than that. He said, "Your words are sweet, but you don't know what pain they mean. I wish they were as sweet as this candy we are eating."

In the third simultaneous session Jim said, "I am really and honestly going to be my own absolute self in talking to you." He then made a barely perceptible hissing sound as he had done in the past when imitating the needle scratch on records. I told him that this sounded to me like one more record and referred to how he had always tried to make me and everyone else into machines and that he seemed to be making himself into a mere record instead of a real live person. He launched into his various imitations and I said that he was not Shelly Berman, nor Franklin D. Roosevelt, not Thomas A. Edison, but his own self. He then spoke into the dictating machine, imitating various other people while saying that he was not any of them. He then said, "Mother, can you come over and act something out? (Mother mumbled something in the background.) I hope you enjoyed it very much" (laughter).

Dr.: Jim, what was it you wanted Mother to say in here?

J.: She wanted to say, ask you . . .

Dr.: What did *you* want her to say?

J.: I don't know because she didn't pay much attention to the recording except that she laughed at what I said that was funny.

Dr.: Now, wait a minute, Jim . . . I said, "What did *you* want

Mother to say?" and you said, *She* wanted to say" as if you . . . .

J.: Were what?

Dr.: As if there were no difference between what you wanted and what she wanted. Now, actually, she didn't want to talk, you wanted her to talk, and then she said, "she wanted to say something" when she didn't want to say anything.

J.: Well, that takes care of everything today, Dr. Gordon.

Dr.: No, wait, let's not polish it off that quickly. You see, you are you, she is she, and I am I. We are three different people. Here, in this room. Now.

J.: Well, that's all right. Well, how is it today, Dr. Gordon, in this room?

Dr.: And only three, only three.

J.: Well, that just about takes care of that so in thirty seconds we'll hear it back. One, two — THREE!

Again I said that he was himself. He then talked in a frightened boyish voice and said, "You're really so right, Dr. Gordon." He went on to talk for some time about how frightened he really was and that he still did believe that nonsense was better than nothing. I agreed with him. He said that I did not agree with him, that I thought that nonsense was the worst thing in the world. I pointed out how in his letter to me the previous week he had accused me of brainwashing him and of attempting to force him to give up his "nonsense." It was as if no matter what I did, he was going to try and make me think I was bad and feel guilty. I expected that he did this same thing to his mother and through playing on her sense of guilt pushed her into doing all kinds of things for him which did not really help him but kept him from growing up. At this point his mother added here that this was very much so and that in the past three weeks she had been able to stop some of the things she was doing but had a long way to go before she stopped all of them. For instance, until three weeks ago, she was bathing Jim. She stopped and his first bath alone took three hours and made a great wet mess. He now took about an hour to bathe himself but caused no more floods in the house. She stopped brushing his teeth for him. She said that she had suddenly become aware of how he would shout that he could not see to find a suit of his in the closet; so because of his poor vision she would come running to help. Yet she realized that for years now he would be laughing as she came in to help him and would actually be holding onto the very suit that he was asking her to get for him. In thousands of ways he would manage to get her to do for him. I asked her what this behavior reminded her of. She said that this was what happened between mother and baby, that this had been going on for sixteen years with Jim, and she was sure that this was a very bad thing for him.

Jim and his mother then both told me about his going to a public school music class the day before. When I had suggested that it was time for him to give up mother and to attend regular classes in school, he fought bitterly against going and was terribly frightened. He parodied Billy Sunday with "The return to school will mean the end of babysitting in America. Do you want your children to grow up to be Phi Beta Kappas and college professors, well-adjusted and creative citizens? I'll kick it as long as I have a foot . . . I'll punch it as long as I have a fist . . . I'll bite it as long as I have a tooth . . . and I'll fight to create an America which is so ignorant, so stupid, and so anti-Semitic that you will have to prime a man before he can think." However, he did go to school and did well, participated as a regular student in the classwork, took careful notes, and was most pleased with his performance. Both Jim and his mother expressed pleasure over the fact that Jim was able to master something and enjoy mastering it on his own. This very disturbed boy continues to develop as treatment progresses. However, even though he has decided that "sensibleness is better than nonsense" and is doing well in school, he is still an obviously disturbed person.

This situation appears to be one in which the mother responded to the child's need to continue the symbiotic union of infancy by functioning as ego for the symbiotic unit. The boy's efforts to grow out of the symbiotic unit showed up in a teasing kind of dependency. His increasingly apparent helplessness and dependency led to ever greater efforts on her part to act as auxiliary ego which aborted Jim's efforts to use his own ego. The symbiotic union which the boy fostered and prolonged was seen by him as a threat to his survival, to which he responded with autistic defenses (20). Whey they were confronted with the pathological relationship and it was interrupted, the mother was able to act as an individual person instead of an extension of the boy and to allow him to seek help for his own problems.

DISCUSSION

Perhaps the most striking phenomenon observed during simultaneous treatment is the emotional impact of insight manifested by amazement on the part of the mother. This could be called an "insight jolt" which is most dramatic and appears to have a profound therapeutic force. This is so even in cases where the mother had previously spoken of understanding how she and her child were stuck together in an impossible situation. Perhaps it is due to the primitive nature of the closeness of mother and child that it requires a living experience in therapy to make it truly conscious. Once mother and child become aware of what is going on, they usually bring constructive efforts into play to create a better living relationship. It is probable that primitive and highly cathected relationships between parent and child are involved in a host of behavioral and psychosomatic syndromes and that the existence of a symbiotic type of relationship between people has different implications and consequences in each stage of life. A study of this should lead to an understanding of those situations in which the simultaneous observation of two people would be therapeutically advantageous (11).

Burlingham (8) described a case which she supervised where a child and mother were analyzed by different analysts. She discovered that mother and child lived in a *folie à deux* where the mother was controlled by unconscious fantasies and the child's behavior was in reaction to her unconscious provocation. Sperling (23) reported findings from simultaneous analyses of children and their mothers in which the child's behavior was in response to the mother's unconscious wish. Sperling saw the mothers and children separately and the children were not told of their mothers' contact with the therapist. Johnson and Szurek (15, 16) have demonstrated that certain disturbed and delinquent children act out their parents' unconscious wishes. Schwarz (22) showed that having the mother in the consulting room could illuminate the mother-child interaction and obviate loyalty conflicts. Elkisch (10) used simultaneous treatment to observe and treat the disturbance in the mother-child relationship; this is, I believe, the essence of simultaneous treatment. Buxbaum (9) has demonstrated that with the mother present the child can obtain her approval and permission for his feelings and thoughts. Ackerman (1) believes that one can obtain therapeutic results in this way which are not possible otherwise. Other studies of this approach have been made by B. Bornstein (6), S. Bornstein (7), Jackson *et al.* (14), and Kolansky (17). In addition to these published papers, it is my impression that all child therapists utilze some simultaneous observation of mother and child whether it be observing their behavior in the consulting room, the waiting room, or on a home visit. Being present at the moment when a particular dynamic interplay comes into being allows one to see what goes on when it goes on. The therapist can confront the disturbed pair with these forces and interpret them. One can strike while the iron is hot to help them resolve the pathogenic relationship.

During the first year of life, the normal infant and mother develop an extremely close relationship which is mutually gratifying. This has been described by Benedek (3) and Mahler (18) as a symbiotic type of relationship. The mother supplies ego functions for this unit. Through doing certain things for the child to relieve his tensions the mother relieves her own tensions and obtains a kind of gratification. During the second year of life, the normal child becomes increasingly independent and begins to give up his mother as auxiliary ego as he develops ego functions of his own. At this time, regression to the primary, undifferentiated symbiotic stage appears to make the child feel threatened with the possibility of reengulfment and loss of identity (20). While some children appear to be unable to establish a symbiotic union with mother in the first months life, as is the case with the autistic type of psychotic child, others, for some reason, seem to be unable to function without a continuation of the symbiotic union and do not separate from their mothers and individuate. They later defend themselves against the symbiotic union with certain autistic defenses ("Nonsense is better than nothing") as is the case in the symbiotic type of childhood psychosis. Jim, case 3 in this chapter, appears to fall in this group of children.

In addition to these classical types of childhood psychoses, there is a large and diverse group of children with ego defects — (19), (21), and (27). Ego defects apparently can be due to inadequacy of function or absence of the mother in her role as auxiliary ego in supplying vital needs and healthful stimuli (24, 25, 26) or in providing a protective barrier against excessive stimuli (13). But in other cases, children respond to a need of a parent to continue the symbiotic union and may fail to individuate and will be infantile or psychotic for the parent (e.g. the cases of Stanley and Lois). In the latter group there is much acting out on the parts of both parent and child *(folie a deux)* and they appear to be able to understand the primitive impulses of each other (4, 2, 5, 8, 15, 16). The closeness which originally provided for the survival of the infant becomes the source of maladaptation. The child is caught in an impossible conflict: a) if he tries to go ahead and grow up, he fears he will be demolished either by the threats of the massive retaliation he expects due to opposing mother or by instinctual anxiety (12) caused by the new tendencies emerging due to normal libidinal development which he is not helped to control; b) regression to the symbiotic union also is seen as resulting in annihilation (20). The child then may resort to autistic defenses and so becomes psychotic. In certain cases, when the interaction between mother and child that has necessitated, the autistic defence on the part of the child is clearly delineated *in situ* for both, the mother's behavior may change, and the lack of necessity for the defense becomes clear to the child.

SUMMARY

Simultaneous treatment of mother and child appears to be useful in understanding and modifying disturbed mother-child relations. It offers a frontline observation post where one can see powerful forces interacting between parent and child. The immediacy of the situation appears to have a profound effect on the perceptive apparatus of all concerned and facilitates acceptance of the meaning of the perception. Understanding what they are doing can help both parent and child to interrupt their disturbed relationship, so that they each can begin to live as individual persons rather than acting out their lives playing a part in *folie à deux*. The parent who has been coercing her child into psychosis can begin to let him live his own life and the reluctantly involved parent who has been sucked into a *folie à deux* with a psychotic child can get out of the situation. Appropriate individual therapy can then be instituted.

REFERENCES

1. Ackerman, N. W.: *The Psychodynamics of Family Life*. New York: Basic Books, 1958.
2. Altman, L. L.: On the oral nature of acting out; a case of acting out between parent and child. *J. Amer. Psychoanal. Ass., 5:*648-662, 1957.
3. Benedek, T.: The psychosomatic implications of the primary unit: mother-child. *Amer. J. Orthopsychiat., 19:*642-654, 1949.
4. Benedek, T.: Parenthood as a developmental phase. *J. Amer. Psychoanal. Ass., 7:*389-417, 1959.
5. Bird, B.: A specific peculiarity of acting out. *J. Amer. Psychoanal. Ass., 5:*630-647, 1957.
6. Bornstein, B.: Phobia in a two-and-half-year-old child. *Psychoanal. Quart., 4:*93-119, 1935.
7. Bornstein, S.: A child analysis. *Psychoanal. Quart., 4:*190-225, 1935.
8. Burlingham, D.: (In co-operation with Alice Goldberger and Andre Lussier), Simultaneous analysis of mother and child. *The Psychoanalytic Study of the Child, 10:*165-186, New York: International Universities Press, 1955.
9. Buxbaum, E.: Technique of child therapy: A critical evaluation. *The Psychoanalytic Study of the Child, 9:*297-332. New York: International Universities Press, 1954.
10. Elkisch, P.: Simultaneous treatment of a child and his mother. *Amer. J. Psychother., 7:*31:105-121, 1953.
11. Fisher, H. K.: Personnal communication, 1961.
12. Freud, A.: *The Ego and the Mechanisms of Defense*. New York: International Universities Press. 1946, pp. 63-64, 1936.
13. Gordon, K. H.: Child with a defective stimulus barrier: Ego development during treatment. *A.M.A. Arch. Gen. Psychiat., 4:*483-493, 1961.
14. Jackson, D., *et al.: The Etiology of Schizophrenia*. New York: Basic Books, pp. 37-39; 323-440, 1960.
15. Johnson, A. and Szurek, S.: The genesis of antisocial acting out in

children and adults. *Psychonal. Quart., 21:*323-333, 1952.

16. Johnson, A. and Szurek, S.: Etiology of antisocial behavior in delinquents and psychopaths. *J.A.M.A., 154:*814-817, 1954.

17. Kolansky, H.: Treatment of a three-year-old girl's severe infantile neurosis: stammering and insect phobia. *The Psychoanalytic Study of the Child, 15:*261-285. New York: International Universities Press, 1960.

18. Mahler, M.: On child psychosis and schizophrenia: Autistic and symbiotic infantile psychoses. *The Psychoanalytic Study of the Child, 7:*286-305. New York: International Universities Press, 1952.

19. Mahler, M., Furer, M., and Settlage, C. F.: Severe emotional disturbances in childhood: psychosis. *American Handbook of Psychiatry, 1:*816-836. New York: Basic Books, 1959.

20. Mahler, M., and Gosliner, B. J.: On symbiotic child psychosis: Genetic, dynamic and restitutive aspects. *The Psychoanalytic Study of the Child, 10:*195-211. New York: International Universities Press, 1955.

21. Rank, B. and MacNaughton, D.: A clinical contribution to early ego development. *The Psychoanalytic Study of the Child, 5:*53-65. New York: International Universities Press, 1950.

22. Schwarz, H.: The mother in the consulting room: Notes on the psychoanalytic treatment of two young children. *The Psychoanalytic Study of the Child, 5:*343-357. New York: International Universities Press, 1950.

23. Sperling, M.: Children's interpretation and reaction to the unconscious of their mothers. *Int. J. Psychoanal., 31:*36-41, 1950.

24. Spitz, R. A.: Hospitalism: An inquiry into the genesis of psychiatric conditions in early childhood. *The Psychoanalytic Study of the Child, 1:*53-72. New York: International Universities Press, 1945.

25. Spitz, R. A.: Hospitalism: A follow-up report. *The Psychoanalytic Study of the Child, 2:*113-117, New York: International Universities Press, 1946.

26. Spitz, R. A.: The psychogenic diseases in infancy: An attempt at their etiologic classification. *The Psychoanalytic Study of the Child, 6:*255-274. New York: International Universities Press, 1951.

27. Weil, A.: Certain severe disturbances of early ego development. *The Psychoanalytic Study of the Child, 8:*271-287. New York: International Universities Press, 1953.

Chapter 15

Treatment of Under-fives by Way
of Their Parents*

ERNA FURMAN

W ORK with young children by way of their parents has been used widely both for prophylactic and therapeutic purposes. One of the basic premises for such work is the unique relationship between the mother and her under-five, an interaction characterized by an unusual mutual unconscious closeness. For this and other reasons the mother is in the position of under-standing and influencing her child during his first five years to an extent which will never be possible for her again. The under-five is particularly sensitive to his mother's feelings and attitudes. His relationship with her often brings to the fore aspects of his mother's personality which are not so readily affected by her other relationships. With the onset of latency the child's personality structure changes and his relationship with his mother loses these earlier striking qualities. The methods employed in working with mothers and young children are all based on the concept of the early mother-child relationship. Yet they vary considerably in different centers, and even from worker to worker, according to their interpretation of this concept and according to the aims of their work.

Roughly speaking there are three main approaches: a) To advise the mother directly as to educational methods, to suggest specific ways of handling certain situations, e.g. feeding, toileting, and to give her intellectual understanding of the child's emotional needs in his different developmental phases. This approach presupposes that the mother is emotionally capable of absorbing and utilizing

Note: Reprinted by permission of the author and the *Psychoanalytic Study of the Child, 12:*250-262, 1957.

such knowledge to the benefit of the child and without causing an untoward upheaval in her own personality. b) To treat the mother — by psychoanalysis, psychotherapy, or various social work techniques — in order to bring about changes in her own personality. This will in turn enable her to alter her attitude to her young child and effect changes in his behavior without direct educational advice. The approach assumes that the mother's relationship with her child is primarily shaped by deep-rooted unconscious factors and that the mother can, and will, change her actual handling of her child only after she has gained insight into her own early conflicts. c) The third approach is more difficult to describe. It aims at keeping the focus of the work centered on the child. In the process of enabling the mother to understand her child emotionally and to help him effectively with his difficulties, one uses direct advice at times. At other times one uses the child's material, and the mother's unconscious closeness to it, in order to give her some insight into herself as a mother and into the nature of her interaction with her child. One here expects that a mother of relative emotional health can utilize given advice effectively in some areas. Moreover, one presupposes that her uniquely close bond with her young child makes a mother capable of recognizing many of his unconscious feelings, thoughts, defenses, and of using them with insight to help him. This can be achieved only if the work is conducted in such a manner and at such a pace as to make it possible for the individual mother to profit from her instinctual closeness to her child without unduly mobilizing her deeply unconscious conflicts — otherwise one would threaten the structure of her adult personality and interfere with her ability to respond to her child's immediate needs. It is this last approach which has been taught at the Hampstead Child Therapy Course in London and which had been applied and elaborated under Dr. A. Katan's direction at the Cleveland center. I am most grateful to Dr. Katan for her assistance with this work throughout the past years as well as for her discussion with me of this particular report.

Here I should like to present some aspects of this work as it is practiced in conjunction with University Hospitals Nursery School. Some years ago Mrs. J. Benkendorf, Mrs. A. Rolnick and I pooled our experiences with mother-guidance work and jotted down our thoughts about it. I have received their kind permission to include many of their ideas here. Unfortunately the scope of this report does not permit a detailed discussion of technique, essential though this would be to a fuller understanding of the work.

At University Hospitals Nursery School mother guidance consists of weekly fifty-minute interviews which are usually continued throughout the child's one to two years' stay. Our work with mothers is adapted to its special setting. It differs in many respects from similar work practiced in child guidance clinics and outpatient departments. Some of its features are advantageous to the work, while others create certain difficulties.

The nursery school is of invaluable help to the therapist. By observing the child there directly herself, and by obtaining the detailed reports from the director and teachers, the therapist gains a much fuller picture of the child's personality. One is also in a much better position to judge the positive or negative effects on the child of the work with his mother and to gauge its possibilities and limitations.

The nursery is most helpful in another way too. It assures understanding education of the child outside his home. The close contact between parents, teachers, and therapist makes it possible for the teachers to adapt their handling of the child to his needs at any given time. The nursery supports the mother's efforts by making the child aware of his problems and, in appropriate situations, by reminding him of some interpretations which his mother has already discussed with him at home.

Incidentally the child's mere stay at the nursery is often welcomed by the parents because it relieves them for a stretch of time of his trying behavior. For this and other reasons connected with nursery attendance, mothers tend to be more willing to continue with the mother-guidance work through difficult stages, whereas in an outpatient setting they may at such times become so resistant as to interrupt the consultations.

Yet the nursery school also brings its own problems with it. While in some cases mothers are happy to find that relative strangers are, or are not, able to deal with the child apparently more effectively, others resent it greatly and it increases their hostility to the therapist. The same is true of all the additional information on the child which the school brings to the mother's notice or which the therapist presents to her. Some mothers can objectively be interested and appreciate getting a fuller picture of the child; with others it is just such new aspects of their child's personality which upset them to such a degree that they are unable to tolerate the knowledge and incapable of working with the therapist on the related problems. In a child-guidance setting mothers come to work on those difficulties of their child which acutely concern them. They are satisfied with the outcome if such manifestations are relieved. At our nursery the mother often finds herself confronted with problems, and is expected to work on matters, which she did not regard as pathological at all and which in fact she sometimes could not bear to see changed, e.g. this frequently occurs in cases where the mother would like to help her child with some fears or eating disturbance but cannot observe or acknowledge his underlying aggression or passive character formation.

By continuing the work with the mother over a long period of time and by attempting to get her cooperation in helping her child with all aspects of his disturbance, one important factor of mother guidance becomes greatly intensified and burdened, namely the mother's relationship with the therapist and the transference contained in it. Jacobs (5) stressed in her article "Methods Used in the Education of Mothers" that the working relationship with the mother is least complicated when the consultations continue over a short period of time so that the positive transference is uppermost and helps the mother to identify with the therapist in her understanding of the child. In our work, resistances arising from the transference, from the material and from reality, are very prominent. It has been one of our main technical interests to learn about them and to find ways and means of coping with them.

In evaluating and studying these implications of mother guidance, we receive great practical and psychological help from the fact that we do not have to make mother-guidance work. Our facilities are such that each child can receive individual psycho-analytic treatment if necessary — either during his stay at the nursery or in his latency years if that seems more advisable — and each mother who wishes and requires psychiatric help for herself can be referred for analysis or psychotherapy to the adult clinic. At any time during the mother guidance we may change our goals to fit the individual case, e.g. mother guidance may be used as a preparation for child analysis. Often we are quite contented with achieving such a limited goal from the point of view of mother guidance. The main value of such cases lies in the fact that they, more than the apparently easy and successful ones, help us to pinpoint facets in a mother, or child, or in the nature of their relationship which cannot be dealt with through mother guidance. The selection of cases from the point of view of the mother and child is of utmost importance. We are constantly trying to recognize better and to learn more about which cases can or cannot be helped through this form of work and why.

Jacobs (5) suggests that from the point of view of the child the most suitable cases for mother guidance are mothers of very young children with incipient developmental disturbances, e.g. feeding or sleep problems during the first two years of life, training difficulties as they arise in the latter part of the second year, and some early fears. Jacobs' suggestion can be amply comfirmed by our experiences. The children attending our nursery do not fall into this group, but they invariably have one or more younger siblings whose problems the mothers discuss as part of their work with the therapist. It is with these siblings that the best results are often achieved. It is difficult for us to know whether many children in the three- to five-year age group may not be equally ideal cases, for the children at University Hospitals Nursery School are in a sense preselected. They are referred by pediatricians or agencies because their work with the parents or child failed, or the children come because they could not adjust at one or more previous nurseries. Others come almost directly from the medical or surgical wards of the hospitals having undergone extensive physical treatments. These children therefore tend to be more severely disturbed and their difficulties are of longer standing. Also their parents often come to us with the feelings they entertained toward the previous people they worked with or at least with the intensified feelings which their child's rather long-standing problem aroused in them. Such selection, however, is purely the outcome of practical circumstances. It does not bear on the theoretical principles on which we try to base our work.

In general it is easier to assess a suitable case from the child's point of view. The mother consciously wants to give full information about him and our direct observation of him at the nursery helps to complete the picture. The selection of the child is based on the criteria outlined by Anna Freud in her paper "Diagnosis and Assessment of Early Childhood Difficulties" (3). We accept for mother guidance primarily children whose conflicts lie between themselves and their environment, or those whose disturbance is only partly internalized. Among the latter we try to make sure that their inner conflict is of recent origin and not rigidly defended. Further, their instinctual and ego development, as well as the nature of their object relationships, should be relatively adequate for their age level and still show progression.

Betty, on whom I shall report at some length, was considered suitable for mother guidance. Her case may also serve to illustrate briefly some aspects of our work. Betty and Bobby were twins who entered the nursery shortly before they were three years old. Mrs. Benkendorf worked with their mother during the first year and a half of their stay at the nursery. I then continued to work throughout the following year and their period of adjustment at the kindergarten. Mrs. Benkendorf has cooperated with me in describing Betty and our respective work with her mother. Tempting though it seemed, we have largely omitted discussing the mother's personality, the technique used by the therapists as well as Bobby's disturbance and his interesting interaction with his twin sister.

Although Betty was a pretty girl, she presented the picture of a whiny, unhappy child, babyish in appearance and behavior. Whenever she felt in the least frustrated, she resorted to vigorous thumb sucking. At such times she withdrew and seemed tired and listless. Betty had not yet attained bladder and bowel control. She had been a colicky baby for the first seven months and consequently had been carried and held a great deal. Her persistent demand to be picked up still characterized her relationship to both parents and was also aimed at preventing her twin brother Bobby from gaining parental attention. Betty's relationship to Bobby was quite submissive. Due to his better coordination and more advanced development of skills Bobby directed all of his sister's activities and often even acted for her. Bobby needed this arrangement in order to feel adequate; to Betty it proved her inferiority. As a playmate to others Betty was unsatisfactory. She lacked initiative, had no ideas to contribute, just offered herself as she was used to in her relationship with Bobby.

Betty's wetting and soiling was the first topic of the mother-guidance work. Whereas Bobby had been reliably clean for some time, Betty did not actively resist the mother's attempts at training but did not comply by performing. Once when placed on the toilet Betty said, "I am sticking in my penis." The mother realized herself that Betty had much feeling about being a girl and she wondered "how to make the situation more acceptable to Betty." In response to mother's verbal sympathy for her unhappiness Betty made a bowel movement in the toilet saying, "Look at my broken beeny, Bobby keeps his in his tushi." She also wished to check the bowel movements of all the family members to establish their difference and informed the mother that Bobby and father had a penis outside, whereas she and the mother had theirs inside. After discussion with the therapist the mother was able to talk with Betty about sex differences and to interpret her confusion between bowel movements and genitals. Betty responded by having all her bowel movements in the toilet. For the first time she could have a daily bowel movement and, to her delight, became dry by day and night. Although Betty's conflict no longer interfered with her mastery of bladder and bowel functions, her intense envy of boys continued to disturb her relationships and impeded the progress of her ego activities and sublimations.

Betty now became overtly jealous of her brother, saying that she too "will look like Bobby one day, right now." Much to his distress, she critized his appearance whenever undressed. So far Betty felt quite unconcerned about sucking her thumb and lately masturbated whenever she felt like it. The latter was clearly related to her penis envy. She called masturbating "making a beeny" — her term for a bowel movement. One day on finding herself excluded from the company of Bobby and a visiting boy friend, she was seen rubbing herself and said, "All little boys have a penis, I am only a little girl." In addition to helping Betty with the feelings which caused this behavior, the mother was advised to suggest to Betty that she touch herself in private.

The thumb sucking proved to be of a more complicated nature. Betty clung to it tenaciously. On close observation it could be seen that Betty used her thumb to avoid expressing unpleasant feelings, particularly anger. While sucking she was like a baby who could not talk; besides, the thumb in her mouth prevented all angry words from emerging. With much skill and understanding the mother gradually helped Betty to express her anger verbally. This was especially difficult as most of Betty's aggression was directed against her mother. Betty revealed her anger first in connection with her interest in babies and their origin. She blamed her mother openly for making her into a girl and told her that she herself had babies in her tummy, but they were two girls. It was particularly hard for Betty to be a twin and yet be different at the same time.

Betty's relationship to her father was not a happy one at the time. Her babyish behavior disappointed him as it lacked all the qualities he admired in Bobby. In order to gain the father's favor Betty would have to be able to enter into competition with Bobby and emerge as the victor. Even at the nursery, however, Betty was reluctant to try new activities since there were bound to be some children in the group who had already mastered them successfully. It helped Betty to be told both at home and at school that little girls could be as quick and skillful as boys in most areas.

As Betty became more contented with herself as a girl and learned to cope better with her anger toward her mother she made great strides. She turned into a happier independent child, developing new skills and social accomplishments and showing a surprising amount of imagination and humor. One also began to see signs of a new relationship toward her father. She who had always been the last ready in the mornings, started to get up early to keep her father company and prepared breakfast for him herself. She liked to learn to cook. Once when her mother asked her to leave the kitchen because she was in the way, Betty said, "But mommy, how will I ever learn to be a mommy if you don't let me work in the kitchen?"

About the age of four years, however, the impact of her oedipal feelings, coupled with the problem of being a twin, overwhelmed her. This was marked by a recurrence of her earlier difficulties and defenses. Unable to express her anger to her mother verbally, she reverted to being tired, listless, and regressed in speech and activities. She attempted to get her father's loving attention by again getting him to treat her like a helpless baby. Her inability to compete effectively with her mother extended into all areas, e.g. she professed to like being the loser in all games. Both she and Bobby resumed their old exclusive relationship in which Bobby domineered and Betty acted as a passive follower. Yet the type of family games they played revealed a new motive for their clinging to each other. Whenever interrupted in their play Betty claimed innocently, "Bobby said we should play that"; and Bobby similarly used Betty's partnership to halve his guilt. The mother showed Betty that she had again become a follower because she feared to choose the role of mother in games. When Bobby openly showed his affection for his mother, Betty did not dare be angry with her because she feared that her brother might really usurp her place with mother. It took a long time before the mother could persuade Betty that she would not lose her mother's love even if Bobby was so nice to her while Betty abandoned her in anger.

Betty's overt masturbation also increased again during this phase. She did not use it as a form of consolation, however; instead she masturbated provocatively to attract her mother's attention. When the mother pointed this out to her, Betty told her fantasy: "I think I am a big mommy and go to the store to get a beutiful red dress. It fits perfectly and then I come home and cook the dinner." The mother appreciated Betty's verbal account and reassured her about her guilt. Gradually Betty was helped to accept her conflicting feelings. She expressed herself in words instead of behavior and asserted herself in constructive activities. When the mother had to be hospitalized unexpectedly for a week, Betty blossomed out as a little housewife and later relinquished her new role only reluctantly, making sure that mother should get all the required bed rest.

Just before their fifth birthday both twins had to undergo a tonsillectomy and adenoidectomy because of impaired hearing. After her first long discussion about this with mother, Betty reacted with reversal of affect, saying, "And can I put on my party dress to go into the hospital?" Yet she took in all the steps of the procedure as the mother outlined them to her and questioned everything in detail. Whereas Bobby's fearful fantasies emerged prior to the operation, Betty's reaction set in afterwards. Although she recovered well physically, she regressed to being tired, helpless and very irritable with her mother. When the mother asked her what made her so angry and suggested that she thought there still was something wrong with her, Betty told her mother how very mean she had been to send her to the hospital because "it wasn't at all the way you said, mommy; now they took it away and I won't ever be a mommy and have babies." Betty's fantasy of having a penis-baby inside had been reactivated and had to be worked through again. About the same time leaving the nursery brought out Betty's apprehension about growing up. On the one hand she enjoyed her visit to the kindergarten and chose to be in a class without Bobby, on the other hand she stated that she was too tired to attend the nursery and had trouble leaving her mother in the mornings. Betty could be openly sad about leaving the nursery and planned many visits to keep up her contacts. She adjusted well at the public school and has begun to enter the latency period.

As to her progress I quote from her mother's recent letter: "Betty is the verbalizer of the family. In addition to voicing her feelings and fears, she has developed quite a facility in the use of words and is curious about everything. She made great strides at school. In fact, her teacher considered her to be the most mature child in her class and made her representative to the student council. She makes friends well and also found a little boy in school whom she insisted was her boy friend. At least now she doesn't have to pine for men who are already married, although she assures her daddy he is still her favorite and shows it in a very affectionate way."

In conclusion a word about the mother. It is evident that Betty's mother is an unusually understanding, capable and insightful parent. In relation to Betty she was aware of feeling badly for having made her a girl. This she called her "original sin" and Betty of course was sensitive to this attitude in her mother. The only time when the mother's feelings momentarily interfered with her ability to help her children was after their operation. She called the therapist in panic blaming her that nobody had told her they would be in pain. It was pointed out that the twins had been prepared for just that and the therapist asked the mother whether she could not recall this from her own tonsillectomy. The mother then remembered that indeed no one had prepared *her* at that time and that she suffered from severe hemorrhages. She was greatly relieved and able to manage again. At all other times the mother coped extremely well with the difficult task of helping twins of the opposite sex over their acute developmental difficulties at the same time.

The case of Betty was used here mainly to exemplify the type of problems in a child which may be treated through the mother. I should now like to turn to the selection from the point of view of the mother, a problem which is of equal importance. To select suitable cases from the point of view of the mother is considerably more difficult. Dr. A. Katan finds that the initial psychiatric interview is not always a reliable indicator because it does not necessarily reveal those aspects of the mother's personality which will prove of greatest importance in her ability to work on her child's problem. Mothers who appear insightful and generally balanced may have difficulties in just the area in which their child too has trouble, others seem unaware of their child's feelings and incapable as educators, yet a very minor personality shift in the initial stages of their mother-guidance work makes it possible for them to cooperate effectively. Frequently it is possible to assess a mother's capacities only after a period of working with her.

John's mother illustrates this. She was an extremely well-dressed, intelligent but aloof young woman when John, aged four, entered the nursery school. Though highly intelligent, he was withdrawn, depressed, and incapable of any creative activity. His mother had left his constant wetting and soiling unattended for so long that he suffered from large bleeding sores all over his buttocks which made it impossible for him to sit or run. The mother also had not trained or weaned two younger siblings. While she reads novels, the three children would incessantly scream, fight, and seriously hurt one another. John's mother described all this without affect and seemed incapable of actively stepping in or making any effective demand on her children. During the first few months of mother guidance she could verbally express her great hostility toward her children. She stated that she had never wanted even one child and knew it would be "bedlam" if she did. She blamed her husband for inflicting this calamity on her and then absenting himself on frequent business trips. After these outbursts she changed remarkably and became one of the most understanding and effective mothers. She was able to help the two younger children herself — they are now both in public school — and she has cooperated very well with John's analysis.

Some types of unsuitable mothers can be excluded fairly readily at the start. Such are psychotics or borderline cases, and extremely infantile personalities who usually simply wish to hand their child over to a person in authority. Into this group often also belong mothers who maintain allround sadomasochistic relationships (in contrast to mothers who have a sadomasochistic interplay only with one child), and mothers who do not themselves see the need for help for their child but come at somebody else's behest.

In contrast to these mothers with overall disturbances or attitudes, it is much harder to assess particular personality traits in mothers who appear generally balanced. Certain traits have been found to interfere greatly with a mother's ability to profit from mother guidance. When a mother and child use prominently the same defense mechanisms or suffer from identical symptoms, or when the child has a symptom which his mother used to suffer from in her childhood, e.g. soiling or bed wetting, the mother's capacity to help her child is invariably so impaired that assistance through mother guidance is not worth attempting. Then there are mothers for whom the child or his difficulties have an important but pathological unconscious meaning; e.g. the child represents part of the mother's person or he stands for the partner in one of her early object relationships. In such cases the unconscious tendency counteracts the mother's conscious efforts too strongly to enable her to alter her attitude.

Some mothers need to maintain their child's problem for a different reason, namely, they are too narcissistic to be able to face their own guilt which would overwhelm them if the child improved. Mrs. M. Flumerfelt worked with one such case and has kindly allowed me to use this aspect of it as an example.

> Debby was a bright pretty girl of four years who suffered from severe temper outbursts and tried her parents with unmanageably difficult behavior. Her mother could cooperate rather well as long as the problems persisted. As soon as Debby improved her mother became extremely hostile to the therapist and to the teachers and went out of her way to bring about new upheavals or to recreate the previous difficulties. She reacted similarly with an angry and punitive attitude to Debby when strangers in the park commented what a nice little girl she was. It turned out that this mother could deny her guilt as long as her child was irrevocably problematic. The mere fact that Debby had some pleasant qualities and could get better confirmed to this mother her feeling that she had caused all the troubles.

Further, there were several mothers who cooperated apparently very well, but one found in time that they merely imitated the therapist and were incapable of carrying on what they had learned once the contact with the therapist was interrupted. Earlier indications of such an attitude vary. Sometimes one could detect an extreme dependency on the therapist, sometimes such mothers had to overstress their superficial imitation of the worker by adopting her manner of speech, hair style, or buy similar clothes.

The different types of maternal traits which I have listed here at random are among the more typical. With all of them mother guidance does not prove effective and, unfortunately, all of them are difficult to detect at the outset and can be assessed in the individual constellation of a mother's personality only after working with her for some time. There surely is a much longer list of unsuitable cases which is beyond the scope of this paper.

Although I have dwelt on the topic of "unsuitable" mothers at some length, I should like to stress in conclusion that, in our experience, there is a large percentage of mothers of under-fives who are very well able to cooperate with the method of mother guidance which I have tried to outline. These mothers derive great satisfaction from learning to help their children themselves and from the improved relationship with their young child which they are able to establish on the basis of their deeper understanding.

REFERENCES

1. Burlingham, D. T.: Present trends in handling the mother-child

relationship during the therapeutic process. *This Annual, VI* 1951.

2. Coleman, R. W., Kris, E., Provence, S.: The study of early variations of parental attitudes. *This Annual, VIII.* 1953.
3. Freud, A.: Diagnosis and Assessment of Early Childhood Difficulties. Paper read in Philadelphia (unpublished), 1954.
4. Fries, M.E.: The child's ego development and the training of adults in his environment. *This Annual, II*, 1946.
5. Jacobs, L.: Methods used in the education of mothers. A contribution to the handling and treatment of developmental difficulties in children under five years of age. *This Annual, III/IV*, 1949.
6. Thomas, R. and Ruben, M.: Home training of instincts and emotions. *Health Educ. J. (London)*, 1947.

Chapter 16

Emotional Aspects of
Rheumatic Fever in Children*

T. BERRY BRAZELTON, RICHMOND HOLDER, AND BEATRICE TALBOT

E MOTIONAL factors have long been considered to be of importance in chronic illness, but the extent of this importance has been difficult to evaluate. To obtain a clearer picture of the role emotional factors play in such an illness, a team of investigators at the Massachusetts General Hospital has studied a group of twenty children with rheumatic fever and their mothers over a period of a year and a half.

The team was composed of four part-time psychiatrists, a psychiatric social worker, and a part-time psychologist. Two of the psychiatrists and the social worker interviewed sixty-eight mothers and children at the time of their appointments at the Rheumatic Fever Clinic. Some of these children had been seen only once a year in the Rheumatic Fever Clinic, others once every week or two. Their cooperation was solicited on the basis that the investigators were interested in knowing about the experience of the patients and their families with the hope that the illness might be made easier for others. The only criteria for selecting patients were that they be between the ages of 5 and 17 years, live in the Greater Boston area, and have had a diagnosis made at one time of rheumatic fever with or without heart disease.

In the group of twenty discussed here, nine of the children had

*Note: Reprinted by permission of the author and *Journal of Pediatrics, 43:*339-358, 1953; ©The C. V. Mosby Co., St. Louis, Mo.

From the Child Psychiatry and Children's Medical Services, Massachusetts General Hospital, and the Departments of Psychiatry and Pediatrics, Harvard Medical School.

Material on which this study was based was obtained with the aid of funds from a USPHS grant.

rheumatic fever with heart disease, three had rheumatic fever without heart disease, and in eight a diagnosis of rheumatic fever was suspected but never confirmed. As the study progressed it became apparent that the group without heart disease did not differ appreciably from the others in its psychological reactions since all twenty of the children had been treated at one time as if they actually had heart disease. There were eleven boys and nine girls, all of whose medical records were reviewed and the diagnosis rechecked by Dr. Gertrud Reyersbach of the Children's Medical Service of the Massachusetts General Hospital.

Of the sixty-eight mothers approached originally, only forty-three were interested in entering the study and of these only twenty maintained enough interest to continue throughout the eighteen months of study. In general, the children were first seen in the Rheumatic Fever Clinic. Three of them, however, were interviewed while they were still hospitalized. The latter continued in the project after their discharge and return home. For the most part both mother and child were seen weekly for hourly interviews, the mother being seen by the social worker while the child was being seen by the doctor. An average of 19.3 hours was spent with each mother and 16.8 hours with each child. Nineteen of the twenty cases chosen were followed for over a year with five coming to the hospital weekly. In addition to this, five other children with rheumatic fever histories were seen for an average of seven hours each. The mothers of these children did not come in for one reason or another and hence they were not included in the study.

PROCEDURES

Before the main study was started, a pilot study was carried out on twenty children with rheumatic fever at a nearby convalescent hospital by another psychiatrist and the psychologist. Twenty children on the orthopedic wards of another hospital were used as controls. Three areas were studied:
1. The effect of the illness upon the attitude of the child toward himself.
2. The effect of the illness upon the attitude of the child

toward his parents and his feelings about their attitude toward him.

3. The attitude of the child toward medical care, hospital, doctors, and nurses.

This study led the investigators to conclude that the most important way to gain accurate information from such children was by establishing a good relationship with each child. The two hours spent with each child in this preliminary study were not enough to establish such a relationship. This was emphasized when one of the children, after he had come to know the psychiatrist well in the main study, said in reference to his earlier experience in the pilot group: "I told that other doc just what he wanted me to when he asked me all those questions. Us kids knew it was the best way to get it over with." He went on to relate how he and the other kids got together "to dope out the right answers for that guy."

A. Psychiatric Approach

The psychiatrist's first aim was to establish a relationship with the child. This was done by using play situations involving toys or games suitable to the child. During the early interviews the conversations were nondirective with the child leading the way. After he had grown to trust the doctor, the latter pointed the play and discussion toward the illness, the hospitalization, the separation from parents, and feelings about rheumatic fever. Often such things did not come up until after ten to fifteen hours of interviews.

B. Social Worker's Approach

The social worker, like the psychiatrist, used an indirect technique in her interviews with the mothers. However, when the illness of the child was brought up the worker encouraged a discussion of the subject. She often had to make a consistent effort to focus attention on the child and the mother's feelings about his illness, as the mothers tended to use the situation to discuss their own problems. As time went on, the research aspects of the case work often gave way to a more typical social worker-client relationship in the face of practical difficulties which arose. In such cases the worker often helped the mothers with outside problems in an attempt to keep the relationship firm. This activity helped the mothers produce more material and was a factor in surmounting the difficulties which arose from the fact that their cooperation had been solicited by the project and that they did not originally come for help themselves.

C. Psychologist

Objective material about the child's psychological processes was obtained by a battery of tests administered by the child psychologist. The tests included the Wechsler Intelligence Scale for Children, the Rosenzweig Picture Frustration study, the Rorschach test and the Draw-A-Person test.

THE MOTHERS

The mothers who joined this study were self-selected as most of them seemed to have emotional needs which they felt the project would meet. In addition to those who sought help in handling their children, there were those who sought help for themselves. Their attitude toward their problems had been such that none of them had ever sought psychiatric assistance nor had any of them been referred for such assistance from the Rheumatic Fever Clinic. With mothers who were unable to tolerate the psychiatric approach, the contact with the study was intermittent and frequently could not be maintained for more than a few interviews. Other mothers whose problems were unusually severe were so threatened by the study that they were unable to go on after the first interview.

1. Relationship with the child prior to illness.

The mothers' relationship to their children prior to the onset of rheumatic fever was of prime importance in determining subsequent handling of the total illness situation.

An example of this is a mother who had her first and only child at the age of 45. His arrival was unexpected and unwelcome since her marriage had been strained for some years by her husband's constant infidelity and incompatibility. From the beginning, therefore, this mother felt resentment toward her small son. She viewed him as an additional burden on her already unpleasant life, yet compensated for this feeling with oversolicitude. This resulted in constant struggles between them during the first three years of his life, with the mother projecting her negative feelings about her husband onto the child. This hostility in turn gave rise to guilt in her. When the boy developed rheumatic fever and the doctors insisted that he be hospitalized, the mother was overwhelmed by these feelings. She felt she was responsible for his illness. This made it impossible for her to give him up to someone else's care, and she busied herself making amends for what she thought she had done by "curing him at home." Thus, for the next two years she fought to keep him out of the hospital, and during this period their stormy relationship became even worse, with daily battles over his behavior. At the same time she brought out in her interviews that she should not have kept him at home in bed but should have hospitalized him as the doctors wished. "If only I hadn't kept him home all that time he wouldn't be so bad now."

This case and others like it illustrate how a disturbed pre-illness relationship of mother and child produces a disturbance in handling the illness. Another instance occurred in a family where the favored son was suspected of having developed rheumatic fever. Even though there was little objective evidence to substantiate this, the mother insisted upon having him hospitalized at once. After his hospital stay which failed to confirm the diagnosis, she supervised his every move, insisted that he take long rest periods daily and prevented him from participating in sports even though the doctors specifically said he could.

When the rheumatic fever brought out the already existent difficulties between mother and child, the mother could then blame the illness as being the cause of their troubles. This happened again and again even though the material clearly showed that the pre-illness relationship had been a turbulent one. The mothers, however, repressed this.

In the instances where there had apparently been a good parent-child relationship prior to illness, the mothers also felt the child's personality had changed owing to the rheumatic fever. However, these mothers were able to accept the changes and help the child to adjust to them.

2. Concept of the origin of the illness.

No two mothers had the same concept of the origin of rheumatic fever despite the similarity of what the doctors told them. Their ideas varied according to many factors, some of which were correlated. These included the following: a) The amount of information given by the doctors as to the cause of the disease; b) past experience with rheumatic fever in their own families, and hearsay from relatives and friends; c) concepts resulting from unconscious conflicts within the mothers.

(a) Information from doctors:

The doctors were, of necessity, vague in their explanation of the origin of the disease. This vagueness acted upon the mothers in different ways. In some instances it caused a minimum of anxiety and the mothers merely regretted the lack of definite information, expressing confidence in the available treatment. In other instances it marshalled tremendous anxiety and forced the mothers to put considerable pressure on the doctors for more specific information. The more specific the information, the less threatening it appeared to be. When they were told that the origin was unknown and uncertain, they would come out with such statements as: "My doctor told me you got it from a cold," or "The doctors up in the clinic said it was a germ."

In common with most mothers of sick children, those mothers who developed anxiety about the origin of the illness sought external causes to blame, the most frequent being the cold and the damp. Eleven of the twenty mothers brought these factors up as not only being connected with the origin of the illness but also with its recurrences. Over two-thirds of the cancellations for appointments in the study were due to the mothers' telephoning that the weather was too cold or too wet and they feared their child might suffer a relapse if he went outside.

(b) Past experience with rheumatic fever in own family:

Since there was a history of rheumatic fever or rheumatic heart disease in eleven of the twenty cases studied, many mothers had ideas about the origin of the illness which predated the birth of their children. This of itself is not peculiar to rheumatic fever but is found in any chronic illness whose origin is obscure, such as diabetes or rheumatoid arthritis. One such mother attributed rheumatic fever to accidents and cited as an example her sister who "fell off a pier one day and the next day she got rheumatic fever." She then linked this with her son: "That's how Eddy got sick. His foot was run over by a car and that was an awful shock. Shocks cause heart trouble."

Another mother who had developed rheumatic fever with heart disease at the age of 14 was convinced that her son inherited his rheumatic fever from her. "How could he help but get it when I've been sick all my life?" she asked. This concept of inheritance was especially strong in families with multiple experiences with the disease, even though the mother herself might never have been sick.

(c) Concepts resulting from unconscious conflicts and needs within the mothers:

In common with most parents these mothers developed guilt feelings about sickness in their children. Rheumatic fever, however, presents a more complex picture than other illnesses because of its obscure origin and recurrent nature. Perhaps because of this these mothers blame themselves more than usual for having allowed the children to become ill. Thirteen of twenty mothers were able to verbalize this directly, and the remainder said so indirectly, voicing their guilt in different ways. For example, one mother stated, "Laura would never have gotten rheumatic fever if I hadn't let her catch poison ivy the day before." Another said, "I let my child run around naked all summer long. He caught rheumatic fever from that." A third blamed the child with the comment, "He should have obeyed me when I told him not to go out in the rain."

Each mother handled her guilt according to her own personality make-up and background. Some attempted to manage their feelings by overconcern for the sick child, occasionally at the expense of the well ones as in the case of the mother who said, "We saw to it that Mary got the food the Rheumatic Fever Clinic recommended even though the rest of us had to go without."

One mother told how her son had wanted a bike very much

though the father had been opposed to his having it. Despite the father's objections the mother bought the bike. Soon after that the father developed cancer of the throat and died within the year. Three months later the youngster came in following a bike ride complaining of aches in his legs. Rheumatic fever was diagnosed and the mother's explanation of the origin of the disease was, "I suppose he'd have been okay except for the bike." Here guilt over having countered the dead husband's wishes influenced the mother's concept of the origin of the illness.

3. The concept of rheumatic fever.

The mothers presented many concepts of the nature of rheumatic fever. Each mother interpreted the process in her own way, with the ideas and accompanying fantasies having their origins in her past experiences. Three examples seemed to show this: At the time one child (Joe) developed rheumatic fever, the possibility of chorea was mentioned to his mother. "When they said to watch for chorea it scared me stiff," she said, "because I knew two ladies who weren't bright who had it and maybe this means Joe isn't bright." Throughout the time she took part in the study she indicated frequently how mental deficiency had become equated in her mind with rheumatic fever and chorea.

A second mother and her twin brother had rheumatic fever with heart disease, and the brother died from it just before the patient Jim was born. Subsequently Jim developed rheumatic fever without heart disease. His mother believed firmly that rheumatic fever meant heart disease and an early death. In fact she described Jim as being "born with heart disease," despite medical evidence to the contrary. Discussion of her feelings about this brought out her early attachment to her brother who had dominated her entire life.

Finally, a third mother who appeared to be one of the best adjusted in the study linked her concept of the illness to her experience with her husband. The latter had rheumatic heart disease and was emotionally disturbed. During the course of the study he died under circumstances which suggested suicide. The mother felt he must have been insane because "only insane people kill themselves." She then became terrified that her daughter Louise would become insane too, since she felt that insanity was in some way linked to rheumatic fever. She projected numerous difficulties on Louise which were characteristic of her husband. For instance, when Louise had trouble with her eyes, she said, "My husband had eye trouble which gave headaches. It was all part of being nervous." She would then attempt to convince herself that her husband's death had been due to a heart attack.

Much of the confusion surrounding the concept of the disease seemed to stem from the mothers' inability to accept the doctor's explanation of the disease process. Nineteen of the twenty mothers kept asking the investigators, "Just what is rheumatic fever?" This was in spite of the fact that they had apparently asked the same question of numerous other doctors and other workers in the field.

Part of all concepts of the illness were ideas that since it involved the heart it meant death. Fifteen of the twenty mothers stressed the fear of death in connection with the disease. One doctor sought to alleviate a mother's concern in this area by showing her the child's heart through a fluoroscope. Her reaction was, "I'd never seen anything but a chicken's heart before and Jane's heart looked so big it frightened me." This led to unnecessary restrictions on the child for the first time because of the mother's anxiety over the incident. Discussion of her attitude toward this child indicatd that she had always feared the child was not "normal." Apprehension centered predominantly about her size, maturity, and eating habits, anxieties which she did not have about her younger child.

Almost all the mothers in the discussions would use the word "heart" with more meaning than ordinarily. Their preoccupation was shown by remarks such as, "It frightened the heart out of me" or "I felt so low in the heart."

4. Hospitalization.

Of the patients included in this study, fourteen went away for care. In most instances the mother made the decision whether a child would stay at home or go away once the doctors recommended hospitalization. In instances where the child was hospitalized she was forced to assume the role of a rejecting parent. This added an extra burden to such a decision. One mother described a violent conflict with her husband, ending in her taking the 6-year-old son away to the hospital during the day when the husband was at work. The father continually reminded the child thereafter of how the mother had been responsible for sending him away.

Another 8-year-old child was placed away from home against her father's wishes, but only after the mother had worn herself out trying to care for her at home. "I could never sleep through a night when she was sick because I was always afraid that she would need something and hurt herself trying to get it." This child and her father were very close to each other. The day she was transferred to the hospital, the father had a psychotic episode. Many of his thoughts centered on his guilt at feeling he was the cause of her hospitalization.

The mothers interpreted a recommendation for hospitalization according to their individual needs. Those who had the greatest difficulty allowing their children to be placed were the ones who had a neurotic need for their child to depend on them. Most mothers were able to prepare a child for separation from home and let him go away with a minimal amount of conflict, since they realized that it was impossible for them to give him the necessary care. Those who had difficulty in releasing their children were often able to do so after a period of home care had proved to be too difficult for them.

It sometimes appeared as though the mother felt that the doctors thought she had been a "bad mother" in that she had allowed her child to become ill; therefore she had to keep him home and give him exquisite care to prove she could be a "good mother." In some instances this feeling led to an intense need to prove her worth and a mother would give her sick child all the attention she had previously spread among her other children. "I never left Susan day or night. Whenever she was lonesome I would go and lie on her bed. She got the best food there was even though the others had to go without." Some mothers felt compelled to refuse hospitalization because they could not stand the pressure from the children to keep them at home. The pressure was usually in terms of the child accusing the mother of not loving him enough. Then it was necessary for her to prove her love and interest by keeping him at home and by overindulging him. Once the decision to hospitalize the child had been made, however, the mother seemed to feel relieved of some of her guilt and anxiety over his sickness. She was able to transfer a good deal of her concern over her child's welfare to the hospital staff and to feel assured that the case was under control.

Although the parents had mixed feelings about their forced separation from their ill child, in every instance but one they based the final reason for placement on medical needs. In this one case the mother said, "We thought it would be good to get her away from home for a while. We hoped they would teach her good manners, and not to be sassy to her mother." After she returned home from placement the mother said, "It was a lovely place. They taught her to wash her hair."

5. Convalescence and return home.

The mothers who kept their children at home seemed to have the greatest difficulty in allowing the children to become mobilized. They tended to center their interests on them after any need for overprotection existed. One mother, whose 16-year-old son had been kept at home, laid out his clothes each day in the convalescent period to be sure he was dressed warmly and would not catch cold. Several years later another was constantly reminding her child to wear rubbers lest he become sick again.

The coming home of the hospitalized child seemed to affirm in the mother's mind that he was better and hence could return to normal activity safely. For one thing the mothers were glad to have their children back because their homecoming marked an end to the anxiety-provoking separation. The return also ushered in the beginning of what the mothers could consider recovery.

On the other hand, this could be overshadowed by the fear of recurrence which was usually emphasized by those in charge of the case. The mother's anxiety resulted in restrictions which were inexplicable to the child, as in the case of 10-year-old Joe whose mother said, "I don't dare allow Joe to ride his bicycle. The streets around our house have so many cars." She later admitted, however, that she could allow her other children to ride their bikes and she really worried that Joe might "drop dead" from his rheumatic fever. Another mother, who worked to support her family, said, "I need to keep Fred home from school next winter because he is so helpful looking after the younger children while I work." Subsequently, she confided that her real reason for keeping her son home from school (despite the clinic's recommendation that he attend) was that she was afraid of his getting an infection there with recurrence of his rheumatic fever. This mother was proud of the fact that the boy stayed in bed every Sunday and usually one or two days a week, "whenever he felt tired."

In general, problems which arose when a child came home were reactivations of old difficulties between him and the parents with a new intensity. One mother had always preferred her son George to her daughter Jane. After Jane returned home following hospitalization the mother blamed the illness for all previous difficulties she had had with her. At the same time she indicated she had always preferred George and found him easier to take care of long before Jane became sick. Still another mother who had always been markedly hostile to her 11-year-old daughter would lean out the window to scream at her, "Don't skip rope, Margaret, or you'll drop dead."

The children provided new problems on their return by making excessive demands on the family as if they were seeking retribution for having been exiled. These demands were frequently difficult to meet, especially when they conflicted with other members of the family. One child, for example, was not supposed to walk upstairs and the mother was told he had to be carried. This added attention made his two healthy siblings jealous. His mother solved the conflict by carrying all three children up four flights.

Another aspect of the convalescent period was seen in those children who had been placed in a medical foster home instead of the hospital. In two such instances the children developed warm ties to their foster parents which was threatening to their real parents on return home. To combat this the mothers did everything they could to make their homes like that of the foster parents. One family moved to another house and chose it "because it had a porch around it like the one at Mrs. Murphy's." The other mother allowed her son to eat gigantic amounts of food whenever he wanted to because "he told me that Mrs. Jones used to let him eat all the time."

6. Reactions to illness.

Those mothers who were themselves the most disturbed handled their children's rheumatic fever with the greatest anxiety for the child. The mothers used the ever-present danger of recurrence and the other aspects of the disease in a way that suited their own neurotic needs in handling the child. A mother, whose 14-year-old son was suspected of having rheumatic fever, insisted on having him sleep with her because "Dickie might have a heart attack in the night." This mother's husband had deserted her and her only other son had been killed in World War II. She apparently utilized the rheumatic fever to keep the remaining child near her constantly.

"John has been sick and we can't expect as much from him," explained a mother whose son was a constant truant from school and was unable to pass in his school work. Although this boy had had rheumatic fever, he had never developed heart trouble but his mother continually stressed the condition of his heart. She explained that her own heart had been severely damaged by rheumatic fever when she was a child. She seemed to be treating him as the cripple she visualized herself to be.

There were other cases in which rheumatic fever was suspected but never confirmed. These children were treated as sick by the mothers who clung to the diagnosis. By contrast, other mothers who had less anxiety could give their child considerable reassurance by sharing their knowledge or lack of knowledge with him in a less threatening way. Apparently there was no correlation between the amount of anxiety a mother had and the actual severity of the illness in the child. Many mothers whose children had few symptoms reacted far more strongly than the mothers of the sickest children. In turn the ability of the parents to handle their own anxiety reflected itself in the child's ability to handle his illness. All too often the mother's feeling of bewilderment and loneliness in managing her problems showed itself in the child's own reactions. "My mother seemed so scared, I got scared, too." said one little girl.

7. Recommendations in working with the mothers.

It seems important that the medical team discover what the

diagnosis and suggested treatment mean to each mother from the time she first hears about the illness throughout the subsequent months. From the moment of the first diagnosis, one person should be in continuous contact with the mother. The importance of the continuity of contact cannot be overrated. Mother after mother would say, "We saw so many different people," or "We'd just get used to someone when they'd change and we'd have to begin all over again."

Perhaps the most important contact with the doctor is the first one, when he tells the mother of the diagnosis. At this time after she has talked with him she would have an opportunity to discuss her feelings more extensively with a social worker. The latter, in cooperation with the doctor, could evaluate what aspects of the illness situation this parent could accept, with particular attention to the mother's concerns. Later, the same social worker could talk with the mother about subsequent plans for the child, and attempt to help her with the doctor's recommendations for care. By this time she would know the mother well enough to evaluate her reactions and, if necessary, steer her to further psychological help.

In this manner, the mother could be helped in preparing the child to meet the various pitfalls the illness presents. The question of hospitalization and the meaning of separation would be worked through for the parent as each step is taken. From the experience gained in this study it would seem that such casework could alleviate the guilty feelings which arise from the mother's having sent the child away, as well as her overreactions to other aspects of the problem, such as undue concern about recurrence and restrictions on the child's activities. Equally important is helping the mother in handling the difficult transition from hospital care to home convalescence. The worker could prepare the mother in advance for her role in this phase of the illness and support her emotionally throughout the long and trying period. Many mothers voiced the complaint that so often they had no one to turn to and they "didn't know what to do," thereby expressing their desire for such help.

From the social worker's viewpoint in this study, one of the most impressive findings was the real relief expressed by the mothers in discussing their feelings about the most threatening aspects of the disease. Many of these mothers, because of their inner reserve and apparent capability in dealing with their emotions, were never referred to a social worker at any time during their child's illness. The uniformity of their appreciation for the help given by the study showed that contact with a social worker could be of great value to all parents of chronically ill children.

THE CHILDREN

The work with the children produced material which closely paralleled that brought out by the mothers and helped to demonstrate how closely knit the mother-child unit had been in its reactions to the illness and its attendant anxieties. Whereas the mothers could eventually verbalize some of their feelings, the children were rarely able to express themselves as directly. For them a play situation was an easier medium of expression than words, but even this indirect expression of their underlying feelings was only possible after becoming confident of the doctor as a friend. At that point the play became more meaningful and could be directed toward areas which revealed the children's true feelings about the disease and the aspects of it about which they were concerned.

1. Relationship to parents prior to illness.

The investigators felt that the relationship of the child to the parents before the illness greatly influenced the way he subsequently handled his disease. This is well illustrated by a 16-year-old boy whose mother had overprotected him even prior to illness because of her fear that he would develop heart disease such as his father had. When he actually did contract a mild case of rheumatic fever, his reactions were out of all proportion to the illness and continued long after he was well. Instead of running upstairs he would walk. Instead of going out to play with the other boys after lunch he would rest for a full hour, and so on. It seemed clear that he had actually developed a neurosis with anxiety attacks and constant fear of death.

The mother's handling of her anxiety at the time she was informed about the child's illness was important. Grace, an

11-year-old girl, said, "When I say my Mommy was scared, I became real scared 'cos I knew it must be bad." A smiliar type of communicated anxiety was seen in war experiences by Anna Freud (5) and could be correlated with the degree of anxiety in the grownups around the children rather than with the severity of the actual situation. In the present study a 14-year-old-boy, in whom the doctors did not make a diagnosis of rheumatic fever but mentioned that they were "ruling it out," remembers that his mother collapsed and wept. He was terrified and said, "I knew something was wrong with my heart. It pounded so hard." Thereafter his mother often brought up rheumatic fever to him despite the fact that the diagnosis was not confirmed and that the doctors assured his mother he did not have heart disease. His mother continued to think of him as a cardiac cripple. The boy's statement was, "I'll never be able to be a carpenter like my father. Every time I get up on a ladder my heart pounds away and I get too dizzy."

By contrast was a mother who had always had an excellent relationship with her 9-year-old daughter Laura. When Laura was brought to the hospital in cardiac failure the mother asked to be allowed some time alone with her "to explain what was going to happen." In the next half hour she explained how she would have to leave her for a while and the fact that she would come back to see her often. Although Laura wept for a while she was able to gain her strength from the fact that her mother wanted to come back to see her all the time and had told her what to expect. Subsequently when something happened in the course of her treatment for which her mother had prepared her, Laura would brighten and repeat with some pride, "My mommy told me this would happen."

2. Concept of the origin of rheumatic fever.

Nearly all children develop a good deal of guilt over having become ill and express it in different ways. These ways often determined the child's concept of the origin of his illness, a reaction not at all peculiar to rheumatic fever. Many expressed the idea that the illness was a punishment for their wicked deeds or thoughts. An 11-year-old boy said: "I stayed out playing in the rain after the baby sitter told me to come in. My mother says that's why I caught rheumatic fever."

Some bodily inadequacy or weakness appeared over and over again as a basis for the child's explanation of why he contracted the disease. A 10-year-old boy who had spent nearly five years in the hospital, flatly stated, "Those that get rheumatic fever must have a weakness in the first place." Turning to the doctor he then inquired anxiously, "Is it a germ that eats inside you and decays like losing a kidney?" This was symbolic of his fear of mutilation which was predominant in his make-up.

Still others blamed their parents, especially when the relationship between them had been a disturbed one. Eight-year-old Laura, who was involved in an intense oedipal situation with her father and whose mother had rejected her prior to her illness, played out some of her feelings with a set of dolls. At the start the mother and father dolls were on the floor lying next to each other. Then the little girl doll came forcibly between them, and the mother was taken upstairs to bed with a "heart attack." The little girl in turn had to be quickly sent off to the hospital because she was "sicker than her mother, as she had rheumatic fever."

When the mothers or doctors were able to give the child an explanation about the origin of the disease which did not imply responsibility on his part, the youngster was freed of a good deal of anxiety. This is turn seemed to enable him to adjust more easily to the disease. Conversely, it seemed that a child who suffered deeply from guilt attributed to the disease might handle the disease poorly, whether consciously or unconsciously. The 8-year-old girl above had a difficult convalescence in the hospital and, when she seemed to be improving, she began to rebel openly, got out of bed too early, and in general seemed consciously to interfere with her own progress. Though her problems were intense, it seems possible that the mechanisms involved might be applicable to less disturbed children.

The guilt which follows the anger at parents for their desertion in the hospital in chronic illness could be seen in those few who were seen in the hospital (13).

3. Concept of the illness.

The children's concept of rheumatic fever and rheumatic heart disease was difficult to investigate primarily because of their strong defenses. They seemed to fear talking about it and, if the subject was brought up too early, would often close up for several interviews.

Each child's concept of rheumatic fever was as vague as the mother's. Among the children who verbalized their fears well was an 11-year-old who became sad and pensive when the doctor brought up the question of rheumatic fever. She stated, "It's so awful to have it hanging over you. Maybe some day you'll have it again. It's terrible. I knew that it was heart trouble because they came to my house just to listen to my heart and never looked at my tonsils or anything like that. I thought it was something like chicken pox — contagious. The other girls would be afraid of you because it was contagious. When they found out it wasn't, they would either feel sorry for you and make you angry, or they wouldn't be sorry enough and then they wouldn't want to see you because there was something wrong."

Other children looked upon the illness in different ways. "Rheumatic fever is just like polio," one of the older girls told the doctor. "You don't know if you'll get it or not. It's mysterious. The boy across the street had it. It didn't leave me a cripple, though, like polio does. That boy had one leg shorter than the other." She laughed and explained that rheumatic fever is "aches and pains. It means being in bed. I didn't think it was much of anything 'cause I thought they knew what they were doing. They said it would take a long time to heal. You've just got to take things easy with lots of rest. If you don't you might get sick and get it again or get heart trouble."

It was in this often expressed fear of heart trouble that many children felt most anxious. Their anxiety was frequently heightened by the classification of potential rheumatic heart disease. They expressed the feeling that being followed in the Cardiac Clinic meant that they must have heart trouble. Although they strove to conceal their underlying fears occasionally they would come out with a statement like that of Gerry, who at the age of 10 had severe cardiac damage and told the doctor, "My grandfather had a shock so he was brought to the Massachusettes General Hospital. They kept him from dying of the shock. If you have heart trouble and have a shock you die. My grandfather collects stamps and so do I."

The concept of heart trouble was a difficult one for the child to grasp although each one knew it as a crippling lesion. A 9-year-old boy, who had spent three years in the hospital and who was still in the second grade, said, "When my heart trouble comes back again I guess I'll be put back another year in school." Later he asked "What can a guy do who has a weak pump?" Fear of death was equated to fears of mutilation and of being different.

4. Hospitalization.

Of the seventeen children who had been hospitalized, four were seen while they were still in the hospital. When first contacted these patients had little to say, but as their confidence in the doctor grew a great deal of material came out. One boy, aged 10, said in his first interview, "The days really fly past fast." Later on when he had gotten to know the doctor better he said, "I felt I was never going to get out of the hospital." This same patient in the beginning had no derogatory comments to make about either the doctors or the nurses. In his eighth interview when he had been discharged, he said, "I don't look back at the hospital at all. I just don't want to think about it, especially the old nurses. They break your toys and bother you a lot. They make you do all sorts of things and get in your way." In his tenth interview he said, "The doctors don't know much. They thought you liked it there; I hated it!" This same patient later on managed to bring out that he was never given much information about his sickness. "Nobody told me nothing. One day I heard two docs say I had rheumatic fever. They just made things up. They're crazy." He elaborated on this by saying that he felt the doctors kept him in the hospital because there weren't enough other sick children to fill the beds.

Another boy, aged 16, recalling his life in the hospital when he was 7 said, "The nurses kissed us all goodnight. There was candy in a big can and four boys in a room." He went on to say that he always wanted to go home but "I never said nothing to nobody about this. I figured I probably couldn't go anyway. I thought I might be there forever." Like many of the other children one of his principal dislikes of the hospital was "sticking needles in my arm" and another was staying in bed. He, along with most of the children, emphasized the hospital's insistence on watching their time up. He felt that they used this as a kind of weapon and resented this technique. "They keep you in bed longer if they don't like you or what you do."

These children often equate the duration and severity of their rheumatic fever to their badness in the hospital. "I got out of bed once when I wasn't supposed to, and the next day they said I was worse and put me in a room by myself. That's when I really got sick." The restrictions which were placed on them in the name of their heart disease seemed to impress them as much as any actual concept of the disease itself, and constantly reminded them of their illness.

Often in this disease, pressure is put on the child to eat. Improvement is often equated with appetite, or, as is more often the case, to the patient's willingness to eat in spite of severe anorexia. An example of what this sort of pressure means to a child was shown by an 11-year-old boy with severe heart damage, who said, "I knew I would have heart trouble. The nurses told me I'd never get well if I didn't eat. Instead I threw the food out the window when they weren't looking. I'm bound to have heart trouble."

The necessity for putting pressure on children to adhere to restrictions became a source of conflict. The passive children seemed to interpret the restrictions as punishment rather than as measures necessary for their well-being. The more active children rebelled against the restrictions but in so doing appeared anxious. Their bravado broke down all too easily in the interviews. As one 11-year-old said: "If I act scared, then I ain't got a chance. Them docs will slap on all they can. They got my Ma scared but not me. Sure, I got something wrong, but that don't mean it's quits – not yet, anyway."

Separation from home was expressed as the most serious aspect of the hospitalization. This was often necessary in an acutely ill child without adequate preparation. Inability to understand this formed him to find reasons for the sudden removal from home. Eight-year-old Lucia elaborated about why hospitalization was necessary in her case and how it became a further form of punishment for her misdeeds. In a play interview she brought her doll to the doctor, saying: "Dolly's been sick four weeks with a cold and a temperature. She's had rheumatic fever before. It was mild but the doctors said that she had a heart murmur. They didn't tell her what that was, just told her it was something wrong with her heart. She was in the hospital a short time — a few months — as she wasn't very sick, and they said she got over it okay. But I was always afraid of this, that she'd catch another cold and get it all over again. Dolly's such a bad girl. She always does what I tell her not to do; she never wears her rubbers."

Doctor: "Is it Dolly's fault she got sick?"

Lucia: "Oh, no it's her mother's. She should have made her wear her rubbers, but she didn't. Now if she should be sent to the hospital you send her. She'll get better there. Anyway I can't keep her here. She's too much of a brat. She never minds me. Keep her there a good long time so she'll be a good girl when she gets home. I don't want her home. She's too bad at home and I've got a boy at home who's good."

Doctor: "What if you don't come and get her?"

Lucia: "She can just go to an orphan asylum. The doctors don't want her if she's well: no one wants her if she's sick."

Doctor: "But she's been in 6 months already. That's a long time to a little girl like Dolly."

Lucia turned to the doctor and said earnestly, "I hated being in. I was in for a whole year, too. No one came to get me."

This feeling of desertion by the parents constantly recurred in each child's recollections of the hospital stay. The child's need for dependence on his parents to support him under such a stress situation is well understood. Separation from them at such a time amounts to a weakening of the child's capacity to deal with the problems of adaptation, and his anxiety about the separation and about the illness becomes increased. The nurse, doctor, or attendant can function as a parental substitute, but visits, letters, and real contacts with home are essential to the child. Frequent visits by the parents during hospitalization do much to overcome this feeling of desertion and enable him to handle his illness better. The crying which follows such visits is often felt by some to be detrimental to the child's condition. From an emotional standpoint this crying may serve as a valuable release for his misery. The attempt to suppress such feelings is a real drain on his resources, and it appeared that the longer the interval between visits the more emotion the child had to release.

5. Convalescence and return home.

Following discharge from the hospital with its limiting environment, the child often burst forth in a surge of activity when he reached home. This proved to be upsetting to the mother who was cautioned about the restrictions she must place on the child, and, in her apprehension, she reacted to his behavior by imposing even more restrictions. To a child who has longed to come home for many months and envisaged a life free from regulation, this reaction was both baffling and disappointing. On the other hand, overindulgence on the mother's part may be upsetting to the patient, who feels he must be sick indeed to be treated in such a fashion. This overprotection augments his fear of being damaged or different because of the rheumatic fever. One child defiantly said: "They won't spank me; they wouldn't dare. I've been sick." At the same time she expressed her anxiety about the parents' change in attitude toward her. One can guess what abolition of discipline accompanying this overprotection might mean to a growing child.

Again, the anxiety implied in the changed treatment was a source of concern to the child. The extent of the anxiety is expressed in a 9-year-old boy's remark, "Now that I'm home again the outside world seems sort of strange, and a lot bigger than I remembered it. My mother says I've got to rest a lot and get big and strong before I can go out and play again."

The children who were kept at home for their convalescence seemed to fall into a rather homogeneous group. They expressed fears which were tied directly to their parents' overprotectiveness. In general they were a passive, dependent group. Their rebellion, which might have expressed itself against the hospital and personnel, had to be quelled in home convalescence. It had to be expressed in subtler, less open ways. For example, there was the 8-year-old who "led her parents around by their noses because she'd been sick and if they didn't give in to her she'd kick and scream and cry and get sick all over again."

The returns to the Rheumatic Fever Clinic for checkups seemed to frighten them all. They were afraid of the bad news of recurrence and the fear of being suddenly hospitalized again.

Visits to the therapists of the study assumed the same significance. A 9-year-old girl expressed her feelings as follows, "What am I coming here for? Are you going to give me tests with needles and things, or are you just going to watch me to see what's wrong? They never tell you anything at the Rheumatic Fever Clinic either. They don't tell you what they are going to do. They block your eyes and say you won't feel it. (Going on to a doll) She hates hospitals. She does feel it, but they tell her she's not going to. Open your mouth wide so I can pull your teeth out. They're not going to tell her anything about what they're going to do and then they're going to pull her teeth out. They forced her to take her aspirin. She hated them. But they made her better. She doesn't have heart trouble though. I don't hear a thing. Now she's practically well. Let's close the case."

6. Reactions to the illness.

Any severe illness such as rheumatic fever with its implications of heart damage seems to serve as a real trauma which lowers the capacity of each child to withstand the tension of day-to-day living and separation from his family. However, rheumatic fever seems particularly hard to endure because of its constant threat of recurrence and the possibility of death. In these respects it is much like cancer and one is struck with the remarkable similarities between the findings in the current study and those reported by Shands and associates (10). They stated that "The difference in behavior and affective state of patients with psychoneuroses and those with somatic illnesses are largely differences in the intensity and duration of certain observable phenomena rather than differences in kind."

In those children whose prior adjustment to life had been an effective one, the reaction to rheumatic fever was minimal, whereas in those children who had previously shown evidence of emotional disturbance, the reaction was more marked. Between these two appeared to be a group which developed a type of reaction under severe stress that Ferenczi (3) called a "patho-neurosis."

As in any stress situation the patients reacted with various adaptive mechanisms with varying degrees of success. The particular type of adaptation chosen, as Fenichel (2) among others has pointed out, "depends, of course, on the total structure of the personality, its history, and its latent defense struggles." The following were the principal types of reactions found.

Denial.

This was one of the most common defenses. An insecure 10-year-old boy, whose family was made up of six sisters, mother, and alcoholic father, said, "I ain't never been sick." This was despite the fact that he had spent nearly four years of his life in the hospital. Seeming to find some explanation for his comment he went on to say, "The docs just made it up. I guess they needed kids for the hospital."

Regression.

Eight-year-old Charlie typified this reaction. He had always been bullied by a hostile, overprotective mother who never allowed him to grow up. When he was put to bed he soon began acting like a child of 2 or 3 with baby talk, thumb-sucking, and infantile behavior. His was not an isolated case but something seen more in the hospital setting than afterward.

Identification.

The study found children who relieved their anxiety about their illness by identifying with children who had been sick with rheumatic fever and had then become well. This was especially true in the hospital where frequent references were made to those patients who had gone home.

Another use of identification in handling anxiety aroused by the illness and the doctor as typifying the illness was by identifying with the aggressor. Several examples of this have already been seen wherein the child played doctor and performed tests on a doll similar to those she had experienced in the hospital and the Rheumatic Fever Clinic. This assumption of the controlling role instead of the passive one was of great comfort to the child.

Repression.

An occasional child repressed all feelings about his illness. Elise, who had been in the hospital nearly sixteen months, kept answering the doctor's questions by saying, "I don't know" or "I don't remember." It was not until after she had been seen for over a year that she began to recall details of the hospital life and how badly she had felt there. During the early months of her interviews she appeared baffled by the doctor's interest in her illness and kept saying, "nothing ever happened in the hospital. There isn't anything to tell." Later on she recalled vividly how her radio was taken away as a punishment for overactivity, with her time up reduced for naughtiness, and how few and far between the visits were.

Isolation.

As a defensive measure isolation appeared most frequently in the children's follow-up visits to the Rheumatic Fever Clinic. They would be given appointments and then simply not appear. This would often happen three or four times in a row. When questioned they might put the blame on the weather but more likely they would say, "Why should I go back there? It just reminds me that I'm sick and I don't want to hear about my rheumatic fever any more."

Sublimation.

Only a few children were able to use this successful defensive reaction. A 13-year-old started drawing pictures of her dreams during the long months in bed at home. These seem to be closely linked with her fears and worries over the illness as seen in her interview material. When she recovered, her interest in art continued and finally she sought and obtained a scholarship in a local art school.

Whereas healthy children might have a basically optimistic attitude toward competition and punishment for being bad, these children were fatalistic and looked for punishment in terms of certain recurrence of disease. One girl of 12 said, "I feel that if I don't do everything the docs say I'll get sick again and that will be it. Then I'll never get big and marry like my sister." Competition with other children their own age was tinged with this same fatalism. Many of them seemed competitive on the surface but under a rather thin veneer one felt an incapacitating fear of losing which rendered them failure-prone. The threat of recurrence of the disease became symbolically associated with punishment for any successful aggressive approach on the part of the child. George, 10 years old, said, "I wanted to pitch in our ball game the next day when that night I woke up and had a pain in my elbow. I guess that is when my rheumatic fever started."

Some children make conscious use of the illness. Roberta, an 8-year-old girl, typified this when she said, "I make my father do what I want him to. When he won't I just grab my chest. He knows I might die any time!" A less conscious use of the illness for secondary gain seemed to be present in George, who had many "false alarms" in his hospital record. Along with two prolonged hospitalizations for active rheumatic fever, he was admitted overnight to the emergency ward on six different occasions for a question of recurrence of his disease. All tests proved negative and his mother pointed out that each episode followed some failure in school or with his contemporaries. He was a passive boy who refused to compete in school with his classmates or in checkers with his therapist. When he did win, he became anxious and wanted to play another game to lose. His fatalism about recurrence of rheumatic fever was in the same vein.

There did not seem to be anything peculiar to rheumatic fever patients in the use of these defense mechanisms. Any sick person, as Freud (6) pointed out, "relinquishes his interest in things of the outside world." The somatic process occupies his entire interest, and his handling of it reflects many factors in his background and personality.

In this study the conclusions drawn by Josselyn (7) in her paper on rheumatic fever were borne out. Rheumatic fever seemed to add pressures and anxieties to an already existent weak psychic structure.

7. Recommendations for the children.

It is of advantage to a child with rheumatic fever to have someone, preferably a parent, stand by and explain as much as possible what is going to happen to him. The details of hospital life and the procedures he may expect can be elaborated upon. Later the child finds security in his parent and the memory of having been prepared. Each new event reminds him of his parent's explanation for it and gives him comfort. The doctors and nurses have a responsibility to give the parents information so that they in turn can pass it on to the child. Likewise, the various members of the hospital can act as substitute parental figures for the child. Warm, sympathetic, and flexible nursing personnel can alleviate the double psychological trauma of a) the loss of parents, and b) the guilty feelings brought out in the child by having become ill.

The realistic difficulties and restrictions of rheumatic fever seemed less crippling than the fantasied ones. Realism, however bad, has a more reassuring quality for children than the fear of the unknown. Talking to a child about his illness is reassuring to him. An understanding doctor encourages ventilation of these fears, anxieties, and questions from the child. This leaves a valuable bond for communication. The child can then express his anxieties as the illness and convalescence progress. It greatly facilitates helping him to deal with them as they arise.

The admitting procedures can be conducted in a friendly fashion, and parents can be urged to bring in a child's favorite toy, to write him postcards, and bring him reminders of home. In making recommendations for the hospitalized children one must consider the need for restrictions imposed by the limitations in any hospital. The investigators feel strongly that more frequent visiting by the parents would do much to overcome feelings of desertion. Since abandonment was the principal trauma leading to these children's neurotic difficulties, one would be striking at the very source of their troubles by promoting continuous contact with their parents who are their main source of strength. Many hospital personnel feel that the crying which follows parental visits is detrimental to the child's condition. From an emotional standpoint, however, this crying serves as a valuable release for the child's miseries. It is his method of dealing with his inner feelings of desertion and rejection. His attempts to suppress such feelings are a real drain on his resources.

Often the children interpreted as punishment their being kept in bed, having needles or necessary procedures or having their "time up" taken away. This is helped by sympathetic explanations from the doctor or nurse as to the need for restrictions which did not imply criticism of the child.

A normal child's mischievousness and restless impulses usually find an outlet in agressive play. He is deprived of these outlets in a confining illness like rheumatic fever. Unless constructive ways are found to deal with this energy it may build up to a level difficult for the child to handle. His response to this is frequently to withdraw or regress. If this accumulated energy could be directed into acceptable channels, such as group play or even group therapy by a psychotherapist, these deleterious reactions would be by-passed. This in turn would decrease later reactions to his hospital experience and make him less fearful of recurrences with their attendant hospitalizations.

The isolation of a newly admitted child for twenty-four hours can be traumatic. The frightened child who feels guilty and deserted has to endure a period of isolation in which he can enlarge upon his fears and loneliness. This may set the stage for regression and withdrawal. These are severely debilitating to the child's total personality and may do him permanent damage psychologically.

Finally, it is important to have a constant person in the hospital to whom he can turn to ventilate his grievances, fears, and fantasies. This will make the child feel that he is not deserted. Such a person would serve as a liaison between him and the outside world. He will thus be better able to resume his place in it when his illness is over.

The child must be prepared for his return home and for the restrictions which will prove necessary. Otherwise he will be disappointed because he is not able to lead a normal life immediately. Again, it is important to emphasize the need for these restrictions without implying criticism of the child. Factual explanation of the disease and the chance of its recurrence must be given. This can be done without suggesting constant impending disaster. A child can flourish emotionally despite a crippling physical disease, if he is given reassurance in an understanding way.

REFERENCES

1. Dubo, Sara: Psychiatric study of children with pulmonary tuberculosis, *Amer. J. Orthopsychiat. 20:*520, 1950.
2. Fenichel, Otto: *The Psychoanalytic Theory of Neurosis.* New York, W. W. Norton & Co., p. 257, 1945.
3. Ferenczi, Sandor: *Further Contributions to the Theory and Technique of Psychoanalysis.* London, Institute of Psychoanalysis and Hogarth Press, 1926.
4. Freud, Anna: *The Ego and Mechanisms of Defense.* London, Hogarth Press, 1937.
5. Freud, Anna: *War and Children.* London, 1945.
6. Freud, Sigmund: *Collected Papers.* London, Hogarth Press, Vol. IV. p. 39, 1949.
7. Josselyn, Irene: Emotional implications of rheumatic heart disease in children, *Amer. J. Orthopsychiat, 19,* Jan., 1949.
8. Langford, W. S.: Physical illness and convalescence: Their meaning to the child, *J. Pediat., 33:*242, 1948.
9. Montefiore Hospital, summary of unpublished material.
10. Shands, H. D., Finesinger, G., Cobb, S., and Abrams, R. D.: Psychological teachings in cancer patients, *Cancer, 4:*No. 6, Nov., 1951.
11. Unpublished data from the Massachusetts General Hospital, period from 1950-1951.
12. Unpublished data from the Massachusetts General Hospital Psychiatric Service.
13. Van der Veer, A. H.: Psychopathology of physical illness. *J. Child Behavior, 1:*55, 1949.
14. White, Grace: The role of the medical social worker in the management and control of rheumatic fever and rheumatic heart disease, *Amer. J. Med., 11:*628, 1947.

Chapter 17

Group Therapy for
Mother and Children in Parallel*

H. BEVAN JONES

The author describes the use of parallel therapy groups for mothers and children in dealing with childhood psychiatric problems, particularly those related to separation anxiety and school phobia. The therapy groups have proven successful in cutting down the treatment waiting list and in providing a new source of group therapy manpower from among the mothers.

For the past 20 years I have worked at the Southend Child Guidance Clinic as consultant psychiatrist and medical director three days a week. The clinic provides psychiatric services for the 37,000 children of the borough under the age of 16. The total population of this area is some 200,000.

The clinic staff consists of two educational psychologists, two secretaries, and myself. Until 1961 there was a psychiatric social worker on my staff, but since the psychiatric social worker retired, we have been unable to get a replacement, such is the current shortage. One of the secretaries has now been with us for five years and during this time, as she has shown a special interest in clinical work, she has learned to supervise a play group of children and to report back to me on their behavior with reliable accuracy. The second secretary has learned quickly to help in a similar way.

When in 1961 I found myself without a psychiatric social worker, I felt I should seek a different approach in trying to help

---

Note: Reprinted by permission of the author and *The American Journal of Psychiatry,* *125:*1439-1442, 1969; ©1969, The American Psychiatric Association.

Read at the 124th annual meeting of the American Psychiatric Association, Boston, Mass., May 13-17, 1968.

the children and their mothers. It occured to me that great economy would be achieved by seeing mothers and children in groups. I have always spent some 50 minutes in seeing every new case referred to the clinic and, in each year, the average number of new cases I see, largely in a diagnostic and couseling service, is some 160.

THE BEGINNING

From the beginning I usually selected for group help mothers with children aged seven or under needing help with (among other problems) learning to separate from their mothers. I planned to run the mothers' and children's groups in parallel, the children's group being supervised by an adult in a free play situation. This arrangement provided an ideal practice ground for children with separation difficulties to learn to leave their mothers.

The layout of the clinic has played an important part in the way the groups developed and behaved. My consulting room is occupied by the children as a playroom when groups are being held. The door to this room is usually open so that children, particularly the two-year-olds, can easily toddle out across the corridor, through the swinging doors into the waiting room, which is the space we first took over for our mothers' group. In the waiting room there is a square area bordered on two sides by a seat. I sometimes sit between mothers on this, but the seat which I most favor is a child's chair on which I sit close to floor level. This I did at first intuitively in an attempt to seem more approachable to the mothers and to adopt a role in which they could feel less threatened, and even perhaps helped, by looking down as they spoke to me.

It is difficult to describe adequately the atmosphere I try to develop here. What I aim at in the mothers' group is an atmosphere of laissez-faire and freedom from convention or professionalism. Under some circumstances the use of professional control may be necessary or helpful to the patient or the therapist, but usually I do not regard the area of our mothers' group as the place for this. This free, open, elastic group atmosphere is very important and is something we can demonstrate to visitors to our group more easily than describe in words.

The mothers all know that they can see me on their own at any time after or even during the hour-and-a-half group session if they request to do so. These interviews take place where mothers most naturally seem to want to talk. Some mothers talk most easily on their own in the corridor with the children playing around them as if in a playground.

For instance one mother, who had attended the group for some months and had been very inhibited in the group, talked to me one day in the corridor about her problem with sexual inhibition. While she was talking her young son approached us with a golf ball I had given him on a previous occasion, which he always brought back with him to the clinic. As the mother reached a crucial stage in confiding her problem, I threw the ball down the corridor so that the child ran out of earshot to collect the ball.

PROGRESS OF THE GROUP

From the beginning of the group three years ago I have dictated a report after each week has finished. From my weekly dictated notes I have extracted some details which are of particular interest to illustrate what has been happening.

The time of arrival of the mothers is elastic, between 11:00 and 11:30 a.m. During the 90-minute session there is complete freedom of movement for mothers, children, therapist, and workers in every direction. If a telephone call comes through I may or may not leave the group to answer it, making the decision in accordance with what may be happening. In this way I have attempted to create a real world situation and have deliberately avoided the more conventional techniques. Sometimes my departure from this group gives them a desirable opportunity to speak in the absence of father, brother, husband, or whatever I represent to them at that time. Often after leaving the mothers' group to go to a child, to take a child back to the children's room, to answer a phone call, or any other reason, my return is greeted by a question which the mothers have prepared in my absence.

In the beginning, if a mother in a group discussion asked to see me alone I agreed to such a consultation. In almost every case the mother told the group afterward what she had consulted with me about. During the last year I have usually, when asked for an individual interview, asked the mother if she could possibly consult me *in the group* so that the other mothers might share the problem. Mothers now almost invariably agree to put the problem to the group without a preliminary individual interview.

From an analysis of full notes on all children attending the group since 1964, some interesting points emerge:

Of the 33 new children treated in the group in the first year, 22 later brought their siblings to the group. Of these 22 siblings, more than 50 percent showed more severe difficulties later than did the original child. In other words, it became obvious that mothers frequently brought the wrong child to the clinic for help first. Of the 33 children seen in the first year 57 percent were first-born, 55 percent were boys, 45 percent were girls, the boys' average age was four years, and the girls' average age was seven years.

On my return from my first leave after starting this group, three years ago, I found that the mothers continued to meet, using their own homes in rotation to further their group discussions – a positive reflection of how much these meetings meant to them.

It became apparent that certain mothers were rapidly becoming capable of helping others. I selected two of these leader mothers to start a second group in 1965. This was designed for children in the latency period and for long-term support rather than active therapy. I have trained three mothers to take charge of three new groups and have other mothers in training to take on further groups under my guidance and observation.

When, after the first year of conducting these groups, I went back to one of my teachers of child psychiatry and described to him what was happening, he encouraged me with the comment, "You seem to have created a living human loom." I like to think that this is a true description.

I have found these groups of great value for teaching medical students. The optimum numbers for groups seem to be approximately four to eight mothers and six to 12 children. For teaching I find that the mothers' group can contain a number of attending students equal to the number of mothers present. Whereas in individual child psychiatric interviews it would be very difficult to have several strangers present, the groups can swallow up their presence and hardly lose their living rhythm at all.

In September, 1967 the mothers developed the idea of forming a closed group to work at a deeper and more confidential level than we had been able to achieve in the elastic situation of the waiting room. They elected, symbolically enough, to meet upstairs behind closed doors. The group meets for an hour and a half and is rarely interrupted by the entrance of children, as the children of these mothers have become free of separation anxiety by the time that the mothers enter this group.

This group is being conducted by a medical officer who previously attended the open group to learn to be a conductor. The senior educational psychologist also attends as an observer with a view to becoming a conductor for a second closed group which is being developed.

THE CHILDREN'S PLAY GROUP

In the play group shy children learn to separate from their mothers and to mix and play with other children. Children with school phobia may be shown younger children actually suffering the anxiety experienced in separation from their mothers, going through the life situation which is represented for all these phobic children in their symptoms of school phobia.

Thus, one day I pointed out to Gary S., a boy of 11 with school phobia, a four-year-old child running out of the playroom in fear when he missed his mother, who had gone out to the mothers' group. I explained to Gary that this four-year-old was now living through what he had seven years ago and that in his school phobia he was now suffering the echoes of that despair. Gary returned to school soon after this because, I think, he had understood his problem from the living example.

I use my children's groups as an aid to diagnosis. I can see for myself how children behave toward others here, and get information which we usually have to rely on school reports for. I always spend some of the 90 minutes of the session in play with the children, and I find this enables me to achieve rapport most quickly with the most difficult children − and I always say good-bye to them at the end of the session.

CONCLUDING OBSERVATIONS

In the mothers' group certain principles stand out most clearly. The group task is ready-made. The mothers learn to search for and find ways of dealing with their own emotional problems and discover how these are being reflected in their own children. The mothers are constantly shown living examples of the children's difficulties by the children themselves, even being graphically shown by visits of their own children. We have observed with significant frequency how remarkably often a child under discussion in the mothers' group will make his appearance, coming from the playroom which is out of earshot as if there is some strange, unproven, telepathic medium by which children, like animals, seem to feel and know that they are being talked about. How strange and complicated must be the matrices of these groups, and so different too the levels at which the groups work, horizontal or vertical, or in our case at Southend Clinic, upstairs and down.

The atmosphere I try to engender is that of home, quite naturally and, though it was not by conscious processes, the atmosphere of freedom is that which I enjoyed as a little boy myself rather long ago. Thus last Christmas time, when some of the children who attend the clinic came to my home for presents from the Christmas tree, I was delighted when one of the three-year-olds asked me, "Why aren't you home today? You should be home for Christmas," and I replied, "This is my home." "Oh no," she said, "Your home is the clinic."

I hope the work I have described suggests a way of creating a closer link in therapy between mothers and children by parallel treatment. It is thus that, through the interaction of untrained patients, certain aspects of experience may be distilled by group discussion. These can later be brought at an appropriate time to a therapist for correct interpretations and advice. This chapter is designed to seek and illustrate a new method in which the long waiting lists common to most understaffed child guidance clinics may be shortened and patients may be taught to help each other.

PART III

THE FATHER IN THERAPY

Chapter 18

The Psychological Role of the
Father in the Family*

O. SPURGEON ENGLISH

THE psychological role of the father in our society has been hard to grasp. Just as his social role has been continuously changing, so his psychological role assumes new forms as customs, beliefs, thoughts, and knowledge change.

Traditionally, Father has been looked upon as the breadwinner. In times past, so much of his time and energy was used in this role that at home he was thought of as taciturn and stern, albeit kind. He was respected but feared by his children who never learned to know him very well. He accepted the fact that he earned the money and Mother cared for the home and raised the children. A stereotype of the Victorian days was the father who was supposed to be very busy and very successful, indulging his children in many things in order to compensate for the fact that he really was not very interested in them at all and preferred the company of older people.

The more modern picture of Father is that of the enthusiastic young man barely out of his teens, interested in his wife and children, who likes his home and likes to work around it. He enjoys helping his wife with household duties and with the routine care of the children. He even likes to take care of them for an evening if his wife needs or wants to go out by herself! We should like to believe that fathers like this are replacing the older types. But facts seem to show that modern fathers do not really understand their role much better than their predecessors did. The purpose of this paper is to indicate why Father has such an

---

Note: Reprinted by permission of the author and *Social Casework, 35:*323-329, 1954.

important role to play in the life of his growing young boy or girl and to emphasize that his role in the family has many facets — he must be husband, father, member of the workaday world, teacher, mentor, and hero. The how, when, and where of his activities will make themselves more evident if the importance of these roles is made clear.

THE CHANGING CULTURE

A great change has occured in this country in the direction of urbanization. According to statistics compiled in 1951, "In 1790, 19 out of every 20 Americans were rural residents; the United States was largely a nation of farmers. At present, only 7 out of every 20 Americans live in rural areas, and, of those, less than half are farm residents. Instead of one out of 20, now 13 out of every 20 Americans are city folk. About half of them live in communities of at least 100,000 inhabitants, and the rest in places with populations ranging from 2,500 to 100,000" (1).

These figures carry with them many implications as far as the role of the father in the family is concerned. In the past, not only were many of these rural families farm families, where the children worked much of the time beside their parents, but in many instances Father lived near his work, was home for the mid-day meal and did not spend an hour or more each morning and evening in traveling to and from his work. These circumstances made Father more of a tangible, living entity in the home. At least he had more time to be with his children and they to be with him. He did not have to plan to be with his family; he was just always there. He may not have been actually aware of the "acting out" of his parental role, but his children saw him at his work and even helped him with it. They saw him with his friends, his neighbors, and business acquaintances. He communicated his philosophy and opinions of life in the ordinary course of living. They saw male friendliness, kindness, and justice in actual operation. They formed a definite image of how a father should behave. Moreover, in the rural areas of twenty-five or more years ago, entertainment

(1) Dublin Louis I. and Spiegelman, Mortimer: *The Facts of Life: From Birth to Death.* Macmillan Company, New York, 1951.

was scarce and what there was of it was likely to be of the "homemade" type in which the child was more often a participant than merely an onlooker. The church, the schoolhouse, and the grange hall were centers that encouraged cohesive relationships. Leisure-time activities were a group affair with Father serving as leader. He was a positive (even though stern) influence in shaping his children's personalities. He knew his family as people, as individuals with their limitations, accomplishments, needs, and abilities.

Modern urban life has changed this. Today members of a family may sit together in front of a television set or at an outdoor movie but they are not actively communicating with each other. They are not getting close to each other; instead, they are losing touch. They are communicating with an image on the screen rather than with someone real — and there is a great difference in what results. What a child shares with his father could be more conducive to security and to sound, practical knowledge of people than all that cinema and television combined can give. E. E. Cummings says it this way:

> "Why (you ask) should anyone want to be here, when (simply by pressing a button) anyone can be in fifty places at once? How could anyone want to be now, when anyone can go whening all over creation at the twist of a knob? . . . As for being yourself — why on earth should you be yourself; when instead of being yourself you can be a hundred, or a thousand, or a hundred thousand, other people? The very thought of being one's self in an epoch of interchangeable selves must appear supremely ridiculous." (2).

It would seem that our changing culture has tended to fragment family life. An increasing number of diversions for both adults and children cuts down the time a family spends together. Movies, adult classes, an education trip, television — each has its inherent value in developing personality, yet each tends to isolate and divide the individuals within the family.

These cultural changes and this fragmentation of family life, coupled with modern knowledge of the personality needs of growing children should indicate quite clearly that parents of

---

(2) *Six Non-Lectures.* Harvard University Press, Cambridge, Mass., 1953.

today must compensate for some of these social changes by an enhanced quality and quantity of interest in their children. And Father, who for one reason or another has defaulted in his role as parent, must enter the picture again to give his children help with the many emotional and psychological problems of growth.

This means more intensive parental participation in order to neutralize the effects of these influences; this means also that Father must work more intensively and cooperatively with his family. Not only must he replace some of this impersonal kind of entertainment which has diverted the child from participating in the "business of living" that characterized family life in the past, but he must augment and strengthen the pattern of family life as a whole.

FATHER AS A HUSBAND

One might well ask at this point — "But what is unique in the role of Father in the family? What does he do that is over and above complementing or supplementing Mother's role? He can provide an extra pair of hands but would not any good maid be of far more practical value?"

Life and personality development are composed of more than kind treatment of a full stomach, and diversion, important though these things may be. There are some facets of personality that grow and develop only in a home where there is a father playing his various roles in a mature way. When he is a genial participant in family life, he serves to introduce these elements more surely into the life of the growing child.

We live in a world of two sexes, with the man and the women performing certain unique functions, some of which are mutually complementary and others mutually exclusive. The mature mother, for instance, is warm, tender, affectionate, and attuned to the basic needs of her infant. She understands his rhythms of eating, sleeping, playing, and eliminating, as well as his emotional needs for touch, fondling, and companionship. It is probably within the potentialities of male psychology to perform these functions also, just as it has been possible for women to enter the realm of man's activities. But the fact that anatomically and physiologically man does not function in such a way as to bring him into close contact with the infant has prevented him from even having been tested out in these areas. Moreover, it seems unlikely that he ever will perform these womanly duties in rearing the young. Just as the mother is anatomically and physiologically adapted to coming into close contact with the young from birth — and before — so it is logical that she have the psychological equipment to use her talents for giving loving, tender care in the difficult human task of getting the psysiological rhythm of the infant's body regulated. Freud's contribution in this area has been invaluable, and it is quite generally accepted that a warm, friendly, accepting psychological climate is necessary in order to promote physiological health and freedom from psychosomatic illness. It is not so well understood that this climate is necessary for a healthy emotional feeling tone which will lay a firm foundation in the infant for happiness, a sense of well-being, and confidence or "mind strength."

In order for the mother to accomplish these things properly and consistently there are certain contributions that a father should make. In this role he may not mean to be directly "fathering" his children yet actually he is doing so. His strength and power are passing through the mother to the child or children. He is keeping her in the mood for her job by consistently providing material comfort for her through his labor. He gives her security and freedom from anxiety about food, clothing, and shelter. Further, he shows an interest in her activity, her creativeness, her work, and her needs, both emotional and physical. He "loves" her in that he satisfies her, stimulates her, comforts her, and assists her in the realization of her personality. This he does uniquely, as a male, in the fulfilment of his role in society. A maid, a sister, a friend, or a mother can perform these duties only partially, and it is neither socially acceptable nor biologically consistent for them to be done by a person other than the father of her child.

Since the pattern of society is heterosexual, a women, if she is normal, can accomplish a more complete emotional fulfilment and wholesome personality growth through the father of her child than from any other source. A woman is so dependent upon "psychological sets" in her personality than even if persons other than her husband could fulfil as much as 90 percent of her needs, she would reject them as inappropriate sources.

FATHER AS A PARENT

So much for the father's psychological role as it functions through the mother toward the infant in the early days and weeks of life. Father must, in addition, play his own psychological role with his child. He should prepare himself to teach, mold, influence, inspire, and develop his child so that the child may become a mentally healthy, good citizen who will be able to love and be loved, to enjoy life and be creative. By showing interest early in the life of the infant he awakens a corresponding interest in the infant toward him. In the beginning this may be only a small awareness, but it is an important one. Boys and girls develop their earliest and most decisive ideas about masculinity from their fathers. It is Father who evokes a process in his child which might be called "animating the mind" toward the male sex. If he delays showing enthusiasm and interest in his child too long, it becomes harder to create a "depth" of relationship with him which will make it easy for the child to grow in a healthy and happy manner.

As the child moves out of infancy it is essential for Father to continue to show interest and thereby make his boy or girl feel important. It is not enough for Mother alone to try to create this feeling of importance; Father needs to join her in this. One of the most common lacks in the human personality is a feeling of worth, of what might be called confidence or self-respect. Scarcely any child develops enough of this commodity and both Mother and Father should do more to ensure its presence. Just as Mother helps, Father, too, can help with his child's small problems. Dressing and undressing, helping with toys, teaching adeptness with objects around the home or in the yard are pertinent examples.

Let it be clearly emphasized that it is most important for Father to play the same role in the life of his daughter that he does in the life of his son. In some families there seems to be an unwritten agreement that Father shall avoid the domain of the females. The tacit assumption seems to be that the girls belong to Mother and that if Father has any time at all he will give it to the boys; nothing need be expected of him in relation to his daughter or daughters. Few adult women feel real closeness and comfort and understanding in their relations with men. One of the reasons for this is that an opportunity to develop these feelings was just not given to them early enough in life. Consequently, it is important to remember that the emotional development of girls calls for just as much interest, attention, and concern on the part of the fathers as is given to boys.

All children between the ages of 3 and 7 have the problem of learning the difference between masculine and feminine traits and patterns, and of incorporating them into their own personalities. It is in this phase of development that the oedipus complex is usually solved. Although many people question its validity, astute observers notice that a real problem exists here in learning to love and learning to relate oneself to the parent of the opposite sex. Until this phase arrives, a boy, for instance, has usually received a great deal of attention from his mother and many of his needs have been met by her. He now begins to view his father as a rival for his mother's affection. He shows this in a variety of ways such as being fretful, antagonistic, moody, unhappy, critical of his father, or, perhaps, unusually aloof. Father needs to understand the conflict the child is going through and must exercise patience. He should foster his son's identification with himself in a friendly manner and try to draw him into masculine interests both within the home and without. The solution of the oedipus complex for the boy is a gradual "giving up" of his mother and an acceptance and desire to be like his father. This is made easier when the father becomes someone that his son would like to emulate. To misunderstand, to scold, or to criticize the child tends to slow up or interfere with normal psychological growth processes.

By the same token a girl can learn to understand the pattern of life and can see that the attention of men brings with it prestige and pleasure. She, too, during the oedipal phase, has a sense of rivalry, this time with her mother, which makes her vie for her father's attention, wanting him exclusively for her own. She feels jealous of her mother and often acts in an antagonistic and hostile fashion toward her. She will talk about marrying her father when she grows up. To some this sounds like accidental childish prattle, but to others it has considerable psychological significance. We believe that solving the oedipus complex is an important and profound psychological experience which requires wisdom, tact, and understanding of the part of fathers as well as mothers, in order to have it run a satisfactory course. The oedipus complex is, of course, not a new phenomenon. For centuries, friendly and intuitive parents have seen it in action, have understood it and have helped their children through it without giving it any name or thinking about it in an unusual way except as a normal growth process.

It is important to emphasize again that children learn to love when quite young. Mature love and social harmony develop only if both sexes are taught how to love. Consequently, Father, as well as Mother, must be a participant in the child's development. If he does not understand his role or retreats from it, he then makes development all the more difficult or forces some kind of repression and immaturity. He should permit his son to love his mother but want the youngster to join him in masculine interests as well. He should help his daughter to know and enjoy men, setting himself as the first example.

FATHER AS COUNSELOR

Father can be of great help with the grade school child during the time when the child, whether boy or girl, feels unsure of himself, and when he must, to a large extent, be under the direction of women. A child can easily develop resentment at the imposed learning process when he is surrounded by women almost to the exclusion of men. What with Mother at home and the female teacher at school — both eager for him to learn and progress — it is easy to see how he can feel smothered by women. Boys in the lower grades are afraid of being "sissy" and any innate lack of grace or docility is often implemented by an inhibition or even refusal to accept the female orientation of the teacher as to what constitutes acceptable behavior or performance. Here Father can help, explain, encourage, approve, teach various skills, and share in a host of activities that will help popularize the learning process which the female teacher is trying to accomplish. He can attend Cub Scout meetings. He can help with the chauffeuring of the children to school events if this is the customary way of transportation. He can take an interest in his child's friends and share some experiences with them. He can approve educational activities. He can help to see that work gets done. He can set little tasks about the home and make sure they are completed. He can inquire whether homework is done — listen to reading and spelling if necessary and give approval and at times a reward when diligence brings results. This interest helps to make work a pleasure rather than a drudgery and makes cooperative effort easier for the child all his life.

Fathers are often less well acquainted with educational procedures than mothers. In line with the dictum that people are generally critical of the things they do not know about, the uninformed father, rather than admit his ignorance, is often negative in his attitudes toward modern education. Think of the father, for example, who utters disapproval of classes in art, dancing, or dramatics without first trying to understand their value; and think of how a child is handicapped in participating by his father's attitude that these things are for sissies and are based on women's whims. It has been suggested that the increased number of boys in special classes for retarded children is due in large measure to such conflicts in the young male.

Grade school children have a good deal of free-floating aggression and their sense of justice and fair play is in a somewhat rudimentary form and needs direction and strengthening. Father should talk to the child of this age about future plans and grown-up activities in order to bring to him an awareness of the various activities, values, and drama of the world outside the home.

Somewhere in the growing-up process, Father can and should help his child get acquainted with his sexual self. Father carries equal responsibility with Mother in answering questions or giving information. It is not suggested that there is a specific time for Father to take an interest in this subject of sex. Sexual activity begins in infancy and questions play a continuous part in the child's growth. Sex should be discussed freely and questions answered when and as often as a child asks them. It is important to remember that the term "psychosexual development" implies that sexuality runs through all of a child's development. The time to be aware of it and to help the child with it is all the time.

During puberty and adolescence the growing child of both sexes is beset with insecurity, uncertainty, inadequate self-esteem, questions about his life around him, problems of ethics, as well as thoughts for the future. Father should be ready to give counsel about choice of a vocation and to stimulate as many interests in the outside world as the youngster can comprehend and make use of. Too much stress cannot be laid upon the fact that the growing male child needs plenty of opportunity (provided by his father) to identify with a male. Life is long and hard and full of decisions, and it is important for a young man to feel confidence in himself — a confidence that he gains through the continuous, friendly, interested contact with his father. A girl, if she has a good relation with her mother, will of course tend to identify with her — and needs to do so. Father, however, can, through his interest in her, make it easier for her to be at ease with members of the opposite sex and to learn cooperation with them. Father will need to have had a good relation with his daughter during puberty and adolescence to be able to relinquish her to her male con- temporaries — a psychological role, incidentally, which fathers have not handled too well in the past. The doting father is prone to feel that no boy is good enough for his daughter. The father who has never enjoyed his daughter's companionship may resent anyone else's doing so and, unless he has been close to and had a friendly and trusting relationship with her, he may be overstrict and prevent her from having the wholesome experiences of adolescence which lead to maturation.

A father can further guide his children during adolescence in vocational choice, and he can make them aware that responsi- bilities await them in a world for which they need to be well prepared with a strong personality, as well as with whatever special training will be required for the fulfilment of their vocational aims.

So, it can be seen that personality development is a complicated affair into which elements from both sexes must enter in order to give the greatest strength and greatest understanding, the most wisdom and versatility. The world is demanding more and more of people. Since it is a world that is socially and biologically dependent upon the two sexes, both sexes must play their roles in accordance with both traditional and modern demands in order that the growing child may see how this is done. He must get the feel of it from the home, in which the mother is made free by the father to play her role and where the father demonstrates a clear picture of the best in masculine traits. Father's ways of loving his children and helping them to grow may not seem so very different from those of the mother. For instance, Mother cooks things the child likes to eat, darns his socks, and nurses him when ill. Father, too, shows his love by working for the family, fixing a broken toy, or bringing home to the dinner table an interesting story from the outside world. They both teach such things as fair play and responsibility. Yet, the father does have his own role to play; it differs in many ways from that of the mother. And while he plays his role he dresses differently, his voice sounds different, his body contour is different, and his ways of looking at things are different.

It would be unfair to say he is a "symbol" in one sense of the word. He is not merely symbolic since he is very human and real. Nevertheless, he does play a unique part in nature's plan for reproducing the young and helping them to grow up. The American father cannot afford to be a nonentity in the family. He cannot leave child rearing so much to the women of our nation. Such a division of labor is likely to produce lopsided personalities.

VARIANTS OF THE FATHER'S ROLE

Because Father's role in the family now seems to be pointed toward a more cooperative, socially integrated pattern it is hard to formulate. We still lack the proper terms to define our acceptance of what seems to be his more passive, flexible role. It is all right for Father to enjoy more tender feelings toward his children, but how do we express this? How do we compensate for our old ideas of masculine ruggedness and aggressiveness and substitute new concepts of tenderness which will not be considered feminine or oversoft? Perhaps we just lack the names for these changed relationships. Or perhaps there are too few words that can convey the meaning of these new roles. We are almost tempted to say that Father is not doing a better job in child rearing because we lack the ability to formulate his significance specifically. When we can realize and define the importance of his role we shall soon have concepts and words for the needs of the child and for the feelings of the father who responds to them. If we were to try, we might suggest the following as being variants of the father's role:

1. Companion and inspiration for the mother.
2. Awakener of the emotional potentials of his child.
3. Beloved friend and teacher to his child.
4. Ego ideal for masculine love, ethics, and morality.
5. Model for social and vocational behavior.
6. Stabilizing influence for solution of oedipus complex.
7. Protector, mentor, and hero for grade school child.
8. Counselor and friend for the adolescent.

This effort to define the psychological role of the father brings up certain questions for future investigation. So far in the study of the psychodynamics of mental disease we have prescribed the pathological factors under the name of environment, family, and parents and we have talked of rejecting mothers and stern fathers. Little effort has been made to *quantitate* the role of the father psychologically as follows:

1. How much of the psychopathology in a given case has been due to the absence of the father?
2. How much of the psychopathology in a given case has been due to the indifference of the father to the mother even though he was devoted to the child?
3. How much of the psychopathology has been due to the favoritism of the father for a certain child in the family?
4. How much of the psychopathology of a delinquent child can be shown to be due to the indifference or unwise management by the father of the child himself?

Since the mother plays such a large role during the feeding and toilet training, she undoubtedly is a crucial factor in producing some of the health or psychopathology of that period. But, as we hope we have shown, the father's influence is definitely not absent even then, and he plays an increasing role as time goes on. If a mother, for instance, is sufficiently orally depriving to produce alcoholism or schizophrenia in her progeny, could the father, if he knew enough, prevent this catastrophe, or could he mitigate its severity, and if so, how would he go about it? These areas of family living need some good research work, utilizing the psychiatrist, social worker, and psychologist. Such quantitation of the father's role in abetting the production of illness may indicate how much more seriously the American father must take his role in family life.

Much has been said about the role of the mother in producing greatness in the human personality but very little has been said about the role of the father. The men of this nation have made excellent use of the natural resources of their country. They have taken the coal, the oil, the metal, the wood and have accomplished amazing things. They have paid less attention to human resources. The time has long since arrived when they should take more interest in their offspring and participate more actively in their personality development. Father is a definite entity psychologically as well as in reality. He should be more conscious of what his role is and play it with greater pleasure and distinction.

Chapter 19

The Role of the Father in Families
with a Schizophrenic Patient*

MURRAY BOWEN, ROBERT H. DYSINGER, AND BETTY BASAMANIA

THE father often plays a peripheral part in the intense conflict in a family with a psychotic patient. The intensity of conflict between mother and patient can defocus his importance in the family problem. This chapter will focus on the function of the father in 10 families currently participating in a clinical research study. Lidz (5) was one of the first to focus specifically on the role of the father in these families.

Four families, consisting of father, mother, and severely impaired schizophrenic patient have lived together on a psychiatric ward in a research center and participated in family psychotherapy for periods up to 2 1/2 years. An additional 6 families with fathers, mothers, and overtly psychotic schizophrenic patients have been treated in outpatient family therapy for periods up to 2 years. The details of the theoretical and psychotherapeutic orientation have been presented in other chapters (2, 3). Theoretically, the psychosis in the patient is regarded as a symptom of a process that involves the entire family. Psycho-therapeutically, the family is treated as if it were a single organism. This report contains material from all 10 families. Detailed 24 hour daily observations have been made on each member of the inpatient families. The study is thus a longitudinal one in which the day to day adjustment of the families has been followed for fairly long periods.

This chapter describes the father as he functions in the day to day life of the family. We believe there are theoretical and

Note: Reprinted by permission of the authors and *American Journal of Psychiatry,* *115:*1017-1020, 1959.

therapeutic advantages in viewing the family as a unit and also in following the family as it functions under varying situations over a long period of time. In our experience, each family member functions in a variety of ways, determined quite as much by the reciprocal functioning of other family members as by forces inside himself. For instance, we often hear that "the father is jealous of the mother's attention to the patient." In these 10 families, this might be descriptively accurate for a single situation but descriptively misleading if applied to a total family adjustment. To summarize this point, the father is viewed as he functions as part of the family unit over a prolonged period of time.

The primary family threesome is father, mother, and patient. Normal siblings have also participated in the family studies but the intense conflict remains pretty much confined to the father, mother, patient group. Another clinical point has been most striking. The family members are quite different in their relationships to figures outside the family than they are toward those within the family. A parent might function successfully and efficiently in outside business and social relationships and yet, within the family group, find self paralyzed by indecision, immaturity and inefficiency.

Functionally, there is a marked emotional distance between the parents in all 10 families. There is considerable variation in the way the distance is maintained. One set of parents had a positive but very formal and controlled relationship. They had few overt differences, saw their marriage as ideal, and reported an active and satisfying sexual relationship. They used conventional terms of endearment with each other but wide areas of personal human experience were obliterated from their thinking and discussions. At the other end of the scale, another set of parents could not remain long together without arguments, shouting, and disagreement. In social situations they were congenial. In the middle of the scale, 8 sets of parents had adjustments with varying combinations of controlled positiveness and overt disagreement. They were aware of differences but consciously avoided touchy points. They maintained sufficient impersonal distance to keep disagreements at a minimum.

The fathers and mothers appear equally immature. The surface distance controls a deeper interdependence on each other. One parent denies the immaturity and functions with a facade of overadequacy. The other accentuates the immaturity and functions with a facade of inadequacy. In their day to day living, the overadequacy of one, functions in reciprocal relationship to the inadequacy of the other. Ackerman (1) and Mittelman (6) are among those who describe reciprocal functionings in marriages. A clinical manifestation of the problem is the "domination-submission" issue. The overadequate one is seen as "dominating" and the inadequate one as "forced to submit." Both complain of "domination by," and of being "forced to submit to" the other. Both avoid the responsibility of "dominating" and the anxiety of "submission." Another clinical issue involves decision making. The families are incapable of decisions that are routine for other families. One father stated this clearly when he said, "We cannot decide together on anything. I suggest we go shopping Saturday afternoon. She objects. We argue. Neither will give in to the other. We end up doing nothing." This example is characteristic of other decisions, both minor and major. Important decisions can remain undecided to be resolved by time, by circumstance, or the advice of an expert. Decisions that are "problems to be solved" by other families become "burdens to be endured" by these families. This paralysis of indecision creates the impression of "weak families." The paralysis subsides when one parent "dominates" the family.

In all 10 families the parents hold emotionally charged, intense, opposite viewpoints about the proper treatment for the patient. This conflict exists when there are no other conflicts. One father said, "The only question on which we never agree is how to raise children and how to raise parakeets. Neither ever changes a stand and neither ever gives in." The mother most often gets her way while the father opposes, either actively or passively. After her way has failed, the father institutes his plan while the mother becomes his critic and the predictor of his failure. The cycle repeats over and over.

There is a constant family relationship pattern in all the families. The parents are unable to have a close relationship with each other but each can have a close relationship with the patient, if the other parent permits. The mother is usually close to the patient and the father is excluded, or he permits himself to be excluded, from the intense mother-patient twosome. The term "intense" describes a close ambivalent relationship in which the thoughts of both, either positive or negative, are invested in each other. The pattern is most frequently changed by the mother, who withdraws from conflict with the patient, and leaves the patient with the father. In this situation, the father functions as a substitute mother. The father may change the pattern with his own activity but he cannot win the patient until he has somehow dealt with the mother's opposition. In such a situation, the father may become cruel and dominating and the mother inadequate and whining. The patient's psychosis is an effective mechanism to rearrange family patterns. In our experience, it is easier for the mother to win the patient from the father than for father to win the patient from the mother.

The fathers and mothers often divide the patient's time just as divorced parents share their children. This has been striking in the 5 families with schizophrenic sons. The parents had long been concerned about the sons' attachments to their mothers. The mothers blamed the attachments on the fathers' lack of interest in the sons. Both parents agreed that boys needed close relationships with fathers. All 5 fathers tried hard to get this closeness. One became a Boy Scout troop leader to encourage closeness with his son. Another father maintained a regular schedule of father-son activities. Another tried "to be pals" with his son, and another tried a continuing "man-to-man" approach. The mothers approved the father-son efforts, but they did not give up their prior intense attachments, and the fathers' efforts all failed. To summarize this point, the parents have an emotional divorce from each other but either parent can have a close relationship with the patient, if the other parent permits.

The family configuration emerges clearly in family psychotherapy. All 3 members attend therapy hours together. The therapeutic effort is to analyze the existing intrafamily relationships. There are periods when one of the threesome is absent from the hours. When all 3 are present, when the therapist does not structure the hour, and when the family follows the plan of working on its own problem in the hour, then the family group cannot avoid running into intense family conflict. This results in high anxiety, action, and progress in therapy. Any 2 members of the family threesome can successfully avoid anxiety issues and the therapy becomes a more intellectual, more sterile, and less profitable pursuit.

The relative functioning of the father has been revealed clearly in the sharp changes that occur in the course of family therapy. The usual family begins therapy with a compliant, non-participating father and a mother locked in emotional turmoil with a hostile infantile patient. The initial hours deal with the conflict between mother and patient. When the father begins to participate, the conflict shifts to the father-mother relationship. As the father begins to assert his strength, the mother becomes more aggressive, more challenging, and then more overtly anxious. Her anxiety and tears can cause him to retreat from his stand. When the father can maintain himself as head of the family in spite of her anxiety, the mother develops intense anxiety. One mother who had been aggressive, hostile, and dominating, changed in a few days to a kind, objective, motherly person. She said, "It is so nice to finally have a man for a husband." Another mother said, "I was so happy to see him stand up for himself. I couldn't help fighting him. It was automatic. All the time I was hoping and hoping he would not get concerned about my anxiety and the things I said." Another mother said, "If he can keep on being a man, then I can be a woman." These changes can last until the parents encounter anxiety. Then they revert to their former way of functioning but the changes repeat with greater frequency and less turmoil. The pattern suggests that a fairly normal family is a flexible one in which parents can shift their functioning according to the prevailing reality without threatening either of them. The first change in these families has been the parent in the inadequate position, whether it be father or mother.

When the parents change their functioning, the patient becomes more disturbed. The first real change in the patient takes place when the mother can maintain a firm stand against the child's infantile clinging. During one change in the parents, the staff referred to the parental closeness as "the honeymoon." When the parents can maintain a closeness in which they are more invested in each other than either is invested in the patient, then the patient makes rapid gains. When either parent becomes more invested in the patient than in the other parent, the psychotic process becomes intensified.

There was a different change in one family. A son dominated a home with his psychotic demands. His parents, especially the father, were fearful of physical harm if they opposed him. The anxiety reached a peak in which the father took a stand. The patient attacked. The father subdued the son physically. There was immediate peace and quite in the house. Within a week the patient's psychotic symptoms subsided and he returned to school. The father policed the home for a month. His relationship to the son had changed and the son's relationship to the mother had changed but there had been no change between father and mother. The father said, "I can't take it any more." He gave up his strong stand, the mother resumed her picking on the patient, and the patient resumed his psychotic behavior. The parents had each changed their relationship to the son without a change between themselves.

SUMMARY

A small number of fathers, mothers, and their schizophrenic children have been studied as a group and treated in family psychotherapy for periods up to 2 1/2 years. The view of the family as a single organism provides a broader, more distant perspective than is possible with close up views of individual family members. An effort is made to avoid the use of terms and descriptions that are associated with the more familiar individual perspective.

The father is described as he is seen to function in terms of the broader family perspective. Several prominent patterns have emerged when the family has been viewed from this position. The family members, particularly the father and mother, function in reciprocal relation to each other. They are separated from each other by an emotional barrier which, in some ways, has characteristics of an "emotional divorce." Either father or mother can have a close emotional relationship with the patient when the other parent permits. The patient's function is similar to that of an unsuccessful mediator of the emotional differences between the parents. The most frequent family pattern is an intense twosome between mother and patient which excludes the father and from which he permits himself to be excluded. The family pattern changes under varying individual and family circumstances in the course of daily living.

REFERENCES

1. Ackerman, Nathan W., Behrens, Marjorie L.: *Amer. J. Orthopsychiat., 26*:1, Jan., 1956.
2. Benedek, Therese: The Emotional Structure of the Family, in *The Family – Its Function and Destiny,* edited by Ruth Nanda Anshen, New York, Harper, 1949.
3. Bowen, Murray: Family Participation in Schizophrenia. Paper presented at annual meeting American Psychiatric Association, Chicago, May, 1957.
4. Bowen, Murray, Dysinger, Robert H., Brodey, Warren M., Basamania, Betty: Study and Treatment of Five Hospitalized Family Groups each with a Psychotic Member, read at the annual meeting of the American Orthopsychiatric Association, Chicago, Ill., March 8, 1957.
5. Lidz, Theodore, Cornelison, Alice R., Fleck, Stephen, and Terry, Dorothy: *Psychiatry, 20:*4, Nov., 1957.
6. Mittelman, Bela: Analysis of Reciprocal Neurotic Patterns in Family Relationships, in *Neurotic Interaction in Marriage,* edited by Eisenstein. New York, Basic Books, 1956.

Chapter 20

The Role of the Father with
Chronic Schizophrenic Patients*

A Study in Group Therapy

GUY DA SILVA

BOSTON State Hospital has a relatively long tradition of interest in the group psychotherapy of psychoses. Observations have been reported by Semrad (18), Mann (15), Arsenian (1), Blau (3), and others of various aspects of the group treatment of psychotics, while Limentani (12) has discussed the symbiotic identification between the schizophrenic patients and their mothers.

This chapter is in the same tradition of interest but focuses the attention on the role of the father. It will be the question of the role of the father mostly as it was possible to perceive it through the eyes of the patients and the patients' mothers.

In fact most of the fathers themselves were inaccessible for direct observation by the therapist and the importance of their "role" appeared at times to be in almost direct relation with its nonexistence.

In spite of the apparent contradiction it appeared to us that the role of the fathers in the maintenance of the illness of male chronic schizophrenics was essentially the fact that they had no role; that they were either physically or emotionally absent as fathers and that if present they were expected by both patients and patients' mothers to play a substitute mother role.

Glassman, Lipton, and Dunstan (8), describing "group psychotherapy with a hospitalized schizophrenic and his family" wrote: "The primary conflict area in this family . . . focused on the father's passivity. It was the topic most often alluded

Note: Reprinted by permission of the author and the *Canadian Psychiatric Association Journal, 8:*190-203, 1963.

to . . . and it was the topic which evoked the most intense emotions." Their observation reveals that the "group session highlights the acute feelings of aloneness and lack of support that the father's inadequacy elicits in the male patient during the pubertal and adolescent years . . . . The clash (between parents) as seen by mother had been a continuous effort to regain what she felt was lacking by constant recriminations, criticisms, and nagging in a furious attempt to activate the father." Ruth and Theodore Lidz (11), were of the opinion that "had there been a stable father . . . the patient would not have been so seriously affected by the mother's difficulties." To which we would like to add: indeed the mother's difficulties in separating herself from her child would not have been so great.

We believe further that the term "schizophrenogenic" mother is a poor one as it tends to overemphasize the role of the mother alone in producing a schizophrenic process in her child and tends to underestimate other factors which may also come into play before schizophrenia appears and maintains itself.

Eisenberg (6), remarks that "the psychiatric literature is rife with studies of childhood disabilities in which detailed attention is given to personality traits in the mother presumed relevant to the disorder in the child . . . (while) the father is the forgotten man." He feels that writers in psychiatry have pursued with great verve the theme that if something goes wrong in this world: *"cherchez la femme! . . ."* Morris Parloff (17), comments on the same subject: "The patient's mother appeared (in the psychiatric literature) to have the remarkable knack of being able to produce, single-handedly, neuroses, psychosomatic syndromes, psychoses or even juvenile delinquency with equal facility and from either side of her ambivalence." Leo Bartemeier (2) remarks that "while it is true a woman's attitude toward pregnancy, childbirth, and motherhood has been definitely moulded and determined by her relationships with her own parents and siblings, it is equally true that . . . how adequately or inadequately her husband's relationship with her satisfies her own needs, determines how well or how poorly she functions as a mother to their children."

METHOD

This chapter is essentially a product of the present writer's frustration when he was given the responsibilities as ward physician for a population of 250 extremely regressed male schizophrenics on the chronic service of Boston State Hospital.

Working with these chronic patients, one begins rapidly to feel that one is living in a museum of psychopathology and that, in order to shake the dust off some of the specimens of the collection amassed over the years, one had better concentrate one's energies on a few of them.

In an attempt to find out what made these patients "wish" to stay in the hospital I began to comb my population of patients in search of suitable patients for a small ward of only 23 beds, staffed with one registered nurse, one male and one female attendant during the day shift. In order to be a candidate for transfer to this ward, a patient had: 1) to be fairly young, 2) without brain damage, 3) to be a chronic schizophrenic with whom previous attempts at therapy had failed. In fact, most had had group therapy or individual therapy, EST, insulin therapy at some time or other in their hospital careers. All had multiple types of drugs; 4) there was another important prerequisite: all patients were chosen by the writer on the occasion of trips through the chronic wards but at least one member of the staff had to have some liking and interest in the patient: if there was any difficulty on the ward, that particular person would be responsible for handling the patient. These were the only criteria established and except for what has already been mentioned no attention was given to any particular personality characteristics or historical data in the patients' background. Indeed these were largely unknown at the beginning of the project. It is only as our study progressed that some common denominators began to emerge.

After our group of 23 patients were assembled on the ward, it became obvious that they were extremely ill: only one patient was capable of working in the hospital industry, nine were mute, four were incontinent of urine and another incontinent of urine and feces. They were all chronic schizophrenics and the breakdown by diagnosis gave: nine catatonics, ten undifferentiated schizophrenics with hebephrenic or paranoid features, and four paranoid schizophrenics. Their age range was from 18 to 48 years while the average age was 30. The average duration of hospitalization was six years eight months, with a range from one to seventeen years. We realized also that we were in the presence of a particular group of patients who had "come to the hospital to stay": 19 out of 23 patients had never been released and were still hospitalized under their original admission. Our group of patients was also remarkable for the high incidence of paternal deprivation: eleven fathers were dead, three were divorced, three had been chronic alcoholics for years, one was blind and a chronic invalid.

Most of the patients chosen were extremely regressed. For example, M.J.N. was a 31-year-old catatonic schizophrenic who had been hospitalized continuously at B.S.H. for the previous 14 years. In the course of his hospitalization he had remained unchanged, in spite of all types of treatment, becoming on occasion assaultive or a feeding problem. Most of his days were spent lying on the floor, incontinent and mute. A second patient M. Ed. McD. was transferred to B.S.H. at age 19 from another hospital where he had been for five years. He had remained at B.S.H. continuously from age 19 until 29 at which time he was started on our project. He was transferred to our ward from the cottage where he was living on the hospital grounds with other chronic patients, after I had surprised his mother in the cottage basement during visiting hours, along with her son whom she had undressed and was giving him a bath as one does an infant. The patient was lying nude on a table while mother was using oil and baby powder, vigorously cleaning his penis!

The group therapy sessions with the patients consisted of a weekly ward meeting of one hour during the morning, attended by all 23 patients plus the day shift personnel and the student nurses rotating in groups of four every four months. Minutes of the meetings were taken by one student nurse. The meetings were held in a relatively small room so that it was possible to watch the interaction in spite of the large number of people attending. Following the meetings, the personnel met together for a one hour discussion of what went on and for reading minutes.

Besides these weekly morning meetings, another group therapy session was held during the evening, every other week, also for a period of one hour and with the patient and evening shift personnel attending. A discussion period of one half hour with the personnel followed each evening session.

A total of 94 group meetings were held from March 1958 until July 1959.

A daily report of the patients' behavior was also kept on a 24 hour basis so that correlations could be made between the behavioral communications of the patients during the week and their verbal or nonverbal communications during the group meetings.

The group therapist was also the ward physician and spent two to three hours per week seeing patients individually for medical problems and crises on the ward.

The first five months of meeting with the patients was a period of complete despair and frustration for the therapist. Through this period patients remained withdrawn, isolated, sleepy, mute, and generally disinterested in the psychoanalytically inspired interpretations of the therapist! The monotony of the meetings was only occasionally broken by anxious laughter of a student nurse, a patient "bumming" a cigarette from the therapist instead of insight, or a sudden outburst of "barking", assaultiveness or incontinence.

PARENTS PARTICIPATION

The patients' mothers appeared omnipresent and disruptive, demanding immediate medical attention for a callus developing on their sons' toes, carrying bundles of food so that their sons could "survive" from one visit to the next or, in the case of one mother, establishing quarters in the male patients bathroom every visiting day to take her own bath with state soap and water!!

After five months of trying, almost consciously, to avoid the parents it became increasingly clear that they needed to be seen if one was to understand something of the psychopathology of their sons. Observation had also been made that when the mothers were given plenty of time to listen to their complaints regarding the alleged mismanagement of their sons they would very quickly stop being so troublesome and disruptive. It had become equally apparent that they were competing for the attention given to their sons and that an interview granted to discuss the patients would often end up in discussion of the mothers' own problems.

An invitation was therefore sent to all parents to meet with the patients' therapist, and the ward nurse acting as an observer, in group sessions of parents only. Meetings were held for one hour every week on visiting day. The reason given to the parents for the meeting was the therapist's feeling that having a son in the mental institution must bring questions and problems for the parents and the therapist's willingness to discuss these problems and to try to be of help if he could.

Out of a possible total of 31 parents: eight (seven mothers and one father) were faithful members and almost never missed a meeting; seven other parents (six mothers and one father) came intermittently to the group; another nine parents (seven mothers and two fathers) could not come to the meetings because of their work but were seen regularly and individually twice a month while another father maintained sporadic individual contact. The other six parents were either never or only rarely seen.

There was a total of 42 group therapy sessions held with the parents in the course of one year from August 1958 until July 1959.

SUMMARY OF THE MEETINGS WITH BOTH GROUPS

The patients' reaction to the announcement that their therapist would also begin meeting with their parents was a violent one. One patient, H.R., whose childhood had been marked by several surgical interventions and whose mother was working as an aide in an operating room while father was a diamond cutter, announced that he had a knife to keep the women away and cut someone's head off. He suggested that all patients "burn some rotten eggs to smoke them all out of here." Following this statement all patients grouped together and remained silent for the 35 minutes that was left of the meeting in spite of my attempts to get them to verbalize their feelings. Even the therapist's cigarettes could not bring a word from them as no one wanted to be a scab and break the strike. But they did not only go on a silence strike, they also went on a hunger strike. Nine of them refused their meals that day while one patient refused to eat for three days. I was extremely worried and was almost ready to give up my plan to meet with the parents. An interview was scheduled with every one of them individually and recommendation was made to students and personnel to spend a great deal of time with them. The strike ended promptly and at the next meeting they began to talk, mostly asking for some reassurance on my part that *"their needs would come first."* Concerns were expressed about confidentiality, and fear of being "double crossed." They talked about surgery, having stomachs being taken out and legs cut off. One patient said: "you were a good father to us but we don't understand you any more."

In spite of patients' verbal opposition to their therapist meeting with their parents there was one encouraging fact; while during the previous five months there had been only isolation and regression and withdrawal during the group sessions, for the first time the patients were able to react as a group in their opposition to the therapist. The silence strike was actually the first time that members got together.

Fourteen people attended the first parents meeting: 13 mothers and one father, M.D. who also was accompanied by his wife. Confusion characterized this first meeting. M. and Mrs. D. launched an attack against drug experimentation. Mrs. M., the intellectual of the group, delivered a speech whose title could have been: "Parents are to blame for whatever happens to their children" while the whole group listened, terrified. The focus however was on Mrs. C. who was completely deaf but insisted on knowing what was happening. Mrs. F. wanting to be helpful (!) suggested that, maybe, I could, in the course of the meeting, write to Mrs. C. things I wanted to say. She did not think it would be disruptive to the meeting as I could limit myself to writing only the *important* things! . . .

At the next meeting they talked about *someone influential* referring to the nursing supervisor who was, just as they, concerned about new rules regarding shaving. Their sons were too regressed to shave themselves and might kill themselves with the razors: if they did, the therapist would be held responsible. In fact, both patients and parents tried frequently to get the therapist to fight with the nursing supervisor and to test which one was really the supreme power and had the greater authority. They talked about doctors who have nervous breakdowns and doctors telling them that their sons hated them. Mrs. F. said: "How could they hate us? Mothers are all good, mother means only goodness." After a bitter argument with Mrs. M. who repeated her speech blaming mothers for all the ills of their sons, Mrs. F. corrected her previous statement and declared that: "at least, all the mothers who are here today are good." The blame switched to the Hospital and the doctors who were killing their sons by making them work in the hospital industry. They also wondered about what their sons were saying during the ward meetings.

One month later, Mrs. F. predicted the therapist's failure with her son and Mrs. B. made a slip saying that her son refused to go back "home" after a week-end visit. Home being actually the Hospital. When the slip was pointed out, they agreed that the Hospital was their sons' home. In fact, this slip was made repeatedly not only by the parents but also by the personnel. Mrs. B. cried and complained how different her situation was from that of her son who was cared for while she had to go out and make a living for herself. Repeatedly, they complained that life had been unfair to them: why did they have to work while their sons were taken care of. Mrs. M. said they felt like coming and forgetting about their responsibilities. Actually, nine mothers had been working for years, either because their husbands were dead and they had no support, or because husbands had abandoned them or were chronic alcoholics. The therapist's attitude was to repeat that he was not here to blame but to help, since it must be very difficult for a mother to have a son in a mental hospital and be also working to provide for herself and receive no support from parents or husband.

They developed a pattern: instead of facing a group issue, they would displace it to their sons and reproach them for doing what they were doing themselves. Frequently, they used their sons in order to express their own feelings towards the therapist or towards each other. For instance, after Mrs. W. had complimented Mrs. D. on a new hat, Mrs. D. answered her: "My son seems to like your son." In another instance, Mrs. M. and Mrs. McD. had a violent argument in a meeting. During the following week, Mrs. M's. son assaulted Mrs. McD's. son. At the following meeting, Mrs. M. apologized to Mrs. McD.: "I am so sorry my son punched your son on the nose last week." To which Mrs. McD. replied that, "it had not really hurt"!

In a recent book edited by Don Jackson, *The Etiology of Schizophrenia*, Murray Bowen (4) reports the same kind of mechanisms occuring frequently in the 14 families of schizophrenics he studied. The mother would deny a feeling or sensation in herself, for instance a sensation of hunger and then would go and feed her psychotic child. So that "a situation that begins with a feeling in the mother becomes a reality in the child."

In our own two groups, we were further impressed how frequently the same topics were brought up with the patients and with the parents, even though both groups had had no contact.

In the same time that they would talk about themselves through their sons, they would also, as if to counteract this fusion of identity, place some distance between themselves and their sons. Mrs. McD. for instance never said "my son Edward" but would say: "my patient Edward." Mrs. M. once said that sometimes she wonders if she was really her son's mother because "he really looks like the people on my husband's side of the family."

Thanksgiving was the occasion for much talk about their incapacity to rejoice on holidays. For years they had been coming to visit their sons, never missing a visiting day. How could they take a vacation and celebrate during the holidays; when there is a corpse in the house, it's time for mourning not for celebrating. And there was a corpse in their house. Mental illness is worse than death; when one dies, grief passes after a short while but mental patients keep dying without really passing away. There was a consensus of agreement when Mrs. D. said that their sons would be better off dead. And Mrs. McD. added: "At least when they are in the cemetery, you know exactly what they do and where they are, you can visit the grave and bring flowers; but when they are mentally ill you always wonder how they are and if they get hurt." Their sons were poisoning their lives.

Christmas time reminded the mothers that they had failed in their progeniture. Jesus was born to be a great man but their sons reminded them of their worthlessness as mothers.

Three fathers attended the group meetings, two of them intermittently. One of the two was a chronic alcoholic who was blasted for his "vice" each time he appeared. The other was suffering from stomach ulcers and would talk only to express his somatic complaints; he was listened to sympathetically and treated like a baby. The only father who came regularly was M.D. Each time he would try to say something, he would promptly be shut up, often by his wife. When it was learned he had a car he became the chauffeur for two other ladies of the group. In the group, he was largely ignored and the therapist's attempts at supporting him were met with fierce hostility. One day, he was absent and when the therapist remarked about it, his comments were at first ignored. Finally the mothers asked: What good are men for any way?

They said that men were useless in the house and did not even know how to take care of babies. Men were good for nothing. The therapist had better not continue on this subject because they would "pin him down." In subsequent meetings, more of the same feelings were expressed and always with the most intense emotions: men were just like kids, always in need of praise and support. If they had had a girl instead of a boy, things would have been different. Some said that they had given to their sons the name of their husband and that was why they became sick. They had been deceived by men and were bitterly disappointed in their marriage. Many had lost their husbands through death soon after their marriage and had been obliged to carry the burden of raising a family alone. It was unfair to women to get impregnated and then get stuck with kids. Others were abandoned through divorce and separation. Still others who were living with their husbands complained that they were receiving no support or encouragement from them. It was not the mother's fault if she had to wear the pants in the house; they were forced to do it because their husbands were not capable of taking their responsibilities. Men were animals and their sons were really like animals: regressed, voracious, and incontinent. They had tried at first to change their husbands but had given up because "how do you change a man"?

They felt guilty at the same time for having lost their husbands. Mrs. M. said her son accused her of having killed his father, and Mrs. McD. had not told her son that his father had died "because he would have killed me." His father had died two years before but the therapist was the first person to announce it to him. At the same time they would accuse their sons of being responsible for the death or divorce of their husbands or for their general indifference towards them.

On the ward with the patients there were frequently the wishes expressed by the patients that "men outnumbered women." They demanded of the therapist that he bring more male personnel on the ward. Referring to female personnel and student nurses, they complained that women were just capable of caring for babies, and they were tired of having to ask permission of women all the time. There were too many of them in the hospital already. Women did not wear "make-up" on their face but "war paint." If they were to learn to work outside the hospital they needed men to teach them. They were extremely depressed when a male attendant left and they accused the nurse in charge of being responsible for driving him away. The nurse and women in general were like monkeys. The men came from the women and came also from monkeys. Both women and monkeys ate "bananas." The therapist should provide them with more "bananas" and with more male attendants.

As was mentioned earlier, the therapist's attitude with the patient at the beginning was very noncommittal, interpretative, and with no results. Probably as a consequence of the work with the parents, who alternately infantilized their children or expected unrealistic achievements from them, the therapist became more aware of his own unrealistic expectations of the patients and began to focus more on little reality problems in their everyday life and less with their unconscious. In response the patients began to improve. The unhealthy aspect of their personality was constantly in front of them. They did not need to be reminded of it. More benefit was obtained when more focus was given to the little areas of the personality which had been left intact in spite of the chronic psychosis and deterioration.

The patients reacted as if dealing with women and dealing with their unconscious, provoked too much rage at unsatisfied dependent wishes and this rage was so overwhelming it could not be handled. They claimed that they wanted to deal with men but it seemed that their desire to deal with men was only a denial of their very intense oral wishes which could be expressed more safely with men, as if dealing with men was delaying the regressive trends to be like babies. They demanded of these men, however, that they take care of them, protect them, and "mother" them better than they felt their own mothers had done.

They were able to talk about how much they missed their fathers and those who had lost their fathers were hoping to be reunited with them. They never said that they missed their mothers since they were fused with them. Both patients and mothers complained about the absent fathers. It was he or whoever he represented that they said they wanted.

The patients' feelings of despair when discussing having been abandoned by their fathers were extremely poignant. The world looked cold and empty without a father. Historically in several cases, the appearance of acute psychiatric symptoms had followed a desperate attempt at trying to identify with father in a manly endeavour, usually the beginning of work. Patient H. B., 27 years old, exemplifies this dramatically: his father, a chronic alcoholic, had constantly ridiculed him because "he was not a man." He would expect him to perform unrealistic tasks and then tease him in front of his friends and frequently beat him physically when he failed. The patient's acute symptoms appeared on his 21st birthday when father forced him to come to work with him. He has been hospitalized (six years) ever since. A similar case is patient O. McA. who proceeded to expose himself to little girls in a park after father made arrangements so that he could begin to work with him. He has been hospitalized for ten years.

It might be that these desperate attempts at trying to identify with father were really desperate attempts at cutting themselves off from mother.

Some of the greatest benefits in treatment arose when the patients' and the parents' attempts at manipulation and at stirring confusion and conflicts between the different members of the personnel failed. Repeated attempts were made in both groups at blurring the lines of authority. At one point, the therapist had to take a strong stand regarding the patients' care and make a decision to oppose some decisions taken by the female supervisor of the building after she had been pressured by some mothers of the group. We believe it is important to note here that these decisions involved the patients' care in specific ways: in these instances where conflicts occurred, the therapist was in the position of giving or wanting to give more food or privileges, while the supervisor and the mothers of the group were in the position of refusing to give. These incidents actually took place after we had challenged the parents' opinion that their sons were hopeless.

On the ward patients saw the therapist's attitude as evidence that he was determined to protect them. They talked about the "man being the boss," and began to show considerable improvement: assaultiveness disappeared completely, ward meetings were friendlier, some began to work and we saw the formation of friendships. Prior to this, every patient had been very isolated and there were few exchanges between them. Now all of them, except one patient, began to pair off. At first, there was some rigidity and exclusiveness in the pairs of "friends," each pair defending its unity against outsiders. Many were seen holding hands and walking together for a long period. Later, however, they stopped holding hands and pairs began to join so that small groups of four or five patients could often be seen together. Still later, these groups began to mix.

In the group of parents, they discussed the therapist's attitude as a "revolutionary change." One day, they all lined up along the wall facing him instead of sitting in a circle as usual. Mrs. M. wanted to organize a fund-raising drive, to get care for their sons in a private hospital so that they could get better treatment. Mrs. B., who was a nurse and considered herself best qualified, discussed plans to open a house for care of the mentally ill. Mrs. M., who had been previously obsessed with the fear that her son might hurt himself with a knife during meals, brought him a cake and a knife. Mrs. F. brought in a newspaper article saying that schizophrenic patients who commit suicide are not responsible themselves, since they are simply executing the hidden wish of a relative who then becomes guilty of psychic murder. She wanted me to state if I agreed with this article. Mrs. D., who had been absent for months, stormed in, delivered a speech in Russian and Yiddish in a prophetic tone and when asked to translate it, said it meant that she had had a heart attack recently and if her son came home, she would have another one and die. She then quickly rushed out of the meeting.

The mothers felt they had been cheated; the therapist was guilty of treason and they wanted him to state if he was for them or for their sons. They had great difficulty accepting that he was "for" both.

When termination was announced, the mothers talked about being forced to take responsibilities all the time because nobody else did. Their husbands abandoned to them the whole burden of decision and the care of the children. Similarly, if the therapist was taking his responsibilities seriously, he would not abandon them and leave to work elsewhere. At the last meeting, they came in with bags of food, saying that their sons or the therapist could eat and have a party but there was no party for them as long as their sons were sick. As the therapist focused on the meaning of the food instead of eating it, Mrs. M. said she meant to tell them that they too had the right to enjoy parties and have things for themselves so that they will be better able to give if they could learn to receive. M.D., the father who attended regularly, offered the therapist a gift, a pen, which he had bought after collecting money from the members.

On the ward, the last meeting with the patients was a very sad one. A group of patients on the ward started a song about a father who had died and about his son who was terribly lonely. To console him, father appeared to him and promised him that one day they would again meet and never separate. M. M. asked repeatedly when he could join his father who was now dead and in Heaven. He felt restless waiting for his father as he had a terrible longing for him.

In January 1962, two and a half years after termination of the group another meeting was held with 15 patients attending. A meeting was also held with the parents, ten of whom attended. A few patients and a few parents could not be reached. The first question was the same in both groups: they wanted to know if the therapist was going to resume work with them.

Some patients showed the therapist blisters and scars they had since "we had last met"; another patient left, slamming the doors, (he came back later). The other patients thought that he was angry because the therapist had walked out on them more than two years before. One patient said he wanted the therapist's identity, his life, his glasses. He wanted to be in the therapist's shoes because "I feel I am in you, Doctor." Another patient kept rocking himself and, looking at the therapist, was yelling: "Eat, drink, eat, drink!" Several talked about homosexual maniacs who sucked men and several complained with anguish of stomach aches and ulcers.

In spite of the separation of two and a half years or maybe because of it, they immediately and directly verbalized their unsatisfied hunger. At the end of the meeting, one patient, who suffers from a conversion reaction affecting his legs, had to be carried out.

Ten parents (eight mothers and two fathers) were present in this "follow up" group meeting. They all appeared glad to meet again with the therapist, shook hands with him and commented that he looked fatter and that it was becoming to him. They were very interested in what the therapist had done during his absence and what his plans were for the future. They teased him, saying that he had invited them to find out if they were still holding on or if they had broken down after the termination of the group. They said they were holding on but Mrs. F., the mother of the patient who could not walk, told of her own inability to walk for a while after she had been in a car accident. But she thought her son's inability to walk was "all in his mind." Another mother, Mrs. D., showed a pair of crutches: she had broken her hip in a fall one and a half years ago and now she could not stand on her feet but had to lean upon her crutches and her husband. Mrs. M. said that her husband had changed to the point where he even spends money on her now.

They wanted the therapist's address in Montreal when he leaves Boston. Mrs. S. D., who, three years earlier, had said in a prophetic voice that she would die if her son left the hospital, now said that she wanted to see the therapist once more before dying. Now that her wish had been fulfilled she could die peacefully. As she talked, the other members listened approvingly. The whole group appeared agreeably surprised and very much pleased when the therapist reminded them of the pen they had given him and showed them how beautifully it still worked. Mrs. R., a former regular member who could not come that day, called and wanted the therapist to know she had changed her job. In the past she had been an aide in an operating room which used to scare her son who had multiple surgical interventions during his childhood years, but soon after termination of the group she had started working for the Family Service Association. Her job, she said, consisted of talking with people who felt lonely and needed encouragement and companionship.

DISCUSSION

To the question raised earlier in this chapter: "What keeps these patients in the hospital?" I would like to propose a tentative answer: It is my feeling that the *absence* of the father was an important contribution to the maintenance of the illness of our male chronic schizophrenics. The word *absence* here is understood as meaning not only the physical distance such as death, divorce, separation or long rravels but also as an emotional distance characterized by a lack of involvement as leader of the family unit. Our patients acted as if they did not want to go back to the outside world where there was no father, and chronic hospitalization was felt as the only way of escaping the absolute and overwhelming control of the mother with whom they had symbiotic ties. The relationship between parents was characterized by active attempts on the part of the mother to eliminate father, out of mother's anger at his lack of support for her, and by inability on the father's part to resist successfully this process of elimination. The women in the group saw their husbands, their therapist and men in general as maternal figures, mother substitutes who, like their own mothers, had not done enough for them, were depriving and ungiving and therefore useless. In the same way that they felt abandoned by their own mothers and later again had been abandoned by these useless men, their husbands, they were now being abandoned by their therapist at the group termination.

The past history of the mothers in our group revealed that they have had to endure great emotional deprivations and isolation, both as children themselves and later as wives. Several had lost their parents early in childhood and later in life had lost their husbands soon after their marriage and had been forced to work in order to support their children. Nine mothers were still working when the group started even though most were in their fifties or sixties. The more one listened to the mothers, the more one became impressed by their achievements in the face of great difficulties, deprivations and almost total lack of encouragement and support from the fathers.

In our sample of 23 chronic schizophrenics, there were 14 fathers who were completely absent (11 dead and three divorced), another three fathers who were chronic alcoholics and another one who was blind and a chronic invalid.

The percentage of paternal mortality in our sample of patients is about double the one found in the average population: 47% among our patients versus 25% in the general population.* (By comparison among 69 medical students, only 17% had no father, according to Lidz, (11), and among 22 residents in psychiatry of the Boston State Hospital with an average age of 31 only five or, 22%, had no father.)

The percentage of parental divorce and separation is also more than double than is found in the general population of parents of the same age: 13% versus 5%.*

We took a random sample of another 23 patients in the same male chronic service with a similar average age of 31 years and hospital stay of six years and eight months and found again a high incidence of "absent" fathers: 15 out of the house (13, or 56%, were dead and two divorced.)

In our own 23 patients we see some correlations between the total physical paternal *absence* (father dead or divorced) and an incomplete paternal absence, (what we called earlier emotional

*Henry S. Shyrock, Jr., acting chief, Population Division, Bureau of the Census: in a personally written communication. Jan. 30, 1962.

distance, meaning father is at home but he is drunk, invalid, passive or indifferent), and the length of hospitalization. We find that the length of hospitalization climbs from the average of 6.6 years to 8.2 years when there was a physical *total* absence, but goes down to 3.7 years when there was an emotional or "incomplete" absence. When calculated, this finding is statistically significant at the 0.01 level of confidence.

What is even more impressive is the fact that the paternal deprivation in our 23 patients was early; before they reached 15 years of age, seven had lost their fathers through death, another two because father had deserted the family, three had already a chronic alcoholic father and one a blind and invalid father. If we take into account only the nine fathers who were completely out of the house before the patient became 15 years of age, we obtain a figure of 39% of total paternal absence. The comparable figures for normals by other investigators were below 15%. Others give similar figures to the ones we found: Wahl, (19) studying several antecedent factors in the family histories of 392 schizophrenics reports 43% of them had lost one parent before age 15. Lidz (11) in his study of 50 schizophrenics found that 40% lost at least one parent before age 19.

According to Fisher (7), as quoted by Wahl (19), the incidence of orphans (who had lost one or two parents before 18 years of age) in the general population is 6.3%. In our sample of patients it was 30.4%.

Some workers have also reported a high incidence of parental loss among disturbed populations: Lindeman (13), among psychosomatically ill and Glueck (9), among delinquents, as quoted by Wahl. What we think is striking in our patients is that the parental loss was a paternal one. This paternal loss occurred early and it appeared that there had been no substitute paternal figure to support both the patient and his mother.

For the purpose of our study we chose as a criterion of maturation, the patient's ability to start working and maintain work because of the identification to the working father and because we felt it indicated a beginning of renunciation of the pleasure principle or as Joost Merloo (16) puts it, a beginning of renunciation of the *realm of the mother* and a willingness to accept demands of the reality. In the course of the life of the group seven patients out of 23 started to work, either in the hospital industry (four patients) or outside the hospital (three patients) even though they never were particularly pressed to work. *Every one of those seven patients had a relative who had regular contact with the therapist,* five of them whose mothers were coming regularly to the parents' group.

We feel that if the chronic schizophrenic is to improve and start working after months and years of inactivity and complete regression, it is necessary for someone, a father substitute, to fulfil some of the mother's need for support, encouragement and help in decision-making about the child. This someone should be willing and available to "step into the mutual relationship between mother and child and cut the symbiotic umbilical cord which retained the child to the world of the unconscious represented by the mother, and prevented him from moving into the world of the conscious represented by the father"(16).

If the father is not there to do this specific job of stepping between the mother and child and *cutting the cord* or "if the father is too weak or too busy to do the job, if he is either physically or emotionally distant, then the dependency upon the mother remains relatively too strong or too lasting" (16). Neither child nor mother can alone free themselves completely of the ties that join them.

We have noted earlier that the greatest benefits in the patients were derived after the therapist was forced to clarify, without doubt, the lines of authority and dispel the confusion of roles among the different people in charge of caring for the patients. One person has to be clearly in charge of the others. Many workers have described the pathological system of interaction going on within the families of schizophrenic patients.

According to Haley (10) "each member of the family, mother, father and schizophrenic child, is unable to acknowledge responsibility for his actions and each will disqualify the attempts of any other to announce a decision."

Murray Bowen (5), gives an excellent example of dramatic disappearance of psychotic symptoms in a schizophrenic boy after the father, in spite of his fear of his son, took a strong stand and asserted himself as the head of the family. The son reacted by assaulting the father, but the father was able to control him physically, after which the psychosis subsided and remained quiet as long as the father continued to police the house. His relationship to the son had changed, but because the father's relationship to his wife had not changed, father could not maintain his strong stand more than one month. After a month, he gave up his leadership, the mother resumed her picking on the patient and the patient resumed his psychotic behavior and his crazy demands on the mother.

The more we listened to the mothers, the more sympathetic we became to them until it was impossible to feel at all critical of them for the illness of their children.

Marguerit Mahler (14), in her work with schizophrenics and autistic children, observes that "there are infants with an inherent ego deficiency" (who do not appear to perceive the ministration of care by their mothers). Similarly there are also adult chronic psychotics who do not appear to perceive the ministration of care by both parents and hospital personnel.

It might be that the mothers in our study were forced in a symbiotic fusion with their sons because of the schizophrenic process in them and that they could not resist involving themselves in this mutual parasitosis because there was no father to cut the cord and protect them.

It might be that the only way one can protect oneself from the fantastic withdrawal and enormous demands of chronic schizophrenics and still live with them over a long period is to withdraw also and stop making demands on them for improvement. It is hoped that studies involving long treatment relationship over periods of several years between chronic schizophrenic patients and experienced therapists could be set up so that more could be learned about ways to maintain demands on patients for improvement and resist the immense frustration generated by their enduring chronicity.

SUMMARY

The author accepts the concept of symbiotic identification

between the chronic schizophrenics and their mothers. However he feels that the term *schizophrenogenic* mother is a poor one as it tends to overemphasize the role of the mother alone in producing schizophrenia in her child. He makes the point that the role of the father has been too neglected in the psychiatric literature and agrees with Marie Bonaparte's* comments that "psychiatrists have killed the father in the psychiatric literature." The role of the father as contributing to the maintenance of the illness of male chronic schizophrenics is studied through a clinical experience in which group psychotherapy is conducted with a group of 23 male chronic schizophrenics and another group with their fathers and mothers. This clinical experience is reported extensively. In the discussion part of this paper, several points are made, with statistical data and review of the literature to support them: a) the *absence* of the father, whether it is a physical absence (death, divorce, long separation) or an emotional absence (lack of involvement as leader of the family unit) appears to contribute significantly to the illness of the son; b) if the child is to grow up independently, it is necessary that someone, a father substitute, do the specific job of stepping between mother and child to cut the symbiotic umbilical cord uniting them. Neither child nor mother can alone free themselves completely from the ties that join them; c) the point is made also of the necessity, in order to make therapeutic gains, to clarify without doubt the lines of authority among the people caring for the patient so that the confusion of roles could be dispelled and so that the pathological system of interaction going on in the families of schizophrenic patients could not be repeated among the personnel involved in caring for these patients. d) A last point is made concerning the fierce competition between mothers and schizophrenic children. The fathers and the therapist are seen by the schizophrenic children, and their mothers as maternal figures, depriving as their own respective mothers were, and a fierce struggle goes on to obtain from these men as much as they can. This competitive struggle is intensified by the feeling that "there will not be enough for everybody around."

It is postulated that if there had been a more *present* father,

---

*As reported in a personal communication by Dr. J. B. Boulanger.

such a father could have prevented the mother from becoming so involved in a symbiotic fusion with her schizophrenic child. It is observed that when coping over a long period of time with the fantastic withdrawal and enormous demands of chronic schizophrenics, it is almost impossible to resist the temptation to stop making demands on them for improvement and to capitulate to the illness. Experienced therapists must find new ways to resist this temptation.

REFERENCES

1. Arsenian, J.; Golner, J. H.; Geddes, H.: Notes on the use of recorded minutes in group therapy with chronic psychotic patients. *Psychiat. Quart., 33;* April, 1959.
2. Bartemeier, Leo: The contributions of the father to the mental health of the family. *Amer. J. Psychiat., 110:*277; 1953.
3. Blau, David; Zilbach, Joan: The use of group psychotherapy in post-hospitalization treatment. *Amer. J. Psychiat., 111;* Oct., 1954.
4. Bowen, Murray: A family concept of schizophrenia in *The Etiology of Schizophrenia,* edited by Don Jackson. Basic books, Inc., New York, 1960.
5. Bowen, Murray; Dysinger, Robert; Basamania, Betty. The role of the father in families with a schizophrenic patient. *Amer. J. Psychiat., 115:*1017, May 1959.
6. Eisenberg, Leon: The fathers of autistic children. *Amer. J. Orthopsychiat., 27:*715, 1957.
7. Fisher, J. J.: *Soc. Sec. Bull, 13:* 13, Aug., 1950, see in Wahl.
8. Glassman, Rebecca; Dunstan, Paul; Lipton, Herbert: Group discussions with a hospitalized schizophrenic and his family. *Bedford Research.* V. A. Hospital, Bedford, Vol. 6, no. 3, June, 1960.
9. Glueck, S.: *Unraveling Juvenile Delinquency.* N.Y., Commonwealth Fund, 1950.
10. Haley, Jay: The family of the schizophrenic: a model system. *J. Nerv. Ment. Dis., 129:*357, Oct., 1959.
11. Lidz, Ruth; Lidz, Theodore: The family environment of schizophrenia patients. *Amer. J. Psychiat., 106:*332, 1949.
12. Limentani, Davide: Symbiotic identification in schizophrenia. *Psychiatry, 19:* no. 3, Aug., 1956.
13. Lindemann, E.: *Arch. Neurol. Psychiat., 53:*322, April, 1945.
14. Mahler, Marguerit: On child psychosis and schizophrenia. *Psychoanalytic Study of the Child, 7:*286, 1952.
15. Mann, James; Rosen, Irving; Standish, C.: Further observations on organization and technic of group therapy in psychoses. *Dis. Nerv. Syst.,*

*10:*3, Dec., 1959.

16. Merloo, Joost: The father cuts the cord. The role of the father an initial transference figure. *Amer. J. Psychother., 10:*471, July, 1956.
17. Parloff, Morris: The family in psychotherapy. *AMA Arch. Gen. Psychiat., 4:*no. 5, May, 1961.
18. Semrad, Elvin: Some difficulties in Group Psychotherapy with psychotics. *Amer. J. Psychiat., 109:*283, Oct. 1952.
19. Wahl, E. W.: Some antecedent factors in the family of 392 schizophrenics. *Amer. J. Psychiat., 110:*668; 1953.

Chapter 21

The Fathers of
Schizophrenic Patients*

BENJAMIN B. WOLMAN

THE present study is a product of clinical experience in individual and group psychotherapy practiced in institutional and private settings. Although the reported conclusions are based on over two decades of clinical experience, the present study is devoted mainly to 33 schizophrenic patients seen by this writer in the last eight years. After twenty-five years of observations, starting with cases of childhood schizophrenia (24) the writer developed certain ideas concerning etiology and dynamics of schizophrenia (30). These ideas have been put to a test eight years ago in a series of carefully planned interviews with 33 patients and as many members of their families as have been available. Shorthand notes have been taken and the data obtained from an individual checked against the information obtained from the interviews with members of his family.

> The 33 subjects do not form a sample. They represent the total number of schizophrenic patients seen by this writer for periods of time of varying length, some in individual and some in group psychotherapy. The 33 subjects are divided into 14 males, and 19 females. Their age varies from 15 up to 47 years; 3 are in teens, 22 in twenties, 6 in their thirties, and 2 in their forties. This age distribution enabled the writer to observe the family relationships on various age levels.

The present study could not be called experimental. It has no control group, although some manic-depressive patients studied by a similar method have been used for comparison. This study, at best, comes close to an ex post facto type of experiment. This

*Note: Reprinted by permission of the author and *Psychotherapy and Psychosomatics*, 9:193-210, 1961.

writer believes in the superiority of the experimental and quantitative method (33); however, the data reported here is of suggestive clarity, and fully corroborates this writer's previous and unplanned observations on a greater number of patients, and they are in a striking agreement with empirical findings of several excellent studies (9, 12, 14, 23). Thus, in the current discussion revolving around the etiology and dynamics of schizophrenia (2, 4, 3, 5, 7) the present study highlights one of the important aspects of this discussion. The writer's theoretical interpretation of the data is new.

From the methodological point of view, the dependent variables are represented in this study by the well-known symptomatology of the latent and manifest schizophrenic behavior, easily observed in all 33 subjects. The independent variables are numerous and controversial. For research purposes, one variable has been isolated; the father of the schizophrenic patient, and his relationships with the patient and the other members of the family, has been the variable investigated.

The intervening variables have been drawn from two sources. One was Freud's theory of personality with some modifications introduced by this writer (33) and the other was the writer's theory of social relations developed in a series of observational and experimental studies (27, 29, 31). As it will be later shown, these two approaches are almost isomorphic; what the clinician could see "from within," the experimentalist "saw from without." The results obtained by these two methods did not contradict each other; the data yielded seemed to complement each other; thus increasing the belief in the fruitfulness of combining the experimental and the psychoanalytic approach (21).

RESULTS

Objective Data

The fathers of 33 subjects represent an occupationally atypical distribution, but probably quite typical in the private practice of individual and group psychoanalytic psychotherapy. Eight of the fathers were professional men (25%), seven business executives (21%), five operated their own small business (15%), seven have been skilled workers, office workers, etc. (21%), and six unskilled workers (18%).

The interviews with the patients and their families inclusive of the fathers disclosed certain peculiarities in the behavioral patterns of the fathers. Only 13 out of 33, i.e. 39% of the fathers used to eat dinner with their families on week days. The remaining twenty fathers never or on very rare occasions ate at home on a weekday. It would be difficult to assume that dining out was an absolute necessity for none of the fathers in our group has been a traveling salesman or a pilot or a sailor, or of any occupation requiring long periods of absence from home.

Moreover, only 11 out of the 33 fathers (33%) used to spend weekends at home with their families, while 22 of them, i.e. two-thirds never or on very rare occasions did it. Most of these fathers explained to the writer that they had to work 6-7 days a week to support their families. Some stated that they had to meet friends for business purposes or to keep up with people, or visit their own parents; or just to have a good time, play golf, drink, play cards, gamble, etc. All patients complained that their fathers never did anything for them. One patient complained that her father used to work at least six days a week; whenever home, he went to bed and slept. Another patient said her father played golf every Sunday; he used to leave home early in the morning and come home late at night. This patient's older sister had been hospitalized for the last ten years with the diagnosis of catatonic schizophrenia, but the father did not miss even one Sunday meeting with friends. Those fathers, who used to stay home on weekends, did not participate too much in family affairs. The two college professors amongst our 33 fathers used to lock themselves up in their studies, appearing to the family only at dinner time, and quickly withdrawing after the dessert was served. The two writers in our group did the same; the dentist and the others somehow managed to avoid the company of their wives and children, or indulged in bitter Sunday fights. The rare family outings brought more dissension then fun. Only six fathers out of 33 ever spent a summer vacation or winter vacation with their families. Considering the fact that our population has been mostly middle class, and that almost all of them used to leave town for vacations, the ratio of fathers who spent vacations together with their families seems to be exceedingly low (18%). Most of the fathers used to send their wives and children away. One of the fathers put it in a way which is probably typical for most of them: "You feel in the summer like a bachelor."

It has been rather impossible to trace the amount and nature of child-father communication (3) but from the statements made by the schizophrenic subjects, their fathers, and other family members, certain facts became obvious. Practically all patients stated that their fathers have shown no interest in them; rarely took them to a doctor; never spent a sleepless night at their beds; the fathers did not notice, did not care or at best dismissed the child's diseases with a cliche: "you'll be all right." Most of the subjects told with resentment that their father never paid attention to their birthdays; eight of the fathers (25%) could not figure out the age of their children. The fathers rarely brought gifts and rarely if ever praised scholastic achievements of their children. The patients tried very hard to reach their fathers, but always met with lack of interest and understanding.

> Once a patient, when she was graduating from high school, insisted that her father listen to her short story which won a prize. Father showed neither any interest nor patience but upon the insistence of his wife, he sat through the reading. When the girl finished her father asked: "You mean to say that for 'that' you won a prize? How old are you, by the way?"
>
> A few days later the girl ran away from her home. Her older brother has been on and off in mental hospitals. The diagnosis was the same for both; simple schizophrenia.
>
> A 26-year-old hebephrenic was brought to the writer's office by his father who was dean of a college. The father presented to this writer the problems of his son in a cut and dry manner: "My son is lazy, so he failed in school; he is crazy because he masturbated. Doctor, see to it that he gets married soon." That's all that the dean and professor knew about his mentally sick son.

Fathers as Described by the Patients

In accordance with the patient's description which has been corroborated by interviews with the fathers and other family members in almost all cases, all their fathers could be divided into four groups. The first group forms the fathers called by the patients "babies." These fathers are likable, pleasant, usually listen to their wives, often do things around the home but they "do not behave as fathers do."

> One father would on rainy days expect his wife to leave home and wait for him with an umbrella at the subway station. It was a four-block walk and the father "could catch a cold." The same father demanded considerable attention from his children. He was the "poor

hard working man" and his children were forced to sympathize with this "sweet, nice, good daddy." He was "the baby of our family" said his son.

Another father never allowed his wife to leave home at evening to play cards with neighbors, because he would feel lonely. Later on he extended this demand to his daughter too. On trips his wife and daughter carried suitcases; father was too tired and too weak to do so. Occasionally he had fights with his daughter at the dinner table. The bone of contention were dessert and cookies.

Another father refused to be bothered on weekends by his wife and children. His excuse was that he was working very hard and needed rest. His job was, so he said, "exceedingly responsible, complex, and nerve wrecking." He has been a cook in a restaurant, had a very good income, but was always complaining about hardships.

One of the fathers, shopkeeper, kept his store open unneccessarily till 10:00 PM. He walked miles to save a few cents for a bus. He saved money on food, clothing, and medical care. His wife complained that he did not take care of himself. He was often sick. His daughter had her first nervous breakdown at the age of 16, when her father was brought home very sick.

One of the fathers has a heart condition. He never forgets to remind his family about it and make them feel guilty; three other fathers do the same; one is really sick, the others are probably not.

To the other group belong fathers who behave in their home like a spoiled "prodigy child" or "favorite son" who expects all the attention in the world.

Let us start with a father of a 32-year-old man, who spent a year in a private hospital in intensive shock and psychological treatment; presently he is in remission with a very precarious mental balance. His father, a business executive, seems to believe that he is the wisest man in the world, and an unusual and unique case of a successful man. He told that he made a small fortune "all by himself," nobody helped him and his wife was, of course, "always a hindrance." Both his children are schizophrenics.

One of the fathers, a college professor, believes that he deserves the Nobel Prize. Apparently he could not spare his precious time in the company of his "hopelessly stupid" wife and their two children. The daughter is paranoid schizophrenic; no definite information about the son has been obtained.

One of the 33 fathers is a pharmacist and a "scholar"; so he says. Two fathers in this group believe that they are geniuses. One of them spent most of his income on a library of several thousands volumes in all possible fields of knowledge. The other keeps writing books in a dozen of specialties; none of the books has ever been published.

The third group is formed by fathers who act as if they were "rebellious boys" who fight against their mommy but would not dare to leave her for good. They would never miss an opportunity to criticize their wives or to make derogatory remarks in public. Some of them resorted to physical violence directed against their wives.

> One father openly hates his wife. He thinks she is a stupid, selfish, narrowminded, old woman. He told the writer that he himself reads many books in psychology. But his wife, he said, is "old fashioned" and "she made the 'kid' (patient) sick." He struck his wife a couple of times and the "kid" too, but it was all their fault.
>
> Another father is a drunkard, who lives with another woman but visits his home frequently, rapes his wife, and beats her whenever they go into an argument. When sober, he complains and cries and feels sorry for himself.
>
> Another father, who is highly competent as a dean of a college, behaves at home like a "bitter old man" and demands that his wife cater to him. The patient, the oldest son, was afraid of his father's bad temper and worried that his father may kill his mother or be killed by her.
>
> Another father has bad temper tantrums, hates his wife and both of his daughters. Fist fights occur frequently. The patient has been hospitalized and twice underwent shock therapy.
>
> One of the fathers is a seemingly quite well-behaved business executive; at home he demands all the attention of his wife. They fought bitterly, till finally after twenty years their marriage ended up in a divorce. Both their children are schizophrenics.

The subjects whose parents belong to this group are the most serious cases. Most of them have been hospitalized with schizophrenic personality deformation, some are out-patients who represent a great challenge to one's therapeutic skills. One is tempted to say that the more overt hostility and physical violence in the family the more severe was the case. Since the overt expression of hate is less inhibited in the lower social classes, one could not be surprised to find among them a higher incidence of severe schizophrenia (10, 13).

To the fourth group belong the fathers who do not care and do not participate in their family. Those fathers have very little in common with their wives and even less with their children.

> One of those fathers owns a restaurant and somehow manages to keep himself away from home seven days a week. "I never had

320 Counseling Parents of the Emotionally Disturbed Child

anything to do with my father," said his son, a schizophrenic in relapse. The father, to the contrary, boasted that he was always a good father who worked very hard to provide all the necessities, but his wife and children have been ungrateful.

These fathers live their own lives although legally and often physically they are still at home. One patient described her father as "a bachelor with six children." This father was a skilled worker who worked overtime, six days a week, and never went out together with his wife nor took his children out. He himself had his group of friends; at home he slept, sometimes ate, but never participated. Two of his children are schizophrenics.

Another father, a business executive, comes home regularly; twice a week goes out by himself, never with his wife. At home all his time is devoted to the reading of the Wall Street Journal and other business publications. He did not notice that there was anything wrong with his daughter. The only thing which annoyed him were the constant quarrels between his wife and daughter. In the interview with this writer he was unable to relate any information concerning his sick daughter.

These four groups are not discreet and closed categories. There is a great deal of overlapping between the various types, and some fathers represent a combination of two or more types. Moreover, all the four groups are mere variations of the same nonfatherly attitude.

The main common denominator of all the 33 fathers was their failure to behave like husbands and fathers. All of them seem to compete with their own children for their wives' attention.

Whenever one of the young girl patients brought good marks from school, her father interrupted the conversation telling about his own successes. Another father could not stand his son's "boastful talk."

Many fathers resented their children's college when they themselves could not make it. None of them offered to their children protection and guidance, none of them made the child feel secure at home. All four groups of fathers acted as if they were the children of their own wives.

The first group tried to win their wives love and attention by playing the poor, sick child. The second group tried to accomplish the same by playing the prodigy, favorite child. The third fought, tooth and nail, for their social position at home as the favorite son. The last group gave up the fight but did not give up the hope. The methods used by the fathers have been variated, but the objective has been the same: *each of them apparently wished to be the beloved, admired, only child of his wife to the exclusion of his own child.*

Marital Relations

This peculiar type of relationship between the parents of the 33 subjects has been observed in all cases, corroborating the data obtained by several workers (8, 12, 14, 30).

All these authors, describing different aspects of fathers behavior, disagree with one another on several points; but on one point all of them agree unanimously, i.e. that the fathers of schizophrenics lamentably failed in performing their role as husbands and fathers.

The cases reported in this chapter do not differ significantly from cases reported by other workers. There is a great variety of behavioral patterns in the present study, starting from an overt and constant battle between the parents up to an apparent submissiveness of the father combined with a not too well hidden resentment. None of the fathers reported here seemed to be happy in this relationship; all of them bitterly complained against their wives and no one had shown respect for his wife or for her judgment. Some fathers spoke about their wives with overt hate; some ridiculed, some cursed them. Those who have shown overt submissiveness to their wives, either denied it in the interview with the writer, or apologetically stated that this was the only way to keep the house together and they did it for the children's sake.

> Only three out of 33 divorced his wife after 18 and 20 years of marriage respectively. Two left their spouses temporarily, but did not sever the relationship; one of the cases of divorce took place when the wife was taken to a mental hospital. A few fathers had extramarital affairs, but did not break away completely, despite all their unhappiness. As Hill (9) amply pointed out, all those fathers acted as their wives unhappy agents. In view of all this it seems rather surprising that the ratio of divorces has been so low.

Since none of the fathers in the present study ever proved to have concern for his children, the only possible alternative is that all these fathers have been *overattached to their wives*. Their marriage was never a give and take relationship as the usual marriage is. They clung desperately to their wives the way an infant clings to his mother. The infant may cry, scream, even rebel and strike, but he cannot leave mother. He may alternate his methods; he may try to win her approval by fight or by submissiveness, but he could not run away too far.

The Mother-Father Relationship

Apparently all the 33 fathers reported have wished the wives to act as if they were *mothers of their own husbands*. Some mothers have been all too eager to accept this role, but none could play it too well. Their husbands wished them to be "ideal mothers," i.e. omniscient, omnipotent, protective, and yet absolutely permissive and bending to the whims of the beloved child-husband. As one of the fathers remarked, he would like to "have" his wife but not to have any obligations or any commitments; to have her, so to say, "at his disposal," but she had to be able to disappear whenever he was "tired with her."

It takes two to develop such a relationship. As it has been reported by several workers (14, 16, 18) the mothers of schizophrenic patients are domineering, self-righteous, over-demanding, and dictatorial.

In an earlier study this writer (30) reported on mothers of 16 latent schizophrenics. All these mothers let their child know that his mother was a poor, rejected, suffering human being. All the mothers have been self-publicized martyrs who said that they gave away their life for their children. All the mothers have been overprotective, restraining the child's freedom, and restricting his social contacts. All the mothers have been moralistic, self-righteous, dictatorial, and demanded perfection from the child. Moreover, the schizophrenic patients have been exposed in their childhood to a constant threat that unless they display an unlimited gratefulness to their self-sacrificing mother, they will be blamed for mother's sufferings, misery, and inevitable death. "I am going to be very sick and die because you are so bad," that was the way the mothers of the schizophrenics used to talk to their children.

This domineering, absolutistic, "imperialistic" attitude was directed by those mothers to their husbands also. In all cases observed by the writer, whenever the father was the leading member of the family, no schizophrenic development has been observed.

> It is worthwhile to mention at this point the study of the Hutterites in South Dakota (6). The Hutterites, a small Protestant sect, came to the United States in the 1870's and developed a social system of "patriarchal democracy." In this patriarchal society the ratio of schizophrenic is 1.1 per 1,000 population, as compared to 4.6 per 1,000 in rural Sweden, 4.5 per 1,000 in rural Norway, and 1.7 in rural Tennessee, U.S.A. (15).

In the 33 cases reported here the mother actually took over fathers' social role. Most mothers treated their husbands as if they were children; the mother censored father's behavior, sent him for errands, controlled his little expenses, and checked his purses and pockets; some mothers tore their husbands down in the presence of children, criticized them publicly, ridiculed and belittled their achievements, rebuked and insulted them daily. Some of the 33 women used to "punish" their husbands by refusing sexual relations. Some used to expel their husbands from home at any slightest argument. Seventeen of the 33 mothers overtly incited their children against their own father; eight put their husbands on a safe and distant pedestal, "so he should not mix" and told the children that father is "too busy to be bothered."

And yet most of the mothers meant well. Some mothers explained that they had no other choice but to take over the role of father and mother. Some did it unwillingly, some eagerly. All of them somehow managed to force their husband out of his usual role as the leader and protector of the family (1, 19). No women could have accomplished it without her husband being her tacit or protesting accomplice; those 33 fathers, wittingly or unwittingly, helped their wives in this morbid process.

Patient-Father Relationship

While the 33 fathers showed very little concern for their children, all the patients expressed great concern for their fathers. All the patients harbored resentment against their mothers, but none of them expressed such hostility to their fathers, and talked of their "poor daddy." Many of them complained about their father's lack of interest, but no one really hated the father. The prevailing emotions have been sympathy, with occasional outbursts, "Why doesn't he care!" Whatever resentment there was against the father who apparently failed the patient, it was always accompanied by a warm, almost "parental" feeling of the schizophrenic patient toward his or her father.

The subjects whose fathers belonged to the first group ("the sick baby") voiced a great deal of sympathy for their "poor" fathers. The patients often resented their mother's harsh treatment of "poor daddy." Most of them blamed themselves for their father's true or imaginery sickness or failures.

The subjects whose fathers belonged to the second group ("the prodigy child") felt they have been in their father's way and probably prevented his great accomplishments.

> One borderline patient whose father used to spend most of his own and his wife's income on buying of books, said to the writer, "I am the daughter of a beauty and a genius. I shall never forget the sacrifice of my father. Because of me he did not finish yet his great work."

The patients of the third group ("the rebellious boy" type of a father) remembered with horror the family fights, and yet felt sorry for their brutal fathers. Even the children of the fathers of the fourth group ("the run-away boy") expressed mixed feelings of resentment and longing after the fathers who have always been distant and not interested in the patient's life.

Apparently the social roles in those families have been confused. Mother played the role of father and mother; father behaved like a child; and the child worried about both his parents as if he were their parent.

Father's Personality

The remarks on personalities of the fathers are based on interviews with them and observations and descriptions of them by their children, the subjects and the other members of their families. Naturally, these remarks lack scientific precision. None of the fathers were hospitalized and as far as this writer knows only two are currently undergoing psychotherapy. It would be, therefore, impossible to be sure that all or some of them were psychotics or neurotics.

The interviews and the description of their life patterns led to one general conclusion. All of the fathers have been *exceedingly selfish,* overconcerned with themselves, and not too concerned with the well-being of their families. Most of them, 21 out of 33 (64%) have worried about their own physical health. Some fathers brutally fought for the sole possession of their wives; some envied their children; some competed with their children; some have been aggressive, some not; many of them had superior intellectual abilities, some were men of social stature and commanded public respect. It is not true that all of them failed in life; it is apparent that many of them function reasonably well outside their family circle. But all of them failed as husbands and fathers.

It seems that in our 33 cases not the father's personality *per se* was schizogenic, but rather the peculiar family constellation had to be blamed. And this is exactly the conclusion arrived at in the present study. Some fathers probably represented pathologic features, two of them were paranoics, one probably schizoid or latent schizophrenic, three probably borderline cases of manic-depressive disorder, three seemed to be psychopathic. No clear-cut uniform personality pattern has been observed. Thus one cannot present father's personality structure as a direct cause of schizophrenia in their children. It seems that far more important was the father's childish attitude to his wife and his non-fatherly and not protective attitude to the child. And whatever the origin of this husband-wife, father-child attitude was, it has invariably led into a schizoid personality distortion in the child in all 33 cases.

These conclusions are shared by several workers in this field. Let us quote some of them:

> The etiology of schizophrenia . . . requires also the failure of the father to assume his masculine controlling function . . . to produce schizophrenia it appears necessary for the mother to assume father's role," stated a group of experts (23).
>
> Arieti (2) found the following marital combination most frequent: "A domineering, nagging, and hostile mother who gives the child no chance to assert himself is married to a dependent, weak man, too weak to help the child."

Hill (9) quoted a description given by Dr. W. Elgin who was in charge of admissions to the psychiatric ward. This quotation is worthwhile to be quoted again. Dr. Elgin observed in his office of admissions, that if, "mother sat in one of the two chairs at his desk and father sat off in a corner, it usually followed that mother took over the discussion, did the talking, made the arrangements . . . Father meanwhile looked unhappy and was silent . . .". Dr. Elgin came to know that "the odds were that the patient would be schizophrenic." In later interviews father was often aggressive, but "his belligerence was that of a very unwilling agent of his wife."

Since schizophrenia is, most probably caused by a peculiar family situation, it is not surprising that it runs in families. The thorough studies in heredity (11) have been critically evaluated (20), and there is no conclusive evidence on this point (1/). One feels like paraphrasing Freud's dictum to say that neuropathic parents have a much shorter way than genes.

This writer has observed over a quarter of a decade a great many cases of schizophrenic siblings, ten of them in this study. So has the writer observed a great many manic-depressive siblings. However, there are many manic-depressive parents of schizo- phrenics and many schizophrenic parents of manic-depressive patients. Apparently, a certain family constellation is conducive to one disorder and excludes the other. There is no evidence that a certain personality type of parents cause schizophrenia in children; it is rather the *sick family*, the perverse social roles, the morbid family relations that makes the child sick (1).

But family constellations are changeable. Nor is the family situation the same for all children in a family. Five subjects out of 33 have been only children, 28 had siblings, ten of them known to the writer as manifest schizophrenics. But 18 subjects had nonschizophrenic siblings, at least it is not known about their being latent schizophrenics. Eight of them, seen by the writer, are probably relatively well adjusted with no schizoid type of development.

One of the subjects, a 28-year-old, was the first child. Father and mother fought bitterly. When mother was pregnant with the second child, the parents separated, and mother moved in with her mother and uncle. The younger child had quite a peaceful childhood with the uncle playing the role of father-substitute.

Another subject was the second child in his family. His older sister was born when parents lived friendly and peacefully with one another. The fights started when our subject was 1-2 years old, and was fought around the problems of educating this child.

Often the difference in age, in sex, in looks may save a child from the devasting influences of his parents. Apparently, the same parents do not treat all their children in the same way.

THEORETICAL INTERPRETATION

Power and Acceptance

The observed phenomena can be explained in a continuance of independent, intervening, and dependent variables. Let us assume that the family situation is the independent variable, and the schizophrenic symptoms are the dependent variable; then, the intervening variable must represent a hypothesis or a series of constructs. The choice of the intervening variable cannot be an arbitrary, for the three variables together have to fit into a causal chain of causes and effects.

One way of explanation has been developed by this writer in a series of observational and experimental studies in social psychology and especially in experimental work with small groups (26, 27, 28, 29, 31). As soon as the human infant is capable of perceiving or "empathising" other individuals, he probably becomes aware of two facts. First, that some individuals or "significant persons" are able to help him and satisfy his needs and some not. Those who can satisfy the infant's needs or deprive him of their satisfaction, are *strong*, and those who cannot are *weak*. A mother is perceived by the infant as a strong person, while an old grandfather is probably perceived as weak.

Strong and weak are the dimensions of *power*. However, those in power are not always willing to satisfy the infant's need. Soon the infant learns to distinguish between those who are willing to help, the *friendly* individuals and those who are *hostile,* i.e. unwilling to help, or willing to hurt. Thus the social perception of the infant deals with two dimensions, the dimension of power (strong vs. weak) and acceptance (friendly vs. hostile).

Three Types of Relationships

Usually the child is the taker, and the parents are the givers. Life starts as dependency upon the organism which gave life, and the infant continues the parasitic type of life even after birth, after physical separation from mother's body. Let's call this attitude *instrumental,* for the parents are instrumental in the satisfaction of the infant's needs and are perceived by the infant as sources of support.

As the child grows, he learns, probably both through maturation as well as through learning, to give and not only to take. According to Freud, this attitude starts at the *anal* stage. As a rule the friendship relations in adolescence are based on *mutual acceptance*, on a give and take basis (26, 28). At a certain point of development, young people of the opposite sex become ready to live together. Marriage is usually a mutual acceptance type of relationship.

The infant-mother attitude represents the instrumental attitude; friendship and marriage represent usually mutual acceptance; parenthood introduces a new relationship, the *vectorial.* The infant is a taker, the parent is a giver. The vectorial attitude is the readiness to give without expecting reward; it is the readiness for self-sacrifice for those one loves and cares for.

Adults participate in social relationships of all three types. When a man looks for a job, or makes an investment, his aim is to take and his attitude is instrumental. Whenever a man forms a genuine friendship, or marries out of mutual love, or forms a partnership, his aim is to give and to take, and his attitude is of mutual acceptance. Whenever a man gives away his time, his money, his health, or his life for the dearest ones, for his family or his country or his religion, and his aim is to give, his attitude is vectorial. A well-adjusted individual is capable of all three types of relationships.

The Hypervectorial Attitude

The empirical observations of this writer led to the conclusion that it is essential for the child's mental health that his parents should act in such a way as to enable him to perceive them as strong and friendly and their attitude to the child as vectorial. In cases where the parents are weak and their attitude has been instrumental, the child's progress from instrumentalism toward the ability of functioning in all three types of relationship becomes badly impaired. When parents act as if they were the infants and force the child into a premature vectorial attitude, schizophrenic processes start in the child's mind (30, 32).

A further analysis of the impact of the morbid parental attitudes upon a child's development requires us to go beyond the observed phenomena and to use some psychoanalytic concepts (5). One of the most fruitful concepts of Freud has been the concept of cathexis. Cathexis is the investment of emotional energy, libido, borrowed by Freud from inductive electricity. The little child is narcissistic and his libido is self-cathected. The adult's libido is partially self-cathected and partially object cathected or invested in the images of those whom the individual loves.

All children are born narcissistic and it takes both libido-development through biologically determined stages and learning by environmental experiences till the individual attains some balance between self and object cathexis. But in cases of parents who force the child to renounce narcissism too early and induce the child to take a protective, parental attitude towards them, the normal processes of maturation and learning become disrupted. The child is forced to hyper-cathect his love objects at the expense of self-cathexis (7).

The future schizophrenic starts his life in the same way as any other child. He is helpless and depends upon help from outside. His attitude is instrumental, and he depends upon "narcissistic supplies."

However, the future schizophrenic soon realizes, that there is something wrong with his parents. He lives under constant threat of loss of his martyr-type mother and nonparticipant baby-father. The loss of support means death to the infant. All schizophrenics, as Sullivan amply observed, are panic stricken (22). The child starts to worry about his parents, feels sorry for his father, blames himself, and takes a protective hyper-vectorial attitude. In order to survive he must protect his protectors. *Vectoriasis praecox* is the essence of schizophrenia.

The process of symptoms formation and deterioration in schizophrenia has been explained (30) as a continuous struggle against the fear of death. The more demanding the mother, the less protective the father, the more serious the disorder. Whenever violence between the parents makes the threat of their death more realistic, the more severe the disorder and greater the danger of a complete collapse of personality structure.

SUMMARY

Fathers and other family members of thirty-three schizophrenic patients were interviewed. All these fathers failed in their social role as husbands and fathers. Normally, intraparental relationships (in terms of Wolman's theory of power and acceptance), are *mutual,* i.e. give and take. The parents versus child attitude is *vectorial* i.e. giving, protecting; and the child versus parents is *instrumental,* i.e. taking.

In the schizophrenogenic family neither mother nor father are vectorial. The mother demands love from the child and the father takes on the role of a sick, prodigy, rebellious or run-away child. The father competes with the child instead of protecting him.

The child is forced to take on the protective, giving, *hyper-vectorial* attitude toward parents. The child worries about his parents and is terror-stricken. This abundant object hypercathexis and impoverished self-cathexis lead inevitably into schizophrenia named *vectoriasis praecox.*

REFERENCES

1. Ackerman, N. W.: *Psychodynamics of Family Life.* Basic Books, New York, 1958.
2. Arieti, S.: *Interpretation of Schizophrenia.* Brunner, New York, 1955.
3. Bateson, G., Jackson, D. D., Haley, J., and Weshland, J.: Toward a theory of schizophrenia. *Behav. Sci., I:*251-264, 1956.
4. Bellak, L. (Ed.): *Schizophrenia: A Review of a Syndrome.* Logos, New York, 1959.
5. Bychowski, G.: *Psychotherapy of Psychosis.* Grune and Stratton, New York, 1952.
6. Eaton, J. W., and Weil, R. J.: *Culture and Mental Disorder.* Free Press,

Glencoe, Ill., 1955.

7. Federn, P.: *Egopsychology and the Psychosis.* Basic Books, New York, 1952.
8. Gerald, B. L., and Siegel, J.: The family background in schizophrenia. *Psychiat. Quart., 24:*47-73, 1950.
9. Hill, L. B.: *Psychotherapeutic Intervention in Schizophrenia.* Chicago Univ. Press, Chicago, 1955.
10. Hollingshead, A. B., and Redlich, K. C.: Schizophrenia and social structure. *Amer. J. Psychiat,* 110, 1954.
11. Kallman, F.: *The Genetics of Schizophrenia.* Augustin, New York, 1948.
12. Kohn, M. L., and Clausen, J. A.: Parental authority, behavior and schizophrenia. *Amer. J. Orthopsychiat., 26:*297-313, 1956.
13. Lemkau, P. V.: *Mental Hygiene in Public Health.* McGraw Hill, New York, 1955.
14. Lidz, Th, Fleck, St., Cornelism, A., and Terry, D.: The intrafamilial environment of the schizophrenic patient: IV. Parental personalities and family interaction. *Amer. J. Orthopsychiat., 28:*764-776, 1958.
15. Lin, T. Y.: A study of incidence of metal disorder in Chinese and other cultures. *Psychiat., 16:*313-336, 1953.
16. Marck, J. C.: Attitudes of mothers of male schizophrenics toward child behavior. *J. Abnorm. Soc. Psychol., 48:*185, 1953.
17. McDonald, R. K.: Problems in biologic research in schizophrenia. *J. Chron. Dis., 8:*366-371, 1958.
18. Nutfield, E. J.: The schizogenic mother. *Med. J. Australia, 2:*283-286, 1954.
19. Parsons, T., and Bales, R. F.: *Family, socialization and interaction process.* Free Press, Glencoe, Ill., 1955.
20. Richter, D. (Ed.): *Schizophrenia: Somatic aspects.* MacMillan, New York, 1957.
21. Sears, R. R.: Survey of objective studies of psychoanalytic concepts. *Soc. Sci. Res. Coun. Bull.,* No. 51, 1943.
22. Sullivan, H. S.: *The Interpersonal Theory of Psychiatry.* Norton, New York, 1953.
23. Whitaker, C. (Ed.): *Psychotherapy of Chronic Schizophrenic Patients.* Little, Brown, Boston, 1958.
24. Wolman, B. B.: *Neurasthenia in Children.* (Polish). Unpublished thesis, 1933.
25. Wolman, B. B.: Medicine and therapeutic education (Polish). *Szkola Specjalna, 14:*18-25, 1938.
26. Wolman, B. B.: Friendship (Hebrew). *Hachinuch Quart., 18:*1-16, 1946.
27. Wolman, B. B.: *Freedom and discipline in education (Hebrew).* Massada, Tel-Aviv, 1949.
28. Wolman, B. B.: Spontaneous groups of children and adolescents in Israel. *J. Soc. Psychol,* 171-182, 1951.
29. Wolman, B. B.: Leadership and groups dynamics. *J. Soc. Psychol.,*

*43:*11-25, 1956.

30. Wolman, B. B.: Explorations in latent schizophrenia. *Amer. J. Psychother., II:*560-588, 1957.

31. Wolman, B. B.: Instrumental, mutual acceptance, and vectorial groups. *Acta Sociol., 3:*19-28, 1958.

32. Wolman, B. B.: Psychotherapy with latent schizophrenics. *Amer. J. Psychother., 13:*343-359, 1959.

33. Wolman, B. B.: *Contemporary theories and systems in psychology.* Harper, New York, 1960.

Chapter 22

The Fathers' Group

An Effective Therapy Medium for Involving Fathers in a Child Psychiatric Clinic Treatment Program*

GEORGE CHALPIN

THIS chapter draws principally on my experience at the Douglas A. Thom Clinic as therapist of an ongoing open-ended fathers' group over a period of four and a half years. The chapter also draws on a background of a two-year leadership of a fathers' group at the Putnam Children's Center, on familiarity with eight other fathers' groups through four years' participation in seminars on fathers' groups led successively by Drs. James Mann and Max Day, and on my supervision of other fathers' groups at the Thom Clinic.

THE COMMON DILEMMAS OF THESE FATHERS

Experience at the Thom Clinic and the Putnam Center indicates that the clinic fathers commonly share symptoms of angry passivity, and either a withdrawal from or an immature form of involvement with both their families and the treatment program. They have brought into their present families their rather dismal childhood *Weltanschauung*. This often includes a limited range of functioning for the fathers as both a husband and a parent. The woman, past and present, frequently continues to be perceived as the dominant object. These fathers relate to their wives and children in a hazy, immature way because they themselves are unclear about their own identities and afraid of their potential adult functions in the family. They avoid the anxiety of dealing with their libidinal and aggressive impulses were they to relate in a

*Note: Reprinted by permission of the author and *Journal of the American Academy of Child Psychiatry*, 5:125-133, 1966.

more intimate way. They often tend to bury themselves in their work and in their newspapers and television at home. By doing so, they escape the humiliating state of feeling like "trapped kids in the doghouse" whose wives and children only wish "to hound them." Underneath, most of them share a Chekhov-like despair of feeling doomed to bleak lives. Their only apparent solution is to retreat: retreat from the seemingly insoluble bind of having to be reined in by their wives and harnessed by guilt to a negative identification with the worst versions of their own fathers.

A father in such a predicament is hardly equipped to resolve the family dysfunctions that led to a neurotically involved mother bringing her disturbed child to the clinic. Rather he often tends to reinforce pathogenic aspects of his wife's emotional world. In reaction to his lack of support, she all the more angrily perceives males as disappointing and displaces onto the disturbed child unresolved problems with her original family and with her consequently unsatisfactory marital relationship.

In relationship to his children, the father is often characterized by a relative unavailability or unsuitability as an object of identification for his sons. For his daughters, he either minimally enhances or complicates their confidence in their developing femininity.

The major goals of the fathers' group are the following: a) to reverse these trends in the fathers; b) to increase their family involvement by the parallel path of group involvement; c) to improve the quality and efficacy of the father's relationship to both wife and children; and d) to capitalize on changes in the treated child and wife who often become more capable of switching over to a more healthful relationship with the husband father.

A TYPICAL FATHER'S EXPERIENCE IN THE GROUP

Surprising as it may seem, and in contrast with the mothers, a cross-section of our fathers yields many common character- istics. One might then formulate a "typical father" from these common characteristics among fathers in families serviced by such community clinics as the Thom and Putman

Center (1). The typical father enters the group quite ambivalently. Unlike the mother, he often feels consciously remote from the neurotic dilemmas of the child and mother. Despite feeling diffusely guilty about his implications in his child's problems, he is apt to be several steps away from appreciating that he could benefit from some kind of therapy to help himself and thereby his family. He usually joins the group mainly out of compliance with the clinic's recommendation that he too should be involved in the treatment program in order for the child to progress.

He is initially anxious in the unstructured group setting with six to nine other strangers and the leader, but he shortly finds there is much in common to share and talk about. In the free interchange of experiences about their families and especially their children, he is relieved and gradually hopeful to find so much universality in what he had felt were problems unique to himself. The others, too, are afraid of most of their feelings, have trouble setting limits for their children, and dealing with the latter's aggression, sexual curiosity, etc. As they talk about their children, he gradually eases his concerns about his own child-parent relationships and about closeness and hostility toward the other members and the leader. He is angry with the leader for not giving him the things that he always wanted and felt he never got enough of from his parents. He deals with this anger by banding together with the other fathers and pretending to shut out the leader. He also deals with his aggression by forming an essentially hostile, compliant identification with what he feels the leader expects of him. Gradually the father voices more of his feelings in the group. In rivalrous interchanges he finds that one can make a hostile remark without destroying the other person or seriously alienating him. He also finds that no violent homosexual explosions occur when he consciously likes or seems to dislike homosexuality tinged behavior by another member toward him. The leader does not appear hurt nor does he retaliate when the father makes a cutting remark about the latter's resented "aloofness" "superiority," and

---

(1) The findings of this paper would seem to apply more readily to fathers at other community clinics similar to the Thom Clinic and to have less correspondence with, for example, city-hospital-affiliated clinics where families are often less intact and the fathers more apt to be out of the house, alcoholic, or otherwise grossly irresponsible.

ungivingness, or when he attempts to bring the leader down to his own felt lowly status by calling him a novice.

Increasingly he develops trust in other members and the leader and commits himself to being a part of the group. He acknowledges that he has many problems and that he is now seeking help from the group and the clinic to resolve them. He exchanges more personal explorations into his and the others' difficulties at home and in the group. The others will not let him get away with convenient distortions, projections, and rationalizations. Instead they persist in exposing what the father is really afraid of. And rather surprisingly, the father often accepts these confrontations from his peers.

He hears another father ask, "What is a normal adult male?" and verbalizes that he too has always been perplexed by mouse-bear-Neanderthal man alternatives to his identity. Associations lead to mutual memories of, and angry or disappointed feelings toward, their own fathers, and eventually to the recognition of the transfer of these feelings and quandaries onto the leader. The father becomes uncomfortably aware of the childlike status he has assigned to himself in his family. He realizes how he sets his wife at home and the leader in the group up above him, requiring their approval, seeking their protection, and resenting the cage he thus creates for himself. As the group interweaves past with present, the leader interprets one of the father's most guilt-laden reactions to taking his own father's place in the home. He learns that he has angrily assigned himself a self-devaluated role buttressed by his wife's ambivalent version of him. He may be one of those fathers who discover that their own taciturnity and aloofness at home repeat what they felt was dealt out to them by their own parents.

As he rebels more in the group and dares to be more assertive in his work ventures, his distrust, awe, and fear of the leader partially dissolve. He perceives the central figure more realistically as an ally in helping him face himself and his dilemmas. Along with the greater communication developed in the group he finds more areas of intimate and frank communication between himself and his wife. The wife, while threatened by her husband's greater assertiveness in the home, has a chance to resolve her conflicts in her own therapy. Hopefully, she is then able to do what she has always yearned to do – to respect her husband and to turn to him for mutual adult interdependence. This marital improvement often tends to precipitate dramatic improvement in the child in treatment.

The above description is of course a rather idealized, simplified version of the experiences of any one father. Many fathers have severely entrenched problems and do not progress in this uncomplicated fashion, but a number of these emotional steps do occur in varying degree in a large segment of the fathers we have seen.

THE SUITABILITY OF THE GROUP MEDIUM FOR THESE FATHERS

The group setting capitalized on the common denominator of interpersonal experience that is at once most familiar and acceptable to these fathers. Since early latency they have participated in social and work-oriented groups with other males. I believe that this extensive background facilitates the fathers' handling of the new and unprecedented experience of relating to others in a less structured, permissive atmosphere. In this setting they are likely to be most motivated to utilize object relationships for therapeutic purposes. One might speculate here that the group experience recapitulates, in a more controlled, integrated, and purposeful way, the growth aspects of these fathers' latency and adolescent group experiences with peers. Just as in the past, they turn to one another for help and mutual identification to resolve issues of identity and related conflicts over dependence versus independence, aggression, and sexuality. Yet, unlike past group experiences, the group provides the added presence of the central figure, the transference to whom is a fundamental of the group experiences.

The fathers share not only common neurotic dilemmas but face these dilemmas in the context of similar family and life functions as fathers, husbands, breadwinners, all with a child in treatment reflecting their common feeling of defect. I believe that an effective group composition should have a relative homogeneity of neurotic dilemmas and life situations and a reasonable variety in the ways of handling these problems. The typical fathers' group within limits meets this definition.

The father's growing attraction to the group endows it with a special kind of leverage for therapeutic purposes. The kind of involvement these fathers least object to committing themselves to results in their greater readiness to progress to a different form of involvement. This new involvement, which they did not quite count on, is with the many neurotic problems they have always tried to evade in the past. And the group setting itself confronts them concretely with a capsule version of the life issues they have been afraid of.

The aforementioned trends help explain the presence of two phenomena in the fathers' groups: the development of marked conscious libidinal investment in the group and of increasing reality-based hope. Whereas these fathers, feeling underneath so abandoned and lonely, have felt so little hope by themselves, they now find new hope, which is of course a *sine qua non* for effective therapy.

The diluted transference medium of the group would appear to be a preferable one for many of these fathers; it enables them to deal more flexibly with their ambivalent transference to the therapist. In individual casework or therapy, at this stage of their fence-sitting, it is quite threatening to deal with the undiluted transference situation which includes both the unresolved infantile transference to the passive father and to the frightening or resented parent-authority figure. Instead, the group medium substitutes a more easily manageable situation in which the father feels the support of the others in the same boat, and may at his choosing vicariously experience hostility through the attacks others make on the leader. He can also deflect hostility onto other members until the leader, when the timing is appropriate, confronts him with the displacement.

The unconscious of each of the fathers seems to act more in unison with the others than that of the average outpatient group member. This is probably because of the uniqueness of their sharing both dilemmas and life functions. At times one feels there is an almost inevitable sequence of emotional issues which develop from session to session. A recent event in my own group pointed up this phenomenon. One father, Mr. S, who had missed two successive sessions, was anxiously trying to catch up. Unknowingly he brought up in sequence the two major group concerns discussed in the meetings he had missed. The subject of the first meeting, Mr. S had missed had been the conflict about wanting to push their sons ahead in curricular and extracurricular achievements. This wish had reflected abdication of possibilities of their own achievement and a vicarious transfer to their children who instead might achieve for them. The subject of the second missed meeting, which occurred after President Kennedy's assassination, dealt with their resentment toward their fathers and employers (several members have their own fathers as employers). When Mr. S returned, he first anxiously brought up his concern over his son's recommended promotion in school. Then he turned to his uneasy relationship in his business with his employer whom he had been ribbing, devaluating, and rivaling. This monologue occurred in a vacuum created by numbed, guilty reactions of the other fathers over their death wishes toward their fathers and employers expressed in the previous meeting. These latent death wishes had been in part stirred up by the later discussion, in the midst of the session, of the President's assassin. When I, as the leader, confronted Mr. S and the group with the phenomenon of this father's unconscious repetition of their concerns, they were quite surprised.

Many of the fathers often have a remarkable degree of insight into the problems of other fathers with whom they are attuned. It may well be that these insights come as a peculiar by-product of their problems in identity; usually the father having the insight is a considerable distance away from perceiving emotionally how these insights apply to himself. But I believe that this attunement to each other's neurotic dilemmas is another fortunate result of the homogeneity of these fathers' difficulties.

Perhaps above all, the fathers learn the value of communication of both their thoughts and feelings. Many fathers have driven their wives to distraction and to added pathological involvement with their children by their uncommunicativeness and hostile silences. They now learn that rational communication clears the air and has possibilities for resolving their often restricted and stalemated marital relationships. Many transfer this newly found entity of communication into their homes where they become less afraid of removing their protective barrier of emotional distance.

Finally, the evolution of the transference to the leader recapitulates more successfully some of the aborted phases of these fathers' psychosexual development in relation to their own fathers. The fathers, of course, begin with the angry dependent fantasy that the leader will provide for them the wished-for omnipotent function of supplying an external source of unending nutrition, guidance, and strength. The bubble necessarily bursts with angry reverberations occurring for many months afterward. But the leader helps the members perceive that one of the reasons for these wishes is sensible, namely, that they wish to become more adequate male adults. There is a gradual transition from the initial unhealthful hostile identification with the central figure to a more genuine positive identification with him. In this process they have also introjected his belief in their ability to master their problems. The significance of this identification with the male leader and of their partial identifications with other fathers is all the more central when one notes the fact that most of these fathers have had a remote, tenuous, or otherwise unsatisfactory relationship with their own fathers.

THE MUTUAL COMPATIBILITY OF THE FATHERS' GROUP WITH THE CHILD CLINIC

The fathers' group offers a reasonably impressive economic advantage as a treatment medium in relationship to the time required of staff and training personnel. A clinic is understandably concerned about restricting the number of families treated because of the personnel time required. One can, however, involve the fathers of a considerable number of families in treatment with a relatively low investment of personnel time. At our own clinic, for example, we have four fathers' groups and one mothers' group (forty-five parents) meeting weekly for one-and-a-half-hour sessions; these are weekly seminars of the same length of time, and time must be available for communication between the group and family treatment teams. This is at the cost of about thirty personnel hours divided between nine staff personnel and trainees.

The fathers' group is also adaptable to the varying purposes of the clinic and its community requirements. For example, the clinic might see fit to establish a group of fathers from only those families who are known to be terminating within the next several months. A relatively short-term group could then be formed with the more specific goal of pointing toward the time when the family will finish its contact with the clinic. It would then devolve back upon the father to play a more responsible role with the treated mother and child.

I have had most experience, however, with the open-ended group in which the group itself continues while the average member's participation may last as long as two to three years. The life of the open-ended group is analogous in some ways to the life of the child clinic where it takes place. In the clinic, families come and go and the staff and training personnel also change. But the traditions and expertise of the clinic, which have developed through the years, continue. So with the group the membership changes and the leadership itself may change. These events, traumatic as they are, can of course be turned to therapeutic advantage (dealing with the arrival of new siblings and the loss of a parent). The carefully selected new members quite often respond to the stimulus of the advanced functioning of the group by moving more rapidly into facing their problems then they would in a beginning group. The continuing group takes on new members as the caseload of clinic families changes (although fathers often may continue after the child is terminated). It also continues to develop its hard-won qualities of skill in communication.

I would caution that a newly undertaken group therapy program, by its departure from tested, accepted therapeutic procedures, requires patience through the period of skepticism attendant any new treatment medium. Initial deterrents to the successful continuity of such a program include the relative inexperience of its participants, their difficulty in interpreting the therapeutic process of group to the rest of the clinic, and the handling of new problems in the communication of family information with treatment team members. In addition, one may encounter problems in continuity because of changing personnel. Also, adequate supervision, a requisite, may be difficult to obtain. Finally, one must anticipate the reluctance of some clinics to acknowledge the importance of the clinic father: the least understood entity of the family. Only recently have many clinics recognized that the typical clinic father may prove, through clinic involvement, to be a father-lode instead of a nonfunctioning lodestone.

REFERENCES

English, O. S.: The psychological role of the father in the family. *Soc. Casewk., 35:*323-329, 1954.

Foulkes, S. H.: Group analytic dynamics with specific reference to psychoanalytic concepts. *Int. J. Group Psychiat., 7:*40-52, 1957.

Mann, J.: Some theoretic concepts of the group. *Int. J. Group Psychother., 5:*235-241, 1955.

Mann, J.: Psychoanalytic observations regarding conformity in groups. *Int. J. Group Psychother., 12:*3-13, 1962.

PART IV

GROUP THERAPY WITH PARENTS

Chapter 23

Parallel Group Psychotherapy
with the Parents of
Emotional Disturbed Children*

JACK C. WESTMAN, EUGENE W. KANSKY, MARY E. ERIKSON,
BETTIE ARTHUR AND ANN L. VROOM

REACHING the parents of emotionally disturbed children is an important challenge for child psychiatry (1, 12, 18). A variety of methods is available for gaining leverage on pathogenic forces in the family through the treatment of parents (3, 4, 7, 8, 10, 14, 15, 16, 19, 20, 21, 22, 24, 26). This chapter describes a plan of treatment built around parallel psychotherapy groups for mothers and fathers and specifically designed to meet common problems in clinical work with families. Three of these important difficulties are the following: a) parents' lack of motivation for psychotherapy for themselves, b) faulty communication between family members, and c) impaired coordination of the therapeutic team in the clinic.

Achieving maximum effectiveness in the therapy of a child depends upon attracting both the father and the mother to the treatment process, but motivation problems in parents are often intensified when attempts are made to involve the father actively in treatment. The reluctance of the mother and father to share an interest in therapy frequently reflects pervasive faulty communication patterns within the family (1, 5, 9, 11, 13, 23, 25). As a gross example, one father did not appear at the clinic because his wife had not told him of his scheduled appointments.

If communication patterns are teased out of the complicated matrix of family relationships, one can distinquish conscious and unconscious communication. Both verbal and nonverbal messages

*Note: Reprinted by permission of the authors and *International Journal of Group Psychotherapy, 13:*52-60, 1963.

are transmitted at each level. In our clinic families, potent unconscious communication occurs between family members, while contradictory, inconsistent, or inadequate messages are transmitted at the conscious level. For example, one set of parents was enmeshed in a "cold war" in which underlying hostilities rarely broke through superficial pleasantries. At the other extreme, another family was in continual surface conflict but was held together by strong unconscious bonds. Most often the marriages of our clinic families are quite stable. As an illustration, if a wife projects her hostility on her husband and he characteristically turns his hostility against himself, a mutually satisfying relationship exists. If both parents project their hostility to a child, the marriage is compatible, but the child develops symptoms. In each case the parents have blind spots for their dominant unconscious communications. The projecting wife with a masochistic husband has no opportunity to become aware of her projections since they are readily accepted and unchallenged. Parents dominated by unconscious neurotic bonds cannot rationally deal with each other at a conscious verbal level, and thus they are handicapped in psychotherapy, which depends upon rational analysis and understanding of their behavior in each other's presence.

A third common problem is difficulty in making clinic teamwork a smoothly operating reality (6, 17). Szurek (1952) points out that failures in the treatment of families may result from faulty coordination in the clinic. At times a disturbed family induces a similar disturbance in the therapeutic team, staff rivalries and personality differences providing fertile soil for the family's manupulative tendencies. The very contagiousness of family disorder brings into bold relief the necessity of effective coordination of the therapeutic team.

In order to meet these problems, our strategy called for a therapeutic design which would capture the interest of both mothers and fathers, stimulate conscious verbal communication between parents as a basis for psychotherapeutic insight, and facilitate coordination of the team in the clinic. The ultimate goal was to raise parental communication from a blind, unconscious level to a more rational, conscious plane on which the parents could look at themselves and at each other more objectively.

METHOD

Group psychotherapy was chosen as the core of the program because of its usefulness in rapidly achieving a high degree of motivation in patients. Closed parallel groups of mothers and fathers were formed, tapping the natural curiosity spouses feel when each is in a similar but separate activity (Fig. 23-1). Periodic merging of the groups, it was decided, would stimulate intergroup interest and give the parents an opportunity to see each other in action.

The clinic team consists of a separate therapist for each group, with the same observer in both groups. Weekly stereoscopic meetings of the group therapists, observer, and child therapists are scheduled for sharing information within the team and comparing material from the separate group sessions. The children are treated individually as their needs indicate.

The material for this presentation is drawn from five families followed for two years in the parallel group therapy program. The groups met weekly for ninety minutes, with merged joint meetings at three-month intervals. Families with parents between the ages of 25 and 40 and with some college background were selected from the waiting list of the Out-patient Service of Children's Psychiatric Hospital.

At the beginning of therapy the overall plan illustrated in the diagram was introduced to the parents. The channels of communication in the clinic were described. Appropriate respect for confidentiality outside of the families involved was requested, but confidentiality within the clinic-group-home system was not expected. Although they were not encouraged to discuss the group meetings at home, the parents were told they need not avoid discussions outside of the meetings. We did not directly encourage discussions at home because of the possibility that such a suggestion might cause or prevent outside interaction in an effort to please or frustrate the therapists.

OPEN CHANNELS OF COMMUNICATION
IN PARALLEL GROUP PSYCHOTHERAPY

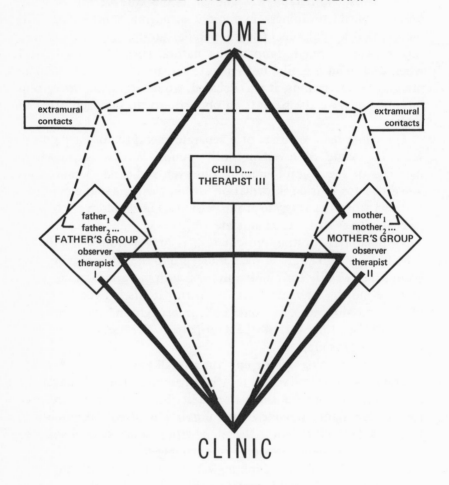

Figure 23-1. Open channels of communication in parallel group psycho-therapy.

OBSERVATIONS

The observations here are limited to the unique features of this structured treatment plan. We omit reference to the psychoanalytically oriented group therapy process and the treatment of the children for the sake of clarity.

The Hale family was referred because their six-year-old daughter developed the school phobia syndrome after entering the first grade. At the time of initial evaluation, both parents were harmoniously preoccupied with their daughter's unhappiness and somatic symptoms. Because of the severity of her symptoms, Carol was enrolled in the hospital's day school. A part of the pathological interaction between parents and child was their mutual projection of their hostility onto the child. With Carol's improvement in the hospital school, open conflict appeared between the parents as they shifted their projections to each other. At this point, they entered the group therapy program. Carol was discharged from treatment several months later.

As the Hales became involved in their respective groups, "gossip sessions" after the group meetings began to replace their arguments at home. Mr. Hale told his wife of the faults and peculiarities of the other fathers. Mrs. Hale spoke bitterly of the other mothers. They began to displace their projections from each other onto members of the groups, permitting the return of relative harmony at home. In the fathers' group, Mr. Hale's projections were repeatedly interpreted. In the joint meetings the other fathers saw his wife's distortions and later demonstrated them to Mr. Hale. As he recognized his underlying hostility toward himself, he became clinically depressed. Mrs. Hale, at the same time, intensified her projections onto the other mothers as her husband was less inclined to return her hostility. Her accusations against the other mothers became so irrational that she was forced to face her own infantile conviction that she was unlovable. As Mr. Hale recovered from his depressive symptoms, Mrs. Hale began to show overt depression. She was continued in individual therapy for six months after the couple's two-year course in the parallel groups.

Although there were variations, the outline of the course with the Hales was repeated in other families. With the exception of one case, the children left treatment prior to the parents. All five families terminated with evident clinical improvement in their children and marriages.

The following tentative phases may be distilled from our experience with the five families.:

Phase I: The Family Neurosis

On entering therapy each set of parents showed meshing of their neurotic personalities. Both of the Hales were basically infantile, passive-dependent persons who maintained a stable marriage by projecting their hostility onto their children. Their conscious communications centered around worry about their children. At an unconscious level numerous messages revealed their hostility for the children and each other.

Phase II: Displacement to the Group

Projections were readily displaced from family members to the groups, resulting in improved relations at home. "After-group" discussions at home began with gossip about the other families and the transmission of messages between groups. For one couple the discussion of group meetings was the first interaction they had shared without leading to an argument in seven years of married life. The Hales' conscious verbal communication shifted from their children to criticisms of the other parents in the groups.

Phase III: Mirroring in the Groups

Married couples are handicapped in analyzing their relationship because of the blind spots created by the unconscious fit of their defenses. At home their pathological bonds are not recognized because they serve mutual neurotic needs, but in the group these bonds do not fit as well with other members and stand out as inappropriate. With the aid of the therapists and the other group members, the parents begin to see themselves as others see them. Mr. Hale could not continue to remain unaware of his low self-esteem when a mirror was repeatedly held for him at group meetings.

Phase IV: Intrapersonal Change

With parallel groups the separation of spouses permits the gradual working through of insights at a rate consistent with the individual's tolerance of painful affects. The option of temporarily retreating to the old, but partially gratifying, neurotic interaction at home is always available. On the other hand, periodic confrontation with the spouse in the joint meetings keeps the focus on the husband-wife relationship. As the Hales were confronted with their own psychopathology, their conscious communications at home centered on themselves individually.

Phase V: Interpersonal Change

The ultimate goal of this program was to establish a new equilibrium in the family based less on unconscious neurotic bonds and more on mutual conscious tolerance and understanding. In the Hale family the first change was seen in the daughter who quickly improved when she was relieved of the pressure of the parents' projections. Mr. Hale's depression deprived his wife of his hostility which had given a core of reality to her projections onto him. With his later improvement and the appearance of her depression, Mr. Hale was able to partially fill his wife's dependency needs. In this family clinical symptoms shifted from the daughter to the father to the mother, ultimately exposing the mother's chronic depression which was the core of the family neurosis. After this was worked through, the family reached a new equilibrium, with visible evidence of less unconscious mutual hostility.

DISCUSSION

Both mothers and fathers showed a high degree of interest in the therapy groups. The mothers had initially expressed their desire for help through bringing their children to the clinic. The fathers were less involved in the clinic referral and less motivated for treatment for themselves. Meeting in separate groups offered the parents an opportunity to share feelings of guilt and failure with peers. The fathers saw their group as according them recognition equal to that given their wives. The parents supported each other in dealing with their spouses during and after the joint meetings. This was particularly true in the case of a passive father who used the other fathers' encouragement to stand up against his wife.

The curiosity stimulated by the separate groups heightened interest and opened channels of communication at home. For example, the mothers used each other as messengers to learn what their husbands were doing in the fathers' group. Husband and wife compared notes about the other families. As they did this, they found themselves talking less about dissatisfaction with their own children. Information transmitted between the groups underwent distortions that labeled the defenses of the bearer. As an illustration, Mrs. Hale repeatedly complained to her husband about another "rude, inconsiderate" mother. Mr. Hale gradually learned from the other fathers that his wife was in fact the "rude, inconsiderate" member of the mothers' group.

Although they came to the clinic because of their children, the parents rarely mentioned their youngsters as they became involved in the groups. Merging the fathers' and mothers' groups tended to focus the content of the parallel meetings and conversations at home on the marital relationship. The periodic joint meetings followed by separate sessions directly contrasted images developed of opposite partners with first-hand observations. For example, one father portrayed himself as the dominant force in his home. Witnessing his "puppy dog" behavior with his wife in a joint session led the other fathers to challenge his pseudomasculinity at the next fathers' group meeting. Several joint exposures and the working through of this confrontation during separate meetings were necessary before he could accept this unconsciously mediated pattern. In his wife's presence, he was unaware of his obvious submissiveness. The parents' unconscious interaction was modified first by conscious attention to the marriages of the other parents, second to themselves individually, and last to their own marriages.

The weekly team meetings in the clinic were leavened by the observer's reactions from her vantage point as a member of both groups. The stereoscopic view of life at home as reported separately by the husbands and wives provided the therapists with useful information for the clarification and interpretation of character operations. How much the open channels of communication in the clinic induced similar channels at home by example can only be inferred. One parent remarked that the presence of the observer in both groups kept her "honest." The clinic team found that this design promoted a harmonious, constructive climate for teamwork.

The usefulness of this program for training group therapists warrants mention. Supervision of two groups can be provided at the stereoscopic conferences. The observer gains experience in group therapy in addition to filling a key position in the design.

SUMMARY

Parallel group psychotherapy is described as a method of inducing change in the families of emotionally disturbed children. The strategy of this program focuses on opening conscious verbal channels of communication between parents as a basis for insight-producing psychotherapy. The structure of the design with separate mothers' and fathers' groups periodically merged in joint meetings tends to keep the focus of therapy on the marital relationship and sharply outlines the defenses of the members. Phases of the therapeutic course with five families over a two-year period are noted. Evidence of intrapersonal and interpersonal change in one illustrative family is presented.

REFERENCES

1. Ackerman, N. W .: *The Psychodynamics of Family Life.* New York, Basic Books, 1958.
2. Ackerman, N. W. (Ed.): *Exploring the Base for Family Therapy.* New York, Family Service Association of America, 1961.
3. Bell, J. E.: *Family Group Therapy.* Public Health Monograph No. 64, 1961.
4. Bellmont, L. P., and Jasnow, A.: The utilization of cotherapists and of group therapy techniques in a family-oriented approach to a disturbed

child. *Int. J. Group Psychother. 11:*319-338, 1961.

5. Beukenkamp, C.: The noncommunication between husbands and wives as revealed in group psychotherapy. *Int. J. Group Psychother., 9:*308-313, 1959.

6. Brody, W., and Hayden, M.: Intrateam reactions: Their relation to conflicts in family treatment. *Amer. J. Orthopsychiat., 27:*349, 1957.

7. Dawley, A.: Interrelated movements of parents and child in therapy with children. *Amer. J. Orthopsychiat., 29:*748-754, 1959.

8. Durkin, H. E.: *Group Therapy for Mothers of Disturbed Children.* Springfield, Ill., Charles C Thomas, 1954.

9. Eisenstein, V. W. (Ed.): *Neurotic Interaction in Marriage.* New York, Basic Books, 1956.

10. Glaser, K.: Group discussions with mothers of hospitalized children. *Pediatrics, 26:*132-140, 1960.

11. Grotjahn, M.: *Psychoanalysis and the Family Neurosis.* New York, W. W. Norton, 1960.

12. Group for Advancement of Psychiatry: *The Diagnostic Process in Child Psychiatry.* Report No. 38, 1957.

13. Haley, J.: The family of the schizophrenic: A model system: *J. Nerv. Ment. Dis., 129:*357-374, 1959.

14. Hallowitz, E., and Stephens, V.: Group therapy with fathers. *Social Casework, 40:*183-192, 1959.

15. Jackson, D. D., and Weakland, J. H.: Conjoint family therapy. *Psychiatry, 24:*30-45, 1961.

16. Johnson, A.: Collaborative psychotherapy: Team setting. In Heiman, N., Ed., *Psychoanalysis and Social Work.* New York, International Universities Press, 1953.

17. LaBarre, M.: Dynamic factors in psychiatric team collaboration. *Brit. J. Med. Sci. 33:*53, 1960.

18. Langford, W. S., and Olson E.: Clinical work with parents of child patients. *Quart. J. Child Behav., 3:*240-249, 1951.

19. Lowry, L. W.: *Orthopsychiatry, 1923-1948: Retrospect and Prospect.* Amer. Orthopsychiat. Ass., 1948.

20. Marcus, I. M.: Psychoanalytic group therapy with fathers of emotionally disturbed preschool children. *Int. J. Group Psychother., 6:*61-76, 1956.

21. Martin, P. A., and Bird, H. W.: An approach to the psychotherapy of marriage partners. *Psychiatry, 16:*123-127, 1953.

22. Mittelmann, B.: The concurrent analysis of married couples. *Psychoanal. Quart., 17:*182-197, 1948.

23. Pollak, O.: A family diagnosis model. *Soc. Serv. Rev., 34:*19-31, 1960.

24. Ritchie, A.: Multiple impact therapy: An experiment. *Social Work, 5:*16-21, 1960.

25. Ruesch, J.: *Disturbed Communication.* New York, W. W. Norton, 1957.

26. Szurek, S. A.: Some lessons from efforts at psychotherapy with parents. *Amer. J. Psychiat., 109:*296-301, 1952.

27. Szurek, S. A., Johnson, A., and Falstein, E.: Collaborative psychiatric therapy of parent-child problems. *Amer. J. Orthopsychiat, 12:*511-516, 1942.

Chapter 24

Group Psychotherapy for
Parents of Disturbed Children*

AL B. HARLEY, JR.

GROUP psychotherapy for parents of emotionally disturbed children is not a new idea, but one whose value warrants continued reappraisal because it helps to clarify the psychodynamics of family interaction. The use of group psychotherapy for parents of disturbed children is based on the hypothesis that children become sick because of their psychological environment. Parental relationships are at the center of this environment, and the child's illness may reflect parental problems. A child is unlikely to get well and stay well unless his family environment improves.

In our own hospital we found that a number of patients in the children's unit were progressing too slowly, with too many setbacks and furlough returns. The basic problem appeared to be related to parental problems. We decided to try group therapy because it is adapted easily to parents and to the usual time limitations of a state hospital.

We decided that the group sessions could best be conducted by two therapists, a man (the author) and a woman. This would provide both a mother and a father image (to promote optimum transference) and enable me to become familiar with the technique of a more experienced therapist. Later we found that the presence of two therapists also afforded an excellent safety mechanism when transference-countertransference became too violent. In some cases I served as therapist for the child and his parents. Although this provided me with firsthand knowledge of

*Reprinted by permission of the author and *Hospital and Community Psychiatry*, *14:*14-18, 1963.

the child, it often led to conflict in the group sessions because the parents thought I was the child's ally and the child thought me the parents' ally.

We organized two groups, each consisting of eight sets of parents. We planned weekly sessions for the convenience of parents, some of whom had to travel great distances and, in many cases, take leave from work. We had already discovered that if we held the sessions less often, parents lost much of their interest and feeling of belonging to the group. Obviously, seeing parents only once a week meant that we could not uncover much anxiety or expose many defenses. However, we hoped to arouse enough anxiety to make progress possible. We included both mothers and fathers whenever possible, to increase the beneficial effect in the child's environment and allow us to observe family interaction firsthand. In both groups wife-husband interaction was extremely interesting and varied, ranging from consolation to outright domestic conflict. As might be expected, mothers attended more frequently. In the first group only two fathers participated and then only minimally. Seven fathers took an active part in the second group.

We felt that the optimum time limit per session should be one and a half hours. One hour seemed too short for real involvement and two hours too tiring both for patients and therapists.

Each session was supervised by an experienced psychiatrist, who met with the therapists immediately after each group meeting for an additional hour and a half. We found these supervision meetings valuable for future planning, interpretation, clarification, and evaluation of transference-countertransference phenomena.

Perhaps the most controversial factor in our plan was limiting the number of therapy sessions to six, but it was necessary because of the many patients in our children's unit — as well as some parents — who needed psychiatric attention. Furthermore, we wanted to see if group therapy, under the pressure of limited time, might yield relatively greater results. We assured the patients in the series, and their parents, that they could return to a later group if necessary. Therapeutic goals were necessarily limited, varying in individual cases from simple clarification and support to open attack on severe neurotic defenses so that the parents would realize their need for help and seek further psychiatric guidance.

In selecting parents for the groups we considered several things. Obviously there had to be a distinct need for therapy, for which the presence of the child in a mental hospital seemed sufficient evidence. We also considered the psychological accessibility of parents to therapy by asking ourselves, Are the parents interested? Are they intelligent enough to benefit from therapy? Do they have enough emotional stability to withstand the anxiety of therapy? (In one case we encouraged the parent to stop the sessions after we learned during an anxiety-ridden episode that she had had a schizophrenic break in the past year.) Could we establish a schedule which would make it possible for parents to attend? In a few cases the possibility of desirable secondary benefits influenced our selections, such as three-day passes for the children or early release from the hospital. We tried to select for each group parents of similar social status, but from different geographical areas to minimize the chances of parents' knowing each other socially.

The parents in the first group were as follows:

Mrs. A was a plump, middle-aged woman from the lower-middle socioeconomic class. She appeared hard-working and practical, and had raised a large family, most of whom were grown. Her youngest son, a boy of ten, had shown moderate difficulties in adjustment, with frequent acting out which had forced his commitment.

Mr. A, an authoritarian, self-sufficient man, came to only one session, but gave the impression of being honest and forthright, with relatively few difficulties.

Mrs. B, a middle-aged, strait-laced woman, seemed inconvenienced by the difficulties caused by her 16-year-old daughter's severe negativism, hostility, and sexual acting out. Mrs. B had been divorced for some years and recently had suffered through her younger daughter's slow death from cancer.

Mrs. C was a middle-aged lady, somewhat shy and almost tearful because her teenage son had shown a great deal of emotional difficulty.

Mrs. D was an attractive young mother whose father had died recently. Shortly after his death, her 12-year-old daughter began to have severe hysterical episodes, usually with auditory and visual hallucinations that her dead grandfather was trying to kill her.

Mrs. E was an anxious young mother who had great difficulties with her 11-year-old son's episodes of aggression and unchecked hostility toward her and the boy's sister. At one point, he had threatened them with a knife.

Mrs. F was a young woman who had spent five years in a mental hospital. She and her husband, who also came to therapy, were of rather low intellectual capacity and were recognized from the beginning as poor selections. However, their 15-year-old daughter's recent schizophrenic behavior indicated definite family problems as the precipitating factor.

Mrs. G had been married several times and had five children, but still seemed to be a very immature little girl. We were treating her 8-year-old son, who was a bright, well-liked child while in the hospital. When outside, however, he stayed in trouble constantly by stealing, breaking windows, and other antisocial activity.

Mrs. H was an apparently self-sufficient, middle-aged woman, who wore a stony expression, masculine suits and heavy jewelry. Her teenage son was severely psychotic. She had been separated for some time from her second husband.

All of these people belonged to the lower-middle-class. Only two fathers participated; the others apparently could not afford time off from work.

At the first session the therapists seated themselves at opposite ends of the table. In the light of later developments it was interesting to note that the parents developed a closer transference to the therapist nearest to whom they seated themselves. After the therapists introduced themselves, the parents were asked to give their names and their children's names. This was done uneventfully until Mrs. F's turn, when she made a loud cry, slumped over the table, and began pounding it with her fist. The therapists were caught off guard. Mr. F tried to comfort her, and Mrs. A came to her rescue saying, "That's all right, dear, we are all in the same boat." Although the outburst seemed to increase the parents' anxiety, it did help to break through superficial social barriers. We then explained that in our experience the child makes more progress when the parents are also in therapy, and that we would all discuss their problems and their relationships to their children's problems. The session was opened for discussion. Mrs. A and Mrs.

D did most of the talking, comparing their children's difficulties, while the other parents remained on their guard. There was little interference on the part of the therapists.

After the first session we evaluated Mrs. F's condition and decided that we had little to offer her. We suggested to her afterward that the long distance she had to travel to get to the hospital might prevent her from attending each session. This excuse was all she needed to escape from an anxiety-provoking situation.

In the second session we attempted to involve the parents more closely in the group. We tried by arousing their guilt feelings to overcome their hesitance to accept the patient role. The parents reacted with a number of defenses. The initial defense might be called the "organic defense": "He fell on his head when he was born." "Do you think this may be epilepsy?" We simply turned such questions back to the group. As these defenses failed, tensions increased, resulting in a frantic groping for other defenses, which were usually easier for the therapist to deal with, such as "My child didn't get sick at home. He got sick at school." By the time these poor defenses were presented, we had picked up from among the other parents several helpers, who were able to point out the fallacies behind this type of reasoning. By the end of this session, Mrs. A, Mrs. C, Mrs. E, and Mrs. G showed signs of stress but were beginning to recognize their parts in their children's illnesses. Despite our efforts to involve them in the group, Mrs. B, Mrs. D, and Mrs. H remained almost silent.

Another defense appeared at the third session: "Well, I've got three other children who are normal, so it can't be my fault he's this way." We had been waiting for this key defense so that we could try to discover what made this child different in the parent's eyes. Mrs. A's anxiety mounted, and, although we could not get her to express her feelings during the session, she did express them afterward to the cotherapist. She had permitted a hysterectomy after the birth of this child, and, being a devout Catholic, she had felt guilty and degraded because of it. She had tried to compensate for this by overprotecting the boy. During the same week Mrs. G told the cotherapist that her son had been born before marriage and that his father was not the man she later married. Apparently the hostile resentment she felt toward the child, because of what he represented, had caused her such anxiety that she reacted by overprotecting him.

During the first three sessions only Mrs. B and Mrs. H remained remote and showed little progress. It became evident in later individual sessions that Mrs. B had invested in her teenage daughter all of her sexual desires and was acting out through the daughter. Mrs. H revealed high expectations of her son; she could not tolerate seeing him as a weak, dependent man. It was clear that her failure in two marriages was due to the inability of her husbands to live up to her concept that men ought to be strong and independent.

Mrs. A worked hard in the group and at home with her husband. She admitted to the group that she had tended to overprotect her child, while her husband demanded that he be self-assertive. This conflict had led to dishonesty. For example, when the father would tell the boy to mop the floor, Mrs. A would tell him to play while she did the job herself. Later she would tell her husband that the boy had done it. With her new-found insight, she was able to correct this pathologic attitude when her child went home on brief visits.

Mrs. C was very frightened and conveyed this fear to her son, making him into a helpless teenage boy.

Mrs. D finally was able to express her own unresolved Electra feelings toward her father, which had compelled her to use her own daughter as an extension of herself to point where the 12-year-old girl had fantasies of sexual relations with her grandfather. We speculated that his death at the height of the child's adopted Electra feelings had created a severe guilt feeling and led to the hysterical reaction.

Mrs. G's immaturity appeared to have been caused by a stern, dominant grandmother, who had raised her and continued to control her even though she had been married several times and had a number of children. The grandmother controlled her through numerous favors. She had given Mrs. G and her husband the house next door to live in rent free, and she had given them money, and she had cared for the children between marriages so that Mrs. G could go husband hunting. After supporting, direct therapy, Mrs. G announced that she had her own telephone installed. Later, she and her family moved to another neighborhood, started paying rent, and began a constructive family relationship.

At the last planned therapy session, we left the door open for those who wanted further treatment. Five of the parents were followed up later and showed good results. We felt that all the parents had profited to some degree. At least they had all become involved more closely in the children's problems. Most of the children also showed decided improvement.

We were quite apprehensive about the second group because it consisted mostly of highly intelligent upper-middle-class parents, most of whom had strong neurotic defenses. Also, their children were more severely ill than those of the first group.

Mr. A was an obsessive-compulsive individual who worked as a lawyer in Washington, D. C. His wife was a meek, nervous woman, many years his junior. Their 16-year-old daughter was schizophrenic.

Mr. B, another lawyer, and his wife also exhibited obsessive-compulsive tendencies. Their son was severely schizophrenic.

Mr. C, who stuttered, appeared to be a weak, spineless man. His wife was a very neurotic, belligerent woman. Their son was a 13-year-old chronic schizophrenic.

Mr. and Mrs. D were soft-spoken parents who were afraid of the world. Their teenage boy was an exhibitionist with a serious stuttering problem.

Mr. E was an insurance claims investigator who had made his way to the top from humble beginnings. He had obsessive-compulsive tendencies. His wife was an attractive, well-mannered, soft-spoken lady who appeared much younger than her husband. Their daughter was suffering from *anorexia nervosa*.

Mr. F was a self-made businessman who had climbed from the slums of New York to a position of high status. His wife also seemed to have a lot of drive. Their 13-year-old son was a severe behavior problem.

Mrs. G was an attractive young woman with few neurotic defenses. Mr. G, her second husband, was a quiet, reserved man. The patient, a 17-year-old boy with behavior problems, was not his child.

Mrs. H, a widow, had previously been exposed to therapy elsewhere. Her 13-year-old daughter was a behavior problem.

The members of this group, particularly those whose children were psychotic, had achieved high professional status. This is an interesting but fairly common occurrence. In 1672, Thomas Willis (1) noted in *De Anima Brutorum* that "Wise men and highly ingenious, do beget fools. For that the parents being too much given to study, reading, and of meditation."

During the first session some parents made vicious verbal attacks against the hospital: "My boy is being mistreated." "My child had on one red sock and one blue sock." "Why does my child take only three baths a week?" "My boy gets beat up by groups over there." Mr. F led the attack, apparently demonstrating his own guilt feelings at having committed his child to the hospital in a fit of anger. The fact that the children had been committed to the hospital did not seem to reduce their parents' demands on them. In a study of 175 such cases, Cohen (2) found that parents who bring their children to a hospital still retain the same distorted expectations of them that caused their illnesses, and transfer some of their expectations to the hospital. This transference seemed to occur in our group. Mr. and Mrs. C joined Mr. F in attacking us, and the three of them dominated the entire first session. However, the show of fireworks so surprised some of the other parents that they dropped their defensive attitudes and became somewhat sympathetic to the undergoing therapists. Mrs. D was horrified and cried openly, once again giving an indication of her fear of the world.

The second session began the same way, until we stated that, if the attacks continued, the therapy would probably be of no benefit. Mr. and Mrs. C complained that they could see no benefit in these sessions anyway. Mrs. C went on to attack psychiatrists in general, listing a dozen who had not helped her boy. She was antagonized even more when I asked her is she had ever listened to

(1) Quoted in P. F. Cranefield: A Seventeenth Century View of Deficiency and Schizophrenia, *Bulletin of the History of Medicine*, Vol. *35*, 1961, p. 4.
(2) R. L. Cohen, I. W. Charny, and P. Lempke: Parental Expectations as a Force in Treatment, *Arch. Gen. Psychiat.*, Vol. *4*, 1961, pp. 471-478.

them or followed their advice. She then described some trouble she had had with her son when he insisted on eating dessert before meals. She had asked the psychiatrist about it, and he suggested that she let him eat his dessert first. When I asked if she followed his advice, she replied, "Of course not. That's silly." The group laughed aloud at this obvious demonstration of her illogical reasoning. Mr. and Mrs. C then demanded that I tell them specifically how to help their child, but Mrs. H, who had had previous therapy, replied that the answer was buried within themselves.

Mr. A showed remarkable improvement during the sessions. When I first met him, he showed me a large collection of papers about his daughter, including a complete medical history, in diary form, listing the frequency of bowel movements, menstrual periods, several electroencephalograms, an electrocardiogram, and typewritten progress notes which he had signed. He had started keeping these records four years before when she had had several *petit mal* seizures. Since then, she had ceased to be a child to him, and had become a medical case which he pursued with great interest. Coupled with his neurotic behavior, the minor physical ailment, which was well controlled by drugs, had led her into a severe psychiatric condition. Although he did not participate actively in the group to any extent, Mr. A was able to drop these habits. He became depressed temporarily, but later recovered. His daughter improved greatly after his change in attitude.

Mr. and Mrs. B began the sessions by taking notes of everything said, in an obsessive-compulsive manner. They soon gave this up, however, and realized that their perfectionistic demands had prompted their son's breakdown. The boy showed a good remission of acute schizophrenic symptoms, and they are now in a guidance clinic for treatment.

Unfortunately, little was accomplished with Mr. and Mrs. C because of their strong neurotic defenses.

Mr. and Mrs. D were able to see that their own fear of the world had been partly responsible for their son's fearful attitude, and both parents and child improved. They were quite earnest in attempting to stop overprotecting him.

Mr. and Mrs. E gained some insight but required further therapy because of the severity of their disorder and that of their child, whom I am still treating in individual psychotherapy. Their needs to excel and to be perfect seemed to encourage the child's retreat into psychosis.

Mr. and Mrs. F remained hostile throughout the sessions, although the dynamics of their relationship became obvious. Mr. F was basically dishonest; he admitted that he always claimed to have a high school diploma but in fact had never finished the ninth grade. This dishonesty was conveyed to his son, whose anxiety was increased by the ambivalence of their perfectionistic demands and their dishonest parental attitudes.

Mrs. G, who had few neurotic difficulties, cooperated well throughout the sessions. Her main difficulty appeared to be a fear of showing her true feelings. This had accelerated her son's feelings of being unloved and unwanted.

Mrs. H gained a great deal of insight and realized that her daughter's defiance and hostility stemmed in part from the mother's separation from her husband because of his drinking. The girl had unresolved Electra feelings. Through therapy, a more peaceful coexistence was established.

Three of the parents went on into individual therapy in our hospital and a fourth sought help on the outside. We observed again that the degree of improvement in the parents had a casual relationship to the child's improvement.

Our experiences lead us to conclude that group psychotherapy is particularly useful with a disturbed child's parents because the child's illness appears to improve in direct proportion to improvement in his parents, and vice versa. We found that our short-term limited therapy produced relatively worthwhile results when cases were selected with care. Finally, we believe the cotherapist approach, under supervision of a psychiatrist has definite merit.

Chapter 25

Group Therapy of Parents Who Have
Children in Residential or
Day Care Psychiatric Treatment*

JAMES BLACK

THIS presentation about group therapy deals with parents whose children are in residential treatment at Child Guidance Home in Cincinnati. This inpatient service for severely emotionally disabled children encompasses therapeutic residential experiences, including special education which is coordinated with collaborative individual therapy for children and parents. In addition, many parents are also seen in weekly group therapy.

The parent groups are planned for eight persons, four mothers and four fathers who are not married to each other. New members are not admitted after the group has begun, and currently there are three groups, each consisting of five to eight members plus two therapists and a recorder. Initially these parents accept group therapy because of their sincere desires to help their children. They are willing to participate in a procedure recommended as part of the comprehensive treatment for their children, but seldom do they understand the process of group therapy or the need for their own involvement in it. In the earliest group sessions the parents are usually blocked in presenting thoughts and feelings which do not seem directly related to the problems of their children. Further, they have even greater difficulties expressing any attitudes or responses to the other members of the group. However, the common experience of having children in residential treatment serves as a unifying force which leads to an unusually early sense of cohesiveness among the group members. Despite the value of their common interests in bringing these parents together

*Note: Reprinted by permission of the author and the *Journal of Asthma Research*, 4:251-252, 1967.

as a functioning group, this unity of purpose eventually becomes a resistance to greater emotional interaction between the members themselves.

In the early phases the parents are often united in viewing the therapists as omnipotent figures of authority from whom they expect ready solutions for their problems with their children. Eventually they discover that the therapists cannot supply any magical answers. They begin, at first indirectly and gradually more openly, to reveal their disappointments, anger and anxieties in fantasies of rejection and punishment and also in direct expressions of irritation and annoyance with the therapists and with each other.

It is then the task of the therapists to help the parents recognize these patterns of interaction, to understand some of their causes, and to encourage further exploration of dynamic involvement with each other. This leads to a shift from the parents' focusing on their children's problems to a more serious consideration of their own feelings and their reactions expressed in relation to each other during the group meetings. The ultimate goal is to help the parents understand that this process reflects the dynamic interactions within their own families and that these insights can be useful in bringing about improved parent-child relationships.

Chapter 26

Group Psychotherapy with Parents of Psychotic and of Neurotic Children*

MAISEN MOE, NIC WAAL AND BJÖRN URDAHL

THE intention of this chapter is to show the differences between two groups of parents, as experienced in group-psychotherapy: a) parents of psychotic children, and b) parents of neurotic children. This difference is to be found, first of all, in the selection of the group members, in the group process, and in the effect of therapy.

We hope to verify the hypothesis, which other authors like Kanner, Pavenstedt, and Rank have asserted, that parents of atypical children are likely to have a personality structure, which − together with other factors − is decisive for the appearance of the specific disease of their children.

Group (a) consisted of 4 couples of parents and one divorced mother. Later on two more couples joined the group. The children brought to the Institute by these parents were "atypical" children, all autistic. Three of these children were clearly clinically autistic, one was autistic on the background of a diagnosed brain damage and decrease of sight, and two others on the background of ego-weakness, and a state of borderline anxiety which had been mishandled.

Mr. and Mrs. A: Their son was referred to the Institute from the Child Psychiatric Clinic of the University at the age of 4 1/2 years. He seemed to have developed normally up to the age of 2 1/2 years, but showed no skill of language. The diagnosis at the beginning was uncertain, mentally deficient or autistic. The patient had two brothers, one 4 and the other 6 years his elder,

---

Note: Reprinted by permission of the author and *Psychotherapy and Psychosomatics,* 8:134-146, 1960.

both seemingly well adjusted.

Mr. A held a higher position in a bank, all his brothers were bankers. He himself was a man with practical hobbies and never satisfied with his position in the bank.

Mrs. A held a higher position in a bank, all her brothers were cashiers in a bank, very efficient and always confident, smiling, positive, however, always extremely ambivalent to the Institute.

Mr. and Mrs. B: Their son was also referred from the Child Psychiatric Clinic of the University at the age of 4 1/2 years, and had shown a seemingly normal development until he was 2 1/2 years, except for his language capacity, which failed to develop. This fact troubled his parents after the younger brother had been born. The patient had been treated as an "out-patient" in the Child-Psychiatric Ward for three-fourths of a year, later he stayed one year in a residential home, after which he was referred to the Institute. The boy showed clear characteristics of an autistic picture. He had one sister 4 years older, seemingly well adjusted. Mr. B was an architect of a high standard. He had a domineering, boisterous, and almost military authoritarian personality. He was the son of a well-to-do farmer.

Mrs. B was a very efficient high-school teacher, her father a college professor. She lived, in a sense, a double life, that is: at home, as the mother of the patient, she showed the image of a Madonna, always smiling sweetly, passive and permissive, while in school, she was a very well liked, active teacher.

Mrs. C: She was the divorced mother of a girl referred to the Institute by Mrs. C's employer, with whom she worked as a housekeeper. Because of the divorce, the daughter, 3 1/2 years old by then, was placed in an old fashioned home for mentally deficient children. The author of this chapter visited the girl on behalf of the mother's employers, and found an extremely autistic child. The child was transferred to a modern institution for mentally deficit children, which cooperated on the line of the autistic problem, and from here she was referred to the Institute for therapy. The mother was the daughter of a very poor fisherman in northern Norway, was married to a brutal skilled worker, to whom she, masochistically, subdued, then left him placing the child in the old fashioned institution. The mother is passive, mute and Madonna-like. (This patient left the group after 1 year.)

Mr. and Mrs. D: Their son was referred to the Institute by the University Child Psychiatric Clinic, diagnosed as autistic. The patient, 5 1/2 years old, showed autistic behavior. He was distant, unruly and obsessive with signs of panic when phobias and obsessions were hindered; yet it was possible during the examination at the Institute to break through his distant and queer behavior periodically. The Institute diagnosed him as a "borderline case with autistic behavior." The patient had developed well in his early years, but started to behave in a queer, panicky, and obsessive way at the age of 2 1/2 years when his younger brother was born.

Mr. D was a seemingly well-adjusted man, but with signs of anxiety neurosis. He was the son of an alcoholic foreman, but had become a well-to-do department director in an automobile-firm. In his business he was very clever, but narcissistic, socially insecure and verbally dominating when stimulated, but without rapport.

Mrs. D was the daughter of a shoemaker, belonging to the lower middle classes. She was "her father's daughter," very insecure, sweet, quiet, and beautiful. Before she married she was an efficient seamstress.

Mr. and Mrs. E: Their daughter was referred by a practitioner, a medical school officer, after having been refused as a pupil in public school in the special classes for retarded children. The patient was at this time 6 1/2 years old, had developed speech, but at the age of 3 years had shown signs of severe anxiety, developing a queer behavior with obsessional demeanor, strange language, and symbolic attitudes. The school psychiatrists diagnosed her as being mentally deficient. The Institute, however, diagnosed her as being a borderline case with autistic features.

Mr. E was a foreman in industry. He was stocky and mute, it was impossible to get real contact with him, although he had a humourous, likable attitude. He was the son of an alcoholic of the lower classes.

Mrs. E was a stocky, very infantile woman, who did home work as a seamstress. She was efficient, humorous; like Mrs. A, she showed a defensive optimism, but with sudden aggression and ambivalence. When the group had been together for nine months, the members decided to accept as new members:

Mr. and Mrs. F: Their son was referred by friends of the Institute as very difficult case because of the father. The patient had been examined and treated at the University Child Psychiatric Clinic. The father was disgusted with the service there and therefore he accepted the transference to the Institute. The patient had developed no skill of language at the age of 3 years, was examined at the University Pediatric Department and first referred to the child psychiatric ward, getting logopedic treatment without results. It was found that the boy had severe widening of brain ventricles and diffuse encephalopathia and was diagnosed as mentally deficient. The parents trained their son by excessive motoric activities, reading, and spelling. At the transference to the Institute the boy showed autistic features. He was obsessive and babyish. He was diagnosed as suffering from behavior disorder and ego-weakness, autistic features superimposed on organic brain disturbance. He also had a severe disturbance of sight and became blind during the treatment.

Mr. F was extremely successful as director of a research institute of industry and held a high academic degree. He was an efficient, brilliant, dominating, and self-conscious man with great talent for organizing.

Mrs. F was the daughter of a cultural upper-class family. Her father was a leader of the silver and gold-industry in Norway. She was her "father's daughter," but was rejected by him. She was a boyish and flirty housewife, socially dominating, but dominated by her husband.

Mr. and Mrs. G: Entered the group after 2 1/2 years. Their son was referred to the Institute by a physician after having been found unable to enter the special school of mentally deficient children. This boy was a borderline case with severe autistic features, obsessive with queer demeanor and panic reactions. He suffered from organic brain disturbance with manifest epilepsy, unruly and distant.

Mr. G was a stocky and humorous, but very defensive, mute police officer, the son of a well-to-do farmer. Mrs. G was a youthful, beautiful and efficient housewife, always smiling – with a pollyanna complex. She insisted that nothing was wrong, and had little contact with children.

The parents in group A were selected for group psychotherapy for the following reasons:

First of all, these parents were found to be extreme in the sense that they all lacked insight into the disease of their children. They were also completely defensive in the course of the interviews. None of them could see any connection between themselves, the family situation, and their atypical and deviant children. Any attempt to change the regular interviews into supportive psychotherapy was unsuccessful. As families they were all socially isolated, but for this they blamed their deviant children. At best, these parents had received from the child-psychiatric clinics and from the professionals, the advice to give their children more warmth and pay more attention to them. This advice, however, had been misunderstood by all the parents. They became more indulgent toward their children to such a degree that they became almost self-destructive. This attitude destroyed their family life and made it difficult for the other children at home. The dominating fathers were either aggressively and unconsciously disagreeing — or behaving masochistically as most of the mothers did, according to their different personalities. All of them had withdrawn from social contact and interaction.

Secondly, one of the reasons why group-psychotherapy of these parents was initiated was that, after the first half year of successful experimental treatment of their children, it came to a mechanical stand-still.

The respective therapists felt is was useless to try to achieve better results unless the parents themselves could be made less ambivalent to the treatment of their children. Thus, group (a) was primarily selected because of the extreme deviant features of their children, and because the parents, individually, were unreachable. Other aspects were that the parents considered their situation as a disaster, that their children had become a curse to them. We hoped to reach them and help them through group method.

Group (b) consisted of 4 couples of parents.

Mr. and Mrs. H: Their son, the patient, was an acting-out type, seemingly ego-weak, but according to examination he suffered from ordinary behavior disorder.

Mr. H was a salesman. Although divorced from his first wife, he was bound to her in spite of his new marriage. He was efficient, smooth, denying emotional conflicts. He was the son of middle-class people.

Mrs. H was a housewife and the second wife of Mr. H. She was jealous of her husband's first wife. She was the second child of middle-class parents, her father being divorced and married twice. She had had a stepmother at the age of eleven. Mrs. H was quite warm, affective, somewhat prudent, using common sense, and had inherent temperament.

Mr. and Mrs. I: Their daughter was a teenager, in opposition to her mother and family, she was diagnosed as having character disorders with psychosomatic complaints. Mr. I was a domineering and strange personality. He was an auditor and cashier in the municipal administration, from a lower middle-class family. His financial operations were dubious and obscure, and his wife never knew how the money was spent. There were marital conflicts.

Mrs. I had a very complicated background. Her adoptive father was a rather adventurous, freelancing businessman in good financial conditions, married several times. Mrs. I grew up partly with adoptive grandparents and partly with stepmothers. She had made several suicidal attempts previously. She was masochistic, and full of repressed criticism against her husband, but tried hard to keep up the economy of the family.

Mr. and Mrs. K: Their daughter, a pre-adolescent girl, with clinical appearing backwardness, was diagnosed as having behavior disorder with pseudodebility.

Mr. K was an independent and well-to-do businessman. He had an authoritarian personality with latent anxiety close behind the surface. He was a competitive type and career-minded. His father was a skilled worker.

Mrs. K was a housewife, socially insecure, subdued by her husband and children. She came from the lower middle-classes.

Mr. and Mrs. L: Their son was diagnosed to have behavior disorder with developing character disorder.

Mr. L had had a military career, but disliked his job. He had been severely dominated by his mother, he was domineering himself, but with rather open anxiety concerning his own problems. Mrs. L had been an immigrant warbride with a white-collar education, she was openminded, full of common sense, but concealed aggressive tendencies appearing as self-assertion.

The parents in *group (b)* were typical of the bulk of parents referred to the Institute. They had emotional and marital problems not differing from the usual type of neurotic parents. The diseases of their children represented the ordinary clinical problems. The neurotic state of their children caused these parents a lot of trouble and unhappiness, but did not represent to them such a fatal catastrophe as the children in group (a) did. The strife to reach a certain social status was common to all the parents in group (b). In personalities they differed a lot in contrast to the members of group (a). They admitted or revealed marital difficulties already during the first interviews.

Group (a) was conducted by the author herself for 3 years. The first year the assistant physician of the Institute together with his wife acted as cotherapists of this group. Then the nursery school teacher of sick children replaced these observers during the second year, and in the third one of the candidates being trained in group psychotherapy was observer.

Group (b) consisted of parents of neurotic children. The group was conducted by two training candidates – a social worker and a male clinical psychologist, both senior psychotherapists, and both were parents themselves (the female leader was a 54-year-old woman with 4 grown-up children, the other was a 30-year-old man and father of a small child.)

The parents in group (b) were very keen to get help with their problems. Several of them had already from the start accepted supportive individual casework. They admitted from the very beginning of the interviews that the neurotic conflicts of their children were connected with their own and their family problems.

The parents in this group were selected according to group dynamic factors after a multi-factorial planning, as has been done in all cases of group-therapy at the Institute, that is: we evaluate and scrutinize diagnostic symptoms, case histories, age, socioeconomic status, emotionality, active or passive type of personality, etc. This system of selection has been constructed according to psychoanalytical as well as sociometric methods. The common factor in group (b) was the motivation to get an insight into their problems and their admittance of the connection between their children's conflicts and their own. They differed in personalities as much as the types of neurosis of their children did.

Furthermore, they shared the feeling, that the marriage represented conflicts, the contents of which was not always known to them. None of them, however, considered divorce. As families they were adjusted socially.

Group (a): Except for one couple, the parents in this group did not reveal their personal conflicts during the first two years, neither in the interviews nor in the group-work. In the beginning of the third year, however, the situation changed totally. Several of them now admitted that they often had discussed divorce long before coming to the Institute. Marital problems then became the main topic of discussions. The case history of the patients had to be rewritten, because the initial stories actually gave a false picture of family surroundings, background, and family situation.

The very first meeting of group (a) was arranged as a party with a meal, snacks, and wine at the office of the leader. This is a drawing room and therefore suitable for the purpose. The parents were asked if they would like to get together regularly, and told that this might help them in their situation, without promising any cure for their children. They agreed to the regularity of the group-meetings and chose the party form themselves. They were also willing to share the expenses of the meetings. No time limit was set for each party, although the leader told them she could stay for two hours. The meetings were not described to them as therapy.

The development of group (a) was characterized by an extreme cohesiveness, but only overtly. The meetings lasted about 3 to 4 hours, until the members almost had to be thrown out. They practically never missed a meeting, and criticized the leader if she did so for professional reasons. After one year they proposed that the meetings should, alternatingly, be held in their respective homes. They started to get together socially, outside the meetings.

They even went on week-end trips to the countryside together.

In the beginning two or three of the fathers in the group were dominating, using a lot of humor, while the rest – especially the mothers – remained passive. From the second year on, considerable changes took place. The men were the most forward in the sociability of the meetings, and soon the women – except for one – became more and more secure and active in conversation, thus the sociogram did not stay as patterned and rigid as in the beginning. From the end of the second year there were distinct signs of loyalty in the group, and they also began to think more socially. They showed more empathy with each other and started also to help the Institute with practical arrangements for their own children. From the third year the members of the group supported each other whenever specific problems of child-training of one of the families were discussed. This development to social thinking and interrelationship was extremely slow, but could be noticed from the twentieth meeting onward.

In order to keep the group concentrated on common subjects during the sessions, the leader had to be alert and active, as smaller subgroups were about to be formed all the time. The leader had to change from being passive into active leadership, but in the second year the members became more and more active themselves in contact with each other. In the very beginning the conversation centered around lamenting their fate, showing constant distrust against the treatment of their children. They showed open fear of the future, and were angry at authorities, which they felt did not help them. During the second year the theme of coversation at the meetings changed to more personal matters. They began to be interested in the effect upon parents having disturbed and unsuccessful children. Now they were able to admit both fear, ambivalence, sorrow, and anger. These personal discussions led to further discussions in the third year touching on their own marriage conflicts and problems of contact.

This development of the group itself, however, did not mean that the members had developed greater understanding of, or contact with, their children, who were the actual patients. They changed very little in the attitude towards their sick children, but seemed to understand their other children better.

In becoming less isolated through the group activities, they dared to let other people take care of their sick children, while they started to "go out," to the theater, movies, and to parties. Some of the fathers and mothers changed noticeably into warmer personalities, which after all affected their contact with their sick children.

It was to be hoped that another year would bring the group nearer the aim of the therapy. In this group the leader met with some of the same problems as in group therapy with juvenile delinquents. The whole process seems to show, in some way, that these parents (as well as the members of the juvenile group) reveal personalities, which had narcissistic, infantile, and immature features.

Group (b) was told, already after a few gatherings, that the aim in forming a group was to start group therapy, and that the sessions were to be limited to 1 1/2 hour. They got only loaf and biscuits and had to pay the usual fee for group-therapy.

Group (b) differed from group (a) in the following facts: The parents in group (b) showed much less formal cohesiveness, but the usual signs of group process, the inner cohesiveness, developed already from the second meeting. Absence from the group of single members was not uncommon. They usually gave as reason lack of babysitters, excess of work, etc. — while attendance in group (a) was much more stable. Transference and interaction between group members was clear from the beginning. Sub-grouping took place much less than in group (a), and they were also better able to concentrate on one particular subject. The leaders of group (b) were therefore able to stick more or less to one technique, namely, the interpretative psychoanalytical technique.

The group was active in discussions of children's problems, democratic versus authoritarian atmosphere in the home, relationship between themselves and their children and also their own problems and personalities. It happened during the debates that family problems were seen in relation to problems in a wider scope, e.g. national and international problems. Their own personal defenses were little by little torn down, and their marital problems were now seen in relation to their children's problems and their own childhood. The therapists children were able to elicit positive alterations in the relationship between the parents and their sick children. All this happened during the first year of the group.

CONCLUSIONS

Group (a) showed an intense formal cohesiveness but practically no inner cohesiveness before the end of the second year, that is, after 26 meetings. Previously, the meetings had been falling apart into subgroups, chattering without concentrating on any particular subject. The leader had to break up, actively, the subgroups and reinstitute the topic, with which they actually should deal. The sociogram remained static over a year and changed only slowly during the second year. The group was "leader-centered" until the third year, the actual group-process started after the 26th meeting, and a real group therapy became evident in the fourth year.

Group (b) did not show any signs of formal cohesiveness, but they showed a growing *inner* cohesiveness and a clear group-process already from the second meeting. The members of the group stuck to one subject, and did it in a fertile way. During the sessions the "leadership" was flexible and changed among the members and the two leaders of the group. The method applied in the group process could therefore be releatively constant, the method of interpretative psychoanalysis.

Group (a) showed an almost tiresome defensive attitude, causing repetition, not seeing any connection between themselves and their children, having very little contact with them. This went on for a whole year. During the second year these parents started to admit their ambivalence and their inner feelings, so that the defenses decreased. Simultaneously they started to show more empathy with each other and a greater social responsibility. Later on, in the third year, they started to discuss each other as personalities, their marital problems, etc. They seemed to change their attitudes towards marriage and conflicts. Thus, as time went on, several of the parents became eligible for individual psychotherapy. Their isolation was decreasing, but all this, only, took place after 3 years. Little by little they changed their attitude towards the other children in the family, but still they showed little change in their behavior towards their sick children, though one could trace more warmth towards them, which was slowly developing.

Group (b) showed already from the beginning that they had some insight into their own and their children's problems and conflicts, and they were consciously struggling to solve them. The children's therapists noticed a change in the parents' way of handling their children, already from the first year with 13 meetings.

It may appear that the parents in group (a) were seemingly well adjusted but with rigid, defensive personalities, in other words, they lived within closed compartments. This personality structure actually shows that they were in reality asocial, narcissistic, and immature, whereas the parents in group (b) had more flexible and richer personalities, although they also had infantile neurotic conflicts, but their defenses were less compact and therefore easier to overcome. They were also more communicative.

Conclusively, we may say that the parents in group (a) actually were resisting treatment, they lacked motivation, and formed a special group-dynamic structure, which seemed to differ from the usual design. They were selected because of need, and the set-up had not been planned. They developed a defensive and rigid attitude, but they needed each other, and therefore gained a certain personal satisfaction and better adjustment. By help of group process, they seemed to get more out of life, but did not change very much in their behavior towards their sick children, whereas the parents in group (b) changed their attitudes rather towards their children than towards their own fate.

Thus, the differences between these two groups seem to confirm what other writers have found: that parents of psychotic and autistic children are extremely deviant themselves, although they function in society in a seemingly normal way. Several authors and other people taking part in this discussion would describe these parent's as latent, but adjusted, psychotics, as for instance Anthony (Maudsley Hospital, London) would say.

I feel that these parents are more like the juvenile delinquents, whom I had under treatment. They are narcissitic, infantile personalities. In contrast to the young criminals these parents behave adjusted, but they show a real lack of object contact, which also applies to really difficult criminals.

SUMMARY

Two groups of parents have been selected for group psychotherapy. Group (a) consists of parents of autistic children. Group (b) consists of parents, whose children were suffering from different neurotic disturbances.

Individual psychotherapy with parents in Group (a) was impossible, as these parents were neither inclined towards it, nor had any insight into their own conflicts, and they did not *feel* ill. Group method was applied, it was not called therapy. Group process did not develop on group (a) till after the 26th meeting. Changes in personalities started to take place decidedly after a period of 3 years.

The parents in Group (b), however, were eligible for psychotherapy, and the method used was psychoanalytical group-therapy. Group process developed already after the second meeting and carried all signs of a usual course of resistance, anxiety, catharsis, resolution of problems.

Thus we can say that parents of autistic children hide severe disturbances behind a hard surface of seeming adjustment of a different character from ordinary neurosis in adults.

Chapter 27

Group Therapy with Parents of Adolescent Drug Addicts*

ROBERT HIRSCH

REVIEW OF LITERATURE

ALTHOUGH much has been written on the parents of disturbed children, there has been relatively little in the group therapy literature on parents of adolescent drug addicts. Healy and Bronner (1) in their study felt that "antisocial children identified themselves with gross ethical distortions of parents"; Johnson (2) saw the mother as unconsciously encouraging the amoral or antisocial behavior of the child. The same author felt that the needs of the parent are gratified by the behavior of the child who blackmails the parent who is guilt-ridden about discipline.

In a series of papers (3-5), Gerard and Kornetsky showed that the relations between the parents of adolescent addicts are poor and grossly disturbed. They saw the addict as unable to break the ambivalent tie with his mother without guilt. Their studies also revealed the strong familial need for high attainment and the inculcating of high levels of aspiration and expectation into the children. In an important paper on moral masochism, Bromberg (6) viewed the mothers of "moral masochists" as people with above average aggressive impulses, narcissistic, hostile, and inconsistent. Bromberg felt that these mothers have a great need to control and that they unconsciously identify the child with one of their own parents or siblings. Berliner's recent paper on masochism (7) came very close to the core conflict of the adolescent narcotic user, as he stated that the very young child

---

*Note: Reprinted by permission of the author and *Psychiatric Quarterly*, 35:702-710, 1961.

misidentifies criticism and punishment as a form of pleasure and thus goes through life reliving (under the repetition compulsion) the original distortion. Berliner went on to state that the hated child denies the parental ill-treatment and accepts hate as if it were love; "suffering is thus libidinized and introjected, and the trauma becomes ego-syntonic."

INTRODUCTION*

On April 15, 1958, a project was undertaken at the Riverside Hospital After-Care Clinic which involved the group therapy of parents of adolescent drug addicts. Riverside Hospital had been opened on July 1, 1952 by the New York City Department of Hospitals for the care and rehabilitation of adolescent drug addicts. The bed capacity is 140; and, since its inception, this institution has had over 1,600 first admissions. The idea of treating mothers rested on firm clinical grounds, since it is basic in psychiatry that the unconscious conflicts of parents have a profound effect on the behavior and feelings of their children, who, upon leaving the hospital, must return to their original environments. It was felt that treating the young addict, either in individual or group therapy, was certainly not sufficient to effect a permanent change or, in many cases, even an alteration in behavior. When this experiment was undertaken, the main purpose was to learn and understand what some of these parental conflicts were; discussions with the addict gave one picture of the parent; the author was interested in hearing from the mother or father.

It became clear almost immediately that the parents were bringing their own neurotic difficulties into the group. Their sense of guilt and their inability to accept the roles of patients made it very difficult to put the group on a therapeutic basis. Almost always, they were looking for judgment and for many weeks the question of acceptance of treatment was the paramount problem

---

*Before giving a brief description of the patients in the project to be discussed, the writer would like to express his appreciation to Miss Hazle Harte, R.N., who is the coordinator of the clinic, and to Dr. Raphael Gamso, director of Riverside Hospital. Without their cooperation administratively, this project would never have become a reality.

in the sessions. Over and over again, the group members denied that *they* needed help, their concern was their addict sons or daughters and how to manage them. Their anger at consistent confrontation caused some of the initial group to flee therapy; actually the inability to accept their hostile aggression was an important source of acting-out in terms of missing sessions, lateness and silences. Early in therapy the group nucleus was formed — four mothers and one father. They looked upon the therapy as a "class" or a "lecture" program, and their acceptance of the patient-role became at once an important area of investigation.

Time and space prevent discussion of the complete case histories of the five group members who constituted a rather permanent nucleus; one of the members died from a fulminating carcinoma, so that three women and one man were left. It was felt that the mobilization of unconscious guilt was not an essential preliminary maneuver, these patients were guilt-ridden from the beginning; but when it became overwhelming, projection of responsibility on others was a prominent mechanism of defense. In general, the group requested advice; for members to focus on themselves became a very difficult task. The selection of the group admittedly was not on any specific basis, circumstances in the clinic made it necessary to select parents who were available and interested; the one variable which is probably the most important and significant dynamically for any group was the various character-structures, and in this group this was evident. Each patient was seen for an hour before admission into the group, some idea of the clinical diagnoses and dynamics was arrived at; and, as a preliminary maneuver, the patient was in a sense "oriented" to what group therapy was and why the project was undertaken as an adjunct to the treatment and rehabilitation of the adolescent drug addict.

The goals, as has been said, were admittedly not definitive. As one essential, the writer wanted to learn if the group helped the patient see that he too had conflicts; this was to be considered a major step. Essentially then, it was hoped that in this project a global or bird's-eye view of this problem as regards the parent-child interaction could be obtained. It was hoped that others at

Riverside Hospital and elsewhere would also be stimulated to work with the mothers and perhaps the fathers of these young narcotic drug users and thus fill in some of the gaps in our knowledge of this ever-increasing problem.

THE PATIENTS

Case 1

A is a 47-year-old, Roman Catholic shipyard worker of Italian derivation. He is short of stature. In the first individual session, he told of how well his two sons played baseball. His son's addiction was a blow to his own self-esteem, which was already low because of his own inability to become a "major-leaguer." He tried hard to impress the writer with his abilities as a member of many youth clubs, where he functioned as a "big brother." His wife's psychotic depression was blamed on his addict son, but in actuality he related to her as an unfeeling man who substituted activity for feeling. He saw his son as "knifing me in the back." He verbalized much anger as he talked about "dope peddlers" whom he wanted to kill. Essentially, A wanted to be a "pal" of his son; he competed with the boy who outdistanced him athletically and angered him on a deeper level.

Diagnostically, A was seen as having a passive-aggressive character disorder with compulsive features; his major defensive structure consisted of denial, intellectualization and projection, along with conscious fabrication. He is a man who feels extremely inferior, and he does much in an ineffective manner in an effort to compensate. His anger toward his son became more and more obvious; and, on not so deep a level, his unconscious hostility (and ineffectiveness) was communicated to the son.

Actually A did very little in a realistic way to help the boy; there were the "pats on the back" and the usual "be a man" cliches; he was superficial, and he generalized often. His hostility to women became clear as he referred to his wife as a "baseball widow" and as a "girl that started my son off on drugs." This was an angry little man protecting himself in the best way he could from the guilt he felt.

Case 2

Mrs. B is a 40-year-old married woman who has a husband and three children (a daughter aged 23 who is making a good adjustment, a son aged 20 who is the addict, and a 5-year-old daughter). She entered with a fair conception of what group therapy was concerned with. She revealed that she was "tensed up" and impatient with her younger daughter. Almost immediately it became clear that her marriage (she was married at 16 because her "father remarried") was a conflicted area; she felt her 50-year-old husband invested very little in the family. Mrs. B, it seemed, was partial to her older daughter who always was a good student; the competition between her son and older daughter was fostered by Mrs. B; and, in therapy, Mrs. B saw this with some affect.

In an indirect way, Mrs. B, like many other parents, "bought" drugs for her son. Such parents supply their children with money, paying for their pawned clothes, etc. (One mother who left the group said, about her nonpsychotic, manipulative son, "I had to give him money when he threatened to kill somebody with a screwdriver.") Mrs. B's sexual adjustment was poor. There had been no orgasm for two years and her complaint was that she couldn't get close to her husband. She had five brothers who "depended" on her and this was a clue to her relationship with her son. Diagnostically she was seen as having a hysterical character disorder with severe Oedipal problems and "acting-out" concerning her son. In the group she was rather verbal, and at times she become the "assistant doctor." Her prominent mechanisms included intellectualization and repression, but she became "motivated" for therapy when she, at long last, saw her own role in the production of her son's psychopathology.

Case 3

Mrs. C is a 47-year-old Jewish saleswoman who has a chronically ill husband (cardiac) and two sons, the younger of whom is the addict. The other is apparently making an adequate adjustment. Mrs. C has been married 26 years to a poor provider, a gambler, and, according to Mrs. C, a pathological liar who impulsively beat his children frequently. She gave the impression of being an angry, repressed woman who is much afraid of her husband and her own aggressive impulses, which apparently were projected onto her son in terms of rejection and inconsistent control. She related warmly and somewhat seductively; she verbalized her guilt and told how she and her own mother had never been close because of the dominating influence of the latter. Her father was reported as an "alcoholic," but, when questioned in detail, she said that he really wasn't an alcoholic — that she had seen him drink once or twice. She was diagnosed as having compulsive character disorder with hysterical and masochistic features.

Her sexual adjustment was poor in terms of orgastic ability. Mrs. C was a hostile, angry woman who had to submit passively. Her guilt was a motivating force in bringing her to therapy, but she, too, became aware of her own role in her son's addiction. During the course of therapy, Mrs. C had her son sent to jail; and, ironically, this was the first protective action performed since her son became addicted; both son and mother felt relieved when this occurred. Mrs. C's defenses included projection, denial, and repression, and she related in the group passively and masochistically.

Case 4

Mrs. D is a 50-year-old married, Roman Catholic housewife, whose only son (legally adopted) is a drug addict of long standing. He is the illegitimate son of Mrs. D's brother (who committed suicide). The mother had given up the child. The boy was told of his adoption when he was seven years old, but he still denies ever having been adopted. Mrs. D has been an ulcer patient on medication for the past four years. Her mother is 72, and she too has "stomach trouble"; her father committed suicide when the girl was 14 years old. A sister, aged 53, is childless; and a single 46-year-old brother has been in a Veterans Administration hospital for 18 years because of a "nervous breakdown."

Mrs. D related to the group in a passive, depressed manner; her denial was excessive but she wanted to enter the group. She appeared helpless, and she constantly saw her son as someone with a "weak mind." Her hostility to the boy became obvious, but she recognized none of it. Her husband is 51 years old and he was seen as a passive man with very little investment in the boy, who was sent to California (by the mother) to live with Mrs. D's sister. She was considered to have a masochistic character disorder with a very low feeling about herself which was unbearable for her to face. Her defensive operation consisted of projection, denial, and repression; in the group, she sought advice, and was rigid and unfeeling for the boy who was always a reminder to her that she was a failure as a woman.

These histories form a brief description of the four parents who were permanent members of the group. There were others who participated for two, three, or four sessions. What follows are the author's observations, which stem from his work with the parents (in and out of therapy) of adolescent drug users. The group therapy lasted for 25 sessions; it was discontinued because of the writer's inability to stimulate a therapist to continue it. The group wanted it to continue, and it was felt that this desire was genuine.

OBSERVATIONS ON PARENTS
OF ADOLESCENT DRUG ADDICTS

As the group sessions progressed, it became quite clear that disturbed people, who had much to do with their children's choice of symptom — namely the use of narcotics in their attempts to cope with their internal and external environment — were being dealt with. To a large extent, the parents were limited in the language of feelings and also in the ability to be introspective; no doubt cultural factors played a great part in how they related; but in addition to this, the orientation was also indicative of defensiveness and pathology. Almost immediately, the group regressed to a "dependency phase" which manifested itself in repeated attempts to get the therapist to answer questions or to advise members about their problems. A phase gradually emerged where they blamed themselves for their children's problems; and this approach gave way to a "my son is weak-minded" attitude.

In all the parents seen, in or out of a therapeutic setting, the one consistent pattern soon established was an unhappy marriage reluctantly entered into by the woman, who is extremely ambivalent toward her children. The mother presents a characteristic picture of narcissism, seductiveness and orality; she is "giving" and permissive only when the addict gratifies her own needs; so, in essence, the child is a narcissistic extension of the mother who actually "gives to herself" when she goes through the motion of giving to her child. The parents of addicts, especially the mothers, constantly allow themselves to be intimidated or "conned" by the narcotic users. Some parents see themselves as "indirect pushers" as they literally run after the addicts, paying their accumulated debts and even giving them money which the addicts always use for drugs. The hidden hostility in this orientation became very clear in the group; and again it became very clear that the mother reacted with rejection and aggression when the addict did not gratify her narcissistic needs.

Mothers of addicts (especially boys) have a powerful need to infantilize their offspring. In doing so, a mother bolsters her own omnipotence, which the addict can never accept in safety despite the intense dependency needs of the child. Since the growth of ego and super-ego depends so much on this acceptance of dependency and trust, it becomes easy to see the sources of developmental retardation here in the addict.

A striking feature in working with mothers of addicts is the fact that the child is like the mother in many ways; many of the mothers had tyrannical parents (usually the mother) to cope with and to rebel or act-out against. Their fathers were weak, ineffectual men and they were seen through the mothers' eyes by the children. For the addict and his mother, the adult world became a hostile, unsafe place, the resultant clinging to omnipotence is a persistent characteristic of most addicts and most mothers of addicts. The identification between the two becomes tenacious and binding, and each wants from the other what each cannot give: namely, one's self in terms of warmth, affection, and trust. The mother's longstanding sado-masochistic pattern, with the guilt involved, results in inability to love and to trust in a mature manner; her constant need that *she* be loved, cherished and admired actually damages every relationship she enters into, including the ones with her children.

The mother as well as her addict son gives the history of being powerless before a rejecting mother. This, it is felt, is where the core of the masochism lies in both parent and child, who in a sense says, "If my mother hates me, then I must be worthless or bad, because every mother is supposed to love her child." Every addict has the uncanny ability to provoke this original rejection in terms of his current environment; both mother and child get people to hate them (society's attitude toward the addict is typical of this); and thus, under the repetition-compulsion, the original parent-child relationship is reenacted over and over again. The transference and counter-transference implications of this formulation are extremely important; and this is one of the main reasons why psychotherapeutic efforts are so difficult with drug addicts in the majority of cases undertaken.

In the group, the mothers banded together for a while reassuring themselves, later blaming each other, and finally blaming society for the dilemmas that they were in. One mother (Mrs. C), after being paralyzed with fear and inconsistency for years, finally "controlled" her son from self-destruction by turning him over to the police and this resulted in a prison sentence. It amazed the group and Mrs. C to learn that her son had always wanted this control. Actually, most of the adolescent drug addicts the author has known ask literally for control, and many times the pleading is not disguised. Mrs. C consequently became quilty and depressed over her supposed "hostility"; but when the reality was pointed out, her mood lifted and soon she became "proud" of her ability to really help her son.

The one father in the group probably inhibited the mothers for a while; future studies should not include both sexes in one group. He, it is felt, rarely did any "feeling" in the group; the verbiage became abundant; his hostility in part was utilized as a defense against loving and trusting. The fathers of addicts are generally passive men who offer very little in terms of identification for their male children. Fathers of female addicts seem very concerned over their daughters' sexual activities, of which they consciously deny the existence. As with the mothers, much marital discord seems to occupy a central position with the fathers.

CONCLUSIONS

As was stated, this project was not undertaken with any definite goals in mind. That parents of drug users, however, are intimately involved with their children's psychopathology was a fairly clear observation after working with these people, who are just as disturbed as the addicts who "mainline." The infantilization of the son by the narcissistic mother, who rejects the child when her demands and needs are not met, is of paramount importance. The unworthiness experienced by drug addicts, the very masochism reflected in sticking a needle into one's vein, typifies the image that the addict sees of himself through the eyes of the mother.

From experience, it is seen that the mother plays a dominant role in the process of identification in the addict; this coincides with the concept that the child identifies with the parent who frustrates him the most. This author feels that the addict's homosexual conflict and passive orientation to women is strongly related to this.

The tremendous guilt experienced by parents of adolescent drug users is seen as a motivating force in therapy; their awareness that guilt is a useless emotion put the group reported here on a therapeutic basis, which enabled them to see, at least partially, their own involvement in their children's problems.

That group therapy for parents is *the* answer to the problem of narcotics addiction is an unwarranted conclusion; there are too few clinical studies to evaluate its merit; but the undertaking certainly rests on sound clinical grounds. This chapter in a sense was written to stimulate the interest of others working in this very difficult field to investigate this approach. If this further investigation becomes a reality, this project will have accomplished its purpose.

REFERENCES

1. Healy, William, and Bronner, Augusta: *New Lights on Delinquency and its Treatment.* Yale University Press, New Haven, Conn., 1936.
2. Johnson, A. M.: Sanctions for superego lacunae of adolescents. In: *Searchlights on Delinquency.* International Universities Press, New York, 1949.
3. Gerard, Donald L., and Kornetsky, C.: A social and psychiatric study of adolescent opiate addicts. *Psychiat. Quart., 28:*113-125, January, 1954.
4. Gerald, Donald L., and Kornetsky, C.: Adolescent opiate addiction: A case study. *Psychiat. Quart., 28:*367-380, July, 1954.
5. Gerald, Donald L., and Kornetsky, C.: Adolescent opiate addiction: A study of control and addict subjects. *Psychiat. Quart., 29:*457-485, July, 1955.
6. Bromberg, Norbert: Maternal influence in the development of moral masochism. *Amer. J. Orthopsychiat., 25:*802-812, 1955.
7. Berliner, Bernhard: The role of object relations in moral masochism. *Psychoanal. Quart., 27:*38-56, January, 1958.

Chapter 28

The Role of Group Psychotherapy for Mothers in a Rehabilitative Approach to Juvenile Intractable Asthma*

THEODORE H. WOHL

REHABILITATION of children with refractory asthma, utilizing the existing facilities of the Convalescent Hospital for Children in Cincinnati, has proved successful and has resulted also in the establishment of a basic allergy and pulmonary function research laboratory. Attained results corroborate those reported by other centers, and the local program is judged to have certain distinct therapeutic and practical advantages. These advantages have been cited in a previous paper detailing an extensive program for the rehabilitation of juvenile intractable asthma (3).

The focus of this chapter is on the contributions that can be made by group psychotherapy with mothers of asthmatic children toward: a) the understanding of family processes, b) helping the mother to face and accept relevant emotional factors, and c) insuring that the patient gets the optimum benefit from his hospital and post-hospital experience.

We feel that the interaction of the child and parent enables the staff to have a closer view of the peculiar relationships of each parent and child. During the months of hospitalization, both parents and children begin to realize fruition of successful treatment, and this mutual insight and change provides a strong basis for ultimately healthier, emotional relationships at home. The dramatic cessation of symptoms so often noted after hospital admission implies the importance of family and interpersonal

*Reprinted by permission of the author and *Mental Hygiene, 1:*150-155, 1963.

tensions in the continuance of severe bronchial asthma.

The nuclear maternal role has been extensively formulated in the literature by French and Alexander (7), Baruch and Miller (11), Jessner (10) and others who feel that the severely asthmatic child is closely dependent on the love of the mother and experiences constant fear of losing her love and support.

Ambivalently, the asthmatic fears separation but protests against the necessity of dependency. The asthmatic child cannot show his resentment because of this dependency and the fear of losing the love and recognition of others. The hostility is then defensively redirected against the self and may often find expression through genetically predetermined vulnerable respiratory tract and autonomic nervous system.

The mother herself has been generally described as "rejecting, immature, over protective, often poorly mated and somtimes unconsciously encouraging her child's illness to gratify certain underlying neurotic needs (10)."

FORMATION AND NATURE OF
THE THERAPEUTIC GROUPS

We accordingly selected psychoanalytically oriented group psychotherapy with mothers of our hospital patients as a major means of working actively with the home environment. We wished to help these women deal with general responsibilities and be more relaxed and comfortable in their parental role. Perhaps even more important — and Durkin (6) states it well — "the members of the therapy group are given the opportunity to gain insight into their attitudes instead of having to make futile *conscious* attempts to improve their ways of handling children, on the basis of advice which, by the very nature of their problems, they are so often unable to follow."

The mothers of our asthma patients have usually experienced years of well-meaning advice from relatives, teachers, and friends; counsel, information, and directives from pediatricians, allergists, hospital resident physicians, and even psychiatrists. Many have done extensive reading on the subject of asthma. Without exception, all had adequate knowledge of caring for the asthmatic child and "allergy proofing" the home. More than half were familiar and agreed with the theory that emotions might play a part in the asthmatic syndrome. Several (even those of limited education) had a reasonably accurate concept of the antigen-antibody relationship.

Yet, as has been stated, there was and is a considerable gap between the intellectual understanding of these factors and appropriate emotional reintegration permitting effective relevant action. Moreover, and despite their "relief" in having their child under the hospital's care, most mothers found it quite difficult to accept hospital policies, conditions, and the parent surrogate role of nurses and practical nurses.

A few verbalized guilt over what they perceived as their temptation to shift all responsibilities onto the hospital personnel. These attitudes and subsequent feelings and problems were exacerbated and otherwise affected by the hospital's policy of frequent daily visiting privileges, allowing free access to all ward areas and nurses' stations, and the close residential proximity of the parents themselves. More succinctly our general goals were as follows:

1. To help mothers acquire an understanding of the problems of the severely asthmatic child.
2. To promote self-inspection and insight into emotional problems.
3. To examine closely the clinical family pattern of childhood asthma and the personalities of the parents of severely asthmatic children.
4. To help eliminate serious interference by the mothers in the hospital treatment of their children.
5. To provide a main source of help for parents after their children have been discharged from the hospital.

Although the importance of including fathers in the overall treatment planning cannot be denied, practical considerations demanded the group therapeutic approach be limited to mothers. We found fathers generally more threatened and resistant to the prospect of "public" discussion of personal problems.

The mothers, on the other hand, seemed carried along on what might be termed their natural concern with child-rearing practices and normal child development. It was felt that a homogeneous female sex group would facilitate the group process and make it easier for a woman to bring up genuine feelings and attain the immediate major goal of a sustaining group.

This was further supported on the grounds of the theoretically greater role played by the mother in the juvenile asthmatic syndrome and the possibly greater facilitation of mutual identification and gross commonality of transference feelings toward the therapist. Thus, the group was organized by the author and an observer-recorder in the autumn of 1957, and still continues as an ongoing process entity.

The group is "open" in structure, although new members are introduced at relatively infrequent intervals. The basis for selection from an average pool of 30 mothers has been the therapist's clinical judgment, somewhat influenced by the verbal facility of a prospective member. The "clinical" judgment" criteria in this case refer mainly to the therapist's evaluation of the prospective group member's motivation to attend meetings regularly, and lack of psychosis, monopolistic tendencies and gross disruptive impulsivity.

There was no attempt to look for certain individual characteristics such as ability to express anger and tolerate the aggression of others, which are thought by several authorities to argue for a more favorable course of treatment. The group might be termed "homogeneous" as defined by Foulkes and Anthony (8): e.g. possessing in common a supposed and subsequently revealed rejection of their children, a conscious wish to help these children, and acute and varied problems resulting from the presence of a chronically-ill child in the household.

Until very recently the group members have been largely representative of lower socioeconomic classes – Hollingshead's (9) classes IV and V – although recently more middle-class (classes II and III) mothers have been admitted (9), stemming from the hospital's successful attempt to demonstrate the usefulness of an asthma program to these families and their physicians.

Meetings are held weekly for 75 minutes. Group attendance has fluctuated from three to ten in number, averaging about six women per session. Forty mothers have been members since the group's inception. The most representative age is 30 years with a total age range extending from 19 to 61 years. The average member of the group has had a tenth grade education but all have been of at least average intelligence. The racial composition of the group has remained constant, equally divided between Negro and White. This proportion was not and is not manipulated.

We have been unable to discern any significant effect on group process resulting from either age or education, while the "mixing" of races has resulted in an interesting although only partly understandable situation. Cincinnati is a geographical and cultural area where one might expect Negro and white therapy group interaction without insulting local mores and consequently impeding group process. Yet, despite interpretation and good humored cajoling, the races generally segregate themselves and frequently face each other across the long conference table. However, this grouping does not seem to affect group process or interaction.

Some of the middle-class white mothers complain bitterly about their children's "forced associates," but this seems more inspired by "lower class aggressiveness" of certain children and is evidently not given a racial label. Actually the above mentioned difference of race, age, and background seems to have a stimulating effect on discussion as the individual mothers become aware of both the urgent freshness and irrationalities of different subgroup mores and child rearing practices.

It is again important to note that the above-mentioned heterogeneity was more apparent than real. There was never a time when a given mother could not count on a potential ally within the group: i.e. another woman of similar socioeconomic, age or education background.

GROUP PROCESS

The therapist was quickly forced to alter his usual procedure in "conducting" the therapy session. These parents, despite their privilege of refusing an invitation to join the group, seek this type of help because the hospital is their "last" hope in dealing with their child's refractory illness: i.e. they join the group more by necessity than by choice.

They come specifically to find out more about asthma, hoping to be *given* the magic key or to obtain another diagnosis or prescription for handling their child's behavior. This attitude is further strengthened by the hospital staff's conceptions of and verbal reference to the group sessions as "classes," thus strengthening the individual mother's expectation of the conventional classroom lecture delivered by a "teacher."

Since the group atmosphere is quickly experienced as *permissive,* with the keynote being group discussion, angry disappointment over this frustration of dependency strivings is inevitable. This is usually manifested in staring silence, denying problems with their children, extensive and sometimes angry ramblings concerning hospital treatment and care of their children, and in directing discussion toward the child to avoid facing their own personal problems.

The author strongly agrees with the view point of Abramson and Peshkin (1) who point out the necessity for involvement in parents' personal problems, even when these problems seem to have little obvious relation to the problems of their children.

During the first year of group meetings, attendance varied widely and only after seven months coalesced into an ongoing stable group. The mothers initially tended to accept the group as part of the overall service of the hospital to be utilized as a convenience or because the hospital seemed to expect attendance.

This was dealt with variously by pointing out that they were a selected few, educative comments regarding the nature of small groups, the effect of absent members on the group process, and interpretations to certain members concerning the possible meanings of their absences.

The group "monopolist" crops up continually despite attempts to exercise preventative screening procedures. This is the mother who reacts to the group situation with fear of attack or isolation and handles this by a determined and sometimes angry bid for the therapist's attention (protection). She must also interrupt the conversation, usually with anecdotes and comments about her child. The effect on the group process frequently has been disturbing, with the group often leaving a session feeling frustrated, angry, and tired. Despite individual counseling with such women, we have had only limited success in modifying this type of behavior, short of discouraging further attendance at meetings.

The manifest content and topical discussion areas of the group sessions agree most closely with the observations reported by the Denver Group (1): i.e. bewilderment and unconscious guilt over the effectiveness of the child's (subtotal) "parentectomy;" disappointment over their child's progress relative to that of another child, concern as to the child's continued health after returning home, the optimal way to "handle" him, and the potential disruptive effect of his return to a home which has changed during his absence.

Yet, the group has managed to evolve through many of the initial "phases" cited by such authors as Bach (2) and Bion (4) and has for some time been working at the "intermediate phase": i.e. they seem to have a readiness to understand that the child's symptoms and mannerisms are meaningful to the child and are able to link their own emotional reactions to the child's symptomatology.

DISCUSSIONS AND CONCLUSIONS

Notable progress has been made toward the realization of our earlier mentioned goals of understanding the child and encouraging self-inspection. The family patterning and personalities contributing to childhood asthma have necessarily emerged. For example, the concept of the "pathogenic family" is strongly supported.

Our mothers are usually nexuses of intra-familial tension. The mother-child bond from the early weeks of the child's life is unanimously strong among the members of our group, although seemingly reflecting various causes, including the presence of such realistic stresses as separation of a husband. Unconscious guilt and rejective attitudes are also prominently manifest, with much emphasis on strict child-rearing procedures and adherence to cleanliness as the supreme virtue.

A major reason for maintaining the group over a four year span has been the reports of our social workers, allergists, and hospital staff that the mothers involved seemed to understand treatment goals and procedures more thoroughly. They are described as much more cooperative than nongroup asthma mothers and more careful and willing to maintain outpatient contact after the child's hospitalization is over.

Social service home visits are more easily arranged, and the workers find these mothers unusually willing to "allergy-proof" the home. They possess an increased willingness to introspect and discuss real problems during periodic individual conferences with a social worker. This is regarded as a significant step toward a successful treatment outcome and is generally credited to their experiences in the group.

From all of this there is a mandate somehow to devise measures of patient-family interaction in order to conceptualize family processes more adequately, and then to relate this knowledge to the identification and treatment of the "pathogenic family." One also realizes that even a two-year period of hospitalization is but a small fraction in comparison to the impact of family life and the involvement in family processes. Indeed, the traces of the involvement persist clearly in the hospital environment and are reinforced by frequent parental visits.

The necessity of systematically studying the process of psycho- therapy and methods of assessing changes in patient behavior has been recognized widely. Yet, there is perhaps a tendency in many of us to collect data endlessly under the guise of rational empiricism, resulting in an unwieldy accumulation of apparently unrelated facts and theories. More systematic and quantitative information is needed within numerous narrower limits.

The work of Saslow and Matarazzo (12) in standardizing therapist's behavior while interviewing, combined with precise recording of predefined variables, and the approach of Chance (5) in combining clinical and research descriptions of child-family interaction seem to favor prediction and the more optimal utilization of current medical and hospital treatment programs. The most important question — whether children of mothers seen in group therapy enjoy a more pleasant and successful course of treatment — is currently being studied.

In conclusion, the application of a group psychotherapeutic technique as an integrated part of a general rehabilitation program must be viewed as having at least functional utility. This argues for more rigorous methods to study systematically group processes and results and supports our opinion that the family must be treated concurrently with the intractable asthmatic child.

REFERENCES

1. Abramson, H. A. and Peshkin, M. M.: Group psychotherapy of the parents of intractably asthmatic children, *Journal of Children's Asthma Research Institute and Hospital, 1:*77-91, 1961.
2. Bach, G. R.: *Intensive Group Psychotherapy.* New York, Ronald Press, 1954, p. 269.
3. Bernstein, Leonard, Allen, J. E., Kreindler, L., Ghory, J. E. and Wohl, T. H.: A community approach to juvenile asthma. A new concept in treatment. *Pediatrics, 26:*586-595, 1960.
4. Bion, W. R.: Experiences in groups I to VII. *Human Relations, 1:*314, 1948; *2:*295, 1949; *3:*3, 1950; *4:*221, 1951.
5. Chance, E.: *Families in Treatment.* New York, Basic Books, Inc., 1959, p.14.
6. Durkin, H. E.: *Group Therapy for Mothers of Disturbed Children.* Springfield, Ill., C. C. Thomas, 1954.
7. French, T. M., and Alexander, Franz: Psychogenic factors in bronchial asthma, Part I. *Psychosomatic Medicine Monograph IV.* and Part II, *Psychosomatic Medicine Monograph,* Vol. 2, Nos. I and II, Washington, D. C.: National Research Council, 1941.
8. Foulkes, S. H., and Anthony, E. J.: *Group Psychotherapy.* New York, Penguin Books, Inc., 1957, 94.
9. Hollingshead, A. B. and Redlich, F. C.: *Social Class and Mental Illness.* New York, John Wiley & Sons, 1958, p. 110.
10. Jessner, L., Lamant, J., Long, R., Rollins, N., Whipple, B. and Prentice N.: Emotional impact of nearness and separation for the asthmatic child and his mother, in Eissler, Ruth S. *et al.,* Eds., *The Psychoanalytic Study of the Child,* Vol. 10, New York, International Universities Press, 1955, p. 355.
11. Miller, H., and Baruch, D.: *The Practice of Psychosomatic Medicine.* New York, McGraw-Hill Book Co., Inc., 1956, p. 21.
12. Saslow, G., and Matarazzo, D.: in Rubenstein, Eli A. and Parloff, M. B. Eds.: *Research in Psychotherapy.* Washington D. C., American Psychological Association, 1958, p. 125.

Chapter 29

Psychosomatic Group Therapy with Parents of Children with Intractable Asthma*

Adaptation Mechanisms

H. A. ABRAMSON AND M. M. PESHKIN

FOR the past three years we have had the opportunity to discuss with the parents of the children hospitalized in Denver their attitudes toward the rehabilitation program (1, 2). Until we spoke to the parents, we had no idea as to how complex the problem of the adaptation of the parents was in terms of giving up their children for about two years. Without studying in detail the transcripts of the verbatim recordings it would be difficult to analyze accurately the frequency of different feelings stemming from the separation. Some of the problems as they have recently developed in the New York area in our parent discussion groups, will be discussed here.

Our parent discussion groups are constructed somewhat the same as Slavson's child-centered group guidance of parents. However, Slavson deals with the parents of normal children. Furthermore, these children are living with their parents. In our parent discussion groups the discussions are "illness-centered" not "child-centered." In addition, the children are 2,000 miles away from home. The parents must adapt not to the children, but to the illness, the letters from the children, the telephone calls, the reports of visitors to the Denver Institution, and other official reports from the Institute. All of these enter into the complex family pattern and are reassembled for the adaption process of the parents themselves. The parents have to reconstruct their lives in

---

*Note: Reprinted by permission of the author and *Annals of Allergy, 18:*87-91, 1960.

terms of their relationships with the siblings of their child at Denver, his other relatives, such as grandparents, uncles, aunts, friends, the local family physician, as well as the other members and leaders of the parent discussion groups. Most striking of all these, we believe, is the reconstruction which takes place in the parents; that is, the father and mother of any particular child, after attending twenty or thirty group sessions.

Our experience runs contrary to that of Slavson (3). Slavson's child-centered group guidance of parents is governed by the theme that "in the technique with which we are dealing here, attention is focused on the child and the child alone. His nature, his fears, his needs . . . " Slavson emphasizes the need for this form of guidance being completely child-centered and avoiding the personal problems of the parents where these have no direct bearing on those of the children. We feel that it is impossible to deal with the relationship of the parents with the intractable asthmatic child without considering the entire interaction of the mother and father of the child as part of the guidance situation. As a matter of fact, many of the couples discuss their relationship with each other quite openly and demonstrate how conflict within the home has intensified the asthmatic process in the child.

One of the more difficult aspects of group psychotherapy is that the procedure requires a transference relationship with the therapist by "self-confrontation" and regression, bringing up matters that ordinarily create both guilt and anxiety. This lengthy process is rapidly catalyzed in our discussion groups by the child's illness leading to a rapid dependency relationship with us. The intensity of this process is so great that painful memories and fears of the parents have often emerged with explosive force in the group sessions. For example, in the past months two of the fathers of children at the Institution wept only when recalling cruelties they experienced as children at the hands of their own fathers. These emotional factors feed back into the group and aid in self-confrontation, which is always permitted by the therapist as far as members of the group or ego permit.

One of the most difficult parts of the adaptation process is connected with the compelling need of the parent to fix into his own concept of what the parent's role is. Misconceptions of the role of the parent in child development and lack of knowledge and understanding of the needs of young children almost invariably lead to a notion of child discipline which embodies punitive measures rather than educational devices. The structured neurotic needs of these parents to strike their children, shout at their children, and deprive their children of commonly accepted rewards, like television, and desserts, must be replaced by reconstruction of the ego accompanied by a change in the psyche of both parents. This, of course, involved an important reconstruction of the way in which the parents react upon one another. It may surprise you to hear that we believe that treatment of the parent's relationship with one another is a necessary condition for the successful treatment of intractable asthma in our children at the Institute.

We have commonly observed in our groups that the intractable asthmatic child has become, so to speak, a part of the pattern of the parent's character (chronus complex) (4). This character structure of the parents who have abused their children is the product of culturally determined attitudes which led these parents to relive with their children the patterns of their own childhood. You may recall that "the sins of the parents are carried into the third and fourth generation." We have seen the sins of the parents carried into the third generation in our own groups. Thus, the mother of one of our asthmatic children has had her own mother living with her ever since she was married. This mother acknowledged that she was completely dominated by her own mother and at no time until she became a member of the group sessions had she ever asserted herself with her own asthmatic child. It was necessary therefore for this mother to give up a pattern of childhood behavior which she had employed up to the age of thirty five. How successful she will be we do not know.

Mothers and fathers exposed to the same cultural and religious forces support one another in their methods of dealing with their asthmatic children. Our parents seem to have been exposed in most instances to cultures believing that "sparing the rod will spoil the child." Razor straps, cat-o-nine-tails, wooden spoons, hair brushes and belts, amongst other weapons have failed ,to cure the asthma. One parent said, "What do you expect me to do — sit up and talk to him until three in the morning?" Another parent expressed her rejection of the parental role and stated quite openly in the group session, "Where the children are concerned, I come first."

Where there is a strong religious vein in the home, the cultural forces are often replaced by spirtual vectors which dominate the interaction of the parents with one another and with their asthmatic child. Where both cultural and religious vectors operate together they seem to synergize one another and prevent the transference relationship from developing. Thus, one couple took the view that the illness of their child was an act of God, that each parent had done the best that he and she could, that they did not see how their attitudes could be changed, and that the beatings the child had received at the hands of the father could not have possibly affected the course of the illness. In contrast to this couple another couple established an excellent relationship with us through an identification process and replaced constant bickering with fruitful discussion between them. They began to project themselves into the nature of their own difficulties and into the needs of their children. The outlook for the second set of parents is good.

One of the most difficult problems in the adaptation of the parents is an error in thinking which has its origins in our culture. It is based upon the belief that when a child's attitude and behavior are so persistent it is believed that children will not change without punitive parental pressure. This fear forces their children to remain in a regressive, somewhat infantile state and interferes with the development of the child both physically and emotionally. At the Institute in Denver the parents know that the independence of the child is encouraged. The parents must adapt to a child who has been subjected not to the neurotic needs of parents to maintain their children at childhood levels, but to demands where every opportunity is given for maturation to proceed uninhibited by parental fears. The way in which parents deal with their anxieties engendered by the Denver Institute is well borne out by two contrasting sets of parents. In one instance the parents "accepted" their healthy child, and, perhaps unwisely, discontinued attending the group sessions. They sent us messages that they were so well oriented that they could deal with all the problems that arose, thus rejecting us as parent figures, and proceeded to manipulate their rehabilitated child's life in their own way. This was also true of a second set of parents, both of whom were highly educated along psychological lines.

Surprisingly enough, the mother who stated, "I come first" has reversed her role to the pressures placed upon her by the group and by the therapist. She and her husband are reporting in detail the nature of the adaptation process which they are undergoing in dealing with their asthma-free child. The father, however, who is very compulsive is unable to cope with his healthy child and spent an entire session discussing with the group what measures should be taken to force his eleven-year-old child just recently returned from Denver to hang his clothes away properly. This has become his new problem.

One of the difficulties of adaptation of the parents is that the parents, in accord with the way in which adults view current events, always orient their thinking in terms of a cure of their asthmatic children. The asthmatic child is preoccupied with the present. Thus, the asthmatic child gears his parents to sources of anxiety which become more and more intolerable as the intractability of the asthma increases.

When the child is removed to Denver, the parents are left with the same anxieties, without the source, the asthmatic child, being available. These anxieties, then, are turned toward one another and toward the other children. Not only are their anxieties oriented within their own home but they also extend to the surrogate parents and administrators at the Institute.

A good deal of maturity is required to exercise the self-restraint needed to permit the rehabilitation program to proceed. The guilt and anxiety produced by the removal of the child may be intensified by any illness of the child during his stay in Denver. A serious illness such as osteomyelitis that recently occurred in one of the children led to the appearance of the parents at the Institute grimly determined to take the child back to their home in spite of the fact that the child was receiving the best possible medical care for this illness. Fortunately, the parents were persuaded to let the child remain and recover.

One of the more difficult aspects of the reconstruction in the adaptation mechanism required for the successful psychotherapy of the parents, is the realization of parents that their parental instincts are sufficient justification of their attitudes toward their children. Most parents seem to be blindly unaware of the effect of their instinctual drives and the special influences these instincts have from culture to culture. Children are brought up very differently because of the modifications of instinct by religions and cultural needs. The complexities of these adaptation processes seem to be very difficult for the members of our group to incorporate without the aid of supplementary reading.

We believe it is important that pressure be brought to bear on the attempts of the parents to reconstruct their attitudes while their children are in Denver. Acting out their feelings with insight is not enough. Understanding the way in which feelings modify attitudes can only be accomplished, however, through techniques which are almost academic in nature. In other words, we believe that these parents have to be told some of the realistic facts as well as develop suitable feelings. The adaptation of the group depends, therefore, on the ability of the parents to deal with abstractions. This is perhaps one of our most difficult stumbling blocks with the rigidly fabricated parent who feels that his parental instinct is sufficient for him to guide the psychosexual development of his intractably asthmatic child.

SUMMARY

Two hundred psychotherapeutic group sessions with parents of intractably asthmatic children hospitalized in Denver are briefly summarized. The parents resided in the area of New York City, with their children, therefore, two thousand miles away. There were always two discussion leaders who coordinated both the immunologic and psychologic aspects of the adaptation process required by the parents, connected with the removal of their children to Denver.

The following briefly outlined items are the subject matter of this paper: a) the "illness-centered" nature of the discussion groups; b) the effect of communications from the children, visitors, and office reports from the Institute; c) the effect on sibling relationships, as well as relationships with grandparents and other relatives; d) the relationship of the parents with one another, incidental to the removal of the asthmatic child; e) the transference problems with the therapist; f) the structured neurotic needs of the members of the group, partly with respect to the concept that parental influence must carry punitive authority; g) the narcissistic needs of the parents; h) cultural and religious factors; i) anxiety produced in the parents by attending the group sessions; j) attitudes toward physical changes in the children while they were in the Denver Institute, and k) the need for development of insight.

REFERENCES

1. Peshkin, M. M., and Abramson, H. A.: Psychosomatic group therapy with parents of children with intractable asthma. *Ann. Allerg., 17:*344, 1959.
2. Peshkin, M. M., and Abramson, H. A.: First National seminar of regional medical consultants. *Ann. Allerg., 16:*473, 1958.
3. Slavson, S. R.: *Child Centered Group Guidance.* New York, International Universities Press, 1958.
4. Abramson, H. A.: *The Patient Speaks.* New York, Vantage Press, 1956.

Chapter 30

Short-Term Group Counseling for Parents of Children in Residential Treatment*

FLORENCE L. CRISS AND RAY C. GOODWIN

OUT of a growing concern for the future of children returning from treatment settings to homes where little observable change in parental attitudes had occurred, a 12-week parent-couple group counseling program was initiated by the Fairfax County (Virginia) Department of Welfare. The program, under the Child Welfare Division, sought to give parent couples a chance to examine their relationship with their children and themselves, and to gain insight into the child's problems as extensions of the total family relationship.

Fairfax County is an upper-middle-class suburb of Washington, D.C., with a population exceeding 400,000 and an average family income that is one of the highest in the nation. The area population is highly transient and growing rapidly. The Department of Welfare is administered by a director and a five-member board appointed by the County Supervisors.

In the parent-couple project, the group met weekly, in the evening, for 1 1/2-hour sessions. The emphasis was on problems of communication. There were two therapists, a male and a female Child Welfare supervisor. The families of girls were chosen from the unit supervised by the female therapist. The male therapist was already working with the residential treatment center where the boys were placed, and had coordinated all applications and financial arrangements made with the center and the families by

---

Note: Reprinted by permission of the authors and *Child Welfare, 49:*45-48, 1970.

the agency. He had done some counseling with the parents.

Eight parent couples and one single parent were invited to participate. Seven couples and the single parent responded. They came from middle and low-middle socioeconomic backgrounds, and their educational levels ranged from the eighth grade through business college.

DESCRIPTION OF COUPLES

Mr. and Mrs. A were referred by the State Department of Welfare and Institutions for financial assistance in placement of their only son, age 15, in a residential treatment center. At the time of application, he was in a state training school. When the group began, he had been in residential treatment 2 months.

Mr. A, 41, had a high school education and worked as an engineering draftsman. In the group he was carefully controlled and conforming. He was content to listen, and he tried to appear uninvolved.

Mrs. A, 33, a telephone operator, was uncomfortable in the group. During sessions she was either withdrawn or gave planned recitations about her family and background. She seemed to feel a need to compensate for the disapproval of her son by the community. Mrs. A had been hospitalized twice, with a diagnosis of schizophrenia.

Mr. and Mrs. B were referred by the Juvenile Court for financial aid in placing their 15-year-old son in residential treatment. He was the middle of five siblings ranging in age from 17 to 11, and the only one acting out in the community. He had been in care about a month. During the parent program he was expelled from the center and placed in a state training school, but the parents continued their participation in the group.

Mr. B was the stepfather of the boy in residential treatment and his two older siblings. Their natural father had committed suicide. Mr. B, 37, was a grocery store clerk, although he was trained as an electrician. He was lazy intellectually, and had a facade of congeniality that seemed a defense against uncontrolled outbursts.

Mrs. B, 35, was a rather sharp, loud, and unfeminine person, who preferred to wear slacks. She was employed part-time as a school crossing guard and spoke of this with pride. In the group she exposed feelings of helplessness and anger about her son's behavior.

Mr. and Mrs. C were referred by the residential treatment center, to which they applied, for financial aid in the placement of Mr. C's 17-year-old son by a previous marriage. The boy's natural mother was reported to be an alcoholic and a drug addict. The child had spent the first 15 years of his life with his natural mother. At the time of the group's beginning, he had been in residential treatment 2 months.

Mr. C, 53, was passive, and related only superficially to the group. Several times there were indications of his drinking prior to group meetings. He was moderately successful as a homebuilder. We felt he had minimal involvement with his son. He seemed content to have his second wife assume the dominant role in the family.

Mrs. C, 36, an attractive matron who wore her hair pulled tightly back from her face, had initiated the referral of her stepson to residential treatment after the boy had involved her 10-year-old daughter in sex play.

Mrs. C attempted to dominate any situation in which she found herself. She tried to play the role of cotherapist, and when she was successful, she was ingratiating, but when frustrated in her efforts, she became hostile and attempted to undermine communication in the group.

Mr. and Mrs. D were referred by military social service for supplementation of military benefits in payment for residential treatment of their adopted 12-year-son, who had been in treatment 3 months.

Mr. D, 56, a retired Air Force enlisted man, worked for the Post Office. He was uncommunicative with his wife and expressed a preference for superficial relationships.

Mrs. D, 56, an obese, unkempt woman who exhibited many masculine gestures, appeared intellectually limited and emotionally starved. She repeatedly discussed a deprived and abused childhood with a grandmother. She used the group largely as a way to feel involved with her husband.

Mr. and Mrs. E were referred by the court for financial aid in the placement of their daughter, 17, in a semicustodial school setting because she was beyond parental control. She was the second of four siblings, ranging in age from 20 to 11. She had been in the school 6 months.

Mr. E, 50, a bookkeeper, had been employed for 28 years with the same supply company. He demonstrated concern about what others thought of him superficially. He saw himself as totally responsible for keeping his family within the limits set by him as sensible. He showed little concern for others. Mr. E attended the group meetings regularly, and was able to relax to the point where he attempted to share feelings with his wife.

Mrs. E, 44, a former hospital patient with diagnosed schizophrenia, tended to overweight, and was casual about her appearance. Sometimes she would slide down in her chair as though wanting to slip out of the group. She was perceptive of the dynamics in the group and helpful to others, but she was unable to work on her own problems. She was apparently able to act out through her daughters.

Mrs. F was referred by the court for financial help in placing her 13-year-old daughter, the oldest of four, in a semicustodial school because she was beyond parental control.

Mrs. F, a 45-year-old waitress, was intellectually limited and emotionally depressed. Although she attended group meetings regularly, she remained generally uninvolved. It was our impression that her daughter acted out for her.

Mr. and Mrs. G were referred by the court for placement of Mrs. G's illegitimate 12-year-old daughter in foster care. In the course of evaluation, the decision was for a semicustodial setting where the girl could get treatment. At the time of the group's beginning, she had been in placement for a year.

Mrs. G, 31, initially looked tense and anxious. She attended four of the first seven sessions alone, with encouragement by the female therapist.

Mrs. G, who had been accused of sexually molesting the daughter, began attendance during the eighth session. Neither missed a session from then on.

In the group, Mrs. G was generally nonverbal, but she was obviously attentive, and a positive change in her personal appearance was evident. This was believed linked to her acceptance by the group. Mr. G, 44, was angry-looking at the first session he attended. But by his third he told the group he had always had problems with authority and felt his wife had, too.

Mr. and Mrs. H were referred by the court for financial aid in the placement of their 16-year-old son in residential treatment. He had been in residential treatment 18 months.

Mr. H, 56, had an eighth-grade education and 20 years' experience as a butcher. He was carefully controlled during group meetings, fearful of hurting others. He told of a background of physical deprivation and many fights. He compensated for his poor self-image by fantasizing successes, past and future. He tried to play "big brother" to his son, and set unrealistic limits for the boy.

Mrs. H, 48, habitually had an angry expression, and was embarrassed and uncomfortable at any expressions of positive feelings toward her by other group members. She expressed a great deal of anger and self-pity. She repeatedly attempted to manipulate her spouse and other members of the group.

EVALUATION OF GROUP MEETINGS

The group spent early sessions allaying their own anxiety by projecting responsibility for their children's problems on schools, police, courts, and community resources. There also were expressions by some parents of anger and feelings that children needed to be punished, and objections that the residential settings were too permissive.

By the third session, problems of communication were being discussed as such by the group members. This came about when the therapists focused on such problems clearly evidenced in preceding sessions. Some parents were able to identify breakdowns in communication between themselves, and between them and their children. The group process provided an opportunity for sharing and clarifying feelings, and for supporting efforts at resolutions.

With the initial efforts at improved communication, there was a shift in focus from children and placement to the parents themselves and the interaction in the home.

The group was tested by various members with angry outbursts and the expression of extreme positions. With supportive responses and an absence of attacks, the use of these defenses diminished. The group members began to feel safer in discussing things about themselves that were anxiety-provoking.

The respect shown the clients tended to humanize their experience. Sharing with and knowing about others directly relieved some guilt and anger. The perceived authority of the agency fell away in the mutually supportive group. This contributed to the high level of attendance. It also enabled the group members to express feelings which, in other settings, they would have suppressed or shown covertly.

With the general lessening of guilt and anxiety came more assurance as parents, and general improvement in self-esteem, as well as more esteem for the spouse.

The feeling of general security in the group then enabled the members to discuss anger as a destructive force and an end in itself. The therapists pointed out that expressions of anger were normal and, when not an end in themselves, could be the beginning of new understandings.

Defense mechanisms used at home were much in evidence in the group meetings, but with the reduction of anxiety, members were able to identify and challenge the appropriateness of these defenses in other couples, to the point where some were able to discard the most unhealthy ones.

The 12 weeks concluded with generally supportive comments from the therapists, and positive reactions from the group.

At the last session, the therapists announced the possibility of another short-term group starting in the fall and invited applications.

Several weeks after termination of the program, there were indications of significant effort toward change in several of the families. One boy was returned home during the course of the project, and maintained himself within the limits of the family and community. There was indication that the father, particularly, understood and acted upon many of the comments directed to him by the group. He assumed a more confident role as father, and with this there was a lessening in his wife's attacks on him, and their communication improved.

One girl was returned home soon after the termination of the program. The improvement in the mother's self-image and the stepfather's recognition of his own problems with authority enabled the couple to relate more realistically to the girl.

IMPLICATIONS

When the program was planned, the agency chose parents who had been in contact with various community resources and were so disorganized in their family relationships that removal of the child to a residential treatment setting was necessary. Nonetheless, of the 17 persons invited to the group sessions, 15 responded.

Attendance remained around 75 percent and most members telephoned when unable to attend meetings. Several members had health problems.

In all instances, the child was too far away for the parents to be actively involved with the treatment facility, and they were unmotivated to contact agencies in the community that might have been able to offer counseling to them. However, they readily responded to and benefited from service in a milieu with which they were familiar. The implication is that the public welfare has a responsibility to move further into the treatment of parents while children are in residential treatment, group homes, or foster care. If the philosophical goal is reorganization or preservation and strengthening of family life, short-term, communication-oriented group work with parents is a useful tool, to be tried and tempered in all kinds of family situations.

Selected Readings

1. Bakwin, Ruth Morris: Attitudes of parents of mentally ill children. *Amer. Med. Women's Ass. J..,* 305-308, 1963.
2. Bartemeier, Leo: The contribution of the father to the mental health of the family. *Amer. J. Psychiat., 110:*277-280, 1953.
3. Bonnard, Augusta: The mother as therapist, in a case of obsessional neurosis. *Psychoanal. Stud. Child, 5:*391-408, 1950.
4. Cooledge, John C.: Asthma in mother and child as a special type of intercommunication. *Amer. J. Orthopsychiat., 26:*156-176, 1956.
5. Cooper, James F., and Kittrell, Elizabeth: One group for both parents: An experiment. *Social Work, 3:*24-29, 1958.
6. Despert, J. Louise: *The Emotionally Disturbed Child.* Garden City, Anchor Books, 1970.
7. Dietz, Chester R., and Costello, Marie E.: Reciprocal interaction in the parent-child relationship during psychotherapy. *Amer. J. Orthopsychiat. 26:*376-393, 1956.
8. Durkin, H. E.: *Group Psychotherapy for Mothers.* Springfield, Thomas, 1969.
9. Durkin, H. E., Glatzer, H. T., and Hirsch, J.: Therapy of mothers in groups. *Amer. J. Orthopsychiat. XIV:*1, Jan., 1944.
10. Egan, Merritt H.: The mother who goes from doctor to doctor with her child. *Children,* 251-252.
11. Elmer, Elizabeth: Obstacles in treatment planning for mothers of little girls. *Amer. J. Orthopsychiat. 26:*613-617, 1956.
12. Eisenberg, Leon: The fathers of autistic children. *Amer. J. Orthopsychiat. 27:*715-724, 1957.
13. English, O. Spurgeon: The psychological role of the father in the family. *Social Casework, 35:*323-329, 1954.
14. Esman, Aaron H.: Parents of Schizophrenic Children. Workshop, 1958, pp. 445-454.
15. Goldfarb, William: The mutual impact of mother and child in childhood schizophrenia. *Amer. J. Orthospychiat. 31:*738-747, 1961.
16. Hallowitz, Emanuel and Stephens, Bernice: Group therapy with fathers. *Social Casework, 400:*183-192, 1959.
17. Hofstein, Saul: Parent-child counseling in a multiple service agency. *Mental Hygiene, 40:*438-449, 1956.
18. Hotkins, Albert S., Kriegsfeld, Michael, and Sands, Rosalind, M.: An interview group therapy program for the waiting-life problem. *Social*

*Work, 3:*29-34, 1958.

19. Kohn, Melvin L., and Clausen, John A.: Parental authority behavior and schizophrenia. *Amer. J. Orthopsychiat., 26:*297-313, 1956.

20. Kubie, Lawrence S.: Resolution of a traffic phobia in conversations between a father and son. *Psychoanaly. Quart., 6:*223-226, 1937.

21. Lidz, Theodore, Cornelison, Alice R., Fleck, Stephen, and Terry, Dorothy: The intrafamilial environment of the schizophrenic patient. I. The father. *Psychiatry, 20:*329-342,1957.

22. Lidz, Theodore, Parker, Beulah, and Cornelison, Alice: The role of the father in the family environment of the schizophrenic patient. *Amer. J. Psychiat., 113:*126-132, 1956.

23. Lippman, Hyman S.: *Treatment of the Child in Emotional Conflict.* Chapter 3, Involving the parents in the child's therapy. New York, McGraw-Hill, 1956, pp. 28-42.

24. Maizlish, I. Leon: Group psychotherapy of husband-wife couples in a child guidance clinic. *Group Psychotherapy, 10:*169-180, 1957.

25. Maizlish, I. Leon, and Hurley, John R.: Attitude changes of husbands and wives in time-limited group psychotherapy. *Psychiat. Quart. Supp., Part 2:*1-20, 1963.

26. Marcus, Irwin M.: Psychoanalytic group therapy with fathers of emotionally disturbed preschool children. *Int. J. Group Psychother., 6:*61-76, 1956.

27. Meerloo, Joost A. M.: The father cuts the cord: The role of the father as initial transference figure. *Amer. J. Psychother., 10:*471-480, 1956.

28. Miller, Hymen, and Barach, D. W.: Psychotherapy of parents of allergic children. *Ann. Allerg., 18:*990-997, 1960.

29. Morse, Joan: Involving fathers in the treatment of patients with juvenile rheumatoid arthritis. *Social Casework, 49:*281-287, 1968 (5).

30. Ogdon, Donald P., Bass, Carolyn Lebo, Thomas, Edwin R., and Lordi, William: *Parents of Autistic Children.* May, 1967, pp. 653-658.

31. Pechey, B. M.: The direct analysis of the mother-child relationship in the treatment of maladjusted children. *Brit. J. Med. Psychol., 28:*101-112, 1955.

32. Peck, Harris B., Rabinovitch, Ralph D., and Cramer, Joseph B.: A treatment program for parents of schizophrenic children. *Amer. J. Orthopsychiat., 19:*592-598, 1949.

33. Rice, Katherine K.: The importance of including fathers. *Int. J. Group Psychother., 2:*232-238, 1952.

34. Sands, Rosalind M.: Method of group therapy for parents. *Social Work, 1:*48-56, 1956.

35. Schwarz, Hedy: The mother in the consulting room: Notes on the psychoanalytic treatment of two young children. *Psychoanal. Stud. Child, 5:*343-357, 1950.

36. DaSilva, Guy: The role of the father with chronic schizophrenic patients. A study in group therapy. *Canad. Psychiat. Ass. J., 8:*190-203, 1963.

37. Slavson, S. R.: Steps in sensitizing parents (couples) in groups toward schizophrenic children. *Int. J. Group Psychother., 13:*176-186, 1963.
38. Speers, Rex W., and Lansing, Cornelius: Group psychotherapy with preschool psychotic children and collateral group therapy of their parents: A preliminary report of the first two years. *Amer. J. Orthopsychiatry,* 1964, pp. 659-666.
39. Straughan, James H.: Treatment with child and mother in the playroom. *Behav. Res. Ther., 2:*37-41, 1964.
40. Tarachow, S., and Fink, M.: Absence of a parent as a specific factor determining choice of neurosis. *Hillside Hospital Journal, II:*67-71, 1953.
41. Wylie, Howard Lee, and Gluck, Martin R.: An approach to rapid involvement of parents in child guidance therapy. *Psychol. Reports, 19:*309-310, 1966.

Index